# More Praise for *What's It All About?*

◆ ◆ ◆ ◆ ◆

"A stimulating and insightful investigation of the diverse ways humans perceive the universe and the deeper mysteries of life. Strongly recommended as an honest, much needed, and thoroughly interdisciplinary guide for persons seeking surer foundations for their personal lives."

—VICTOR R. DEFILIPPIS, PH.D.
BIOLOGIST AND EVOLUTIONARY GENETICIST
OREGON HEALTH AND SCIENCE UNIVERSITY

"A magnificent, comprehensive, and fair-minded account of contrasting views of what life is all about—distilled to their essence and applied to our personal lives. A book of hope and wisdom for seekers who want to judge for themselves what is true and meaningful. Thank you de la Chaumière!"

— HARRY J. LIEBERMAN, M.F.T.

"There is no book quite like this book. It is for intelligent people who want to find answers for themselves, instead of merely repeating the traditional answers offered by our culture. This is a book of philosophy in the original sense of the term: *philo-sophia* is the "love of wisdom," and wisdom is the ability to make wise choices that lead to a good life. Richard de la Chaumière provides guidelines that lead to wise choices. This book is not only a sensitive exploration of the greatest traditions of philosophy and psychology; it also includes the latest and best scientific explanations of world views and human life."

—ROBERT B. ZEUSCHNER, PH.D.
PHILOSOPHER, PASADENA CITY COLLEGE

"At last, here is a book that combines a thorough understanding of the sciences with a deep appreciation of the spiritual quests of mankind. This beautifully written, pioneering work will appeal to reflective adults of all ages, including university students who seek to expand their perspectives beyond their specialized studies."

—CHRISTOPHER T. TREVINO, M.D., PH.D.

# WHAT'S IT ALL ABOUT?

## A GUIDE TO LIFE'S BASIC QUESTIONS AND ANSWERS

Richard de la Chaumière, Ph.D.

Wisdom House Press
Sonoma, California

Copyright © 2004 by Richard de la Chaumière

Wisdom House Press
P.O. Box 1838
Sonoma, California 95476
www.wisdomhousepress.com
wisdomhousepress@aol.com

Publishing Consultant: Linda F. Radke
Five Star Publications, Inc.
Book Design: Barbara Kordesh
Illustration: Jeff Yesh
Proofreader: Sue DeFabis

LIBRARY OF CONGRESS CATALOGING-IN-PUBLICATION DATA

de la Chaumière, Richard
What's it all about? : a guide to life's basic questions and answers / by Richard de la Chaumière.
p. cm.

Includes bibliographical references and index.
ISBN 0-9725777-0-X (acid-free paper)

1. Life.  2. Meaning (Philosophy)  3. Philosophy and science  4. Spiritual life.  I. Title.

BD431.C43 2003                                      128
QBI33-924

2003100387

*For all Truth Seekers,*
*and Esther*

# CONTENTS

## 3   WAYS OF KNOWING: HOW DO WE KNOW WHEN WE KNOW?   55

# PREFACE

If you would like to make up your own mind and heart about some of the basic questions of life, this book is intended for you. If you would like to learn many of the traditional answers, yet prefer to develop your own philosophy of life within or outside these major traditions, this book may not only be helpful but also enjoyable. My goal is to convey to you, at least in a beginning way, accurate knowledge and an empathetic understanding for many of the contrasting views in philosophy, science, and religion, as well as to provide some practical psychological wisdom to equip you a little better for your truth-seeking journeys. My two dominant concerns are truth and truth seekers, and I hope that in this book and in my own inquiries I proceed with all the competence and compassion my limitations allow.

# 1

## *Some Basic Questions*

Sometimes it happens when we awake in the middle of the night. It can happen on our way to work. For some of us, it happens when we are quite young, for others toward the end of our lives. Sometimes it happens in the middle of tragedy. It can happen at the very peak of our success. At these and other often unpredictable times, the question of questions can spontaneously float into our consciousness: What's it all about?

Though this book is not a collection of interviews, I decided to prepare for this work by posing this question to a variety of persons as well as investigating what other fundamental questions they ask about human existence. Not only were most of the interviewees happy to share their questions about life and views of the world, many were relieved to tell me about important, sometimes painful, events in their lives. A senior physicist at a world-famous research institute told me of the rejection he experienced when, at age eleven, in his small Nebraska town, he questioned the existence of

God, declared himself an atheist, and refused to join his classmates in school prayers. As an adult, his personal, family, and professional life is inspired by the mathematical elegance and beauty he found in the fundamental realities of the physical world. Among the Nazi death camp survivors I interviewed, I sat down with a couple who, through the most unlikely circumstances, first met and fell in love as teenagers, talking to each other from the opposite sides of a high, barbed-wire camp fence. One year later, when a German guard seemed to intentionally look the other way for an instant, they escaped together. All that summer and fall they kept on the move in a large forest in order to elude the guards and their vicious dogs. During the winter months, they hid out in a village sewer. As with the other survivors, I asked myself, what *could* they believe after enduring such inhumanities?

I sat down with a Lutheran pastor who told me the questions he asked during his crisis of faith the previous year and his recent experience on a minister's retreat, when he physically experienced the reassuring hand of God on his shoulder. A Catholic housewife detailed how her faith sanctified her daily routine and gave meaning to her life. A former Chicano gang member and heroin addict, now a recognized poet and writer, told me that he found religion to be powerless, but in a drug rehabilitation program he discovered a humanistic philosophy emphasizing self-responsibility that completely changed his life.

I interviewed a French lawyer, an Austrian hotel manager, a Romanian engineer, and a Vietnamese refugee. An American insurance agent related how his twenty years of intensive training in the martial arts and frequent visits to Asia gave him a physical discipline, world view, and spirituality that not only transformed his personal life but also made him a more effective business person. A sixty-four-year-old African-American artist shared with me how the civil rights movement revolutionized his self-image and philosophy of life, and a struggling thirty-three-year-old screenwriter recounted the lasting questions raised when, as a seven-year-old ghetto black, he viewed on his TV the tranquil Buddhist monk quietly setting himself on fire with gasoline to protest the war in Vietnam. I sat down in the homes of HIV-positive young men as well as at the hospital bed of an AIDS patient in excruciating pain. I listened quietly in the bedroom of a fifty-three-year-old nurse, weak and dying of cancer, who reflected on both the questions of life and her twenty years dedicated to nursing terminally ill cancer patients.

A forty-eight-year-old office supply store manager with a great sense of humor chronicled all the big questions he so innocently asked and how he looked for truth in all the wrong places. I shared with him my hypothesis: Scratch a comedian, and you will find a philosopher. His wife described the faith she needed to overcome her alcoholism and the powerful meaning of married love in her life. A physician, who is also an Orthodox Jew, enthusiastically enumerated the miraculous cures and fulfilled prophecies of his rabbi. A psychologist with Jewish origins and a doctorate from Harvard described the questioning of his family's religion as a youth and his conversion to Islam. He became a Sufi sheikh and spiritual leader of a growing Muslim community. After an extended interview in his home, I gladly accepted his invitation to join in the whirling dervish dance with him and his congregation. I met with an eighty-one-year-old American Communist, who during the Depression, dropped out of a prestigious university to dedicate himself to alleviating poverty by trying to reorganize society based on a Marxist world view. A lifelong, full-time organizer, he shared with me the painful disillusionment and self questioning he and other party members experienced when Stalin's brutalities became known. Maligned, imprisoned, he suffered woefully through the McCarthy era while maintaining his steadfast commitment to democratic socialism. Also, I interviewed the seventy-three-year-old labor lawyer who, at great cost to his professional career and personal life, successfully defended him in a landmark case before the U.S. Supreme Court.

A high school science teacher tearfully recalled how as a seventeen-year-old she began to think for herself and questioned her parents' apocalyptic church. They immediately ousted her from the house without any financial or emotional support and would not speak to her for another nineteen years. I interviewed a television actor and an entrepreneur-inventor, both of whom are committed to New Age thinking. They explained to me how their questions about life are answered by the New Age world view and how each of us, solely in our own minds creates all the good and evil and everything else that happens in our lives; thus we are totally responsible for ourselves.

A fifty-one-year-old former accountant related to me how, twenty years ago, he began to deeply question the basic values of his business career and looked for a community with which he could identify. He joined a well-known movement, which offered personal growth and happiness through the purported application of science, psychology, and spiritual principles. He left his job and whole-heartedly committed himself to the organization, eventually becoming chief financial officer. The organization was taking in millions of dollars every month, but little by little he learned that the illustrious founder was a sociopath, secretly and illegally siphoning off millions for himself, brilliantly running a world wide but unrecognized cult, and exploiting innocent people with subtle and powerful brainwashing techniques. A Lebanese jeweler told me that she did not want to question the existence of God because if there is no God, life would have no meaning, and she would want to die.

◆ ◆ ◆ ◆ ◆

Though I do not quote directly from the above or the total array of my interviews, you can hear their voices in the questions assembled below.[1] Also, you will hear questions that I have gathered down through time from philosophy, religion, and science. When you read these questions, take your time. Reflect on them rather than rush. Go to a quiet place within yourself. This inner silence may also evoke your own questions. As a result of your reflections, you will be better able to discern which of your questions and those below are most important to you.

# Is There a God?

Is there a personal, all-powerful, intelligent, and loving God who cares about the cosmos and me personally? Is what we call God or the Great Ultimate part of nature, nature itself, or a force working within nature? Were we created in God's image, or did we create God in our image? Do humans stand alone in a cosmos that is indifferent to human concerns, sweeping everything along on its inexorable course, a Godless universe without morality or reason? If there is a God, why such a hidden God? Is the transcendental urge that some of us so profoundly experience a spark of the divine in us or just wishful thinking? Are prayers answered? Do religious rituals have any power? Do miracles exist? If there is a perfect Creator God, why did God not create a perfect world? How could a good and just God create a world of such pervasive and undeserved cruelty, injustice, violence, ignorance, and self-delusion? Given the existence of so much evil, is it impossible or unlikely that a moral God exists? Or do we live in a divine mystery of ultimate holiness, justice, and love beyond our capacity to comprehend, and which it is sacrilegious to even question?

# Why is There Anything at All?

Why existence? Why is there something rather than nothing? Doesn't it seem more likely that there be nothing rather than something? Isn't it astonishing that anything exists? Isn't existence itself a miracle? Isn't it most appropriate to feel a sense of the sacred in light of the tremendous mystery of existence? Or are these feelings only naïve sentimentality in the face of the harsh realities of a cold cosmos, in which life preys on life in the violent struggle for survival?

# WHAT IS THE ULTIMATE REALITY?

What is the essence of being? Is it material, mental, spiritual, or something else? Is the universe ultimately rational and orderly or chaotic and random? Who or what rules the universe, or does the universe run itself? Is this a God-created and God-infused world? Is ultimate reality a sacred reality? Is love not only a human but also a cosmic phenomenon? From where comes this profound yearning to be in communion with ultimate reality? Is this ultimate reality indifferent, even hostile to our truth seeking, our spiritual, moral, scientific, and aesthetic aspirations? Do we live in a friendly or a heartless and mindless universe? Can we feel at home in the universe?

# WHAT, IF ANY, IS THE PURPOSE OF THE UNIVERSE?

What's it all for? Is there any cosmic design within the universe? Is there a cosmic meaning? Why does the universe exist? Is there any kind of Absolute Spirit or Force guiding the universe toward a certain goal? Why should the universe have a purpose other than simply that it is? If we experience purpose in our own personal lives, why shouldn't there be a purpose in the larger cosmos of which we are a part?

# WHO AM I?

Where did I come from? Where am I going? Who or what put me in this world? Am I only a cosmic accident? Do we humans have a fixed nature, or can we as a species and as individuals create our own nature? Are humans basically good, bad, or just weak and easily influenced? What is the value of one human life? What is this "I" asking these questions? Is there a permanent self at the center of my consciousness, or am I only a transient collection of bones, blood, and brains? Am "I" a transmigrating soul who has and will experience many reincarnations? Is there something of the Eternal and Absolute in the human spirit? What do I really need? Who are we humans that we ask ultimate questions about the universe and our origins, nature, and destiny?

# WHY AM I HERE?

Why do we exist? What, if any, is the ultimate meaning of human existence? Is there any absolute cosmic purpose that we must or should choose to follow? Or do we live in an indifferent or even hostile universe, in which our human challenge is to create our own ultimate nature, meaning, and purpose? What is the source of our longing to create a world of greater love, compassion, and justice? Is there one ultimate meaning for all of us or only individual meanings for each of us to discover or create? What is our place and destiny in the universe? Where do I belong? Do I have a spiritual home? Can I make a difference in the world? What should I do with my life?

# IS THIS ALL THERE IS?

Is there anything beyond our endless struggles of daily life? Is there any transcendent power that can save us from the limitations, sorrows, and uncertainties of the human condition? Any big Salvation beyond the details of our everyday lives or only scattered little salvations of momentary gratifications? Why do so many of us have a transcendental urge for something more? Do we need something transcendent to have truly meaningful lives? What is the source and significance of this profound feeling that some of us have of wanting to serve something greater than ourselves, of even wanting to kneel before, worship, and sacrifice our lives to something greater than ourselves? Why do some of us have an inner sense of the Beyond, a deep feeling of the ultimate holiness of all life, and of wanting to be one with the entire universe? What is humanity's true portion in the universe? What can we hope for?

# IS THERE LIFE AFTER DEATH?

Why death? Why must we die? Do I as an individual self survive death, or do I somehow survive only as dissolved into some ultimate energy, like a grain of salt in a vast ocean? Do we survive only through our children, our work, or our influence? Is the belief in everlasting life or reincarnation just egotistic wishful thinking and vain self-serving delusion? Did we have life before birth? How can human life be fair if there is no afterlife or reincarnation in which perfect justice is finally realized? With recent advances in the biological sciences unlocking the secrets of the aging process, might not we or our children become the last of the mortals or the first of the immortals? What, if anything, is eternal in humans?

# IS LIFE WORTH LIVING?

If we are going to die anyway, why bother to live? Why bother with all the hassles of life? Why have ambitions and projects? Does anything really matter? Isn't human existence only entertaining ourselves until we die? But on the other hand, why not fully live in the present? Why not celebrate the gift of life and enjoy its genuine opportunities and pleasures? Why not join in the human evolutionary adventure and be part of the creative experience of living in the universe?

# WHAT IS THE IMPORTANCE OF THIS WORLD?

In contrast to the vastness of time and the immensity of space, are not we and the planet Earth utterly insignificant? Does human history have any meaning, pattern, or purpose? At some future time, will this planet be considered important only because it was the launch pad for the colonization of space and subsequent co-evolution with other forms of intelligent life in the distant realms of the universe? Is this world only a moral testing ground to gain eternal happiness with God in heaven? Should we be only in the world but not of the world?

# WHY SO MUCH SUFFERING?

Why so much cruelty, violence, injustice, indifference, and apparent evil in the world? Are there no ultimate rewards for virtue or punishment for evil? What is the source of evil? Are good and evil of no importance to the universe but only to humans? Is morality only our human invention? Is some of the suffering I cause others an inevitable result of my own need to survive and develop?

# HOW OUGHT I TO LIVE?

Are there any cosmic laws of the true, the good, and the beautiful applicable to all people? Are there any absolute values valid for all humans? Does our intrinsic human nature tell us how to live, or do we need to be taught what is best to do? Can we discover objective values in our nature, or is it our nature to create our own human values? Why do most of us have a moral sense? Why be moral? Are there any divinely validated norms for morality by which we can judge and be judged? What and whom should I most love? What and whom should I most fear? What are my indispensable human needs? When do I betray my highest self? What should I live for, fight for, and be willing to die for?

# WHAT IS CONSCIOUSNESS?

Where does it come from? Where might it be taking us? Is consciousness physical or metaphysical? Is consciousness the ultimate

SOME BASIC QUESTIONS 11

reality and the essence of human nature? Does consciousness pervade the entire universe, or is it only an emergent property that accidentally evolved in certain life forms on our minor planet? Is God pure consciousness? Is consciousness the divine spark in us? Is consciousness causal in the physical world? Is our fundamental task the evolution of consciousness in the cosmos, and thus are we indispensable for the completion of creation?

# AM I REALLY FREE TO CHOOSE?

Am I free to will what I will? Doesn't present scientific evidence demonstrate that we are totally determined creatures? Are we not sculpted by our genetic endowment, conditioned by childhood experiences, predictably plastic to social stimuli, and controlled by unconscious motivations? Is our subjective experience of personal freedom only a delusion caused by our limited knowledge of brain functions? With increasing scientific knowledge and our ability to change our genetic and cultural conditioning, are we not somehow creating a certain freedom for our species? Though originally all may have been determined, might not freedom become our achievement?

# HOW DO WE KNOW
# WHEN WE KNOW?

What can we know? What are the most reliable ways of knowing? What are my emotional, intellectual, and situational limitations that affect my honest and competent inquiry into asking and seeking answers to the basic questions of life? Must all knowledge come through the senses, or is there a human knowing independent of our senses? Were we born with a certain innate knowledge of reality, or with empty, blank minds? Can we ever directly know reality, or do we know only through our minds' mental models of reality? Is objective knowledge possible? What is the validity of personal, subjective experience? Do our subjective experiences, however powerful or sublime, prove anything about ultimate reality? Do we need faith in order to understand? Do we know not only with our minds but also with our hearts? Why do some of us have this love for inquiry, this love of truth?

◆ ◆ ◆ ◆ ◆

In presenting the basic questions of human existence that I have gathered from interviews, philosophy, science, and religion, my aim has been for you to identify which of these or your own questions are the most important to you. The purpose of the remainder of the book is to assist you to become more informed and competent as you seek answers to your own questions. In the next chapter I provide some historical reasons why people today are seeking fundamental answers about their existence and outline the impact of religion's decline and the advance of science. Then I take up the question of whether truth itself should be of any great importance, alert you to the dangers of asking basic questions, and provide practical wisdom to better prepare you for your inquiries. I conclude by describing some different points of departure for truth seekers and also provide an array of answers that people have discovered.

# 2

# *Why and Why Not Ask These Questions?*

## ALL IN THE FAMILY

Let's begin with the upside. In asking the basic questions of life we are not alone. We belong to a long tradition of humans who have both asked and sought answers to these questions. Some of us have distinguished ourselves as philosophers, religious pioneers, scientists, writers, and artists. Most of us, however, are not publicly identified as professional truth seekers. We all have a certain passion to discover not only what is useful but what is true; and to reflect not only on our personal lives but on life itself. Many of us share a wonder and awe that anything at all exists and strive to understand our place and purpose in the big picture. Down through time, whether we come from the East or the West, whether in loincloth or lab coat, business suit or artist's beret, we come together for the great purpose of applying our heads and hearts to the deepest questions of human existence. We are part of an historic community, a family. Doesn't it seem that we are in rather good company?

# CONSCIOUSNESS:
# OUR GREAT JOY AND SORROW

Among the estimated ten million species on the planet, an unparalleled power of conscious awareness has evolved a unique species— *Homo sapiens*. With exquisitely developed sensitivities, we can delight in the abundant pleasures of our senses. With unprecedented intelligence, imagination, and language capabilities, we can celebrate our creations in the arts and literature, our discoveries in science, our inventions in technology, and the other glories of human culture. With our unique form of conscious awareness, we are not only part of nature, as are other creatures, but with our minds we can stand outside of nature and reflect both on nature itself and on our own human nature. Without parallel among all other life forms on Earth, we have evolved the conscious experience of self-identity as a subject distinct from all else as object. But with self-awareness comes death-awareness. With self-consciousness comes the capacity to worry—increasingly aware that life is full of uncertainties, that life can go wrong for us. In time we discover the Tree of Good and Evil.

Our gift of consciousness is a two-edged sword. While this singular intelligence may be the evolutionary cutting edge for human survival, growth, and happiness, it also brings a sharp awareness of life's terrors. This is the knowledge of sorrow and the sorrow of knowledge. Suffering is the price of consciousness. We may become painfully aware of the apparent fact that we were born into this existence without our consent, are confronted by a world with conditions we did not choose, needs, feelings, limitations, injustice, and violence we did not design, and a genetic time clock of aging and death. We came into the world in pain, and we leave in pain. As soon as we are born, we are old enough to die. While every cell in our body pulsates with the instinct to survive, we humans are conscious that we are going to die. Aware that we live in time, we have an idea of eternity. Unlike our VCR, life has no "pause" button. Whether we are ready or not, life will roll in on us full-blown. Whatever questions we may have about reality, life doesn't stop until we have figured out all the answers. We can't say, "Wait, I'm not ready!" Practical life decisions need to be made for which we may have only habits and hunches but not knowledge.

# RELIGION HAS ANSWERS

Many of us who are convinced religious believers do not need to ask the basic questions of life. We already have the answers! Most of the major Eastern and Western religions teach certain world views, the truth claims for which are often based on divine revelation as contained in sacred scriptures, inspiration, illumination, enlightenment, or transmission through a lineage of masters. The answers to the basic questions in the hands of mystics and theologians can be exceedingly complex and subtle or at the popular level extremely simple and easy to understand. At its best, religion has inspired great and courageous deeds and has attracted and nurtured intelligent, loving, and beautiful human beings.

Moreover, there is no question that religion can powerfully meet basic emotional and cognitive needs. Most religions address in one way or another the need of many to experience a higher purpose and greater significance than is provided by our mundane, everyday lives. Religion can instill hope, sanctify suffering, inspire ideals, and provide a sense of belonging in shared traditions as well as stability and solidarity in a common code of morality and sacred rites of passage. Religion can provide a sacred sense of ultimate realities, a deeply felt shared vision of what life is all about, and a profound psychic foundation for personal lives and entire civilizations.

# THE DECLINE OF RELIGION

In the view of William Barrett, even though the Western religions have millions of churchgoers and still very powerful organizations,

> The central fact of modern history in the West—by which we mean the long period from the end of the Middle Ages to the present—is unquestionably the decline of religion....The decline of religion in modern times means simply that religion is no longer the uncontested center and ruler of man's life, and that the Church is no longer the final and unquestioned home and asylum of his being. The deepest significance of this change does not even appear principally at the purely intellectual level, in loss of belief, though this loss due to the critical inroads of science has been a major historical cause of the decline. The waning of religion is a much more concrete and complex fact than a mere change in conscious outlook; it penetrates the deepest strata of man's total psychic life. It is indeed one of the major stages in man's psychic evolution.... Religion to medieval man was not so much a theological system as a solid psychological matrix surrounding the individual's life from birth to death, sanctifying and enclosing all its ordinary and extraordinary occasions in sacrament and ritual. The loss of the church was the loss of a whole system of symbols, images, dogmas, and rites which had the psychological validity of immediate experience, and within which

hitherto the whole psychic life of Western man had been
safely contained. In losing religion, man lost the concrete
connection with a transcendent realm of being; he was
set free to deal with this world in all its brute objectivity.
But he was bound to feel homeless in such a world,
which no longer answered the needs of his spirit. A
home is the accepted framework which habitually contains our life. To lose one's psychic container is to be cast
adrift, to become a wanderer upon the face of the earth.[1]

A shift from a sacred to a secular society began during the
Renaissance, a cultural movement beginning in mid-fourteenth-
century Italy but spreading throughout Europe, which enthusiastically revived worldly pagan values plucked from rediscovered classical Greek and Roman manuscripts. However, for the medieval mind,
the Renaissance humanists over-emphasized the glory and creative
powers of man rather than the infinitely greater glory of God
the Creator, the dignity rather than the depravity of man, and self-
development rather than self-denial.

While the humanists were rediscovering the past pagan pleasures
of this world, bold adventurers were exploring the entirely new
worlds of the Americas and the Orient, sometimes discovering religions more ancient than Christianity and advanced civilizations at
least or more refined than Europe—all without the saving grace of
Christ and thus challenging their faith. Back in Europe, the minds of
the masses were going on their own adventures through the explosive availability of inexpensive books, made possible by the invention
of moveable type in the fifteenth century. The outpouring of popular religious books with intersectarian denunciations and secular
books with whole new areas of fascination induced doubts about
and distractions from the old unquestioned beliefs and values. With
the feudal system breaking down, illiterate serfs flocked from the isolated drudgery of the countryside to the stimulating new trades,
technology, commerce, delights, and ideas of the flourishing cities. A
new class of people was discovering that this world was not just a

somber, wretched testing ground in the drama of salvation but rather was an exciting, meaningful place to enjoy. Increasingly, religious authority was breaking down in the wake of Church scandals, exhausting religious wars, and bitter disputes among Protestant groups.

# SCIENCE, RATIONALISM, BIBLICAL CRITICISM AND FREUDIAN ANALYSIS ERODE RELIGIOUS FAITH

The decisive loss of innocence for the major Western religions was the arrival of science. Science requires proof. During the brilliant scientific revolution of the sixteenth and seventeenth centuries, a new breed of truth seekers arrived on the scene who did not sit in monastic cells contemplating the laws of Moses but rather actively went out to observe the laws of nature. Many of these pioneering scientists were religious men. They sincerely believed that questions of faith belonged exclusively to religion. Theologians examined the supernatural, scientists the natural. Religion explained the purpose of life, science the mechanisms of nature. Faith and reason were entirely separate domains; thus there could be no conflict between religion and science. Science did not require religious faith; it required objective, empirical evidence. Religion did not require scientific proof; God provided the evidence of faith. The supernatural realm of religion was beyond the range of science.

Conflicts, however, did develop between science and religion, and in the past 300 years when confrontations arose, religion usually retreated, while science advanced. Theology went on the defensive, sometimes redefining religion in terms of science. Inspired by the revolutionary celestial mechanics of the English mathematician and physicist Isaac Newton (1642-1727), thinkers who identified themselves as Deists propagated the view that all of existence is a world machine perfectly designed at its creation by a Divine Architect and inexorably following natural laws. Once set in motion, the world did not need any further application of force. Thus, after the initial creation at the beginning of time, subsequent divine interventions by a Savior God, who performed miracles and answered prayers, were unnecessary and an insult to the perfection of God's creation. The world was like a perfectly functioning clock, which did not need to be fixed from time to time by a Divine Repairman. Devout Christians criticized the Deist God as only an absentee landlord. During the late seventeenth and eighteenth centuries, Deist attacks on revealed religions had a powerful impact on thinkers and leaders in England, Europe, and America, including Benjamin Franklin, George Washington, Thomas Jefferson, Thomas Paine, and Ethan Allen.

Rationalists of the seventeenth and eighteenth centuries found more evidence for faith in the order of nature than in the doctrines of revealed religion. Early belief in the supernatural was seen as based on ignorance of natural phenomena; religion was considered to be a survival of primitive, precritical, prescientific magical thinking. Theologies were ingenious webs of rationalization, clinging to realities that didn't exist. The classical proofs for the existence of God were found to be invalid or inconclusive. With the cold chill of reason, rationalists examined sacred scriptures and found contradictions, absurdities, superstition, and a tyrant God. Revealed religion was not even a splendid error, but rather only pious nonsense.

Western religion was not without its brilliant defenders, but among the educated and in certain pockets of popular society, the tide was turning toward questioning the credibility of religion. Leaders of the eighteenth century Enlightenment, especially the *philosophes* of France epitomized by Voltaire (1694-1778), passionately struggled to liberate the human mind and spirit from the oppressive control and persecution by the official church and police state. They challenged individuals to not be fearful of thinking for themselves. They sought to lead humanity into a new age, enlightened by empirical science and untrammeled reason. They ferociously attacked the ecclesiastical monopoly of education that in their view, stunted and distorted the minds of the young and the innocent. Imprisoned and exiled for free thinking, their books banned and burned, the *philosophes* battled for freedom of the press, freedom of speech, the right to dissent, and religious tolerance. They defied the church in every possible intellectual way, including publishing devastating satire in popular works. Their mocking of sacred beliefs and institutions gnawed away at ecclesiastical privilege, power and prestige.

An increasing number of European scholars applied scientific canons of evidence to prayerful scripture study. What emerged was biblical criticism, demonstrating that various texts could not possibly have been written by the claimed authors, that prophecies were in reality written generations after the predicted events, and that stories of the Creation, the flood, the final judgment, and various biblical prayers believed to be unique to Judaism and Christianity actually originated from surrounding religions and cultures. The origins of Judaism and Christianity were examined in painstaking detail by philologists, archaeologists, anthropologists, sociologists, mythologists, psychologists, and specialists in comparative religions. The more "critical" of these professionals came to the view that the miraculous events of Jewish biblical history and the Christian New Testament were only self-serving stories, fables, and poetry—products of the Middle Eastern religious imagination. For some critics, the Jewish belief that they were specially chosen by God was the result of group narcissism and a vicious self-serving rationalization for their murdering and maiming the ancient and rightful inhabitants of the newly claimed Jewish Promised Land. With fateful consequences, the notion of God's chosen elect transferred into Christianity and Islam, resulting in massacres of the Jews, persecution and wars of religious superiority between Christians and Muslims, and the oppression of peoples encountered in their missionary expansion—all in the name of being God's Chosen People.

Critics doubted or disbelieved the resurrection of Jesus, not only because of contradictory reports in the New Testament and evidence that crucial texts were written as long as two generations after his death, but also because of the suspected motivations of those pro-claiming his resurrection. Examining the religious, sociological, and psychological situation of those times, the critics did not necessarily question the honesty of the early Christians, or claim that they con-sciously intended to deceive people, but neither were they viewed as objective, trustworthy witnesses or transmitters of the resurrection stories. Rather, they were preachers, proselytizers, and propagandists of the superiority of Jesus. With each telling and retelling of the original stories of the death of Jesus, preachers elaborated a more and more miraculous story, including his descent into hell and ascension into heaven at the right hand of God. Subjective embellishments of one generation became objective facts of the next generation. Thus, Hebrew converts to the Jesus sect, (Jewish heretics) could increas-ingly justify their unorthodox faith with miraculous events, and Gentile converts could buttress their faith in the Jewish prophet to compare more favorably with the surrounding pagan religions, myths, and philosophies. Modern mythologists have observed that in various ancient cultures it was common to prove the divinity of a king by claiming that he was conceived not by a mortal father but by a god. Thus, the miraculous conception of Jesus by the Holy Spirit and a virgin was interpreted as a story created to demonstrate the exceptional powers or divinity of Jesus, not to emphasize the sexual purity of Mary.

The onslaught of critical examination of religion continued with the psychoanalyst Sigmund Freud (1856-1939), who expanded some of the influential views of Ludwig Feuerbach (1804-1872). According to Freud, religion has its psychological origins in children's terrifying feelings of helplessness which aroused a powerful need for protection by the father. The recognition of our human helplessness and the felt need for fatherly protection continues throughout life, and theistic religion provides an even more powerful father in a Divine Providence who shields us from life's dangers, guarantees justice, and provides eternal life. For the nontheist Freud, all such beliefs are only humanly created, wish-fulfilling illusions. Religious beliefs and prac-tices are essentially prolongations of childhood ways of relating to the world; the omnipotent parent becomes the omnipotent God who can soothe our feelings and help us meet all our needs. To become mature adults, we need to outgrow the consolations of religious illusions, just as a child must physically leave the warm and comfortable parental home for adult reality. If adults can renounce their infantile wishes and realize that they have nothing to depend on but their own powers, then they can live more effective lives. However, it might be argued that Freud did not consider the possibility that only childlike persons have childlike religions, and that for the psychologically mature individual, religion need not be an illusionary escape from reality but rather a profound quest for understanding and union with the deepest and most comprehensive reality. Rather he considered that all religions were the universal obsessional neurosis of humanity, a mass illusion.[2]

Though I have limited this sample to the effects of science and the secular, critical attitude on Western Christianity and Judaism, the same movements in the name of Westernization have pivotally influenced many educated adherents of Islam and the Eastern religions and cultures. Inherent in the scientific spirit, which originated with the ancient Greeks, is a skepticism, a critical attitude toward claims of facts. When thinkers began to apply scientific methods to assess the credibility of religious claims, unquestioned faith was lost to humanity, the age of innocence ended. Religion was no longer the sole arbiter of truth. Science gave its own account of reality. Some religionists have shunned science and sought inner security in unquestioned piety and strict observance; certain others welcome science in modern life as a way of purifying and evolving their religious beliefs and practices. The eighteenth and nineteenth centuries' heat of battle between science and religion has cooled down, and today there seems to be a gentlemen's agreement that scientists do not publicly question matters of faith and religionists educate themselves in science before criticizing it. Most significant perhaps is that, in their professional work, scientists ignore religion. But might not religion somehow be a leaven for science, challenging and expanding its perspectives and suggesting new areas and avenues for investigation without corrupting science in its quest for truth?

# THREE BLOWS TO THE EGO: COPERNICUS, DARWIN, AND FREUD

For those of us living in Europe before 1543, common sense, science, and religion told us that the Earth was the center of the universe, with the sun, stars, and other planets revolving around us. In that year Copernicus, an astronomer and Catholic canon, published his book *On the Revolution of the Celestial Orbs*. In this work he demonstrated systematically and in detail that the mathematical theory that would most accurately fit astronomical observations required the rejection of the Earth-centered cosmos of the then dominant Ptolemaic system of astronomy and the enthronement of the sun as the center of our universe. The Earth, rather than being an immobile, fixed point around which the entire universe turned, instead became a revolving planet, just like the other planets orbiting around the sun. Previously the sun and planets were "seen" to be going around the Earth because it was not yet conceived that the visual experience could also be explained by the earth's daily rotation on its own axis. This revolutionary perspective gave an entirely new view of the world—and a new view of ourselves. We were no longer the center of creation, no longer the darlings of the universe. Perhaps the cosmos was not made only for us.

There were objections to this disturbing new theory. For example, if as claimed by Copernicus, the Earth was speedily turning on its axis, why do we not feel its motion or a powerful wind or see objects flying off the Earth? Also, the new theory contradicted the long-standing Ptolemaic view and the letter of Scripture. However, the notion of a sun-centered universe, as Copernicus and some of his professional contemporaries knew, went back to the origins of Greek astronomy, including Aristarchos of Samos (310-230 B.C.), but was later rejected. Gradually the Copernican sun-centered system was accepted through the more accurate astronomical observations of the Dane Tycho Brahe (1546-1601), as interpreted and developed by Johann Kepler (1571-1630), a German astronomer and mathematician, and by Galileo, who in 1609 improved the recent Dutch invention of the telescope, turned it to the heavens, and let lay persons and professionals alike see the marvelous evidence for the revolutionary new Copernican theory and the demise of the old world view.

Then another revolution jolted our sense of importance. It was called "evolution." When Charles Darwin and Alfred Russel Wallace in 1858 described their independent codiscovery of the origin of species by natural selection in papers presented before the Linnaean Society, the idea of evolution was already in the air.[3] Lamarck (1744-1829), a French botanist and zoologist, is considered to be the first person to formulate a general theory of evolution, though it was generally rejected as lacking sufficient evidence. Charles Lyell in his *Principles of Geology* (1830-1833), based on a wealth of field observations, established evolutionary geology, at least in the English speaking world. Even Charles' grandfather, Erasmus Darwin (1731-1802), a well-known physician and gentleman scientist, published certain evolutionary views, partly anticipating his grandson.

However, Charles Darwin (1809-1882), who was the first to develop a scientifically credible and systematic theory of biological evolution, began his career strongly biased against the notion of evolution. His opinion changed while doing extensive observations of plant and animal life as well as geological formations in and around the coast of South America during his post as unpaid naturalist aboard the ship the *H.M.S. Beagle* (1831-1836). Also on this voyage, he read Lyell's book, which opened his mind to the slow development of the Earth through vast geological ages and made it difficult for Darwin the devout Christian to continue believing the biblical story of creation. Based on his observations and reflections, he also began to examine his unquestioned belief in the unchanging fixity of species and their special creation, as described in Genesis. Noting both the minute and significant variations among the species in their geographical distribution and living conditions, he returned to England convinced of the truth of evolution.

But Darwin puzzled over what might be the mechanism by which entirely new species develop from an original species. Species change, but how? He carefully studied the work of English breeders and horticulturalists, who were extremely skilled in observing the many spontaneous chance variations that occur in animals and plants and were aware that such variations could be transmitted to their descendents. By a process of conscious and deliberate selection they would mate (or cross) only those individuals with the most favorable variations (e.g., sheep with thicker wool, roses with brighter colors) and thus eventually would produce new and improved varieties. Darwin wondered how nature, by an unconscious natural selection process, developed new species in the way that breeders and horticulturalists used conscious and artificial selection methods.

In October 1838 he found the critical clue when, as he said, he "happened to read for amusement" the *Essay on the Principle of Population* (1798) by Thomas Malthus. In this widely read and influential work, Malthus noted that population tends to grow at a geometric rate, while food supplies cannot grow more than arithmetically. Thus the population tends to grow beyond the available food supply, producing an inevitable competition for limited resources among individuals. A fierce "struggle for existence" results in which only the fittest survive. Darwin had meticulously observed many variations among individuals within species, though he readily acknowledged his ignorance of why they occurred. He reasoned that some of the differences would increase or decrease an organism's chances for survival, and that some of the variations are inherited by subsequent generations. Because organisms tend to produce more descendents than the environment can support, a higher proportion of the organisms with favorable variations will survive and produce descendants than will those organisms with unfavorable variations. Thus, with the accumulation of variations over vast periods of time, the great multitude of presently known species of plants and animals could have gradually evolved from only a few simple life forms. He considered that the spontaneous individual variations (when heritable, now called mutations by modern geneticists) were random. For

Darwin, evolution was an entirely natural process, not requiring any outside force or agency. The means by which evolution occurred were mechanical, not designed, combining chance variations and the necessity to survive for reproduction.

Darwin had a strong distaste for controversy and also was sincere in not wanting to scandalize the public with his evolutionary views, which he knew had revolutionary implications. While he had long reflected privately on man's evolution, he deliberately avoided the matter in his *Origin of Species* (1859). His readers, however, quickly saw the implications of his theory for the nature of humankind. Bitter debate developed when certain of his enthusiastic followers publicly, even pugnaciously, flaunted the notion that humans had evolved from apes, thus refuting the biblical tradition that Adam was the first man, made in the image of God. For religionists, the human was a unique creature, a special creation of God, unrelated to the beasts of the field, who lacked souls. Most religionists believed that human nature was entirely separate and different from the rest of nature. There could be no kinship, no zoological continuity, between human and animal life. Shocking was the idea that man himself, the pinnacle of creation, was nothing more than a remarkably successful ape. Adding fuel to the polemics, it was T.H. Huxley, not Darwin, who in his *Evidences as to Man's Place in Nature* (1863), detailed the similarities among humans, primates, and other animals, arguing that the structural differences that separate the human from the gorilla are not as great as those that separate the gorilla from the lower apes. On the Continent, others, including the German Ernst Haeckel (*General Morphology*, 1866, and *The Natural History of Creation*, 1868), produced a number of studies showing the similarities between humans and apes and proposing various theories of human evolution from earlier forms of life.

Finally, in 1871, Darwin applied his evolutionary theory to humans when he published his *Descent of Man*. With a mass of evidence and detailed argumentation, he proposed the hypothesis that humans are subject to the same evolutionary mechanisms as the rest of nature, and that we, like other animals, descended from more primitive forms. He demonstrated many similarities between humans and the apes, but contrary to popular belief he never implied that we are descended from apes. What he did suggest was that humans and apes descended from a common ancestor. Through natural selection of the survival of the fittest, nonhumans became humans. For Darwin, humans are a species among other animal species. Humans are a part of nature, not separate from nature, not biologically unique. We are animals, but remarkably evolved animals—the most dominant species on the planet Earth.

A third blow to our sense of self was the rediscovery of the unconscious mind, culminating with Freud at the turn of the twentieth century. He demonstrated by clinical case examples that we are not the complete masters of our minds, not the rational creatures that we thought we were. Since at least the beginning of recorded history in both the East and West, many cultures have had myths describing divine, demonic, or natural forces influencing our minds. Before the fuller development of our reflective consciousness and sense of separation from nature, humans experienced their conscious and unconscious mental life more as a continuum along a unified totality. But especially in the West with the rise of critical thinking, science, technology, and the rational ordering of complex social, political, and economic institutions, the unconscious tended to be neglected as a force in mental life. During the Age of Reason in the seventeenth and eighteenth centuries, it was precise conscious reason that was emphasized.

By the end of the eighteenth and especially in the nineteenth century, a reaction against the emphasis on the conscious rational mind developed among thinkers and artists, particularly in Germany and Britain, where there was a widespread interest in unconscious mental processes. Carl Gustav Carus, a physician, painter, and friend of Goethe, began his influential book *Psyche* (1846) with the words, "The key to the knowledge of the nature of the soul's conscious life lies in the realm of the unconscious."[4] Gustav Theodor Fechner (1801-1887), German philosopher and a founder of experimental psychology, described the mind as an iceberg, mostly below the surface of conscious awareness and moved by hidden currents. Nietzsche (1844-1900) provided piercing, poignant, and widely influential insights into the powerful processes of the unconscious.

By the last decade of the nineteenth century, when Freud began publishing his major works, the existence and importance of the unconscious had already become a commonplace among educated thinkers in Europe and England. Freud, a neurologist by training and the founding pioneer of psychoanalysis, sought to understand the unconscious in a more scientific way. For him, the unconscious was a vast cauldron of primitive, amoral animal instincts, repressed urges, desires, emotions, memories, beliefs, and ideas—an entire under- world of powerful forces below the threshold of our conscious awareness, but which nevertheless influenced or controlled our con- scious beliefs, ideas, feelings, and actions. Fundamentally, most of us do not consciously know our deepest psychic selves and the source of many of our motivations. In a more systematic and thorough way than his predecessors, Freud attempted from his clinical observations to construct a theory of the structure and dynamics of the uncon- scious. He expanded our understanding of unconscious motivations, conflicts, fears, and wishes. He showed how our minds, by an auto- matic, self-starting mental process of which we are not even aware, repress from conscious awareness ideas and feelings that are threat- ening or unacceptable to our egos, how without our conscious intent or awareness, we deny or distort painful truths—how uncon- sciously we lie to ourselves and others.

Copernicus, Darwin, and Freud, especially for the Western world, brought about three revolutions, or should we say revelations. With Copernicus we lost our privileged place in the universe, with Darwin we lost our unique place among creatures, and with Freud we lost our God-like rational minds. Each brought in turn a new view of the universe, human nature, and the mind.

Furthermore, modern astronomy and astrophysics have revealed to us the awesome vastness of time and immensity of space. Who can view human life and the Earth quite the same way since July 20, 1969, when men landed on the moon and took those fantastic photos of our magnificent but tiny jewel of a planet from the space ship *Apollo 11.* Even for those of us who only fly commercial airlines, how short have become the times between cities. How small we human creatures appear at 2,000 feet, and then totally disappear at 25,000 feet. These are all perspectives which were unknown to our ancient ancestors, but which impact us today as we, like them before, ask the basic questions of life.

# SCIENCE AND MODERNITY: GAINS AND LOSSES

Saul Bellow said that science has made a housecleaning of beliefs, and Friedrich Schiller in the late eighteenth century had already observed that the result was the "disgodding" of nature. Some of us say, good riddance! We welcome the demythologizing of nature, even at the price of losing supernatural solace in our flawed world. For many of us, religion is the last refuge for primitive animism and metaphysical philosophies that are only disguised theologies. We prefer the controlled experiment over mystical illumination and the mathematical-empirical over metaphysical interpretations of reality, not because we don't sense the terrors and tragedies of human existence, but rather because they appear to be the most valid and honest avenues to truth. Given the brute facts of the human condition, our dignity lies not in seeking a Magic Helper or constructing sentimental idealizations of reality, but rather in mustering all the courage, creativity, and compassion possible to us as humans.

Others of us feel a deep sorrow that science has cast us out of our "enchanted garden" (Max Weber), and that in the heart and mind of modern culture, "God is dead" (Nietzsche). In sacred stories and hallowed traditions, which warmed our hearts and edified our minds, religion gave us a home in the universe, a feeling of ultimate belonging, a sense of significance, and also an identity and role in the universe. With the arrival of the scientific world view, we experienced the loss of a sacred vision and the disenchantment of the world. Many of us, as individuals and even as entire societies, have lost our passionate sense of connection with the Infinite and the feeling that comes from knowing that our deeds are part of an ultimate good. In the drama, grandeur, and mystery of our liturgies, we experienced what seemed to be our deepest, most powerful and joyful selves, a sacred relationship with the cosmos, and a communion with the Divine. In our religious observances we elevated and sanctified even the minutest details of our daily lives, thus uniting the secular and the sacred. Everything was endowed with meaning, everything existed in accordance with the divine purpose. Painful it is to reflect on the changes since former times.

> The medieval view of God as the ground of Being and the Supreme Good toward which human beings were moving, Creator and Sustainer of the Universe, occasionally intervening miraculously in human affairs, was left behind at the end of the Middle Ages. With the development of modern science…the substitutes for God are Nature, Chance and Necessity. The shift from medieval to modern was essentially a shift of interest from final to efficient causality, the world is an accident and has no purpose beyond that accorded by human beings. The medieval picture involved a Universe of concentric spheres with the realm of becoming on Earth and that of static perfection above, a Universe created for Humanity. This view was shattered by the revelation of the scale of the heavens and the concomitant insignificance of humanity. The medieval picture was animistic: Nature is alive and sacred, spiritually significant, and an expression of the Divine. In the modern picture, nature is self-contained, independent and its exploration is not dependent on "the God hypothesis". The scientific revolution brought a desanctification of nature, and epistemology of objectification, a view of nature as passive feminine to be penetrated by the masculine mind.[5]

The Divine, once believed to be an omnipresent force in nature and man, has become "omniabsent". However, in some of the kindest visions and finest myths of certain of our religions, God created the universe and man for a great and noble end. No human life, however pointless it may have seemed, was meaningless, because as part of God's plan every life was assured of significance. Religion gave us the gift of transcendent meaning. For certain past generations and some individuals today, our deepest sadness may be the loss of the belief that existence is ultimately meaningful. Some of us might ask with Nietzsche, "Are we not straying as through an infinite nothing?"[6]

# NEED A NEW STORY?

According to Thomas Berry,

> It's all a question of story. We are in trouble just now because we do not have a good story. We are in between stories. The old story, the account of how the world came to be and how we fit into it, is no longer effective. Yet we have not learned the new story. Our traditional story of the universe sustained us for a long period of time. It shaped our emotional attitudes, provided us with life purposes, and energized action. It consecrated suffering and integrated knowledge. We awoke in the morning and knew where we were. We could answer the questions of our children. We could identify crime, punish transgressors. Everything was taken care of because the story was there. It did not necessarily make people good, nor did it take away the pains and stupidities of life or make for unfailing warmth in human association. It did provide a context in which life could function in a meaningful manner....

*continues*

*continued*

> A radical reassessment of the human situation is needed,
> especially concerning those basic values that give to life
> some satisfactory meaning. We need something that will
> supply in our times what was supplied formerly by our
> traditional religious story. If we are to achieve this pur-
> pose, we must begin where everything begins in human
> affairs—with the basic story, our narrative of how things
> came to be as they are, and how the future can be given
> some satisfying direction. We need a story that will edu-
> cate us, a story that will heal, guide and discipline us.[7]

Plenty of us reject the religious stories as untrue, find the secular stories superficial, consider the scientific stories meaningless, but continue to feel deep spiritual longings. We feel that our entire culture
and we personally have in some profound sense lost the big picture
and our place in it and thus lack the foundations for not only an
ethic and values but also for a spirituality, a mystique to inform and
inspire our daily lives. Plenty of us are looking for a new, comprehensive and valid story or a reinterpretation of an old story that can
give our lives meaning, and provides a map of life that shows where
we came from, where we are, and where we are going.

Some of us will need the emotional courage to face the possibility that there are no genuine replacements for certain high promises of our religions, including the promise of personal immortality.
Professional philosophy as it typically functions today does not provide a comprehensive world view or a practical guide for daily life.

Though many of us may feel a need for a new story, we can't
necessarily predict where it might come from or where it will lead
us. Perhaps it will come from a present religion in a more evolved
form, a radical return to old-time religion, a new religion, art, or an
entirely new philosophy. As fantastic as it may sound, the new world
view may come from contact with highly intelligent extraterrestrial
beings. A meaningful new story might come from science itself,

either in its present or a more highly evolved form. For those of us who are believers in current orthodox science, we might justifiably fear that people will ask of science what only religion, art, and philosophy can give, confuse physics with metaphysics and use science to create a powerful new delusion. However, some of us who love science and are working scientists consider that through science there may emerge a larger story meaningful to mankind, and which will better integrate science and spirituality. And in a time when so many are seeking new answers to old questions and are reaching for a new vision, might not the urgent task of philosophy be to create a meaningful world view based on the results of science?

# WHY SHOULD TRUTH BE SO IMPORTANT?

Is truth so important that it makes a practical difference in our personal lives? Consider some of the alternatives: ignorance, superstition, self-delusion, superficiality, prejudice, false hopes, powerlessness, and blind conformity.

> Can you imagine a world in which nobody any longer asked the philosophic questions, nobody was philosophical? It would be a world in which nobody penetrated below the facts of everyday life to think about what is real, true, valuable, just and meaningful in human life. It would be a world of mechanical men, women, and children moving among physical objects, a world in which we would have become hollow men going through meaningless motions and our speech would be empty chatter.[8]

The spirit of inquiry is one of the perfections of the human race, part of what makes us what we are. At its most idealistic, seeking truth is its own reward and is independent of personal advantage. It doesn't need to be justified by the possibilities of status, money, or fame. Our belief in the primary value of truth is not necessarily based on an absolute certainty. It requires a certain faith, or at least the hopeful hypothesis that in the long run it will lead to something better, if not for us as individuals, at least for our species. For Bertrand Russell, "It is not by delusion, however exalted, that mankind can prosper but only by unswerving courage in the pursuit of truth."[9] For some of us, we have such a drive and passion for truth that we can't stop ourselves. We have no choice; it's our nature, our calling.

Seekers asking the big questions of life have sometimes been described in such grand mythic terms as "on a hero's journey," going through "the great ordeal," on a "vision quest," and as pathfinders on "the soul's high adventure."[10] Truth questers can be considered spiritual pioneers, human treasures, leaders, and a leaven for all society. But even without the mythic dimensions of the search, the very asking of the big questions can add significance and meaning to our lives as we take on a larger identity by relating to the ultimate concerns of life. For some of us the search itself can be a kind of salvation. However, no matter how high our calling, none of us needs to be a snob. Truth seeking is not the only great and grand human activity. Each of us has different talents and resonates to different concerns. As truth seekers we have no need for Lord Ego and Lady Vanity.

Whatever answers we may or may not discover, the very asking of the basic questions has a value. The asking can save us from idolatry. That is, it can protect us from an unbecoming forgetfulness of the miracle of being, preserve in us the primordial awe and wonder that anything exists and the sense that our lives and all of life are sacred. Idolatry is a form of provincialism. Reflecting on the basic questions of life and their profound implications can expand our awareness of the vast context of our lives in space and time and the potential breadth and depth of human life. Such reflection enlarges the perspective from which we view our lives and liberates us from being consumed and trapped by the trivia of our daily, practical lives. We are prevented from worshipping the false idols of taking ourselves too seriously and of mistaking our individual consciousness for the world itself. To deeply reflect on the basic questions is to honor existence itself, to not take it for granted, and to not just go through the motions of living. To ask the basic questions is to not confine our existence to our individual, daily lives but to expand our awareness to the wider connections with the human species, the life community, and the universe.

Furthermore, asking the basic questions is of value in itself because it reveals our ignorance. Typically, the more we ask and even the more we know, the more we become aware of what we don't know. Reflecting on the implications of the questions reveals widening and deepening realms of reality of what we need to know in order to have even beginning answers to the basic questions of life. To ask these questions and work toward answers, if only to reveal our ignorance and limitations, are in themselves valuable truths to discover. We are only wise to the extent that we know our limitations. To know our limitations is to liberate ourselves from false expectations and futile efforts. To know our limitations and ignorance gives us permission to live with uncertainties and ambiguities, allows us to be more modest, less strident and self-righteous in our claims to truth. And perhaps most important, to know our limitations allows us to be more accepting, patient, and loving with ourselves and all other humans who share the same condition of unknowing. To ask the basic questions is to more fully appreciate, not depreciate, life and for many of us to become aware that the mysteries of existence are far deeper and more magnificent than any of the traditional stories were capable of comprehending or communicating.

# QUESTIONING THE GIVEN

To love the true is to question the given. It is to honestly ask the sometimes painful, awkward, and haunting question, "But is this really true?" To love the true is to grow up. It is to no longer be the child passively and uncritically assuming the truthfulness of our parents' definition of reality, to no longer be content with secondhand knowing, with "hand-me-downs" that don't quite fit us or the present realities. To love the true is to wake up. It is to rouse ourselves out of our cultural trance, hypnotized by the repetitious routines of our daily lives. To love the true is to question authority, not only of persons and institutions but also of the accepted ways of knowing. In our not especially caring world, to love the true is not only to be a consumer of the given realities but to be an investor, caring enough to risk our personal assets so that we might base our lives on reality, not just on the superficial and the sentimental. Because we belong to that species most capable of learning sense and nonsense, some of us need to deeply question our central certitudes, so that we don't fall more deeply into error. Doubt is a virtue, not a vice. Doubt is not just a philosophical luxury, it can also be a critical necessity, as when in a personal life crisis events close in on us, and our models of reality prove to be inadequate and destructive. We need to question ourselves, because we have ample ability to deceive ourselves when it seems to be in our own best interest. We tend to believe what we want to believe. In a society, then as now, more acquisitive than inquisitive, Socrates proclaimed that the unexamined life is not worth living. For us, to doubt is a right, a duty, an expression of our love of truth, and the privilege of being part of the human adventure.

Doubters are deviants, and deviants are usually punished. Research demonstrates that when an individual differs from the group norm, the group tends to devalue, ridicule, avoid, discriminate against, oppress, or reject the deviant. Individuals can be punished in all sorts of cruel ways, even for quite minor variations from group norms of beauty, like being too fat or thin, too tall or short, too dark or light skinned, or simply having a physical disability. Even these small physical variations can be viewed as irritating, threatening, or hateful by the group. Most of us as individuals or groups prefer the normal and habitual. We tend toward the comforts of our conceptual prisons rather than the freedom of new perspectives. Doubters can be inconvenient, disturbing, and threatening to the group, because unless we are all in great pain, we incline toward the calm and security of our collective certainty. For most of human history, the group defined reality for the individual; the group judged the individual. Today, with global communication and travel, more individuals are confronted by conflicting world views and cultural beliefs, which in turn evokes self-questioning and critical thinking. Many social organizations have lost not only their exclusive authority to construct but also their power to enforce their models of reality. Rather than embracing groupthink, many of us today espouse the democratic ideal of the self-determining individual and thus the necessity and opportunity of "do-it-yourself" philosophizing. Meanwhile, the existing groups strive to mold us toward conformity.

For a single individual to challenge the group is to possibly risk emotional and financial survival and perhaps to experience self-doubt, depression, disillusionment, confusion, fear, and loneliness. A deep sense of loss can be felt as one is severed from the bonding, belonging, and ties of affection with the group. To question the consensus reality of the group, we need to have faith in the dignity of our individual selves, not as perfect but as honest and competent inquirers. We need to trust our individual powers to know, even if our knowing is only partial, provisional, and imperfect in face of the immensity and complexity of reality. We can still love and feel attached to certain group traditions without worshipping them mindlessly, but as truth seekers we may also originate entirely new traditions. When the going gets tough and we feel very much alone, we might remind ourselves that we have a home in our family of truth seekers with its long and noble tradition.

To be a doubter, to cultivate a critical and questioning attitude, we usually don't need to go out of our way to annoy people, to be a public nuisance. We usually don't need to go out of our way to be an obstructionist and certainly not an exhibitionist! We don't need to create a cult of individualism. After all, we individuals can be as self-serving, self-deluded, and just plain wacky as any group or organization. What we do need is to not only love truth but, as much as possible, to also love people. As we see it, we need not only tolerance but compassion, and not only for others but also for ourselves. We all have our limitations. We are tiny creatures, specks in space and time, quite often with rather murky minds, muddled emotions, and mixed motivations. We are born ignorant, innocent, naïve, susceptible to all kinds of suggestions from those who will love and provide for us. We all remain at least somewhat culture-bound, somewhat asleep in Jung's "collective dream."

To doubt, to honestly question, requires courage. We can put at risk our deepest beliefs and most profound prejudices. An essential component of courage is fear, and truth seekers should be afraid. Raw reality can be too harsh for our tender psyches; it can overwhelm us. The reckless are not afraid, because they are inexperienced and ignorant. They do not believe the danger signs. For some of us, it takes heroic courage to become an adult, to grow beyond the apparent invulnerability of our parents, powerful institutions, and the yearning for structure and certainty rather than to flow with the insecurities of daily life. It takes courage to question widely accepted magical solutions and facile answers to the basic questions of human existence. Part of the uncertainty in our truth seeking can also be that we don't really know for sure if we are a hero or a fool, yet we do know that we don't want to live a lie. To not doubt, to not question the truths given to us, may not only be a transgression against our human abilities but also a repression of the human spirit.

# PREPARING FOR THE PERILS

The questions can be dangerous. While questions may visit our house, we must be careful that they do not take over our house. Without wisdom, truth seekers can go crazy. Asking the big questions can release too many psychic demons. Honest reflection on the basic questions can be disorienting. The discovery of unexpected answers can be disillusioning. If we begin our quest with some cracks in our psyche already, such as psychotic tendencies or excessive neurotic demands, and then add acute situational pressures, we can experience a mental and emotional breakdown.

Freud stated, "The moment a man questions the meaning and value of life, he is already sick..." He went on to explain, "By asking this question one is merely admitting to a store of unsatisfied libido..."[11] From our observations of truth seekers, it seems that the more usual reason for falling into confusion is that we become top heavy, living too much in our minds and so our lives get out of balance. We forget the common sense of meeting our basic human needs, living as though we were pure intellects. The mind is a great place to visit, but no place to live.

To seek truth without wisdom is to invite disaster. To seek truth with wisdom is to cultivate the possibility of great personal happiness. By "wisdom" we mean the practical, psychological understanding of our basic human needs and the skillful means to meet those needs. To walk through life and keep our balance, it is best to have two strong legs: both wisdom and knowledge to guide and protect us. As circumstances allow, meeting our basic human needs is the foundation, the home base from which we venture out in our personal quest for ultimate realities. We not only look up to the great metaphysical heights, but to prevent falling we also look down at our feet, to be sure we are grounded in our fundamental human needs reality. Unlike a particular psychologist who was described as knowing everything about psychology but nothing about people, let us know much about the practical day-to-day world and not only about world views. As truth seekers, we are the primary instruments of our inquiry, and thus we need to take good care of ourselves. We are *human* truth seekers, not just truth seekers, and discoveries are made by persons, not merely by minds. Furthermore, most of us seek truth not only to improve our minds but also to transform our lives. Our intent is not to reduce philosophy, religion, and science to psychology, but neither should we skip psychology. While on our personal quest, we need to live, to meet the many demands of life to assure our physical, emotional, and economic survival. Truth seekers who neglect their basic human needs do so at their own great peril.

Most of us have certain unmet needs, but that doesn't necessarily mean that we should postpone our quest. We don't need to be perfectly equipped, only sufficiently able to meet our basic needs, so that we don't create such emotional desperation and cognitive distortion that we grasp onto any quick and facile answer to the questions of life. The hope is that, along our journey our life situation will improve, and our practical skills will sufficiently develop to better fulfill our needs, resulting in greater psychological freedom and more objective judgments about reality. Below is a description of nine basic human needs and ways they might be fulfilled in a high-functioning person, one whose truth seeking is rooted in abundance rather than from deficiency.

## Nine Basic Human Needs

**Biological Survival**—Certain minimum biological needs must be met if we are to survive. These are not a matter of choice but are a given of our biological existence. They include oxygen, food, water, sleep, shelter, locomotion, and the adequate functioning of our physiological systems. At best, we have a high energy level, our senses of vision, hearing, touch, smell, and taste are intact, and we are free from debilitating physical pain, deep depression, and serious psychotic and neurotic symptoms. At best, we enjoy safety, security, and stability in conditions of peace, justice, law and order, rather than war, revolution, violent crime, and natural disasters. While sexual expression may not be a possibility or a choice for all, reproduction is a necessity for the continuation of the species. Health requires good nutrition, regular exercise, and freedom from polluting toxins, including the abuse of alcohol, prescription and street drugs.

**Relationships**—A sense of belonging and acceptance rather than isolation, loneliness, and rejection. To be noticed and not ignored. To not feel invisible. To feel that we matter and are appreciated. Sharing of ideals and disappointments, joys and sorrows. Common goals, the mutual meeting of needs. Human warmth, emotional closeness, physical touching, giving and receiving gifts, loving glances, sexual pleasure. A support community in time of crisis. The ability to relate to others, mutual caring, concern, compassion, and love. Investing our time and talent for the welfare of others. Leading, mentoring, educating, training, supervising, and coaching the next generation. Recognition and approval. Loyalty, fidelity, and honoring our commitments. Ties of affection, sharing the rites of passage in birth, coming of age, graduation, marriage, honors, sickness, and death. Relationship needs are accomplished through a variety of means including mating, marriage, family, parenting, grandparenting, friendships, companions, work mates, team mates; through a sense of identity with our traditions, trade, industry, profession, social, recreational, and spiritual communities, as well as sense of belonging to our ethnic group, neighborhood, state, region, nation, planet, and universe.

**Self-Esteem**—To feel good about ourselves, to feel that we are O.K. To basically accept ourselves and our physical appearance, assets, and limitations. To feel competent and confident to meet life's challenges. A strong, stable, firmly based, and realistic evaluation of ourselves, which is neither self-exalting nor self-debasing. To like ourselves and feel we are good people. Strong enough to accurately hear disturbing realities and painful feedback from others without extreme, reality-distorting defensiveness. Reality-centered, not ego-centered. Faith in ourselves that we can survive. Resilient, knowing that when we fall we can regroup ourselves and bounce back to full functioning. To not be devastated by rejection. To value ourselves enough so that we don't have to brag and compete with others, feel envy and jealousy, and put other people down. To not feel that we are so very precious, one-of-a-kind, and must be the center of attention and always part of the inner circle. To accept those flaws we can't change in ourselves, and for those flaws that we have overcome, to refrain from feeling self-righteous toward others with still the same limitations. To be free of unwarranted shame, guilt, regrets, and self-hatred. To be able to forgive ourselves and others. To not reject ourselves or others for falling short of our impossible ideals of perfection. To appreciate ourselves, to feel worthwhile and worthy of the goods of life. Much of life is a projection of how we feel about ourselves.

**Self-Reliance**—The power in knowing and liking who we are, knowing what and how to obtain what we need. Not independence, which is impossible, an empty delusion, but rather a productive interdependency based on a mutual meeting of needs. Not power over people, but empowering others with the confidence and skills to better meet their needs. Empowering ourselves and others is essential for a more fully evolved human life. Powerlessness corrupts. Weak people have weak relationships. If we feel like doormats, we will find someone to step on us. When we feel lacking in power, rather than actively and directly taking responsibility for our needs, we often unconsciously or consciously play manipulative games, including blaming, complaining, threatening, avoiding, resenting, pouting, pleasing, putting down, or perfecting the roles of helpless victim, martyr, and hysterical tragedienne. Rather, we enrich ourselves and others, because what we don't have, we can't give. Enough faith in ourselves to challenge our own and others' stories of reality, enough skill and experience to at least provisionally trust in ourselves and our judgment of reality. An inner discipline so we can rely on ourselves to do what we need to do. A certain toughness so we can handle emotional and physical pain, mental confusion, and situational pressures. To have confidence in ourselves that somehow we can survive. Self-initiative, imaginative and enterprising. Active, not passive. Courage and perseverance. Simplicity based not on how much we want but how little we really need. Economically self-supporting through a needed skill, trade, profession, product, or service. Financial self-reliance based not on the amount of money we have but rather on the ratio between the money we earn and what in reality we need to spend. An accurate assessment of our emotional, intellectual and spiritual powers, and avoiding situations beyond our powers. A feeling person but not a slave to our emotions. Emotional self-reliance in connecting but not clinging, appreciating but not craving for external validation. Not robbed of our power by addictions to alcohol, drugs, love, knowledge, status, fame, or fortune. A rich inner emotional, intellectual, and spiritual life rather than a desperate need to fill an inner emptiness. Enjoying being ourselves and being with ourselves; not feeling the need to be someone else or always with others. The ability to meet our basic needs through a variety of means, and different types of persons and situations, rather than by only one way, one ideal person or situation. Through

mutually empowering relationships, we build the foundations for a more secure, efficient, and fruitful self-
reliance.

**Work**—Our life work can be our most personal, powerful, creative, spiritual, and truthful expression of what we
profoundly believe and care for and perhaps even a
unique gift that only we can give. For better or worse,
our work can critically shape who we become. If we
value the purpose of our work, our lives will feel more
significant, and life itself will be more meaningful. At
best, our work is not just a job, a career, but a special
calling infused with love and play. At best, we can earn a
living at what we enjoy most, even though at times the
work is extremely demanding, discouraging, and requiring great discipline. At worst, we have never sought or
discovered our life work, or our jobs are merely means
to survival. Whether we feel alienated or fulfilled in our
work can affect our physical and emotional health, our
self-esteem, relationships, and color our entire outlook
on life. Some of us are fortunate to find our work early
in our lives. Some others of us, because of economic
necessity and other reasons, wait decades before we can
begin our natural work. Some of us, because of lack of
opportunity, fear, real or perceived needs, wait until
retirement to do our most enjoyable and meaningful
work.

**Love**—An emotionally charged bond, attachment, or
attraction. When experienced positively, we can have
such feelings as ecstasy, oneness with the beloved, special-
ness, sexual bliss, creativity, and blessed as if we are in the
company of the gods. Less dramatically, we may experience emotional warmth, closeness, comfort, care, commitment, pleasure, acceptance, safety, peace, and sacredness. Varieties of love can include the romantic, the
committed, the married, the love between parents and

children, and the love for family, relatives, tribe, ethnic group, as well as for friends, colleagues, animals, our work, trade, and profession. We can experience love in camaraderie, sisterhood, brotherhood, and with our neighbors, neighborhood, region, culture, nation, planet, and universe. We can have great love for the Divine, nature, learning, the arts, science, truth, goodness, beauty, and a healthy love for ourselves. On the downside, our "love" can be more of an addiction, a self-serving fantasy, a habit, a trap, emotional and financial dependency. Authentic support groups, beginning with the family, can be circles of love to protect, nurture, and empower us. The experience of healthy human love is vital for most truth seekers, because it provides a secure emotional foundation for our adventures with reality and protects us from becoming desperate prey for charlatans and wishful thinking, which promises to fill our emotional emptiness at the price of our abandoning objective judgment. For some of us, love is the greatest truth a human can discover. For some of us, we instinctively agree with the saying, "Love isn't what makes the world go around. It's what makes the ride worthwhile."

**Play**—To celebrate life, that we are alive! To luxuriously lie in bed some mornings, gently waking, and amused by our minds playfully drifting in and out of consciousness. To breathe in the crisp, fresh air of daybreak as the sun announces the dawn of a new day, and later to quietly experience the peace and magnificence of the setting sun. To wander through the woods, glancing at this, noticing that, breathing in all the fragrances of nature, gently feeling the texture of a flower, and so at peace with nature that a nearby deer is undisturbed by us, trusting that we both can share in harmony this place and moment. To enjoy the strength and grace of our bodies in a long swim, and then to lie on the beach, warmed by the sun, totally exhausted and exhilarated. To enjoy our nature in all its sensuality of touching, tasting, smelling, hearing, and seeing. To marvel at the zest and ingenuity of our children playing, and to join in with gusto and lots of physicality. To play ball, to play music, to play cards, to perform or watch a play, and to engage in sex play with our partners as playmates. Recreation is re-creating the playful spontaneity of the joyous child within. Holidays are freedom and rest from our adult responsibilities to refresh and renew our spirits. Play is part of worship, running, racquetball, skiing, sky diving, shopping; decorating ourselves, our homes, and our workplaces. Play includes the joys of learning new skills like singing, sculpting, cooking, sewing, dancing, and foreign languages. Travel can be the carefree discovery of new people, new places and cultures. To feel fully alive, most of us need times of unpredictability, challenge, the unknown, excitement, thrills, romance, abandon, novelty, and variety. Unrelenting routine leads to boredom, which in turn causes depression. Play changes our consciousness, liberates us from our daily duties, and provides a certain distance from which we can have a more accurate perception of our lives. Play helps make life worth living, energizing us with anticipations of future joys as well as providing pleasurable memories to savor. Play can lighten our heavy ego demands, nurture intimacy with our mates, family, and colleagues, and deepen friendships. Play allows us to be gracious, mindful of the grace of life, and gives the opportunity to entertain by sharing our spirits, humor, homes, and hospitality. As truth seekers asking the basic questions of life, it seems that in order to keep our balance, we must not take ourselves too seriously, but have some laughter and lighthearted fun along the way. Part of enlightenment is to lighten up. There is the joy of wisdom but also the wisdom of joy.

**Purpose**—A reason to live. The reason can be real or delusionary, but we experience the reason as real. It usually provides hope and may give us a sense of significance, perhaps even of being special or sacred. With the hope of a worthwhile, attainable goal, our lives have meaning, direction, and focus. For some of us, the meaning of our lives derives from a transcendent, ultimate purpose. For others of us, meaning derives intrinsically from within the natural order. A meaningful purpose in life may give us a real or delusionary hope for salvation, progress, and a sense of mission. It motivates us toward practical goals in our daily lives and may give a rationale for human ignorance, evil, and suffering. Without an energizing, worthwhile purpose for our personal lives, we can experience depression and despair. A belief in a comprehensive purpose can explain why we and the world are what we are. If we feel lost and aimless, purpose is a beacon that lights our way and orients us through the darkness and unknowns of existence. We might have one overarching purpose or a blend of more limited purposes that infuse meaning into our lives. They can change with our learning experiences, particular situation, and life stages, and they can cover a wide spectrum, including survival, security, status, success, fame, wealth, power, creativity, pleasure, excitement, popularity, love, self-sacrifice, health, healing and helping others, revenge, self-vindication, truth, goodness, beauty, justice, eternal life, enlightenment, spirituality, and union with the Divine. We humans are the species that experiences a basic need for a conscious purpose in our daily lives. If we don't discover it in or create it out of reality, we can fabricate purpose out of our imaginations. It has been said that whoever has a purpose in life can endure anything.

**Self-Realization**—The freedom and skills to be ourselves at our very best. The opportunity and power to activate our natural and perhaps unique capacities. It is not uniqueness for its own sake or for ego glorification but is a result of carefully listening to and following our individual nature in our particular circumstances. It is not necessarily individualism, because in some families, groups, and tribes, we might best realize our potential primarily in service to the communal needs. Regardless of whether the self is an entity or a collection of processes, eternal or transitory, self-realization requires a certain degree of freedom from mental and emotional barriers and external constraints in order to be true to our own nature. We trust and listen to ourselves rather than experiencing self-estrangement, while also recognizing that through self-disclosure to others we can develop self-awareness. We understand that through relationships with others we can learn to better discern our natural calling, talents, and limitations and possibly also discover our own special greatness. Self-realization involves not so much abstract ideals of who we should be but rather the experiential discovery of our own way along the high road of our own nature at our personal best. It uncovers not only our own inherent positive capacity as an individual, but at best it also manifests new possibilities for the human race. It is spirituality, at least in the sense of discovering and living our own human spirits and helping others discover and live their spirits. Self-realization is not just coping. It is creating and expressing ourselves as our most reality-based, imaginative, and ethical selves. Our individual development is part of human evolution.

◆ ◆ ◆ ◆ ◆

The basic human needs are dynamically interrelated. Deprivation or realization of one need can impede or promote the fulfillment of other needs. For example, biological health or illness can not only affect our self-esteem, relationships, and work, but inversely the presence or loss of love, purpose, and self-reliance can nurture or undermine our physical health. Depression and anxiety are the result of unmet biological and psychological needs. Healthy relationships are based on the mutual meeting of needs. If basic needs are not met in a love relationship, the love will wither. Love is perishable.

It is essential to distinguish between needs and wants in order to avoid much unnecessary suffering. Wants are the delicious and exhilarating extras, like champagne and chocolate, but they are not the foundations of human life. Wants can add great pleasure or misery to our lives by flowing with or interfering with our basic needs. Wants can grow like weeds but cannot meet our needs. We can never get enough of what we really don't need.

# WHERE TO START?

Where do we begin or renew our journey in seeking personal, valid answers to the basic questions of life? One place to start is with those questions that are most fundamental to us in our individual lives and that perhaps also are the most disturbing. We can also begin by questioning the answers given to us that we sense may be untrue or no longer seem vital or relevant. Uncovering the stories we unconsciously and repetitively play out at the very center of our psyches can reveal an invisible stew of unquestioned and even conflicting assumptions and beliefs. The world is made up of all sorts of stories that tell us what is important, good, bad and what it's all about. Each of us was born into a world of local, particular stories that we did not choose but that were impressed on our innocent, uncritical minds and hearts as the true, the good, and the beautiful. To discover the stories living in us, it is often enlightening to systematically identify our parent's stories, which gave meaning and direction to their lives. What were the dominant religious, cultural, class, ethnic, gender, and racial stories they were told? We are in a sense what we love. What have we been taught to love? As adults we may have taken on a new story. What now would be the title of our life story? To more precisely discern what we value in life, it can be revealing to identify our heroes and villains. What else do these choices tell us about ourselves?

As we begin our truth seeking journey, we might ask and obtain insights as to why we are asking the questions, what are our expectations about possible answers, and be clear about our life priorities and the time, training and energy we are willing to commit to inquiry. It is essential to ask ourselves if this is, or when would be the appropriate time for our inquiries. If we are in great emotional and mental turmoil, it would be better for most of us to first focus on fulfilling the most urgent of our unmet needs.

Along the way, we can seek out experienced others who might share their wisdom and knowledge. Some of us have been blessed with wise parents, a fact we might not appreciate until later in life. Mark Twain recalls, "When I was a boy of fourteen, my father was so ignorant I could hardly stand to have the old man around. But when I got to be twenty-one, I was astonished at how much he had learned in seven years." Quite often in our extended family there is an uncle, aunt, or other relative who has remarkable knowledge and wisdom to share with us. Furthermore, because they may know us quite well, they can give us valuable feedback for our self-understanding. Sometimes we discover in a chance encounter that a stranger, work mate, or fellow student has an uncommon wisdom. A "simple" pastor or a "common" teacher might give us far more valuable advice than a great theologian or eminent scholar. Sometimes the least educated or even illiterate person can unfold in the simplest way a profound and often overlooked wisdom, because they have less learned ignorance. Sometimes the knowledge and wisdom we need awaits us with the neighbor across the street, the expert across town, or in our travel adventures, meeting new people and living in foreign cultures on the other side of the planet.

For those of us examining the truth claims of religion, we might most respectfully begin by deepening our knowledge and critical appreciation of the particular religion in which we have been nurtured or with which we now experience a special affinity. However, our preference is to also study and experience other religions, with the direct guidance of persons deeply steeped in their own traditions and thus by comparative methods better understand what is unique and shared in each religion's approach to reality. To study philosophy and the history of philosophy, both by reading and with authentic philosophizing philosophers, can be a great adventure in truth and wisdom and excellent training in critical thinking. To understand the scientific method, nothing can substitute for actually doing science, but as to how science might comprehensively help us approach the basic questions of life, we would equally require a study of the history and philosophy of science as a truth seeking venture.

# WHAT MIGHT WE FIND?

Answers to the basic questions range along a wide spectrum, from the brightest and most beautiful colors of the rainbow to the darkest of shadows. Some of us discover that there aren't any answers, there have never been any answers, and there are never going to be any answers—that's the answer. Some others of us find comprehensive and meaningful answers, which are a trustworthy and even inspiring guide for our personal lives. Whether we experience the results of our truth quest on the up or down side can have much to do with our original expectations. Expectations can destroy the experience. For example, if we begin by demanding absolute truth and feel entitled to certitude, but later discover that only partial knowledge, probabilities, and possibilities are within the human range of knowing, we can end in despair. If we begin by assuming that we have only the purest of motivations for seeking truth, we might end up with the humiliating realization that we were more the noble neurotic, avoiding unpleasant truths about ourselves, postponing growing up, and evading basic responsibilities. Contrary to our great expectations, we may feel betrayed, because the ultimate truths we discovered are powerless to change our basic personality and solve our personal problems. Truth has its limitations. Agonizing can be the unanticipated personal sacrifices, painful conflicts, choices, and regrets that knowledge can bring. For those of us who begin with perfectionistic expectations of the highest idealism of what the world should be, our subsequent disappointing discoveries can make us cynical malcontents with bitter cosmic complaints. A more ominous consequence of disillusioned idealism is narcissistic nihilism—if we can't have a perfect reality, then nothing is of value. Love of the ideal turns to hatred of the real. The life instinct becomes dominated by the death instinct. The urge to create becomes the urge to destroy.

After years of seeking, some of us celebrate by teaching or preaching the important truths we have discovered. Others of us find a deeply meaningful contentment in the quiet acceptance of the inexplicability of the last ground of things. Some of us seek ultimate meanings to the last day of our lives; others of us conclude that the notion of "cosmic purpose" is not a component of reality but only a human-made mental construct to meet our psychic needs. Some of us have the tendency and ability to explicitly and logically articulate a conceptual response to the basic questions; others of us dissolve the questions in the context of life, sensing the answers rather than seeing the answers. In other words, life is the question put to us at our birth, and our lived lives are the total response to the questions.

Some of us never sufficiently free ourselves from the soap operas of our lives in order to conduct any sustained, competent inquiry. Some of us become convinced that the basic questions of life are only futile, self-torture questions, a deadly trap like flypaper luring the insect to its unsuspected end. We may also conclude that life is not a problem to solve but rather a mystery to live and that the beginning of wisdom is to enjoy the mystery! Some of us have given up on ever attaining a valid and uplifting world view but may deeply appreciate or find pitifully vain the hopes and efforts of mystics and metaphysicians to discover wonderful happenings in the universe.

After systematically seeking answers to the basic questions of life, we may conclude that nobody but nobody knows the answers, that we live on the crazy planet of unknowing. Some of us become convinced that a certain belief must be true because it is believed by so many people, a phenomenon perhaps best described in the ancient Chinese saying, "One dog barks at a shadow, and 400 dogs make it a fact." So abhorrent may be the answers we find that we cannot consciously accept them. They are too painful. Thus, without our conscious choice, our psyches may protect us by repressing into the unconscious the painful realities that we have discovered. But when we bury feelings, we bury them alive. We can still experience a vague but chronic melancholy, and for those of us who seek the transcendent, we may even experience a kind of cosmic sadness that ultimate reality did not live up to our expectations. With time, healing, and a stronger sense of self, we may more safely and productively renew our journey.

As religious seekers we may lose our faith or deepen our faith. Knowledge destroys; knowledge creates. Some of us are convinced that God will hold us accountable for the rational nature He gave us, that Jesus came to take away our sins, not our brains, and that the Buddha sought to enlighten, not dull, our minds. For others of us, blind belief, not rationally and empirically informed faith, is the answer. Montaigne observed, "Nothing is so firmly believed as that which is least known." Some of us who are spiritual seekers may give over our minds and totally submit to an "enlightened" teacher or guru, woefully too late for Voltaire's warning, "Those who can make you believe absurdities can make you commit atrocities."

As a result of our inquiries, some of us will make better sense of the cosmos and thus make better sense of our lives. Some of us, after a long life of reflection, will sift and winnow all that we have learned down to a few simply stated phrases, which will only seem profoundly true and wise to those who have also thoroughly experienced life. Some of us may conclude our quest with the truthful realization that most fundamentally what we were seeking all along was not truth but rather love, community, and the opportunity to help people. Hopefully, each of us in our own lifetime can attain knowledge and wisdom at least a little more clearly and comprehensively and thus leave a legacy of light rather than darkness for the next generation. Each of us is an experiment as we discover our own way in the laboratory of life.

◆ ◆ ◆ ◆ ◆

The focus of the next chapter is epistemology: the ways of knowing and how we know when we know. I begin by presenting our evolutionary context of millions, even billions of years and provide some perspectives on the evolution of the human brain. Then I trace the origins of Western science and philosophy to the ancient Greeks and tell the story of the scientific revolution of the sixteenth and seventeenth centuries. I follow with the critiques of empiricism by Locke, Hume, and Kant. Finally, I sketch some other ways of knowing and raise the question: How rational are we? The goal of the chapter is that you become more competent in judging which answers to your basic questions about life are possible, probable, true, or not true.

# 3

# *Ways of Knowing: How Do We Know When We Know?*

## THE EVOLUTIONARY CONTEXT

Prior to the late eighteenth century and especially before Darwin in the nineteenth, the evolutionary perspective was unavailable to philosophers, scientists, and religious truth seekers. Today, some epistemologists maintain that the best approach to understand how, why, and when we humans developed our ways of knowing is in the context of evolutionary history. Awesome as is the fact that we are the product of an immensely long evolutionary process, it is perhaps equally remarkable that the modern human is such a recent arrival, our tenure thus far is so brief and yet our dominance so powerful on the planet. Below, I list and date some major evolutionary events. Though experts may assign different dates, sometimes by millions of years in the most distant past, they do share a consensus on the sequence of events. Also, most agree that *Homo sapiens* appeared some 170,000 years ago and had an anatomy and cranial capacity identical with ours today. Since that time, the human species has not evolved biologically in any significant ways but rather has evolved culturally.

| *Years Before the Present* | *Some Major Evolutionary Events* |
| --- | --- |
| 4,500,000,000 | Formation of the Earth |
| 3,500,000,000 | First fossil evidence of life (prokaryotes) |
| 2,500,000,000 | Appearance of significant levels of atmospheric oxygen |
| 1,700,000,000 | Eucaryotes (first cells with nuclei) |
| 500,000,000 | Fish |
| 365,000,000 | Amphibians |
| 300,000,000 | Reptiles |
| 225,000,000 | Age of dinosaurs begins |
| 220,000,000 | Mammals |
| 150,000,000 | Birds |
| 65,000,000 | End of dinosaurs; mammals begin to dominate |
| 60,000,000 | First primates (prosimians, i.e., premonkeys) |
| 35,000,000 | Monkeys and apes |
| 25,000,000 | First humanlike apes |
| 4,500,000 | First hominids (species on the human evolutionary branch) |
| 2,000,000 | *Homo habilis* (tool making) |
| 1,600,000 | *Homo erectus* (upright walking) |

| Years Before the Present | Some Major Evolutionary Events |
|---|---|
| 1,500,000 | First use of fire by hominids |
| 170,000 | *Homo sapiens* (same anatomy and cranial capacity as modern humans) |

| Years B.C. | |
|---|---|
| 40,000 | New stone and bone tool-making technology, blade tools |
| 40,000 | Earliest known representational art (cave drawings, three-dimensional objects) |
| 15,000 | Plant domestication, agriculture begins |
| 14,000 | Pottery invented (clean and durable storage for food and drink) |
| 12,000 | End of last Ice Age |
| 10,000 | Domestication of animals; villages appear |
| 7,000 | Metal-working techniques result in metal tools |
| 5,400 | Invention of the wheel |
| 5,000 | Irrigation begins |
| 4,000 | City-states ruled by kings, e.g., the Sumerian city of Ur |
| 3,100 | Writing invented in Sumeria, spreads rapidly |
| 3,000 | Major developments in metallurgy, bronze tools and weapons |
| 3,000 | Civilizations emerge in Middle East, South Asia, and Far East |
| 2,500 | Wooden boats sailing the Mediterranean |

*continues*

*continued*

| Years B.C. | Some Major Evolutionary Events |
| --- | --- |
| 2,400 | Indus civilization rapidly expands |
| 2,000 | Empires develop from nations in the Middle East |
| 1,750 | Shang Dynasty, first developed civilization in China |
| 1,400 | Earliest alphabetic system, from Ugarit in Syria |
| 1,300 | Moses |
| 1,200 | Iron tools and weapons |
| 800 | The first *Upanishads* |
| 600 | Origins of science and philosophy in ancient Greece, Taoism in China |
| 500 | Buddha, Confucius, Pythagoras |
| 400 | Socrates, teacher of Plato; Democritus |
| 300 | Aristotle, Euclidean geometry |
| 250 | Archimedean physics |
| 27 | Roman Empire established |
| 4 | Birth of Christ |

Carl Sagan calculated a "cosmic calendar" on which he placed the Big Bang of 15 billion years ago at January 1, the formation of the Earth at September 14, and the origins of life on Earth at September 25. The first humans appeared on December 31 at 10:30 p.m., later that evening Christ was born at 11:59:56 p.m., and the experimental method in science emerged at 11:59:59. "All of recorded history occupies the last ten seconds of December 31; and the time frame from the waning of the Middle Ages to the present occupies little more than one second."[1] We are such Johnny-and-Janes-come-lately!

For the evolutionary epistemologist, our cognitive and sensory abilities are a product of evolution, just as are the particular shape and size of our body parts and all other aspects of life. The goal is to bring our understanding of evolution to bear on our understanding of human knowing. Of the estimated two billion species that have appeared on the planet since the beginning of the Cambrian period 545 million years ago, at least 99.9 percent are now extinct. The modern human, along with millions of other species, has survived thanks to sufficiently successful adaptations to at least minimally supportive environments. The knowledge necessary to survive did not drop full-blown out of the sky. Rather, it accumulated little by little over eons of time in response to the demands of particular surroundings. This type of knowledge is adaptive learning, and it must have had a sufficient correspondence with external reality or the organism would not have survived. The immediate environment is not exactly the same for each species, so each species must adapt to those particular features of its own surrounding reality in order to survive and reproduce. Thus the adaptive knowledge of each species is not a general knowledge but rather is species-specific to a particular environment. In short, each species evolves its own cognitive and sensory niche.

For example, we humans can only see less than a trillionth of one percent of the electromagnetic spectrum. This thin slice of reality to which our eyes are sensitive and which we call "visible light" excludes gamma and X-rays as well as infrared, microwaves, and radio waves. Unlike certain animal species, we cannot hear sound frequencies beyond the range of 20 to 20,000 hertz (number of sound vibrations per second) and cannot approach their unique abilities to discriminate a variety of smells, tastes, and sounds. Our everyday lives exist in a world of middling dimensions, a narrow splinter of reality measured in feet, yards, miles, and years, incapable of visualizing atoms, billions of years, the speed of light, or any other micro or macrocosmic phenomena. As a result of natural selection acting upon genetic variation, each species evolves its own practical capacities and ways of gaining knowledge for those aspects of its local world that are critical for its own survival.

To a preeminent degree among the conscious species, we humans not only selectively sense reality, but we also have evolved innate mental categories through which we construct our own species-unique interpretations of reality. We do not directly conceive reality as it is in itself, but only as it is filtered through our mental templates. We can never have immediate knowledge of raw reality, because all our knowing is processed through our inner filters. Each intelligent species evolves its own distinct interpretive categories, because they have adaptive value for survival in their own particular surroundings. Each conscious species puts its own spin on reality. Thus, humans know through one set of mental templates and believe the world is one way; ants have another set of mental templates and believe the world is another way. Especially for humans, thought cannot occur without cognitive categories. We think categorically because a hodgepodge of raw sensory stimuli by itself makes no sense. Thus, for example, we have evolved categories of quality and quantity, before and after, cause and effect, either/or, self and other, good and bad to interpret and control the overwhelming flood of incoming stimuli.

Naïve realism is our instinctive tendency. That is, we assume there is an exact correspondence between what is and what we experience as reality. Usually, our innate mental categories are as automatic and unnoticed as our breathing. In our day-to-day lives we are unaware that the categories created by our brains through which we understand our surrounding reality may not be the objective categories of nature itself. We are unaware that we are imposing our reality on nature, that we live in a highly cognized, humanly interpreted version of reality. It feels only natural to assume that what we subjectively sense is objective reality itself. This is a little trick that nature plays on us, perhaps a necessary trick so we can more effectively adapt to the immediate demands of our particular surroundings. From an evolutionary perspective, the brain's categories of experience evolved not arbitrarily but rather opportunistically in a "streetwise" mode for our immediate survival. Our brains and sense organs do not take picture- perfect snap-shots of actual reality but rather have adaptive adequacy— thus far for most situations. Human cognition is not only input but also output. We are not merely cameras but also creators. In a sense, we invent stories about reality.

# EVOLUTION OF THE TRIUNE BRAIN

Based on his own research and that of many others, neuroscientist Paul MacLean concludes that our human brain actually consists of three sub-brains, each of which is the result of a major evolutionary development. He calls them the *reptilian*, the *paleomammalian* (old mammalian) and the *neomammalian* (new mammalian) brains. Each retains certain characteristics from its origins in reptiles and early and recent mammals, and each shows great differences in structure, organization, chemistry, and function. While all three brains form an intermeshed hierarchy of three brains in one, functioning together as a "triune brain" and not autonomously, each brain can at times act somewhat independently. To a certain extent, we know the world and ourselves through three quite different mentalities, each with a type of thinking evolved from its own ancestral past. The three sub-brains might be regarded as interconnected biological computers, each with its own subjectivity, special intelligence, sense of time, memory, motor and other functions. But the brains do not always communicate with each other and can be in conflict without our conscious awareness. Following is a schematic drawing of MacLean's model of the triune brain.[2]

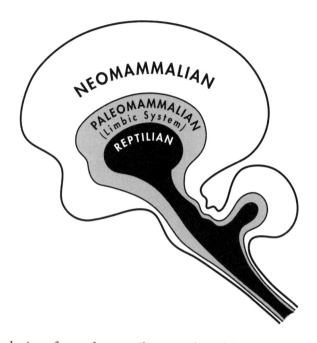

The evolution from the reptilian to the old and then to the new mammalian brain is not unique to humans, but it is common to all advanced mammals. As human and other mammalian brains are examined in the laboratory and from fossil endocasts, we can uncover the historical developments of our brains. For MacLean, the brain is a folded-up record of our evolutionary past. After each evolutionary step, the older portions of the brain continue to function, while the more recent brains layer on new functions. That is, newer brain systems do not replace but rather are added to the older brain system, which to a certain extent continues to function in its more ancient ways. Powerful are the echoes from our ancestral past.

According to MacLean, our oldest brain is basically reptilian, forming the matrix of the upper brain stem and comprising much of the reticular system, midbrain, and basal ganglia. Also called the R-complex, this brain system has its origins some 300 million years past, during the age of the reptiles. In his work with lizards and other extant reptiles, MacLean observed various types of innate, rigidly programmed, aggressive, territorial, dominant, submissive, and courtship ritualistic displays, all of which were instinctive ways of communicating territorial and sexual claims as well as establishing social hierarchies. These behaviors were performed as unvarying routines and in a repetitive, compulsive manner, programmed to better ensure the survival of the individual and the species. For example, dominance and submissive displays avoid unnecessary and sometimes mortal conflicts. These behaviors and the world as viewed through the R-complex have been layered into the brains of mammals, including humans. It is part of our reptilian shadow side. MacLean's goal, however, has been not only to identify reptilian behaviors but also to determine by various experimental procedures which parts of the brain control these behaviors.

The next evolutionary step was the paleomammalian brain, also known as the limbic system and common to all mammals. We could call it the emotional brain, as it is basically involved in the experience and expression of emotions. Ranging from intense fear and depression to joy and ecstasy, emotions have evolved to be experienced as either positive or negative but never neutral. This brain functions as emotional mentation, and its task is to judge all experiences as pleasurable or painful—criteria that have evolved as valid signals toward survival or extinction.

Though scientists disagree about its exact composition, the limbic system is generally considered to include all or certain functions of the thalamus, hypothalamus, amygdala, pituitary, and hippocampus. For MacLean, the limbic system comprises three main subdivisions, each with different functions. The two older subdivisions concern the sense of smell and have been shown to be involved, respectively, with oral and sexual functions necessary for self-preservation and procreation. The third subdivision, which does not appear to exist in reptiles, is concerned with parental care, audiovocal communication, and play behavior. Also for MacLean, clinical and experimental findings indicate that the lower part of the limbic ring fed by the amygdala is primarily concerned with emotional feelings and behavior that ensure self-preservation, including the demands of feeding, fighting, and self-protection. In many warm-blooded mammals, rudimentary or well-developed emotional bonding has evolved between parents and offspring and also among members of the immediate group. With the mammals we find not only the beginnings of the family, empathy, love, and altruistic feelings and behaviors but also a new way through which to experience and view the world. With the paleomammalian brain evolved the capacity to see with feeling.

Arriving late in evolution was a new type of brain which progressively developed in advanced mammals but uniquely blossomed in humans. This neomammalian brain, which is basically identical with the neocortex, is usually described in terms of the frontal, temporal, parietal, and occipital lobes. The human neocortex, including its interactions with the reptilian brain and limbic system, accounts for the unique qualities of humans and distinguishes us from other animals. It makes us what we are and civilization possible.

In the human neocortex evolution took the brain a mighty step further. It is a region of the most complex mental activities that use symbolic processes and made possible articulate speech, language, conceptual thought, and long chains of abstract logical reasoning. Reading, writing, mathematics, as well as foresight, hindsight, and insight became possible. Unique capacities surged in learning ability, curiosity, attention span, memory, imagination, introspection, inventiveness; and the urge to, enjoyment of, and ability to solve complex problems. Religion, morality, a sense of meaning, the arts, science, and technology were all able to develop. Also culminating in humans was a unique consciousness not only in an advanced self-awareness (a sense of "me") far beyond the rudimentary ways evident in some primates, but also an awareness and even the capacity to understand the evolutionary process and our own evolutionary past. According to conventional evolutionary theory, these novel powers of the human neocortex must have contributed to survival in order to have been a product of genetic variation and natural selection. The result is a view of the world seen through an extraordinarily expanded intelligence.

But MacLean is worried. Actually, it's a very old and long-standing worry that has been reflected upon by many thoughtful persons down through recorded history, but MacLean becomes acutely aware of it through his experimental studies of the brain. Simply stated, the reptilian and limbic systems sometimes operate independently and beyond the control of the human neocortex. Furthermore, interbrain communication is hindered because the two older systems are nonverbal, while the neocortex has highly developed verbal capacities. In short, the three brains are not fully integrated. MacLean is deeply concerned about the reptilian brain's instinctively programmed aggressive, territorial, authoritarian, sexual, and reproductive impulses, which at times are beyond rational control of the neocortex and can result in wars, violence, and nonsustainable population growth. His research, however, focused more on the limbic system. Early in his scientific career, McLean did laboratory observations of the limbic storms experienced by patients with temporal lobe epilepsy. What he found so disturbing was that during seizures patients could be utterly convinced of the truth of their thoughts and feelings about external realities, when in fact there was no correspondence whatsoever. For example, some patients during seizures had inexplicable paranoid feelings that certain persons were saying derogatory things about them or that a particular person was standing behind them and about to do harm. Others experienced intense feelings of fear, shame, and guilt entirely unrelated to their personal life circumstances. The patients experienced a broad variety of equally "free-floating" feelings unattached to any particular thing, situation, person, idea, or theory. Occasionally, patients reported mystical experiences, Eureka discovery realizations, revelations of truth; feelings of clairvoyance, of certainty, and that "things are more real, crystal clear" or "frightfully clear." Typical of some patients whose experiences ranged from "an enhanced sense of reality to strong feelings of connection as to what is real, true, and important" is the patient who reported, "I had the feeling that this is the truth and the whole truth; that this is what the whole world is about."[3]

For MacLean, the limbic system looks inward, relying on internal limbic input as its source of information without checking it out with external realities, while the neocortex is primarily oriented to the exterior world, looking outward for information; for example, through vision (the occipital lobes), hearing (temporal lobes), and the receiving and processing of various externally derived sense impressions (parietal lobes). In those instances, when functioning independently, the limbic system is convinced that what it subjectively feels is reality is in fact objective reality. Furthermore, in all instances we must experience the *feeling* that an external thing is real before we can accept it as real. For we humans, "Something does not exist unless it is imbued with an *affective* feeling, no matter how slight."[4] The neocortex, to the extent that it can function independently of the limbic system, cannot experience something as real. In summary, thinking alone cannot be convinced of the reality of something but rather also requires the limbic feeling of reality to have the experience and conviction that something external, is actually real, but the old mammalian brain can be convinced of the reality of something external without receiving feedback from external reality provided by the senses through the neocortex. Though limbic input is an indispensable complement in order for the neocortex to have the conviction of a thing's real existence, the limbic system cannot verbally interface with the neocortex. Hence, the manufacture of belief in the reality, the importance, the truth or falsity of what is conceived depends on a mentality incapable of verbal communication. MacLean expresses his exasperation:

> You know what bugs me most about the brain? It's that the limbic system, this primitive brain that can neither read nor write, provides us with the feeling of what is real, true, and important. And this disturbs me, because this inarticulate brain sits like a jury and tells this glorified computer up there, the neocortex "Yes, you can believe this." This is fine if it happens to be a bit of food or if it happens to be someone I'm courting—"Yes, it's a female, or yes, it's a male." But if it's saying, "Yes, it's a good idea. Go out and peddle this one," how can we believe anything? Logically I've never been able to see

around this impasse. As long as I'm alive and breathing and have a brain to think with, I will never forgive the Creator for keeping me in this state of ignorance.[5]

In MacLean's research, he attempts to trace brain parts and functions as they evolved over the vast eras of time. Also, we can catch a beginning glimpse of how certain errors may inevitably creep into our thinking as a result of the way particular brain structures evolved. Let us now turn to the ancient Greeks, a people who so highly developed the powers of reason and whose legacy includes the origins of science and philosophy, two cornerstones of Western civilization, which in modern times have also so profoundly influenced the East and its ways of knowing.

# OUR GREEK HERITAGE
# IN SCIENCE AND PHILOSOPHY

## THE ORIGINS OF WESTERN SCIENCE

Science and philosophy began with a handful of brilliant Greeks some 600 years before the birth of Christ. It was the beginning of a new direction for Western civilization and a new way of knowing for the human species. Otherwise stated, it was a revolution of the human mind and spirit, the neocortex coming into its own. Though ancient Greek science did not attain the systematic experimentation and mathematization of empirical data characteristic of modern science, we can easily recognize that the Greeks laid the foundations in the questions they asked, in their sources of knowledge, and in their beginning empirical observations and experiments. In those times there was no line drawn between science and philosophy, no exact Greek word equivalent to our modern term "science." Therefore, we might best call these early epistemological innovators scientist-philosophers or philosopher-scientists, to the extent that they emphasized the empirical or rational, the observational or speculative.

Because of the lack of historical documents, we cannot precisely trace all the various influences, contributing individuals, or specific time frame for the emergence of science in Greek antiquity, but it is conventionally agreed that Western science began in the sixth century B.C. with Thales of Miletus and two other Milesians, Anaximander and Anaximenes. Beginning early in the eighth century, Greeks poured out of their home country in search of farmland and trade, and they established numerous influential, semiautonomous colonies around the rim of both the eastern and central Mediterranean. Miletus, on the West coast of Turkey, was one of these major Greek colonies. Founded by Ionian Greeks, one of the original tribal groups of mainland Greece, Miletus along with other Ionian colony cities in the surrounding area became for a time the most civilized and progressive region of the Greek world. Miletus was a large, prosperous, and energetic city of trade and manufacturing. Somewhat infamous throughout the world for its wealth and luxury, it allowed the leisure for the flowering of literacy and the arts—and the beginnings of science.

Though differing in some of their conclusions, the three Milesians shared a new spirit of inquiry that would be a lasting legacy in Western science. First, they had a bold curiosity about the nature of the external world, its origins, its ultimate composition, and how it works. They took the previous science of Mesopotamia and Egypt to another level. Rather than limiting their search to the practical applications of knowledge, which was characteristic of these two predecessors, they also asked and sought to answer fundamental questions about nature itself. Their search for truth was not confined to utilitarian purposes achieved by pragmatic techniques but rather emphasized comprehensive, theoretical understanding explored in abstract generalizations. Because most of us today cannot take ourselves back to the experience of a pretheoretical, prescientific mentality, it is almost impossible to appreciate how radical was this shift in consciousness from the concrete to the abstract and from the useful to a search for truth for its own sake.

The three Milesians are a turning point in Western civilization because of their firm faith in reason to explain natural phenomena and their rejection of mythical, magical, and religious explanations. Though some of their abstract generalizations about reality appear to have emerged from certain mythical-poetic stories embedded in their culture and psyches, Thales, Anaximander, and Anaximenes consciously and deliberately rejected supernatural explanations. Their theory of nature was hylozoist, i.e., all matter has life within it; matter and life are inseparable. Nature is alive as an actual material substance and has within its own intrinsic generative power. Whatever is divine is inherent within, not apart from, nature. Unlike the Hebrews, they had no notion of an external, transcendent God who created the world, gave it life, and from time to time intervened to change natural events. The Milesians' new faith in reason was a break with the past. They were skeptical and critical of their Homeric religion of humanlike gods and demons. Even though we can assume they were familiar with religions of the surrounding civilizations, we have no account of their seeking knowledge of nature from priests, scribes, or sacred texts. Neither do we have any evidence that they consulted with their own religious oracles or invoked the gods of their Greek mystery religions. Rather, they sought naturalistic explanations while living in

a world of anthropomorphic deities interfering in human affairs and using humans as pawns in their own plots and intrigues. This was inevitably a capricious world, in which nothing could be safely predicted because of the boundless possibilities of divine intervention. Natural phenomena were personified and divinized. Sun and moon were conceived as deities, offspring of the union of Theia and Hyperion. Storms, lightning bolts, and earthquakes were not considered the inevitable outcome of impersonal, natural forces, but mighty feats, willed by the gods.[6]

The Milesians addressed their questions not to the gods, but to nature itself. Nature was to be explained within its own boundaries, not by something beyond, and in terms of abstract general principles, not by means of particular gods or goddesses. Furthermore,

> the ancient world was a place of fear. Magical forces ruled it and magic is absolutely terrifying because it is absolutely incalculable. The minds of those who might have been scientists had been held fast-bound in the prison of that terror. Nothing of all the Greeks did is more astonishing than their daring to look it in the face and use their minds about it. They dared nothing less than to throw the light of reason upon dreadful powers taken completely on trust everywhere else, and by the exercise of the intelligence to banish them.[7]

In their pursuit of truth, our scientific ancestors courageously used their wits to unveil the mysteries of nature. Their audacious confidence in conscious human reason, with all its power and limitations, is our heritage in science today.

The Milesians had not only a faith in conscious reason but also a faith in something else, which has continued down through time to be a basic assumption undergirding modern science. Despite all the apparent chaos that their senses perceived in nature and popular belief in the capricious whims of the gods and goddesses, they never doubted for a moment that, underlying all the flux and flow of the observed realities, we live in a world that is orderly and lawful. Nature is both rational and intelligible. Thus, with the Milesians, we find a transition from *mythos* to *logos*, the latter Greek word including the meaning of reason, and from which derives our words *logic* and *logical*. Also, the Milesians represent a transition from *chaos* to *kosmos*, the latter Greek word that has the meaning of the universe as an orderly and lawful system, and from which derives our words *cosmos* and *cosmology*.

In their quest to discover the underlying order of nature, the Milesians sought to explain nature in as few principles as possible. "They looked for something permanent, persisting through the chaos of apparent change; and they thought that they would find it by asking the question:'What is the world made of?' "[8] What is the basic stuff of the universe? They sought the answer in substance. As Guthrie points out, this was not the only possible answer; it might have been structure or form. Or today we might propose that the underlying principle of reality is process, relationships, or a different kind of order.

Though our focus is epistemology, we would like to provide a brief glance at the content of their theoretical results, keeping in mind that all three Milesians were monists and materialists: they believed in the existence of and thus sought a single basic and unifying principle in nature and believed it was material. Their materialism was not the mechanistic materialism of the later Greek atomists but was the belief that matter is alive, active, and contains within itself the power to initiate its own change without outside force. Questionable, fragmentary sources portray Thales (c. 640-546 B.C.) as an astronomer, geometer, engineer, and general sage. Based on his observations, speculation, and critical reasoning, he proposed that water is the single substance that is the fundamental reality of the universe. Because none of his writings have survived, even to the time of Aristotle, we can only conjecture why he chose water. We do know that water was a dominant part of Babylonian myth, that certain Egyptian myths considered water as the principle of all things. Since Aristotle, many have speculated as to why he selected water. One modern theory is that Thales had to account for change in nature using only one basic substance, and he had observed that water changes into different forms of liquid, solid, and gas (water, ice, and steam), depending on the temperature.

Anaximander (c. 610-545 B.C.), a younger contemporary and student of Thales, agreed with Thales that there is one basic stuff, but disagreed as to what it was and the process by which it becomes many. For Anaximander, the ultimate reality of the universe is the *Apeiron*, which translated from the Greek means "the boundless, unlimited." It is eternal, imperceptible, undifferentiated, without any internal parts, unchanging yet in everlasting motion, reaching out endlessly in every direction. It is matter but is distinct and beyond the limits of any human experience. Developing out of this primordial trans-sensory type of matter by a process of dynamic primary interactive oppositions (hot and cold, wet and dry), fire, air, water, and earth are separated out as the four distinct primary perceptible elements. From these energies and consequent elements, he explained the formation of the sun, moon, stars, and earth. For him, the heavenly bodies were not the mythical chariots of the gods but rather were material and measurable bodies. The world that we experience was separated out of the *Apeiron* by a kind of everlasting whirlpool of circular motion, and as the opposites eventually exhaust themselves, the world collapses back into the undifferentiated boundless. Our world is but one of many such cyclic worlds, coming into and dissolving out of distinct, particular being. Supporting his theory of the formation of the earth and animal life, he examined fossilized shells from areas far inland from the sea. Antiquity attributes various astronomical achievements to Anaximander, which would be consistent with his cosmological interests.

The third Milesian, Anaximenes (fl. 535 B.C.), though a friend, student, and successor of Anaximander, found various flaws in his theory of the *Aperion*, rejected Thales' notion of water, and instead proposed air as the fundamental substance. As best as we can conjecture from limited, fragmentary sources, he criticized the boundless and unlimited as too vague, without specific properties, and thus not a real material thing. Though we are not aware of Anaximenes conducting any experiments with air, he did note (incorrectly) that when water is rarified, it becomes fire, and when condensed it becomes cold, changing successively to wind, cloud, water, earth, and stone. Because air is omnipresent and in continual motion, change is constantly occurring. Because it accounts for change in the universe and is essential to the maintenance and growth of all natural objects, including life itself, Anaximenes concluded that air was the only acceptable substance as the underlying reality of the universe.

Though some of the Milesian theories appear to be brilliant speculations, others seem childish and little more than rationalized mythology. To appreciate their originality, keep in mind that these pioneers had no epistemological predecessors with a well-paved path to a store of tested knowledge. Without observational technology or experimental apparatus, they asked and sought answers to very big questions about the ultimate nature of reality. Surely they were not the first ancients, East or West, to ask these questions, but unprecedented was their reliance on human reason and their deliberate and conscious rejection of religious, magical, and mythical explanations. Though today their cosmology and ontology appear naïve, their epistemology was novel. In their reasoned, abstract generalizations, they created theoretical science. In criticizing, revising, or replacing the work of the other Milesians, not only did they begin to build a body of knowledge, but they also originated the tradition of the progressive advance of science. Lastly, we cannot perhaps underestimate the long-term impact of their new epistemology—they made modern science possible. As long as the ancients attributed the cause of natural events to magic and the will of anthropomorphic gods, not only was their knowledge erroneous, but the development of science was obstructed. For example, as long as Zeus was believed to cause thunderbolts, the human species was at the level of divinization, attempting to comprehend the will of the gods rather than developing the science of meteorology to predict the weather.

Following the Milesian tradition of seeking the underlying principles of reality through naturalistic ways of knowing, some successors continued to pursue material explanations, while others developed new explanations in terms of form, thus initiating the classic distinction between materialistic and idealistic world views. For the Pythagoreans, the ultimate reality was in the form of number. The cosmic order has a unity that is mathematical in character; number is at the heart of the universe. The cosmos is an intelligible harmony because it is governed by mathematical law. One of the foundations of modern science was laid as the Pythagoreans in scattered attempts moved beyond exclusively conceptual explanations to precise calculation, thus applying mathematics to understand natural phenomena. They also argued that the earth is a sphere turning on its axis as it revolves and that the universe is not geocentric, theories rejected by most other scientists, but which Copernicus became aware of in his study of the Pythagoreans.

Leucippus of Miletus (fl. 440 B.C.) and Democritus of Abdera (c. 460-370 B.C.) developed an atomic theory that was materialistic and mechanistic and excluded any divine guidance, cosmic intelligence, or purpose in the world. They argued that the world consists of an infinity of tiny atoms moving randomly in an infinite void. Though this theory was not widely accepted in antiquity, especially because of its rejection by the influential Plato and Aristotle, it powerfully reappeared during the seventeenth century scientific revolution. Newton was an enthusiastic atomist, and John Dalton was inspired to found the atomic theory of chemistry. The ancient theory of Leucippus and Democritus, though not identical, is the linear ancestor of modern atomic theories.

Anaxagoras of Clazomene (c. 499-428 B.C.), the last of the Ionian scientist-philosophers and an older contemporary of Socrates by some thirty years, was widely known for his achievements as a physicist, astronomer, meteorologist, and biologist. He distinguished *nous* (mind) from matter. In the beginning, matter had been a motionless mass that was set into motion by a supreme transcendent intelligence, resulting in a nonteleological cosmic order.

Finally, let us not forget Herodotus (c. 485-425 B.C.), "the father of history;" Thucydides (c. 460-400 B.C.), who introduced scientific methods of inquiry into the investigation of historical events; and Hippocrates (c. 460-370 B.C.), "the father of medicine" and his followers who contributed to the Hippocratic corpus beginning in approximately 430 B.C. and continuing for some 100 years. Their goal was to form a rational and empirical medicine liberated not only from myth, magic, and anthropomorphic gods but also from useless philosophical speculation! Their detailed patient observations, daily charting, and case histories can be inspiring to clinicians even today.

Beginning with the Milesians, a tradition of critical inquiry, argumentative debate, and rational clarity developed that would eventually distinguish Western civilization. Along with their reliance on naturalistic explanations, an ongoing debate flourished concerning the valid ways of knowing; some argued for sense perception and observation, some for abstract reason, rigorous logic, or mathematics, and others for a combination of these empirical and rational approaches. Thus far in the evolution of early Greek science, the thirst was for theory, not for the techniques of practical application. With the exception of Hippocratic medicine, the quest was to understand, not to change or control nature. The tone was aristocratic, with many seekers coming from families of wealth or at least sufficient resources to afford the leisure to contemplate basic questions of nature and valid ways of knowing. The appeal was more to the head than the heart, more Apollonian in spirit, with a drive toward order, proportion, harmony, rationality, measure, and intellectual explanation rather than the Dionysian passionate, irrational impulse, craving for the sensuous, ecstatic, and spontaneous experiences of life. The handful of individuals who developed early Greek science did not dent the popularity of the traditional gods, myths, and magic, but they did provide a minority, alternate way of knowing. At the extreme opposite from the fledgling science was a new religious movement that began in the seventh and sixth centuries B.C. and spread in the form of mystery cults promoting the worship of Dionysus. Here the primary theme was

> a yearning for immortality, motivated by a profound discontent with what was felt as the finitude, the defeats, and the inadequacies of this earthly life. This was a religion of redemption—the religion of a savior god who draws his worshippers to him in complete and joyful union.

> The new worship was organized into cults whose rituals were regarded as precious secrets. For this reason there is

*continues*

*continued*

much uncertainty about the details of the worship and about its origins, but it is known that Dionysus was worshipped under various animal forms and invoked by wild dance and song. The ceremonies took place, often at night, in remote places, and women—to the scandal of conservative males—took a prominent part in them. In a frenzy of intoxication the worshipers tore living animals apart, drank their blood, and danced to the point of exhaustion. They felt the spirit of the god pass into their bodies; the union so passionately desired was consummated, and the worshippers exulted in a supreme happiness and utter freedom from any sort of restraint.[9]

## SOCRATES: THE UNEXAMINED LIFE IS NOT WORTH LIVING

To better appreciate Socrates' passionate quest for truth, it is important to know that beginning in the second half of the fifth century B.C., with an expanding economy and political opportunities, a new class of upwardly mobile young Greek men were questioning the practical value of all the speculations about nature, the cosmos, and theoretical mathematics. Confronted with a chaotic mix of conflicting theories about the physical universe and unresolved controversies about whether humans can know such realities, they turned instead to learn practical knowledge in order to better develop their personal, career, and political skills. Some sought to learn and practice the highest moral values, others to only gain wealth, power, and reputation. Previously, such an education was available only to the aristocratic and wealthy few, who quite often engaged tutors to live on their estates. For the new economically emerging classes, there were not yet universities and colleges. To meet their needs, a new educational profession developed which came to be known as Sophists, i.e., practitioners and teachers of wisdom. Some were philosophers; most shared a similar philosophical point of view. Novel for those times was that they were itinerant teachers, whose base of operations was usually Athens, which had become the economic, political, cultural, and intellectual center of the Greek world. These wandering professors introduced the previously unheard of practice of supporting themselves by charging fees for their lectures, seminars, and presentations. They were a diverse group of individuals. Some were of the highest moral integrity, such as Protagoras (c. 490-420 B.C.), the first and most influential Sophist. A few others were more self-serving, primarily oriented toward money and fame.

Plato, who is our principal source of knowledge about Socrates, came from aristocratic and wealthy families on both his paternal and maternal sides. He colored his famous descriptions of the Socratic dialogues with his disdain for the more democratic Sophist educational innovation of serving the practical needs of the rising classes, their charging fees, and their skepticism of any absolute foundations for the existing institutions and traditions. For the Sophists, the skills of political power as well as the practical values of excellence could be taught and learned, and thus were not innate qualities that could only be inherited from aristocratic and wealthy families. To prepare their students for more effective and successful participation in the democratic self-rule of the city-states and in legal and business matters, the Sophists contributed to developments in logic, teaching their students to detect and sometimes practice fallacies, and trained them to argue effectively. With the application of logic to language, they created rules for clarity and precision, thus facilitating a more precise transmission of knowledge. They helped develop grammar and taught effective speaking and writing skills. For some of the Sophists, the education they offered included an entire spectrum of the arts and sciences as well as gymnastics.

Socrates (469-399 B.C.) was similar to the Sophists because he focused on human affairs rather than the natural sciences. A native and lifelong resident of Athens, he also accepted all classes of students. Though of very modest and sometimes impoverished economic circumstances, he never charged a fee, feeling strongly that it was entirely improper. However, what most distinguished Socrates from the Sophists was his belief in the existence of objective, universal moral values, independent of personal opinion, time, and place, whereas the Sophists, as products of and participants in the rising skepticism of the times, taught that values were only relative to each person's point of view. They taught that there are no absolute values, that each person has his or her own true reality deriving from his or her own particular experience. In the end, all understanding is subjective opinion. Objectivity is impossible; truth is individual interpretation. In the famous words of Protagoras, "Man is the measure of all things," meaning that truth is purely personal and human. Reality is what you construe it to be; reality is what I construe it to be. As there are no objective, absolute standards, it is futile to even attempt to prove that my view is true and another's false. However, Protagoras added a pragmatic standard: even though no one version of reality is *truer* than another, one version may be practically *better* or *worse* than another, depending on the particular situation, culture, perceived needs, and purposes. Though the Sophists shared a radical skepticism about the possibility of certain knowledge, nevertheless they insisted that one's values and morals needed to be supported by reasons.

While some of the Sophists provided a wide spectrum of intellectual education, most trained their students in persuasive rhetoric and argumentation to advance their personal and career lives. The focus of Socrates was more limited to logic and ethics, or what we today would call values or practical qualities of moral excellence. In other words, he was concerned with thinking clearly about how we ought to live. As skeptical as any Sophist about what most persons actually know about such matters, he was radically anti-Sophist in his firm belief in the existence of objective values. For Socrates, the Sophist teaching that human values are only a matter of personal opinion and only relevant to a particular time and situation was not only an inaccurate perception of reality but was corrosive to humans as moral creatures. He believed in the reality of goodness and the goodness of reality, and thus we have objective standards by which to judge such values as wisdom, justice, and courage. On what did he base his firm faith in moral absolutes? Not on his observations of the deteriorating personal and political values in an increasingly skeptical and cynical Athens, not on any rational demonstration that he or others could provide, but rather, as best as we can infer, he based his faith on what we could call a religious or metaphysical belief. Like the Milesians, he had the conviction that the universe is orderly and rational but additionally, "He believed firmly in a divine government of the universe, a supreme Reason to which the human reason is akin. Hence rational conduct in ourselves is in harmony with the general scheme of things."[10] Guthrie further specifies his faith:

> Socrates believed in a God who was the supreme Mind, responsible for the ordering of the universe and at the same time the creator of men. Men moreover had a special relation with him in that their own minds, which controlled their bodies as God controlled the physical movements of the universe, were, though less perfect than the mind of God, of the same nature, and worked on the same principles.[11]

For Socrates, objective values exist because they are grounded in the ultimate goodness of the divine reality. We humans can know these values because our intelligence is of the same nature and participates in the divine intelligence. Standing in direct opposition to the general Sophist conviction that, even if such objective values did exist, we could not know them, is Socrates, who firmly believed that such values do exist and we can know them. The problem is not that we can't know them but that we don't know them. For Socrates, the quest for moral certainty is not futile, as the Sophists claim, but rather is possible and also necessary, because before we can be sure we are doing the good we must know what the good is. Furthermore, our greatest happiness is the result of knowing and doing the good. The famous Socratic saying, "Virtue is knowledge," means that if we truly understand the good, we cannot not do the good. A correct and comprehensive understanding of the true nature of any moral value will be so irresistibly appealing that inevitably we must will to do the good. No human would knowingly do what is bad. No human would deliberately reject the good, because of its resulting happiness. Evil, wrongdoing, and harmful intentions are entirely due to ignorance, i.e., the lack of a rational understanding of the nature or the essence of goodness. The Greeks of Socrates' time were keenly aware of the power of emotions to drive us to do things that in our minds we know are wrong; but for Socrates, a true knowledge of the good is more powerful than any contrary emotions. We do evil or lesser goods only because we lack a full and deep understanding of the good and thus act on the basis of only partial or delusionary rewards. If virtue is knowledge, then vice is ignorance, not primitive instincts, evil intentions, sin, disobedience, or the devil; not selfishness, lack of willpower, or the dark impulses of the unconscious mind.

His way of seeking to know the nature of moral values is called the Socratic method, which is also called Socratic dialogue or dialectic. Essentially, it is a process of question-and-answer investigations, usually led by Socrates in discussion with another or several persons, sometimes in the presence of a small group. The goal is to discover objective, unchanging, universally true definitions of the very essence or nature of the moral value under discussion. The spirit is that of a cooperative inquiry, in which Socrates views himself as a fellow seeker, not as an authority dispensing dogma. The purpose is not to persuade or win arguments, skills so often taught by the Sophists, but rather to seek truth together in a common search. His objective was not to teach people what to think but to challenge his fellow seekers to honestly and competently think for themselves. Socrates was fond of relating how he was like his mother, who was a midwife. As with midwives he did not himself give birth to any philosophical conclusions but rather assisted others through his dialectical skills to give birth to their own latent knowledge and wisdom. In fact, Socrates was severely criticized during his lifetime for not arriving at any definitions of moral values. We can better discern his unique contribution if we recognize that his focus was process, a way of inquiring, not the content of a finished philosophical system. Unlike the Sophists, he rejected the role of teacher because he did not believe that moral values could be taught, but rather only encouraged and challenged to grow in each individual. In the finest sense he was an educator, as in the Latin root *educare*, meaning "to lead out, draw or bring out" the unique learning potential of each person and nurture it toward intellectual maturity.

Though the structure of the Socratic dialogues was fairly fluid, it often began with a question of moral conduct and a request by Socrates that his coinquirers voice their opinions. The next step, which is at the very core of the dialogical process, is best understood in the context of a turning point in the personal life of Socrates. While Socrates was in his thirties with already a local reputation as a seasoned seeker of wisdom, his friend Chaerephon visited Delphi, a town at the base of Mount Parnassus and seat of the most famous and powerful oracle of ancient Greece at the shrine to Apollo. Here a priestess, the Pythia, in a frenzied state issued divine pronouncements in riddles. Chaerephon asked her whether anyone was wiser than Socrates. The priestess, who had a reputation for liking to please, replied that no one was wiser than Socrates. As Plato later related, Socrates took very seriously the divine response but wondered how it could possibly be true, as he felt that he had not yet attained any real wisdom. Yet the god would not lie. He asked himself, "What does she mean by saying I am the most wise? What is the answer to this riddle?" He sought to find the hidden meaning in her answer. As Plato tells the story, Socrates systematically went about interviewing many kinds of people from various professions and occupations, all of whom had a reputation for wisdom, to determine how and whether any of them were wiser than he. In the end he discovered that all of these people not only lacked wisdom but, even worse, they and the public were deluded in believing that they had great wisdom. Then with the force of a lightning bolt came the insight providing the hidden meaning: if I am the wisest of all it is because I know that I have not yet attained wisdom, I know that I do not know. Henceforth for Socrates, it was his "divine mission" to convince people of their ignorance, to demonstrate to people that so often when they firmly believe they know something, in fact they do not. As we would say, if we believe that we already have the answers, we won't even bother to ask the questions. Awareness of our ignorance is an indispensable first step toward truth and wisdom.

Thus, early in the dialectical process, Socrates by a series of critical probing questions challenged certainties, unveiled hidden assumptions, exposed all kinds of vagueness, inconsistencies, inadequacies, confusions, contradictions, and absurd consequences to convince his coseekers of their ignorance. This step was to clear the mind of the weeds that prevent the appearance and growth of ideas closer to the truth. To advance the dialectic, Socrates frequently asked his coseekers to provide additional viewpoints, occasionally himself offering suggestions, which he again subjected to his relentless logical scrutiny. He sought to clarify, define, and find agreement on the meaning of words. Sometimes, he employed a rudimentary form of inductive logic by gathering observed particular instances of the moral value in question, noting common characteristics, and then creating general classifications as steps toward his goal of universal definitions. For Socrates, these definitions could express the essence of each moral value, because words are rooted in, correspond to, and express objective reality. Words are not, as the Sophists taught, only subjectively created, conventional interpretations of reality, ultimately just fluff. For Socrates, to reason logically with words was to deal directly with reality.

Though he didn't write anything or establish a school, from his own time through succeeding generations into the present, Socrates has inspired in many of us the philosophical spirit of inquiry. As he walked about his beloved Athens, he was disturbed by the mistaken and superficial notions of success. His yearning for his fellow men was that they seek with him a truer notion of success which could bring a more complete happiness. For both the individual and society, this happiness flows from coming to have a clear conception of the very essence of human moral excellence. Once having this intellectual enlightenment, the vision of goodness will be so overwhelming that we will be unable to resist doing the good. Socrates beckons us to seek first and above all the "goods of the soul"; i.e., to share with him his passion for truth and goodness and his love of wisdom—*philo-sophia*. Money, status, power, possessions, and beauty are goods but only to the extent that they are an expression of moral excellence. The good life is the happiest life and thus we should attend first to the needs of the soul.

For Socrates, the famous Delphic admonition "Know thyself" means to understand our true nature as moral and intelligent beings and thus to realize our purpose and function in our practical lives. "The unexamined life is not worth living," means that we will not realize our greatest excellence and happiness by mindlessly following the current, local ignorance and prepackaged conventional standards of success and the good life. Rather, Socrates challenges us to join him and other seekers in the quest for the absolute foundations of human moral values as the touchstones for our personal and community lives. Edith Hamilton summarizes some of his principal ontological and epistemological beliefs as well as his central mission:

> Socrates believed that goodness and truth were the fundamental realities, and they were attainable. Every man would strive to attain them if he could be shown them. No one would pursue evil except through ignorance. Once let him see what evil was and he would fly from it. His own mission, Socrates believed, was to open men's eyes to their ignorance and to lead them on to where they could catch a glimpse of the eternal truth and goodness beneath life's confusions and futilities, when they would inevitably, irresistibly, seek for a fuller and fuller vision of it. He had no dogma, no set of beliefs to implant in men's minds. He wanted to awaken in them the realization that they did not know what was good, and to arouse in them the longing to discover it. Each one, he was sure, must seek and find it for himself.[12]

Socrates was a complex and controversial personality. With all his faith in reason, he was not a lifeless, one-dimensional intellectual. He was not perfect. His strong suit was his intellectual honesty and moral integrity. Also he had qualities of an advanced martial arts master in his self-discipline, physical stamina, courage in military combat, self-confidence, and a self-containment that detached him from other people's opinions of him. While introspective, he also enjoyed people and had deep, enduring friendships with other men. While living an extremely simple life in terms of material goods, he could fully appreciate possessions without craving and distorting his life for them. While a serious person, he had a great wit and enjoyed parties. By any modern test of "family values," he appeared more invested in the love of wisdom than in loving his wife and three sons. For some, as he hung out in the public places of Athens, often shoeless and in old, worn clothing, initiating conversations about moral values, he must have appeared quite a town character. Some people disliked him for his meddlesome questions, professed ignorance, and ironic humor. For Plato and other student coseekers who became attached to him, they enjoyed, loved, and learned from him.

He was a philosophical pioneer and thus also a deviant. In response to the question we sometimes hear today, Is nothing sacred anymore?, Socrates would have replied with a resounding, Yes! There is an absolute line in our lives which we must not trespass or we lose our moral integrity. In the year 399 B.C. at the age of seventy, Socrates was brought to trial by a political group of Athenians and condemned to death on various charges including "corrupting the young," which we interpret as Socrates' way of encouraging the questioning of adult consensus values. By Athenian law, he could have avoided a trial by exiling himself from Athens, but in his view this would have been to abandon his philosophical mission to his native city. He might have gone to trial promising to keep quiet in the future, thus saving his life. Instead he chose to go to court and confront his accusers. In Plato's famous account of his teacher's trial and execution, Socrates took the court-ordered poison hemlock, thus choosing to die rather than admit guilt and betray his philosophical calling. For Plato, Socrates is a heroic martyr for philosophy; he lived and died for philosophy. He taught us not only by his life but also by his death that philosophy is both a way of living and a way of dying. In concluding his account of Socrates' courageous death, Plato states that he was "of all those whom we knew in our time the bravest and also the wisest and most upright man."[13]

# PLATO: TRANSCENDENTAL IDEALIST AND RATIONALIST

Among those present at the trial of Socrates was his twenty-eight-year-old student, Plato. Inspired by Socrates' truth-seeking spirit, Plato was shocked that a political group in his great city-state of Athens could sink to such a moral low as to condemn his beloved teacher. Because of Plato's aristocratic family, wealth, and political connections, it was expected, and he had intended to pursue a political career, but the execution of Socrates convinced him that he wanted no active part in a political system that could put to death such a man as Socrates. As part of the old establishment, he deplored democracy with its disorder and demagoguery, but he also became disillusioned by the recent tyranny of terror of his own political party, the Oligarchs, which included some of his close relatives. Yet he strongly shared the Greek belief that an individual can only live a good and happy life in a good and just state. For Plato, to actively participate in the existing political system would leave him powerless to reverse the political and moral decay. Confronted also by declining religious values and an increasing opportunism, skepticism, and cynicism, he concluded that he could best serve his city-state by seeking new and absolute intellectual foundations for political and personal life. With Socrates, he believed that people must know the good before they can do the good, but unlike his teacher he further believed that knowledge alone will not inevitably impel us to do the good. Humans must be trained to do the good through a program of intellectual and moral education. With the same passion for truth and certainty as his mentor, but with a more comprehensive genius, Plato (427-347 B.C.) set out on his life mission. He became the first systematic philosopher in the Western world as he developed and integrated his ontology, epistemology, ethics, aesthetics, political and social philosophy, and philosophy of education.

To understand his epistemology, we need to know his ontology. Plato believed that reality is split into two worlds: an invisible, perfect world of eternal transcendent essences (translated in English as "forms" or "ideas") and our daily human world of visible, imperfect, temporal appearances. The ontologically superior transcendent world is the unchanging, ultimate essence of reality and is known primarily through the intellect, while the second, inferior world of appearances contains only imperfect, incomplete images, likenesses, or copies of the world beyond and is known primarily through the five senses. An elite few with adequate intelligence, intellectual education, and character training can catch a glimpse of the transcendent essences and thus have a rudimentary but useful knowledge of the substance of reality. The rest of us are trapped in the chaotic flux and flow of sense impressions, emotions, and impulses, living as though in a deep underground cave, groping about in the passing shadows which we mistake as the substance of reality. In this dualistic theory of reality, the first is the world of being—eternal, perfect, and unchanging; the second is the world of becoming—temporary, imperfect, and ever-changing. In Plato's cosmic dualism, however, unlike in certain Eastern and Western religions and philosophies, our imperfect world is not unimportant. Rather, he attempts to save this world by showing how humans can know the transcendent, perfect essences and thus have a basis for molding the state and individuals closer to the ideal world. Also, with transcendent and absolute standards of truth, goodness, beauty, and justice, the Sophists' corrosive influence can be defeated, along with their claims that truth is purely subjective and relative to each individual's particular experience and interpretation. Plato's goal was not to downgrade but rather to uplift this world to a higher, truer standard.

While Socrates sought universal definitions of such moral values as justice and goodness, Plato went a step further in claiming that the essences of such moral realities are eternal entities, independent of our minds and existing as real but abstract substances in the invisible, transcendent realm of reality. Goodness, justice, and the other moral virtues are genuine and perfect realities that exist in and of themselves, while their manifestations in this world are imperfect, passing, shadowy copies. He also went on to assign independent and real (though invisible and transcendent) existence to the archetypal forms or ideas of material objects in the physical world. For example, the definition of a horse is not only derived through the mental operation of abstracting from particular characteristics, but the essence "horseness" exists as an independent, perfect essence, form, or idea in the transcendent world. Of all the realms of reality, the eternal, archetypal ideal forms have the greatest reality. Sensible things or qualities have reality only to the extent that they embody good copies of the ideal forms. They are real only to the extent that they participate in the transcendent forms. Ultimate reality is formal, not material.

For our modern minds, indoctrinated to reality as material and knowing as empirical, Plato's world of self-existing, transcendent ideal forms seems gratuitously mystical and topsy-turvy. How could Plato, with all his genius, come to believe in such a dualistic world view? One source was the powerful influence on Plato of the brilliant mathematician and mystic Pythagoras, who believed that numbers were the ultimate elements of the universe and mathematics was the key to unlocking the mysteries of the cosmos. The Pythagoreans held the metaphysical belief that numbers were an independent reality, the primary reality, and were the divine principle that gave structure and harmony to the entire cosmos. The human mind did not invent mathematics, it *discovered* it in the absolute, objective mathematical laws hidden behind and transcending the ever-changing material reality communicated to us through our five senses. Deeply impressed by the pioneering mathematical discoveries of the Pythagoreans, and sharing their mystical temperament and close friendships with them, Plato extended their ideal geometrical figures and formal mathematical laws independent of the senses to include transcendent, independently existing ideal forms of the Socratic moral virtues and physical objects in the phenomenal world.

We can better grasp Plato's notion of archetypal self-existing ideal forms if we understand certain aspects of his cosmology. Plato believed that the cosmos was put into a harmonious order by a supernatural intelligence. He portrayed the creative deity, the Demiurge, as a benevolent craftsman who took an already existing mass of primitive, formless, chaotic matter and imposed order according to a rational plan. The universe is intelligible and moral because it is the creative expression of God's rationality and goodness. This is not a perfect world, but it is the best of all possible created worlds, given the inherent limitations of the matter out of which it was created and the immense but limited powers of the creative God. Plato compared this creator Deity with a carpenter who has a mental model (template, form, or ideal) of what a table should be but given the imperfections of wood (knots, discolorations, warping) can never create a table to perfectly conform to the ideal. The world is imperfect because of the imperfections of the raw material with which God had to work. Plato's God cannot make a perfect world out of the pre-existing imperfect elements. In our daily world of matter and sensory perceptions, nothing perfectly replicates the self-existing ideal forms that originated from the divine mind. Everything in this world has reality only to the extent that it is a good copy of the transcendent forms. An eternal ideal presence lies behind our temporal lives, which are only earthly appearances, mere passing shadows of the transcendent reality of perfect forms and perfect knowledge. However, this world is not chaotic but is comprehensible to a limited extent, because sensory things resemble to a certain degree the fully rational and intelligible forms.

In contrast to Plato's cosmology is the world view of the Atomists Leucippus and Democritus. For them, the origins of the cosmos and subsequent ongoing events are the result of blind chance, while for Plato an intelligent and providential power transformed a formless material cosmos into an orderly cosmos with its most ultimate essence in the form of the good. Nature for Plato is not the result of atoms moving mechanistically through empty space, a product of chance, but rather is the artistic expression of a benevolent intelligence in a universe that at its foundations is purposeful, moral, and rational. For the Atomists, the universe is materialistic, mechanistic, without divine guidance or ultimate purpose, whereas for Plato the cosmos is an animated, living being, full of purpose and design with a world soul to govern the world. In Plato's world view, the ultimate nature of the universe in the transcendent forms and human life is a purposeful whole, and our lives have meaning as we participate in the cosmic purpose by striving to realize the ideal forms in our everyday lives. The Atomists' world view has no heartwarming answers to our basic questions about human existence or a purpose for the universe that is humanly meaningful. The Atomists' cosmos does not care about us. We and all there is are only atoms colliding by chance in space. It is a universe without plan or purpose, totally and coldly indifferent to our basic questions and with no answers for our cosmic hopes and fears and our felt need to orient ourselves in a larger, more meaningful context. In opposition to this view, Plato believes we live in a moral and meaningful cosmos in which we can participate in our daily lives. There is no split between warm, human concerns and a cold, mechanistic universe. For the Atomists, seeking ultimate truths offers no hope for most human hearts and only by chance could there be any connection between cosmic and human truth, goodness and beauty. To seek knowledge of ultimate realities offers no salvation in our personal lives but probably only greater estrangement from objective realities. Thus the ancient Greek atomic physicists Leucippus and Democritus ushered in our fateful modern split between objective scientific facts and subjective human hopes, fears, and values. In contrast stands Plato, who with his mystical sense of another, more fundamental and ideal world, proclaims that knowledge can bring salvation by participation in the transcendent form of the good. For Plato, just as the sun is the brightest object we can see and gives light by which we see other sensible objects, so the form of the good is the most intelligible form we can know and makes other forms intelligible.

We are now more prepared to understand Plato's ways of knowing. In the most general terms, he is a rationalist with a mystical temperament, emphasizing abstract reasoning in a quest toward certain knowledge of absolute realities. He finds little or no validity in empirical approaches that utilize sensory input of concrete events. He distinguishes between knowledge and opinion. Knowledge is possible only when the objects of knowing are the perfect, immutable, transcendent forms. By contrast, opinion is when the objects of knowing are the constantly changing and thus unreliable sensory impressions. For Plato, a strictly empirical physics could sometimes provide practical opinions but was "no more than a likely story," because it is based on sensory impressions—incomplete, imprecise moving shadows of the substance of reality, which is the perfect, unchanging, self-existing but abstract realm beyond our senses, space, and time. Knowledge, to be more than opinion, must use reason to reach beyond the phenomenal world of the senses to discover the eternal and invisible beyond the temporal and visible.

Crucial to understanding how we might attain knowledge of the transcendent ideal forms is Plato's pivotal notion that such knowledge is "recollection." From the Pythagoreans, he came to believe in the immortality and transmigration of souls. The human soul (of which for Plato the intellect was the most noble and important part) between its incarnations has clear and direct face-to-face knowledge of the ideal forms. Later, when once again it is imprisoned in a material body, its memory is dulled and dimmed of its former illumination. Our epistemological task as earthbound humans is to reawaken in ourselves a recollection of that former direct vision of the eternal ideal forms. Thus we might have a glimpse of the essence of justice, goodness, or beauty and have an absolute standard for creating a more perfect state, by choosing more perfect political and personal moral values. But Plato was an elitist. He believed that only a minority of us among the masses have the innate intelligence capable of responding to rigorous intellectual and moral training such that we can accurately recollect the soul's direct vision of the ideal forms. Only these elite few (philosopher-rulers) are fit to govern a political state that will be truly good and just.

Plato proposed a comprehensive educational and training program for prospective philosopher-rulers to promote the recollection of the ideal forms, beginning with prenatal care, then early childhood education, and continuing into full adulthood. Not only were the students to receive an intellectual education, but they also were to receive a carefully controlled moral training to instill character and an appreciation of the good. Unlike Socrates, Plato believed that to do the good not only required a clear concept of the good, it also demanded indoctrination, and censorship of harmful cultural influences. Thus as the student developed a moral character conditioned to seek the appropriate earthly goods, he or she also acquired a thirst to seek the souls' recollections of the transcendent good, just, courageous, and beautiful. Physical and musical education and training in the arts also aimed at the improvement of character and a proper harmony of body, mind, and emotions. For Plato, the education of the mind or obtaining expertise was worthless and potentially dangerous, unless the student's moral character was trained to appreciate and seek the good. The student had to be indoctrinated in moral and spiritual values.

As the student matured, the most important intellectual training would be in mathematics and logical dialectics, not so much for their content as to train the mind to think abstractly, detached from the material senses, thus advancing beyond the sensory images and concrete thinking characteristic of the child. The goal was to reorient the mind from concrete to pure, formal thinking so that it might progressively move from the shadows to at least the light of dawn. Then the mind might catch a nascent glimpse of the transcendent forms and thus ascend to a greater reality, eventually reaching full knowledge of the forms—true knowledge—and thus be doing genuine philosophy. Though Plato emphasized that the transcendent ideal forms are intelligible directly to the mind and do not need the mediation of the senses, he rejected Parmenides' position that appearances as presented by the senses are entirely unreal and sense knowledge is totally erroneous. For Plato, sense knowledge can have a certain validity, even if only fragmentary and distorting. Though the senses are usually a dangerous trap that hold us down to concrete thinking about particular images and things, they can also be a starting point from which we can ascend to abstract, formal thinking. Recollection involves receiving sensibles, which remind the intellect of the forms. The sensory world can evoke a recollection of the souls' prior knowledge of the ideal forms, for example in the experience of a sunset or a musical performance, which stimulate in us an aesthetic resonance with the transcendent form of absolute beauty.

As a personality, Plato has for us the flavor of a perfectionist, not only ontologically with his ideal forms but also psychologically in his temperament. Disillusioned by the political and moral collapse of his times, he created a complex theoretical model of the perfect utopian state. Repulsed by the Sophists' subjective relativism and situational morality, he sought objective and certain knowledge in the absolute, underlying reality of the immutable forms beyond the flux and flow of this imperfect, empirical world. Sensing something pure and permanent beyond our bodily imperfection, he believed in the immortality of the soul. With his transcendent sixth sense, he attempted to save the worldly appearances through his metaphysical dualism, questing for the eternal beyond the temporal and valid knowledge beyond "the rabble of the senses." He did not seem to have the temperament for an active political life, with all its painful conflicts and compromises. He did not like kibitzing with all manner of humans in the marketplace, à la Socrates, or sweating out the smelly details of dissecting and classifying animal parts as did his most famous student, Aristotle. Plato had the gift of a great mind, and throughout his long life he cared for us with the very heart of his intelligence. He was a true aristocrat of the rational mind.

# ARISTOTLE: SYSTEMATIC PHILOSOPHER AND BEGINNING SCIENTIST

As a seventeen-year-old, Aristotle was sent from his provincial town of Stagira in northern Greece to study at the prestigious academy founded by Plato in the cosmopolitan city of Athens. As with the Milesian physicists and the Atomist Democrites, he was an Ionian, with the blood of scientists in his veins. Furthermore, from both his paternal and maternal sides, he came from a family of physicians trained in the practical empirical science of Hippocratic medicine. Aristotle's father had been court physician to Amyntas II of Macedonia, who was the father of Philip and grandfather of Alexander the Great. Though Aristotle was born (384 B.C.) into a well-to-do family, both his parents died when he was a child. He was raised as an orphan by a trusted guardian, who sent him to the academy for the best education available in all of Greek civilization. He progressed at the academy from student to colleague, only to leave at the time of Plato's death, twenty years later. During the following twelve years, he toured the Aegean, did biological research, married, and tutored the future Alexander the Great. He then began teaching at the Lyceum.

By all reports, the student Aristotle had a great ambition to learn—to learn everything! Most education in his time was oral, learning by discussion rather than from books. However, Aristotle became also a voracious reader and earned the nickname "the Reader," not only because he devoured every book he could get his hands on, but also because he assembled a personal library of books (i.e., manuscripts), a practice that was yet quite rare. Aristotle eventually became not only the greatest collector and systematizer of knowledge in the ancient world, but also that rare combination of scientist and philosopher, integrating both perspectives as necessary components for comprehensive and genuine knowledge. He was a working empirical scientist in biology (especially marine biology, zoology, and embryology) and also a philosopher of science, writing about the nature of science, the ways of gaining scientific knowledge, and the classification and relationships of the various particular sciences. He is one of the founders of the empirical inductive method and the first to organize cooperative research in a scientific institute. He invented the discipline of formal logic that was the professional standard of Western logic until the nineteenth century. It is taught in introductory logic classes today and remains in various ways the common logic of the modern lay person. In addition to his own original contributions, his goal was to create a critical, grand synthesis of all the best knowledge of his time, not only including what we today classify as physics, astronomy, biology, and chemistry, but also ontology, epistemology, logic, psychology, ethics, political science, and among other things, literary criticism! It all added up to an awesome, grand adventure of an exceptional mind determined to understand all of reality in a systematic way.

Plato and Aristotle had contrasting temperaments, which sent them down different paths of inquiry. Plato was more mystical, the idealist seeking perfect truth, goodness, and beauty in the transcendent world beyond, relegating human knowledge and life in this world as only semi-illusory. Aristotle was more empirical, practical, thoroughly at home in this world. While Plato rejected the senses as basically untrustworthy, Aristotle believed that the senses were the indispensable source for reliable knowledge of reality. Mathematics, lifeless and fixed in its abstract perfection, far removed from the dynamic vicissitudes of everyday life, was Plato's model science. For Aristotle, though he was very familiar with the mathematics of his times, it had no natural attraction. Rather, he was in science primarily a biologist with a burning desire to observe, collect, define, and classify all manner of facts in the world of living organisms. Plato was more of a visionary living in a duality of worlds, seeking epistemological salvation in the ideal presence of a world beyond. Aristotle's nature was one of incorrigible common sense, living in one unified world, discovering reality in the sensate here and now, and convinced that this world is fully real.

However, let us not overstate the temperamental differences between Plato and Aristotle. After all, Aristotle remained with Plato at the academy for twenty years as student, colleague, and friend. While Aristotle's psychological disposition contributed to his rejecting or revising a number of his teacher's fundamental views, Plato's original and fertile mind had a powerful influence throughout most of Aristotle's thinking. Without Plato, Aristotle might never have become both a systematic philosopher and a deeply reflective scientist. Yet as Aristotle's thinking matured, he developed some very different views from Plato about the possibility and ways of knowing. Except for the secure knowledge of the forms attainable by the elite and uniquely trained philosopher-rulers, Plato was a skeptic about the power of knowing for the rest of humanity. The Sophists, with their subjective relativism and radical skepticism about the possibility of obtaining objective knowledge, were in their heyday when Plato was a young man, and they had a mighty impact on him. Plato countered not by defeating them on their own ground but, almost by default, shifting the realm of certain, objective knowledge to another world—the transcendent world of perfect forms. Aristotle, born forty-three years later than Plato, was not so decisively influenced by the skeptical Sophists; their arguments did not take deep root in his psyche. Though a rigorously critical thinker, he was a common-sense realist. He didn't feel any great need to prove that genuine human knowledge exists. Rather, his epistemological preoccupation was to describe what knowledge and its conditions are. Also, he believed that knowledge does not dwell in an abstract ideal world beyond but rather with what is most familiar to us in ordinary here-and-now experience—the concrete particulars. In contrast to Plato, Aristotle believed that, in certain areas of knowledge, commonly shared opinions of ordinary people can represent genuine truths. As to professional opinions, Aristotle typically began a new study with a critical review of previous expert opinions so he could incorporate their valid perspectives, avoid their errors, and to more precisely identify the essential questions and major difficulties. In order to develop an empirically based theory on the types of constitutions that are best for different types of political states, he did not, in Platonic style, spin out of his head a theoretical model of the utopian state. Rather, he started out by collecting and recording the constitutional histories of over one hundred states to learn their positive and negative conceptual characteristics as well as their appropriate applications.

The ontological foundation of Plato's epistemology was his belief that genuine reality existed primarily and most fully in self-existing ideal forms beyond space and time. Aristotle turned this ontology upside down and located reality in the particular things of this world. Whereas for Plato we live in a duality of worlds, for Aristotle there is only one real world—the world of actual individual things. Only an individual horse has full independent existence. A separate form (essence) of "horseness" in a second world beyond does not exist and is a superfluous notion. Reality is to be discovered within the world of sense experience. Placing reality beyond in a transcendent world of independent, invisible, archetypal forms for Aristotle was ontological nonsense. To say that transcendent forms exist and that things of this world exist by mysteriously participating in them is "to use empty words and poetical metaphors."[14] According to Aristotle, Plato came to these erroneous views because he argued too much in the abstract, rather than from empirical facts observed in natural phenomena.

While Aristotle maintained Plato's emphasis on the existence and importance of forms, he radically revised their nature. Rather than accepting Plato's belief in forms as separate, self-existing, transcendent entities, he located the forms as immanent in actual things of this world. All things in the natural world consist of two vital, dynamically intermeshed principles: matter and form. In a general way, we can describe matter as the underlying substratum in which there is an inner striving to realize its form. Though matter and form can be distinguished in thought, neither is an independent, self-existing entity, but rather they are two inseparable, dynamic aspects of the one physical object. Matter is the raw stuff out of which an indwelling impulse actualizes its specific potential form, as an acorn develops into an oak tree or embryo into an adult. Form is not only the actualized shape but also the shaping force. Matter is the potential for form; form is the actualization of matter. In more abstract terms, matter is potentiality and form is actuality. Aristotle's ontology of matter and immanent form in all of nature was influenced by his observations of biological development, as well as by the view of the Milesian physicists that matter is not mechanistic but rather is alive, active, and contains within itself the power to initiate its own changes without outside force.

To understand Aristotle's ways of knowing, it is essential to have at least a beginning grasp of his notion of immanent form. While for the Ionian physicists the essence of reality was in matter, for Aristotle as well as for his teacher Plato, the essence is in form. For Aristotle, to know the fully actualized form of something was to know its specific essence. Furthermore, for both Plato and Aristotle, we can only have scientific knowledge of that which is fixed and unchanging. Matter is that which changes, and form is that which endures throughout change but does not itself change. The Aristotelian form immanent in matter is constant and unchanging, and individual things change as their form actualizes its inherent structure, function, and purpose toward its destined fulfillment.

Scientific knowledge for Aristotle is both inductive and deductive, i.e., both bottom-up and top-down. The knowing process begins with induction. Because sense perception is the foundation of knowledge, the starting point is to use our five senses to carefully observe the particulars of nature. As we compare our perceptions about what is common, constant, and unique in a group of particulars, our minds can then abstract out the immanent forms from the material objects. The process advances from sense impressions of particulars to abstract concepts of the universal. Knowledge occurs when the mind receives the abstracted forms of something into itself. In contrast to other species of intelligent life, the human mind has the unique faculty of intuitive induction, with the power to directly grasp the universal among the particulars, the immanent form common in the concrete particulars. We are not born with an innate knowledge of the essence (form) of things, but we can progress to this knowledge by empirical induction, culminating in an intuitive apprehension. In the ancient Greek world, where the dominant tendency had been to investigate nature in their heads rather than with their hands, Aristotle made induction and empirical facts not only a necessary precondition for scientific knowledge but also intellectually respectable.

The accurate determination of facts in nature by the inductive process of abstracting out the immanent forms from particulars was a necessary but not sufficient condition of scientific knowledge. For Aristotle, scientific knowledge was also deductive. As part of his genius, he invented the syllogism to analyze the forms of valid deductive inference. We will not present a technical exposition of the complexities of his deductive system, but merely describe the syllogism as a kind of deductive proof in which, certain premises being assumed, something else by logical necessity must follow. The syllogism consists of two premises (a major and minor premise) and a conclusion. There are three and only three terms which by certain rules are contained in the premises and in the conclusion. Together, the premises necessarily imply the conclusion. To take a simple example, if the major premise is that all humans are mortal and the minor premise is that John is a human, the logical conclusion cannot be otherwise than that John is mortal. The various forms of syllogism proceeding from assumed premises to inferred conclusions are called "discursive reasoning," as distinguished from intuitive and inductive methods. In contrast to intuition, where there is a direct, unmediated grasp of reality, the syllogistic deduction is a chain of reasoning; and in contrast to induction, which is a process leading from particulars to the more general, a deductive inference often proceeds from the general to the more particular. Though modern logic since the nineteenth century has progressed beyond Aristotle, the basic laws of logical inference systematized by Aristotle, though incomplete, remain valid today.

The goal of Aristotle's deductive logic was not truth but rather validity. The syllogism is not a science but is a mental technique for proving what conclusions must necessarily follow from the two premises. If one or more or the premises are false, the formal logic of the syllogistic reasoning remains valid, but we cannot determine whether the conclusion is true or false. Deductive logic is only a tool for valid reasoning from assumed premises. The formal rules of deductive logic can protect us from invalid reasoning but in no way can guarantee that our premises are true in reality. Deductive reasoning does not discover or determine new facts in nature; it only explicates logical relations implicit in the premises.

Aristotle was keenly aware that if a syllogism was to demonstrate a scientific truth, the premises must be true in reality. But the ultimate, very first premise at the beginning of a sequence of syllogisms cannot itself be proved by deductive reasoning. Its truth must be established by some other method. For Aristotle, science must ultimately be based on certain self-evident, undemonstrable premises which in general are called primary principles. These primary principles are intuitively and immediately known to be true. Though they cannot be proven, neither can they be denied. For example, he believed that there are indubitable laws of thinking that are universally true, such as the principle of noncontradiction: A cannot be both B and not B. Otherwise stated, nothing can be both true and false in the same respect at the same time. Two other laws are the principle of identity (A is A; if a statement is true, it is true; if it is false, it is false) and the law of the excluded middle (A either is or is not B; a statement is either true or false). But these are primary principles that we reason *with*, not *from*. Aristotle also believed that for science in general and for each particular science there are specific, self-evident principles we reason from. For example, he believed that the axioms of Euclidean geometry are true though undemonstrated primary principles and indubitable starting points for geometry. Thus we have an immediate, intuitive grasp of the truth of the statement, "A straight line is the shortest distance between two points." For Aristotle, a primary principle (axiom) in astronomy was that anything which moves eternally must move in a perfect circle; and in biology, every living thing has within it a principle of movement and rest.

The process for Aristotle by which we arrive at indubitable, intuitive knowledge of primary principles requires the indispensable groundwork of empirical observation, induction from particulars, critical evaluation of expert opinions, and examination of the difficulties in attempting to understand the phenomena being studied. Eventually, however, knowledge of primary principles depends on the unmediated intellectual apprehension of *intuitive reason*, which among biological species is uniquely implanted in the human mind. Again, as with the abstracting out of immanent forms from material things by empirical induction, genuine knowledge is ultimately grounded in the unique power of direct, intuitive apprehension by the human intellect. The primary principles are self-evident and need no proof. Thus, scientific knowing is founded on certain, ultimately true first principles. Such is the epistemological faith, thus far, of Aristotle.

Scientific knowledge for Aristotle is not merely description but also explanation. That is, we must not only know *what* the empirical facts are, but we must also know *why*. By explanation, he meant knowledge of the causes. We do not fundamentally know some thing or event unless we know its cause. Scientific knowledge, among other requirements, is always causal knowledge and must include four kinds of cause—material, efficient, formal, and final. They are operative both in natural things, with their own inherent principles of motion and rest, and in artifacts produced by humans. To facilitate our understanding of Aristotelian causes, let's take the example of the construction of a house, where the four causes are most notably distinguished. The material cause is the substratum out of which a thing comes to be, thus, cement, lumber, glass, roofing, etc. The efficient cause (also called the agent, or moving cause) initiates the change by which it comes into being, i.e., the human workers and their various tools. The formal cause is the design (form, essence, or pattern) which is to be actualized. The final cause is that for the sake of which (the end, purpose, or goal) this house is constructed; for example, shelter from snow, rain, cold, and heat. With living natural things, in contrast to artifacts produced by humans, the efficient, formal, and final causes coincide, because the end of a natural object is the actualization of its essence (the form by which it fulfills its purpose), and its moving cause is an internal shaping drive toward its own destined adult form and final purpose, which was inherited from its progenitor. Taken together, the four causes explain the reasons why things or events happen and how they develop from potentiality to actuality. For Aristotle, the four causes are not just mental concepts but rather are actual operating principles producing real changes in the universe.

To understand Aristotle's four causes is to appreciate how profoundly teleological is his view of nature. *Telos* is a Greek word meaning "end" or "goal". For Aristotle, all that is done by nature as well as by human thinking is for some end. Nature makes nothing without a goal, does nothing without a purpose. As a general rule, everything in the world moves naturally toward a specific perfection. Changes in things are not haphazard or accidental but rather are an orderly development directed from within by an inner necessity toward some specific actualization. The teleological purpose is an internal finality achieved through an immanent design, not a conscious purpose in nature, and not an external divine Providence or Mind directing nature from the outside. The ends are intrinsic in the things themselves; the goal is self-actualization. Everything in nature aims toward achieving its form. Final causes in nature draw things to their final purpose by attraction.

Of the four causes, the final cause is primary and the most decisive. The other three are secondary and subordinate. To scientifically know something, we must know its essence, and to know its essence we need to know what it is for; i.e., we must know its end, its purpose. The most profound explanation of things is to be found not in their beginnings but in their ends, not in their potentiality for form but in their final, fully actualized form—in their purpose. In his teleological emphasis, Aristotle was following his teacher Plato, not the atomist Democritus who rejected their concept of nature as a product of rational design exhibiting order, regularity, and purposefulness, and instead viewed nature as inert, mindless, mechanistic, random, and purposeless. For Aristotle, in order to have scientific knowledge, it is essential to know the purpose of any natural thing or event, which is contained pre-eminently in the final cause. Of all the contrasts between Aristotle's concept of science and modern science, perhaps the greatest is his insistence that everything in nature fulfills its proper purpose and any adequate knowledge of the world must include an explanation that involves the principle of final purpose. For Aristotle, to have scientific knowledge, it is not enough to answer the question "how?". We must also be able to answer the question "why?". Since the seventeenth century, orthodox science has adopted a mechanistic view of the universe and has rejected the notion of purpose as relevant and valid in scientific explanation. Strictly speaking, only the efficient cause is today considered to be empirically justified. When we ask about the purpose of human life and how it might be an integral part of a larger cosmic purpose, we are not thinking like a modern scientist but rather more like the ancient Aristotle.

◆ ◆ ◆ ◆ ◆

Aristotle developed a philosophy of human life traditionally referred to as ethics and politics, but with the changed modern meanings of these two terms, these translations are somewhat misleading. Rather than ethics in any restricted moral sense, he meant the study of human character. By politics, he meant what today we would call political science. For Aristotle, as for the great majority of his Greek predecessors, an individual can live a good and flourishing life only in a good and well-governed state. While his politics were concerned with the necessary principles of the good state itself, his ethics formulated principles of the good life as it might be realized by the best person in a good state. Though for Aristotle the individual and government have the same objectives of human happiness and goodness and their study is inextricably interdependent, our focus will be on his ethics, more specifically on the epistemology of his ethics.

Ethical knowledge, for Aristotle, could not have the same degree of precision and rigor in its proofs as mathematics, and it could not, like scientific knowledge, begin with infallible, self-evident first principles, from which universal and necessary truths could be deduced. Rather than universal statements extracted from particulars, ethics deals primarily with individual instances. Instead of what necessarily must be and cannot be otherwise, ethics deals with what may or may not happen and what is not always or necessarily true, depending on particular conditions and contexts. Ethics is about individual persons, acts, and events, not universally true theories. General statements in ethics can be instructive, but alone they are insufficient. They must be applied to particular instances, because truth and reality are closer to particulars than to general statements. While science can make universal statements about what is constant in nature and cannot be otherwise, ethics cannot make exceptionless generalizations with detailed accuracy, because it deals with contingent, ever-changing individual instances. Ethical knowledge is practical knowledge and can be true knowledge, but it cannot meet the criteria of scientific knowledge. As in clinical medicine, the physician's ultimate aim is not knowledge but the right action to heal individual patients; so for Aristotle, ethics was a practical inquiry, and its final goal was not to theoretically know what happiness and goodness are but how to live a happy and good life.

Aristotle's epistemological method in ethics was empirical, inductive, and based on much of the common sense in his culture. It was also rooted in what he viewed as universal human nature. He totally rejected the Platonic transcendent ideal forms as an absolute foundation for human values and instead relied solely on the fluid facts of everyday human experience and human reason. Aristotle did not propose a religious ethic with a divinely ordained system of infallible laws for human conduct. As we saw earlier, he also rejected the possibility of a scientific ethic deduced from indubitable self-evident first principles. For him ethics was a practical inquiry beginning with what is most familiar to us in the everyday phenomena of human life. From this empirical data, we can induce certain general guiding principles of limited validity, but it is always individual human lives in their ever-changing particular context that are nearest to and most decisive in ethical reality. For Aristotle, in order to know the good and how to become good, we must first know the particulars of human nature and the human condition, an approach that can be regarded as a humanistic ethic.

As part of his humanism and in contrast to Plato, Aristotle believed that the starting point for ethical inquiry was not only the views of experts in the field but also the opinions of ordinary persons. This approach would be enough to cause Plato to roll over in his grave because he had emphasized the critical distinction in ethics between opinion and knowledge, the latter could only be achieved by starting out with a search for transcendent absolute truth with the eye of the soul by a uniquely endowed, rigorously trained elite. The Sophists also valued human opinions but ended up with an ethical relativism that said there is no right or wrong conduct, only different subjective opinions, none of which can claim any unique validity. Aristotle rejected not only the Sophists' position but also a conventional ethic in which the good, and right and wrong are only the consensus of popular customs. Instead, he believed that in each particular case, after examining the total context, there *is* a right thing to do. As with a physician treating an individual patient in a particular case, there is a right action to take, and also as with a physician, we do not have an absolute rigorous proof, but only a practical certainty or good probability for our ethical decisions.

In his inquiry into human character and conduct, Aristotle is thoroughly teleological. Everything in nature aims at some end which is its purpose and fulfillment, the actualization of its form. For Aristotle, this final fulfillment of anything can be called its good. He then asks, what is the ultimate good for humans? He agrees with the widely shared opinion that it is happiness, but not just a feeling of euphoria; rather a flourishing and successful life, a life well lived. When people are asked what they mean by happiness, opinions vary widely. Some define happiness as pleasure, others as wealth, or honor, etc. Aristotle further observes that even the same person at different times may define happiness in different ways. For example, when a person is ill, happiness is health; when poor, it is a life of making money. However, says Aristotle, these more specific designations of happiness are not happiness itself, but at best, are only alternative means to the end goal of happiness. Yet to say that happiness is the chief and final goal for humans is still only a platitude.

Happiness, for Aristotle, is the result of the fullest use of our essential human nature. We are happy to the extent that we are doing in an excellent way those properly human functions that actualize the form of humanness implanted in us by nature. Though we share many functions with plant and animal life, our distinctly human form of happiness is the consequence of our unique powers of mind to function according to rational principles. Because we are not only animals but rational animals, when confronted with value choices and consequences we have the reflective cognitive capacity of a moral sense, rather than being blindly conditioned to automatically react to immediate pleasure and pain. Happiness is not merely an emotional, mental, or a passive state but rather a life of activity in accordance with intellectual and moral excellence.

Intellectual excellence, which for Aristotle was above all else proper to humans, is concerned with truth and is of five types: scientific knowledge, productive knowledge for building useful and beautiful things, practical wisdom, intuitive reason, and contemplative knowledge. Moral excellence, which involves the rational regulation of desires and emotions, is identical with goodness of character and is developed by training in good behavioral, emotional, and cognitive habits. Examples of moral excellences include generosity, justice, truthfulness, self-respect, and courage.

Moral excellence involves several necessary characteristics. First, it is a habitual disposition to choose the good. Otherwise stated, it is a stable character trait by which we spontaneously aim our actions toward the good and experience pleasure in doing good acts. This goodness of character is not innate, not inevitable in any of us. For Aristotle, the disposition for moral excellence arises in us neither by nature nor contrary to nature. "Rather, we are adapted by nature to receive them, and are made perfect by habit."[15] Nature provides not only the capacity for moral goodness but also the potential for evil. The disposition for moral virtue or vice is produced in us by practicing it until it becomes habitual. For Aristotle, it is critical that character training begin in childhood, so that children develop ingrained habits of good behavior. We eventually experience pleasure in doing good acts and pain in doing bad acts, and thus develop the internal habitual disposition to be moral. This moral training extends into adulthood by legislation, which reinforces moral behavior and as much as possible its internal disposition by a system of public rewards and punishments. Aristotle sounds much like a behaviorist—we learn best by doing; the practice of good actions, not cognitive insight, is the most efficient means to develop an internal disposition. Moral concepts can provide a deepening understanding and thus a reinforcing encouragement for the person who already has acquired the habitual disposition to desire the good, but theoretical understanding and logical argument by themselves will not change the behavior or disposition of the person who has developed the habit of taking pleasure in doing evil. The acid test of a person's moral disposition is whether or not he or she experiences pleasure or pain in doing virtuous or vicious acts.

However, moral excellence requires not only the disposition to desire the good but also the practical wisdom to select the right means to achieve the good. This practical intellect sniffs out and weighs all the relevant facts in particular and often complicated circumstances, then considers and chooses the best actions to realize the desired moral ends. In the process, many variables are evaluated, including the motivations, temperaments, talents, and limitations of the involved persons, the time, place, costs, consequences, and so on. For Aristotle, the moral virtue or vice of the means is discerned from the facts of the particular circumstances. This is all we have to rely on. There are no certain transcendent foundations, no absolute guidelines, no simple rules valid in all cases. His faith is in the human practical intellect and its power of reasoning and wisdom, at least as achieved by some and even though misused by most. Though for Aristotle there is a right action in every circumstance, he acknowledges that discovering it is no easy task. He observes, however, that certain persons are especially gifted in practical wisdom and recommends that when we reason about the means to attain the moral good we should do so in the way of these exceptional persons. They have a way of grasping the truth about what to do and how to do it in order for themselves and others to have good and successful lives. Their uncommon practical sense is not only the result of a specific talent but also the consequence of a wisdom winnowed out from many years of experience. It is an adult power of discernment in a fully developed person, not the product of youth, naïve intent, or simplemindedness. Their reasoning method and eye for practical reality and effective means is an epistemological process we should emulate to the maximum of our capacities in order to develop good and flourishing lives. Both the disposition toward the potential good and the effective means to actualize it are indispensable and inseparable for moral excellence.

In most circumstances the person of exceptional practical intelligence would warn us to avoid extremes in actions and feelings. Most often, virtue is following the middle way between excess and deficiency, which usually are vices. Thus, courage is a mean between cowardice and rashness, ambition is between laziness and greed, and self-respect is between self-abasement and vanity. The middle way is neither an arithmetic mean between extremes nor a mode of mediocrity. Rather, it most often has the effect of yielding the maximum moral results. Locating the mean depends on many interdependent, dynamic variables, including the qualities and relationships of the persons involved, available action options, emotions, timing—all the circumstances. Moral excellence is to be found in a mean relative to us. For example, if we typically act and feel quite cowardly, the mean for us would be more toward the opposite extreme of rashness to develop the habit of courage. Seeking the mean is not a universal rule. With some moral and immoral actions and feelings, it should not be applied. Also, actions and feelings are not virtuous because they follow a middle way. Rather they are virtuous because they conform to practical wisdom. The goal is to find the right actions and emotions within all the particulars; locating the mean is itself only a helpful method to achieve the moral goal. A final characteristic of moral excellence for Aristotle is that it involves choice. With psychological insight, he developed a complex and subtle theory of choice, including notions of personal responsibility, and voluntary and involuntary action. To bring together and summarize all the requirements for moral excellence, Aristotle defined it as a habitual disposition, "concerned with choice, lying in a mean relative to us, this being determined by reason and in a way in which the man of practical wisdom would determine it."[16]

Though genuine happiness flows from an active life of moral excellence, our highest happiness is a consequence of using what is highest in human nature—our intellect. For Aristotle, the human more than anything else is mind. While happiness and fulfillment can result from various activities of the intellect, including understanding and creating useful things, the most perfect self-realization and consequent happiness is in contemplating the ultimate causes and principles of nature and the cosmos. It is a more perfect knowledge because it is for its own sake, not for some utilitarian end. The contemplation of the unchanging, eternal, and universal realities could include to a certain extent the work of the modern theoretical scientist, ontological philosopher, and transcendental theologian. Aristotle's empirical observations of plant and animal life convinced him that there is a hierarchy of perfection among all living things. We share some aspects of the lower forms of life and thus are animals, but we are superior to other animals in having the power of thought. With this unique intellectual power, we contain something of the divine. Our intellect is the divine within us. Thus on the scale of perfection, we not only have affinities with plant and animal life below but also with the divine above. With the capacity for pure thought and thus for theoretical wisdom, we have a spark of the divine in us.

For Aristotle, all persons by nature desire to know. This desire to know is innate; we don't have to acquire a taste for knowledge. Advancing from ignorance to understanding, even solving simple problems, brings pleasure and delight. If we are seekers and lovers of truth, it is because we are born with a natural disposition to seek and cherish truth. Furthermore, it was because of their wonder that the first humans and succeeding generations philosophized, beginning with the obvious everyday things and advancing to questions about the nature of the sun, the moon, and the origins of the universe. This ultimate truth seeking is motivated by wonder, not merely to escape from ignorance or to achieve practical ends.

To know something of the ultimate truths of the universe is to come to understand something of ourselves, to the extent that we are an integral part of the larger realities. Aristotle's intellectual temperament and talents play themselves out in placing the perfect human life and highest happiness in theoretical inquiry and the contemplation of ultimate truths. Not only is the mind the best thing in us, but the objects of contemplative wisdom are the best objects of knowledge because they are universal, eternal, and unchanging. And to the extent of our individual intellectual capacities, as we cultivate and use our minds we most resemble the gods. Contemplation of the first principles and ultimate causes is closest to the mental activity of the gods, and he urges us to make ourselves as much like the gods as possible. Yet with his characteristic balance and practical good sense, he reminds us that only a part of us is divine—we also are human animals. While the gods can continuously and exclusively live lives of pure contemplation that result in perfect happiness, we as material creatures with animal natures can only hope to attain this contemplative bliss from time to time. Our nature is to be humans, not gods, and thus we must attend to the physical necessities of life, including good health, food, shelter, and sufficient economic resources to have the leisure and serenity for contemplative thought. We are also by nature social animals, and to survive and thrive we need friends, a spouse, family, and a community. We have the capacity and need to be moral creatures and thus must devote time and effort for good and productive interpersonal, community, and political relationships. Human excellence, by nature, requires living a practical life. The pure, uninterrupted contemplative life of the gods is beyond our nature, but contemplative knowing is our highest excellence and greatest fulfillment.

Though part of us is divine, Aristotle rejected the notion of personal immortality along with the transmigration of souls and rewards and punishments in an after life or beyond. His ultimate divinity was the Unmoved Mover, not as revealed in any sacred scriptures, not as the object of faith or hope, but rather as the deduction at the end of a long chain of logical reasoning. He deduced the existence of the Unmoved Mover by applying some of his universal principles of reality, including motion and rest, potentiality and actuality, matter and form, and the four causes. There was no conscious Providence for him, no personal God working in nature who is concerned about us. As a result of its pure perfection, Aristotle's ultimate divinity neither is nor can be aware of the world or of us. The world is eternal and, though the First Mover is not a creator god, it keeps the world going by a kind of magnetic attraction as Final Cause. It keeps the world in motion by the teleological impulse in everything to actualize its potential form through its own proper activity; thus each being realizes its own perfection as an emulation of and attraction to the divine perfection, the Form of Forms. Thus the cosmos is purposeful, orderly, an organic unity, and not a product of chance.

♦ ♦ ♦ ♦ ♦

Aristotle died in the autumn of 322 B.C. at the age of sixty-two and at the height of his powers. During the previous year, his fellow Macedonian Alexander the Great suddenly died at the summit of his achievements. Both had an inquisitive Greek spirit and dared to enter new domains as few had before. They were both remarkable adventurers and conquerors. Both had an unprecedented unifying vision, one to unite disparate peoples and cultures into an enlightened empire, the other to gather all knowledge into a far-ranging, profound, and subtle synthesis. Tutor and teenage student at the royal court some twenty years previous, both were original spirits who left their mark on Western civilization. If Aristotle's thought seems familiar, it is because so much of his terminology has been incorporated into science, philosophy, and our everyday categories of thinking. His physics without experimentation and quantification, his astronomy without such later technologies as the telescope, were based on the best knowledge of the day and lots of common sense—too common, as they have been rejected since the new scientific epistemologies of the sixteenth and seventeenth centuries. However, his scientific approach has, in principle if not always in practice, made empirical facts the critical crucible of theory.

For Aristotle, science and philosophy was an ongoing investigation; his system was never intended to be a final truth. It was a way of knowing. He was a major stimulant for the flowering of a more developed science in the following centuries. He inspired great minds of the Arab and European world. The introduction of his theories into the Christian West during the Middle Ages ignited the inquiring spirit in a number of illustrious Scholastics, including St. Thomas Aquinas, with his brilliant synthesis of faith and reason. We best not confuse Aristotle with Aristotelianism. The awesome power of his system eventually became stultifying to less vigorous minds in the later Middle Ages. They succumbed too readily to Dante's evaluation of Aristotle as "the Master of those who know," forgetting his drive to continually uncover new truths of reality. "It is true that his views became frozen in a monumental orthodoxy that had to be slowly and painfully overcome, but such rigidity and conservatism were totally opposed to the open-minded, intellectually curious, and empirical spirit of the man himself."[17]

Greek philosophy did not end with Aristotle. Among those who followed and attempted to answer some of the basic questions of life were the Epicureans and the Stoics. Also, various schools of skeptical thought developed which questioned the validity of human knowledge, including Arcesilaus (c. 315-240 B.C.) and Carneades (c. 213-128 B.C.) of the Academy and the Pyrrhonian skeptics, who traced their origins back to Pyrrho of Elis (c. 360-270 B.C.) and whose arguments were further developed and synthesized by Sextus Empiricus (c. 200 A.D.).

## THE FLOURISHING OF SCIENCE
## IN THE HELLENISTIC AGE

Within only a few years after the death of Alexander in 323 B.C., some of his generals and closest aides fought among themselves to carve up and rule various parts of the empire, which extended from Macedonia to Egypt, the eastern Mediterranean, Asia Minor, Persia, and even into parts of modern Afghanistan and India. The year of Alexander's death marks the end of the Classical Age of Greek civilization and the beginning of the Hellenistic Age, with its dramatic expansion of Greek culture. Alexander began the Hellenization in the conquered lands with enlightened administration, partnerships with local leaders, and the founding of new cities along important trade routes. This process was accelerated and consolidated by his successors, who brought prosperity and economic opportunity for enterprising locals and the ruling Greeks, especially in Egypt, the eastern Mediterranean, and western Asia. Many of the native upper and middle classes, dominated politically and economically by the Greek occupiers, lost little time in assimilating Greek customs and culture. A Greek dialect became the international language among the educated and influential, forming a widespread cosmopolitan and common culture that would endure for over two hundred years.

No city in the Hellenistic world had more cultural influence than the large, magnificently beautiful, and sophisticated capital city of Alexandria in Egypt. Founded by Alexander himself in 331 B.C., it blossomed into its intellectual glory under the guidance of the Ptolemaic dynasty. Ptolemy I, who was a trusted and personal staff officer of Alexander and an educated man, became the ruler of Egypt and the founder of the dynasty. He began the plan for the famous Museum in Alexandria, which was completed by his son, Ptolemy II. To call it a museum today is misleading. Literally, it was "the shrine of the muses," officially dedicated to the nine goddesses of Greek mythology who presided over and inspired literature, the arts, and the sciences. Operationally, it was an advanced research institute for science and the humanities supported by royal patronage. From all over the Hellenistic world, scholars and scientists were attracted by the facilities and by the opportunity to live and work together as a community, and in addition have access to the library of Alexandria, the most famous and comprehensive in all Greek antiquity. Though the principal and most consistent royal patronage was for literature, a number of important scientists of the third and second centuries, with or without subsidies, devoted at least part of their careers to work at Alexandria.

Science thrived during the Hellenistic Age. Alexandria was its principal but not its exclusive center of research. The Lyceum in Athens did notable scientific work as it carried on Aristotle's empirical spirit and extended his innovation of organized research and an extensive library. Theophrastus, head of the Lyceum for some thirty-six years after Aristotle's death, was an independent, comprehensive thinker who did original and landmark research in botany and petrology. Strato from Lampsacus in Asia Minor, who from 286 to 268 B.C. succeeded Theophrastus as director of the Lyceum, pioneered the use of experimentation to investigate physical phenomena, especially gravity, acceleration, and vacuums. Strato also taught at Alexandria, which increasingly became the hub of scientific work. Euclid (fl. 300 B.C.), who may have been born in Alexandria but certainly spent part of his career there, devoted some of his energies to astronomy, optics, and musical theory but is most famous for his creative and extremely useful synthesis of much of the best mathematical knowledge of his time in his *Elements*, which as an axiomatic, deductive system became the model for scientific demonstration down to the beginning of the eighteenth century, and is a basic textbook for geometry in modern times. A brilliant mathematician far more original than Euclid, perhaps the greatest genius of ancient Greek science and a powerful model for mathematical science, was Archimedes of Syracuse (287-212 B.C.). He made pioneering contributions in mechanics, laid the foundations for the science of statics, and was the founder of hydrostatics (the laws of floating bodies), which had important practical applications. Two other significant Hellenistic mathematicians were Eratosthenes of Cyrene (fl. 225 B.C.) and Apollonius of Perga (fl. 200 B.C.). In addition to his work as director of the library of Alexandria, Eratosthenes applied mathematics to geography and originated the first detailed map of the world based on a system of meridians of longitude and parallels of latitude. He also calculated an amazingly accurate approximation of the circumference of the Earth. Apollonius, who apparently lived a good part of his adult life in Alexandria, wrote a classic in Greek mathematics on conic sections; the terms *ellipse*, *parable*, and *hyperbola* originated with him.

Aristarchus of Samos (c. 310-230 B.C.) propounded a heliocentric system in which the Earth, and presumably the other planets, moves in a circle around the sun, which is fixed in the center of the cosmos. The greatest observational astronomer of antiquity was Hipparchus of Nicaea (fl. 135 B.C.), who demanded an exact mathematical match between theory and observation which radically changed the conception of Greek astronomy. He invented or improved a number of observational and measuring instruments that would be used for the next twenty centuries and also developed a more complete and detailed star map. Some three hundred years later, Ptolemy of Alexandria (fl. 150 A.D.) would synthesize the observational data of Hipparchus and the work of many other predecessors, bringing Greek astronomy to its zenith and making it the standard paradigm for astronomers into the Renaissance. Incorporating the sophistication of previous Hellenistic mathematicians, he brought to astronomy a new level of mathematical power. For him, the only way to achieve certainty in astronomy was through mathematics and mathematical models.

Finally, let us turn to Hellenistic anatomy, physiology, and medicine. Crucial to scientific progress was the practice of human dissection, which began in the third century B.C. at Alexandria. The anatomist Herophilus of Chalcedon (fl. 270 B.C.) and the physiologist Erasistratus of Ceos (fl. 260 B.C.), both also trained in medicine, were the first to do systematic dissection of the human body. Herophilus brought entirely new knowledge to light in his anatomical investigations of the brain and nervous system. He described the cerebrum, cerebellum, and the meninges, identified the connection between the nerves, spinal cord, and the brain, and distinguished the sensory and motor nerves, which expanded the understanding of the functioning of the nervous system. He dissected the eye, giving a good description of the retina and optic nerves; he distinguished arteries from veins, examined the heart valves, and from his studies of the arterial pulse used its variations and rhythms as an aid for diagnosis and prognosis. Erasistratus, somewhat younger than Herophilus, incorporated and advanced his investigations of the brain and heart. He increased our understanding of the vascular system and was perhaps the first to appreciate the function of the four main arteries of the heart. Based on much detailed observation and sometimes speculation, he developed a comprehensive physiology.

Hellenistic medicine reached its peak with Galen of Pergamun (fl. 180 A.D.), an innovative researcher, comprehensive thinker with a philosophical bent, and actively practicing physician. His early education was in mathematics and philosophy, and he received his medical education in his hometown of Pergamun, which was both a major medical and a cultural center, and at Alexandria. Though he made original contributions in medicine and biology and was not merely an eclectic, his voluminous writings synthesized most of the advances in Hellenistic medical research and practice. His important anatomical work was hampered because only animal and not human dissection was considered ethical in his time, though he clearly would have preferred to do human dissection. Both in theory and in practice, he was the dominant medical authority from his time down through the Middle Ages and into early modern times.

With our brief sketch of Hellenistic science now completed, let's note some of the general trends of Greek science that culminated in the Hellenistic age and which in turn will be the foundation for the birth of a more developed science in the sixteenth and seventeenth centuries. Continuing from the time of Thales in the sixth century B.C., Greek science had an indomitable curiosity and an insistence on unfettered freedom of inquiry into the realities of nature, seeking explanations within nature rather than from myth, magic, and the supernatural. In varying degrees, most of these scientific truth seekers placed their faith in reason and knowledge originating in the senses. As Greek science evolved, authority was placed less on abstract argumentation and more on direct observation and the rudimentary beginnings of experimentation. Certain Hellenistic researchers began to quantify empirical observations. As a general trend, Hellenistic science grew more detached from the comprehensive world views of philosophy and was becoming an independent discipline that was the work of technical specialists. Increasingly, science was no longer the rationalization of common sense, and it was developing beyond the comprehension of the untutored layperson. As a spirit of inquiry and a way of knowing, we can recognize in the Greeks our scientific ancestors. Yet there are also differences. In general and with the exception of medicine, the goal of Greek science was to know the world, not to change it, to contemplate nature, not control it. Science was an end in itself; knowledge was its own reward. The life of pure inquiry was viewed as the supremely happy life. By contrast, the later scientific revolution of the sixteenth and seventeenth centuries would also value applied technology and thus had not only the passion but also the power to improve the daily lives of humankind. At its best, modern science has a greater potential for compassion then did Greek science.

## WHY DID WESTERN SCIENCE AND PHILOSOPHY BEGIN WITH THE GREEKS?

Why did the extraordinary phenomenon of Western science and philosophy spring from the Greeks? Why did those indispensable first steps and the resulting unprecedented achievements of the human spirit and intellect not begin in Africa, China, or the Americas? And why didn't the Romans, so influenced by Greek culture and with all their exceptional organizational and administrative skills, ever produce a scientist of genius or a philosopher of any originality? From an evolutionary perspective, the origins of science and philosophy with the Greeks is even more remarkable if we keep in mind that writing wasn't invented until around 3100 B.C. in Sumeria and not until around 1400 B.C. was the earliest alphabetic system developed in Syria. Among the evolving human cultures, why was it the Greeks who had this burning curiosity and thirst to understand reality for its own sake and not merely for survival and utilitarian purposes?

No one can answer these questions with certainty, but our best guess is that a combination of factors coalesced to create this unique evolutionary event. In listing below some of the possible causes, we might use them to assess the climate of inquiry for our own truth seeking. First, let us remember that the entire scientific and philosophical enterprise was the preoccupation of a determined but tiny minority. By whatever degrees, they had sufficiently evolved brains, emotional discipline, and economic resources to afford them at least some leisure to pursue their epistemological passions. Even before Thales in the sixth century B.C., Greeks were pouring out from their tiny, provincial homeland as seafaring adventurers and international traders, exposing themselves to strange and conflicting ideas and customs, thus widening their perspectives, simulating their curiosity, and provoking a cognitive dissonance that drove some of them to construct a more consistent and comprehensive understanding of their intellectual experiences. Though religion was an important part of Greek daily life, there were no forbidden questions or answers proscribed by an organized ecclesiastical authority, powerful priesthood, or infallible sacred scriptures. Absent was any notion of a one true faith, dogmatic orthodoxy, or a tradition of religious fanaticism to trammel the range of their inquiries. In general, Greek culture was exceptionally tolerant to new ideas and usually did not constrict the horizons of the mind. Though with exceptions, the classical Greek belief was that this world and human life have intrinsic value and meaning and are not a mere illusion or a trial to be passively endured in order to earn eternal bliss in a world beyond. The human ideal was not self-abasement but self-development, our task not to waste our earthly lives but to invest our energies for personal and community excellence. Sophocles exclaimed, "The world is full of wonders, but nothing is more wonderful than man." Humans are limited but exalted beings.

Perhaps most critical to the development of free and open inquiry was the Athenian invention of democratic self-government, in contrast to the despotic, centralized rule of the Near East and Orient. Because Athens was a small city-state, it was a direct, not a representational democracy, in which each free citizen was expected to participate in the actual government and to actively debate and vote. Athenians valued freedom for themselves and their city-state. Their ideal was freedom of speech for each eligible citizen, and they expected conflicting ideas and competitive debate. Rational discussion toward consent, not suppression of contrary views, was the classical ideal. This tradition of open, free, and competitive debate rather than obedience to a sovereign's authority became a guiding principle for science and philosophy. In general, the classical Greeks valued individualism, self-determination, and the right to have and express their views in an open forum. For Euripides, "A slave is one who cannot speak his thought." Another thread woven into the fabric of the Greek intellectual character was an unprecedented skepticism and critical spirit toward unsupported claims of truth. Increasingly, they demanded proofs of various kinds, including logical, empirical, and even the beginnings of experimental and mathematical demonstrations. They developed various ways of knowing and characteristically insisted that we have valid criteria so that we can know when we know. Whatever the actual causes for the evolution of the Greek spirit of inquiry, it has had the power to inspire truth seekers down through the centuries.

# THE SCIENTIFIC REVOLUTION OF THE SIXTEENTH AND SEVENTEENTH CENTURIES

## SOME CAUSES AND CONSEQUENCES OF THE SHIFT FROM MEDIEVAL EPISTEMOLOGY TO EARLY MODERN SCIENCE

The European Middle Ages have often been described as the Age of Faith. The ideal was for Christian beliefs and values to dominate all aspects of human life. For individuals, the purpose of human existence was to love God and one's neighbor, live a sacred life of Christian virtue, and thus also attain everlasting happiness in heaven and avoid eternal punishment in hell. For all human institutions, the ultimate goal was to divert mankind away from evil and toward salvation. The intent was to be a religious culture with a saintly ideal. The Church became a powerful, sometimes the most powerful, organization in Europe, able to control personal lives and social institutions. All knowledge, science, philosophy, literature, and the arts, were put in the service of religion. Almost all scholars and teachers were members of the clergy, and schools and universities were owned, controlled, or influenced by ecclesiastical organizations. The medieval synthesis integrating personal, institutional, and cultural life subservient to Christian beliefs made the Church the dominant and final intellectual authority over all of Europe.

Included in the medieval synthesis was the integration into the intellectual establishment of many of the works of Aristotle, including his logic, physics and cosmology; the astronomy of Ptolemy; and the medicine and anatomy of Galen. Generally, this pagan trinity became the dominant authority from the ancient Greek world, and more often than not their writings were accepted as the bible of the natural world. Rather than viewing the Greek empirical methods as only a point of departure to advance their own scientific discoveries, most medieval minds tended to revere the ancient findings almost as infallible dogmas, almost as articles of faith. With notable exceptions, the empirical approach of Aristotle was relegated to minor importance as was his inductive method for arriving at primary principles. Rather, his primary premises tended to be unquestioned as absolute truths, with an emphasis on deductive syllogistic logic. Verbal disputations with great conceptual subtlety became the rule rather than empirical observation and mathematical analysis. The complex and integrated epistemological methodologies developed by Aristotle were most often reduced by Scholastics to a combination of rationalism and authoritarianism. Eventually, the scholasticized version of Aristotle and the teachings of Ptolemy and Galen became so thoroughly entangled with Christianity that most medieval minds could only with difficulty distinguish them. Thus any fundamental challenge to Aristotle, Ptolemy or Galen came to be interpreted by most as an attack on the authority of the Church itself and a threat to the world view and unity of Christendom. But momentous challenges and changes were already well in the works by the fifteenth century. A new age was dawning.

It would be a mistake to assume that the Middle Ages were all stable and sterile. On the contrary, there were plenty of bright and vigorous minds, some of whom devoted critical attention to the details of Aristotelian epistemology. Yet such serious efforts and the resulting conflicts were usually well within the walls of Scholastic Aristotelianism. Rumblings such as these do not constitute a revolution. One authentic revolution that would decisively impact the medieval spirit was Martin Luther's (1483-1546) passionate revolt against Church authority. He preached a complete power shift of the criterion for religious truth from the Church to the individual. To discover the word of God and obtain salvation, he said, Christians must reject the authority of the Pope, the Councils, and claimed tradition, and turn to the pristine, uncorrupted truth in the Bible. No church was needed to mediate the original Christian teachings. Let every person read the Bible, and he or she will find the same

Christian truth. The plain and pure doctrine is directly open to all by following the one, literal meaning of Scripture. The authority of the Bible as interpreted by each individual replaced the authority of the Church. Individual conscience and inner conviction, not the Church, was now the infallible guide of truth. In locating the ultimate standard of religious truth with individual, inner subjective certainty rather than with the ecclesiastical apparatus, Luther breached the unity of Christendom. In his emphasis on returning to the plain, original message of the Bible, he demonstrated to his followers the error and uselessness of Aristotelianized theology. In his individualistic, antiestablishment stance, he would be a courageous and successful model for certain scientific truth seekers, who felt the need to break with the powerful Church-controlled educational institutions, which to them seemed so closed to new ways of knowing natural reality. As with Luther, they would need the firm conviction that they had not only the right but also the power of a surer way to truth than the existing establishment.

What generated the eventual overthrow of the Scholastic epistemology for the new scientific methods of the sixteenth and seventeenth centuries? Several causes seem to be critical besides the background influences of a newly gained cultural dynamism for Europe, a vigorous mercantile capitalism, and a wider assimilation of the classical Greek values of individual freedom, the pursuit of human excellence, and the full meaningfulness of this world's projects and pleasures. In contrast to the more closed and self-contained world of the Middle Ages, a new spirit of curiosity and openness was emerging along with a passion for exploration. Daring voyages of discovery climaxed in the discovery of the Americas by Columbus in 1492 and the circumnavigation of the earth by Magellan's expedition in 1522. How forcefully these discoveries of a vast new world must have jolted the old European mindset, including Copernicus, who was only nineteen when Columbus discovered America. Shocking new facts were discovered by the seafaring explorers. For example, beginning in the early fifteenth century, Portuguese expeditions sailing down the coast of Africa in search of a new trade route to the

Orient were confronted with facts that the ancients were convinced could not exist. With their own eyes, sailors discovered realities that contradicted Aristotle's conviction that the tropics were uninhabitable and Ptolemy's mathematical conclusion that all dry land is limited to only certain parts of the Northern Hemisphere.

The discovery of a mounting mass of new facts accumulated over some two hundred years weakened and eventually destroyed the deep-rooted reverence for the authority of Aristotle, Ptolemy, and Galen. Certain discoveries also challenged religious authority. The Copernican Revolution of 1543, placing the sun rather than the Earth at the center of the universe, not only revolutionized the prevailing world view, and violated cosmological principles of Aristotle and the earth-centered astronomy of Ptolemy, it also contradicted the literal reading of the Bible and the traditional teaching of the Church. The eventual acceptance and empirical verification of the new Copernican world view not only profoundly shook the authority of Aristotle and Ptolemy, but it also introduced a religious crisis. What were Christians to accept as the ultimate criterion of truth—the Bible and sacred tradition or the new facts of natural science?

For the emerging new science, 1543 was a big year, not only for the publication of the epochal work of Copernicus, but also for the *magnum opus* of Andreas Vesalius, *De Humani Corporis* (On the Construction of the Human Body), which marked the founding of modern scientific anatomy. Born in Brussels, educated in medicine at Louvain and Paris, Vesalius completed his studies and became a professor at Padua, the most prestigious medical school in Europe. He broke with medieval tradition by insisting that anatomy be based on human dissection, by himself doing dissections rather than delegating the task to surgeons, and by requiring his medical students to systematically do dissections rather than merely reading ancient texts and occasionally watching others doing dissections. Also, he did pioneering work in comparative anatomy, performing detailed dissections of both humans and animals. Though for well over a thousand years Galen was an unquestioned authority in medieval science,

Vesalius discovered and respectfully reported in his 1543 publication and a later revision that Galen's work was inadequate and had made serious errors in human anatomy, because it was based on animal studies including apes and monkeys rather than humans. Because of his profound reverence for Galen, Vesalius did not see himself as a revolutionary and with great respect and some self-doubt would sometimes follow the physiological errors of Galen rather than his own empirical findings. But the overall impact of Vesalius was to weaken the authority of Galen and launch a new era of detailed anatomical observation and description.

Another revolutionary break with the authority of Aristotle and Ptolemy was achieved by the astronomer Johannes Kepler (1571-1630). A complex personality, he was thoroughly modern in those aspects of his new astronomical system of the universe that are essentially accepted today, combining brilliant mathematics with an unrelenting loyalty to observational data. He was also a fervent Lutheran with an enthusiasm for theology, a firm believer in his own system of astrology, and a passionate mystic influenced by Pythagoras, Plato, and Neoplatonism. While in most ways Copernicus remained conservatively Ptolemaic, the origins of modern astronomy are usually considered to begin with Kepler's revolutionary discovery of the three laws of planetary motion, published in 1609 and 1619. For example, the first law demonstrated that the orbits of the planets are ellipses, thus rejecting the Aristotelian and Ptolemaic doctrine (and Copernicus' assumption) that because the heavens are perfect, their movements must be in perfect circles. In his second law, he showed that the planets move at different speeds, renouncing the earlier belief that because of the perfection of the heavens, all motion there must be invariable. In his great work of 1609, *Astronomia Nova*, Kepler announced his goal to develop a new astronomy, replacing Aristotle's celestial metaphysics with his own physics of the heavens. Though often inspired by a mystical mathematics and a zealous belief in the harmony and simplicity of the universe, he would in his strictly scientific works verify his theories by careful calculations and observational data.

The seventeenth century inventions of the telescope and microscope were unique events in human history. For the very first time, humans could see the invisible! Piercing through the barriers of naked eye commonsense appearances, humans gained access to radically new realms of nature and astonishing new facts. Excitement was in the air as the gates to new knowledge were flung wide open for all to see. This revolutionary empowerment of human vision also revealed disturbing phenomena. In 1609 when Galileo began scanning the skies with his improved version of the recent Dutch invention of the telescope, he discovered new facts that proved false the Aristotelian view that the heavens, unlike the changing and imperfect Earth, are immutable, perfect, and unflawed. For example, he found that the surface of the moon was not perfectly smooth, polished, and spherical but was rather rough and uneven, with mountains, valleys, and even craters, much like the Earth's landscape. Furthermore, he also observed spots on the sun, thus providing further evidence that the heavens were not immaculate and immutable.

In 1610, Galileo discovered four moons near Jupiter, which he concluded were orbiting Jupiter because they changed their nightly positions. Astronomers soon realized that these four moons obeyed Kepler's third law: the square of the moon's orbital period about Jupiter is proportional to the cube of its average distance from the planet. Galileo's telescopic observations and Kepler's three laws of planetary motion were breakthrough events toward the destruction of the Aristotelian doctrine that the heavens have a radically different nature from the Earth because they were formed from an entirely different substance. The new evidence contradicted the dominant belief in a hierarchy of being in which the heavens were qualitatively superior and ascended toward immutability and perfection as they were progressively more distant from the center of the Earth. The heavens, it was believed, were at a uniquely superior scale of being and operated by higher, sublime laws, while the Earth was at an inferior level, operating by lower, material laws. Kepler and Galileo replaced the Aristotelian two-natured theory with evidence for the uniformity of all of nature—a revolutionary change in world views.

A radically new view of the world was also revealed by the microscope. Though we don't know its inventor, it seems to have originated with the Dutch at about the same time as the invention of the telescope. A little more than a decade after Galileo improved an elementary telescope for astronomy, he developed an improved microscope, directed it to the study of bees, and in 1625 was the first ever to publish microscopical observations. Robert Hooke in 1665 published his famous *Micrographia*, the first significant collection of observations with the aid of a microscope. But in the seventeenth century, the greatest improvements in the microscope, along with some of the most astonishing observations, were made by the Dutchman Antoni van Leeuwenhoek (1632-1723). He was a pioneer, leading the human species into the vast, invisible world of microscopic life. He discovered the world of bacteria, corpuscles in the blood, and spermatozoa. The strange, new revelations of the microscope were greeted with enthusiasm by some and with suspicion, disbelief, and ridicule by others. In addition to the telescope and microscope, the inventions of the thermometer, barometer, air pump, and other devices extended the human power to observe and increasingly to measure nature. These inventions revealed things never before seen or even imagined and thus created an excitement that propelled the advance of the new science while, in the minds of many, they discredited Scholastic science as erroneous and obsolete.

The most potent new influence opening up the Scholastic mind may have been the introduction into Europe of an entirely new wave of previously unknown or unavailable ancient Greek philosophical, scientific, and mathematical works, beginning in 1453 with the Fall of Constantinople. Greek scholars fled the Byzantine eastern empire and came west, bringing these texts as well as classical literary works that launched the Renaissance. For the first time, Europeans could read the more complete works of Plato, the Skeptics, the Atomists, the Stoics, and the Neo-Platonists, and newly recovered texts or fresh, accurate translations of Ptolemy, Archimedes, Euclid, and other writers in astronomy, and pure and applied mathematics. Scholastics discovered in depth that Aristotle had important ancient rivals with conflicting views and systems, thus giving some of them the courage to challenge the dominant Aristotelianism. Copernicus was caught up in the stirring recovery of ancient science and literature, learning Greek and translating into Latin a seventh-century Greek author. He was part of the Ptolemaic revival and, with the help of an improved text, his goal was to restore, not reject, Ptolemy's astronomy. As Copernicus became dissatisfied with the Ptolemaic Earth-centered system, he looked back to the ancients for alternative views and found them in Pythagoras and Aristarchos of Samos. Copernicus could now feel emotionally free to correct the great Ptolemy. Vesalius, like Copernicus, shared the same Renaissance respect for antiquity and viewed his epic-making work as a rebirth of Alexandrian anatomy, hoping to at least restore dissection to the level of these ancient scientific models. The year 1543 was eventful for the new science not only for the publication of the great works of Copernicus and Vesalius, but also for the beginning of a new series of widely circulated translations of Archimedes. His mathematical physics provided a revolutionary drive toward the mathematization of nature so characteristic of the scientific revolution and was the inspiring point of departure for Galileo's mathematical and experimental physics. As with the physics of Galileo, most of the breakthrough advances of the scientific revolution were in domains pioneered by the ancient Greeks—as reawakened by the beckoning voice of the recovered texts, beginning in the mid-fifteenth century.

The new scientists continued to maintain that the universe was rational, but it was not the rationality of Scholastic logic but of mathematics. The trend was toward quantitative reasoning, numerical arguments. Syllogistic deductions from self-evident first principles were replaced by mathematical analysis linking provisional hypotheses and generalizations with experimental, empirical facts. The remarkable success of the mathematical interpretation of nature justified the sixteenth century revival of Pythagoreanism, with its belief that nature follows numerical laws. Truth seekers were ushered into a vast new world of mathematical precision. Eventually, mathematics will replace Latin as the international language of science.

Aristotle was not a mathematician; neither was he a mechanist. During the Renaissance, mechanistic and atomistic texts from ancient Greece were recovered or retranslated, and their perspectives became more influential. The new epistemology demanded a new metaphysics. The world came to be viewed as a huge machine, and the new science sought to go beyond common sense to uncover and explain the hidden mechanisms beyond phenomena. The world became a machine, and mechanics became the mathematical science of motion. The new, powerful, productive, and precise knowledge of nature produced a world view that was materialistic, mechanistic, and mathematical. Lifeless matter was set into motion by external forces. Gone was Aristotle's view of the world as organic, alive, and purposeful, drawn by an inner urge to actualize its destined essence, its substantial form. Gone was the search for formal and final causes and explanations in terms of ultimate purpose and ontological essence. Purpose was no longer a primary mode of explanation. The new science explained things mechanistically. Science focused on efficient causes, asking the immediate how, not the ultimate why, of events. For the new scientist, the old Aristotelian categories such as form and matter, actuality and potentiality were pseudo-explana-tions, unproductive and redundant. The mechanistic world and mathematical precision were natural mates, replacing a teleological world and qualitative descriptions. The eventual result was the Newtonian world machine, a clockwork universe. For the Deists, God was not the final cause, drawing each form of life to its own perfection, somehow participating in the divine perfection, but rather God was the efficient cause that provided the initial force to set the universe in motion.

The new scientific method of the sixteenth and seventeenth centuries was a unique event in the history of human evolution. The power of the new method was unprecedented. Among the community of important truth seekers who shaped the scientific revolution, we present below a few introductory, partial perspectives of only five of them, in the hope that it will be helpful to some of us who ask and seek answers to some of the basic questions of life.

## RENÉ DESCARTES: THE METHOD OF SYSTEMATIC DOUBT IN THE QUEST FOR CERTAINTY

If we were to rank truth seekers according to their level of ambition, appearing near the top of any list would be René Descartes (1596-1650). Not only did he seek to construct from scratch entirely new foundations for all human knowledge and the new sciences, but he wanted to do it with absolute certainty. After an excellent education as a boarding student at the newly founded Jesuit College of La Flèche in western France, he studied law at the University of Poitiers, where he received his baccalaureate and license in civil and canon law in 1616. Two years later, while traveling about as a volunteer gentleman soldier, his interest in scientific questions, and mathematical and mechanical problems was revived by stimulating discussions with a new friend, Isaac Beckman. Soon, Descartes began to manifest his mathematical genius. But then it happened. On November 10, 1619, after a time of solitary, exhausting mathematical work, shut away alone in a hot stove-heated room in Ulm, Germany, twenty-three-year-old René had what is variously described as a mystical experience, an altered state of consciousness, or in the words of one biographer, "A nervous breakdown."[18] Whatever the exact nature of the experience, Descartes reports that he had a divinely inspired, exhilarating daytime illumination, in which he had a vision of a universal mathematical science. That night he had three dreams that revealed his vocation to lay systematic, certain foundations for a new science based on a universal mathematics that would unlock the mysteries of nature. He then decided that he would dedicate the rest of his life to establish this new science. With an inheritance from his family, he never needed to work for a living. Being of a quite solitary nature and in order to stay focused on his search, he never married and avoided social commitments other than within a small circle of scientific and philosophical friends. With a disciplined single-mindedness, he pursued his calling to establish certain foundations for knowledge.

Why Descartes' drive for certainty? Today, most Western scientists and philosophers have abandoned as futile his quest for absolutely certain foundations for science and all human knowledge. Many a modern psychologist would view Descartes' passion for absolute certainty as a natural but infantile wish for parental security and an unrealistic expectation, potentially hazardous to adult mental and emotional health. But Descartes lived in a time of crumbling certainties. The European psyche was suffering an agonizing loss of secure certitudes on which individuals and entire cultures had based their lives and world views. The peace of the one, true, infallible Church as the final arbiter of truth was for many shattered into clamoring, competing Protestant sects with contradictory claims of truth. The Copernican Revolution, Kepler's planetary laws of motion, Galileo's telescopic observations of the heavens, the unsettling discoveries of a new world in the West and ancient civilizations in the East, and the dismissal of the trusted intellectual authorities of Aristotle, Ptolemy, and Galen were devastating or at least disturbing events to many a thinking person. Descartes also experienced the traditional, secure foundations slipping away from under his feet. The certitude he was seeking in the sciences was perhaps of the nature that only the divine can give in religious faith. With the rational grounds of religion beginning to be rattled, some religious spirits sought refuge in fideism, discounting entirely the role of reason in religion and trusting solely in the experienced certitude of faith. Powerful and pervasive was the sense of loss and longing for the old certainties.

Compounding the pain of lost certainties was a shock wave of rediscovered Greek Skepticism that resounded through Europe beginning in the mid-sixteenth century and persisted through the lifetime of Descartes. In 1562 a translation of Sextus Empiricus (c. 200 A.D.) was published which contained a presentation of the ideas of the Greek Skeptic Pyrrho of Ellis (c. 360–270 B.C.) and Pyrrhonian thinkers after him through the time of Sextus. Their basic view was that judgment should be suspended on everything beyond immediate appearances. The conclusion was that certainty was impossible, even the certainty that there is no certainty. As examples, they presented evidence that knowledge gained through the senses is unreliable, presented arguments demonstrating the invalidity of induction, and showed that the premise of every logical argument requires a previous premise, leading back to an infinite regress because there is no certain indubitable criterion to judge the truth or falsity of a first premise. Michel de Montaigne (1533-1592) had an enormous influence on the spread of Pyrrhonian Skepticism, which was forcefully sustained by several subsequent French writers. Descartes was acutely aware of and detested the Skeptical movement. He did not want to hear of "suspending judgment" or that knowledge could only be "probable." His goal was to restore certainty to human knowledge.

Descartes turned the tables on the Skeptics. He collected their criticisms, added some of his own, and instead of arriving at the universal suspension of judgment, he transformed systematic doubt into a method for achieving certainty. In becoming more skeptical than the Skeptics, he hoped to preempt their doubts and put science beyond their attacks. His goal was to sweep away not only the Skeptics and Aristotle but all other past authorities and to make a completely fresh start in order to establish new, firm foundations for the emerging science of his time. He was not yet doing science, but he was laying its metaphysical groundwork. To explain his purpose, he used the metaphor of a tree of knowledge. The roots are metaphysics, the trunk is physics, and the branches growing out from the trunk are the other sciences. He criticized Galileo's methodology as inadequate because it explained only particular phenomena while ignoring the important questions about the very foundations of his work. For Descartes, inquiry began with the method of systematic doubt. "The seeker after truth must, once in the course of his life, doubt everything, as far as possible."[19]

> For a long time I had observed...that in practical life it is
> sometimes necessary to act upon opinions which one
> knows to be quite uncertain just as if they were indu-
> bitable. But since I now wished to devote myself solely

to the search for truth I thought it necessary to do the
very opposite and reject as if absolutely false everything
in which I could imagine the least doubt, in order to
see if I was left believing anything that was entirely
indubitable.[20]

Descartes had great faith in the exclusive use of human reason to
establish the metaphysical and epistemological foundations of science and the certainty that valid scientific knowledge is actually possible. Unlike Aristotle, he did not believe that all knowledge must be
derived from sense experience. As the Scholastics would say, there is
nothing in the intellect that did not have its origins in the senses. He
believed that a number of general, fundamental principles of physics
can be discovered intuitively by the mind without input from the
senses because they are innate ideas, implanted in our minds at birth
by God. But beyond these general principles, the truths of particular
phenomena must be discovered and tested by empirical observation
and experimentation. Though scientific inquiry begins with rationally established foundations, the payoff is with the empirical discoveries of the particular sciences. "Now just as it is not the roots or
trunk of a tree from which one gathers the fruit, but only the ends
of the branches, so the principal benefit of philosophy depends on
those parts of it which can only be learnt last of all."[21]

For Descartes, seeking truth should result in some fundamental
certainties. He believed that up until his day the only discipline that
had succeeded in finding certainty was mathematics. If philosophers
would conceptualize in the manner of mathematics—in particular, if
they would employ the so-called geometrical method—then philosophy could be rid of its unending disputations and uncertainties.
Descartes, the inventor of analytical geometry, wanted geometry to
be the ideal model for philosophizing. Certain knowledge is
achieved in geometry by the use of intuition and deduction. Thus,
inquiry should begin with the mind's direct, intuitive apprehension
of independent, self-evident principles, as with the axioms of geometry: for example, a straight line is the shortest distance between two

points. From these indubitable self-evident truths, inferences are then made by strict, logical deduction. One of Descartes' critical tests of truth was to accept as true only what presented itself to his mind so clearly and distinctly that he had no occasion to doubt it. He proceeded to apply his method of systematic doubt by suspending his belief in anything which he could detect or even imagine had the slightest trace of doubt. Sense perception is often found to be illusory and therefore can be doubted. Even the external reality of our bodies and the world can be doubted, as we may only be dreaming. We can doubt the existence of God. Also, we cannot trust our experiences, because an evil demon could be purposely distorting our faculties and standards of evidence, even fooling us into believing basic mathematical axioms such as 2+2=4. Descartes systematically pours on the doubts until we seem to be in an endless stream of universal doubt. Finally, he arrived at one absolutely certain truth, the indubitable axiom "I am thinking, therefore, I exist." (In his French *Discourse on Method,* "je pense, donc je suis," and in his Latin *Principles of Philosophy,* "ego cogito, ergo sum." The phrase does not appear in the *Meditations.)* The process of doubting, which is a form of thinking, makes us aware of our self as a conscious being, that we exist. Even if I am deceived in all my thoughts, I must exist in order to be deceived. No matter how much an evil demon distorted my knowledge, he could not deceive me in my primary intuition, that I think and therefore I exist. Thus far, all Descartes knew with certainty was that he existed. From that inner, subjective consciousness, he then rationally built outward and reconstructed the existence of God, an external world, and the metaphysical foundations of human knowledge.

Descartes found in the contents of his consciousness an innate idea of God as a perfect, infinite, and infallible being, which he proceeded to prove as existing through several rational arguments. Then he noticed that he experienced sensory ideas that he himself did not produce; moreover, he had a strong inclination to believe that such ideas were caused by bodies. He reasoned that a good and perfect God would not mislead him on such a fundamental matter, and concluded that an external world that caused his sensory ideas in fact existed. Thus, he proved the existence of God by logical necessity from his own consciousness and then proceeded to prove the existence of the external world from the certainty of a benevolent God. Furthermore, God is the foundation of human knowledge of the world, because he would not deceive us and let us fall into systematic error if we follow a proper method, in which we accept only what is in our mind doubtless, clear, and distinct. The content of our innate ideas and the world are made for each other; thus, the mind can come to know the world. God is the ultimate guarantor of the rational order of the external world, which the rational mind can infallibly discern in its clear and distinct intuitions. Geometry is the paradigm for the reasoning process.

With the establishment of these metaphysical and epistemological foundations, Descartes then proceeded to build his science of reality, beginning with general laws of physics. "I have noticed certain laws which God has so established in nature, and of which he has implanted such notions in our minds, that after adequate reflection we cannot doubt that they are exactly observed in everything which exists or occurs in the world."[22] Some of these general, fundamental principles include his law of inertia, that the nature of a body consists in extension alone, that the extension of the world is indefinite, and that a vacuum is impossible in space, where there is absolutely nothing. Within the guiding framework of his general laws of physics, the individual sciences then proceed by empirical and experimental methods to discover and test new particular phenomena.

Beginning with his contemporaries and continuing into the present, Descartes was severely criticized for the weakness of his rational proofs for the existence of God, his apparently circular arguments, his vague test of truth in "clear and distinct ideas," and an array of implicit assumptions of which he was unaware and alternate explanations he did not consider. Though most of his mathematical innovations have endured, his rationally derived physics has been considered obsolete since Newton. Yet he is universally considered one of the founders of early modern science for his mechanical and mathematical interpretation of nature. Rejecting completely

Scholasticism's search for the purpose and essence of things, explaining change teleologically as the movement of matter toward the actualization of form, he interpreted nature by the mechanical motion of matter. For Descartes, the search for final causes was utterly useless in physics. In the beginning was God, the efficient cause that set into motion the great and harmonious, mathematically ordered world machine. Replacing the small, finite, and cozy cosmos of medieval Aristotelianism was the vast, infinite, and cold universe of Descartes. The mechanical replaced the organic and the mathematical the mystical.

Descartes' enormously influential dualism revolutionized the traditional world view and radically impacted the Western psyche. In this philosophy, reality is divided into two sharply distinct, entirely different kinds of substances: material and mental. Matter is extended in space, mechanical in motion, and follows mathematical laws. The mental does not occupy space, is not in motion or part of the predictable mechanical realm. The mental, spiritual substance, as for example the soul, has consciousness, thinks, remembers, and feels. Material substances have no consciousness and cannot think, remember, or feel. While the material world is deterministic, the mental, spiritual substance of the soul allows free will; consequently, we are responsible for our decisions and actions. While we humans can be moral or immoral, the physical world is morally indifferent. For Descartes, a human being was a composite entity, made up of a mind and a body. However, it is difficult to escape the impression that he was unable to integrate these two components in a satisfying way, with the result that we are more closely identified with our minds than with our bodies. As minds, we are conscious and have a personality; the body is unconscious and impersonal. The result is a split, and for some a terrifying alienation, between the world of spirit and the world of matter, between the essence of who we are and what the universe is. Spirit and religion are removed from the cosmos, and what is left dwells with a distant God and within tiny human souls. Descartes' world view makes us strangers in a cold, mechanical universe. Left behind is our warm, living bond with the universe and the sacred and endearing realm of the medieval cosmos. His mechanical philosophy of nature was a radical, heart-rending spiritual revolution.

> The scholastic scientist looked out upon the world of nature and it appeared to him a quite sociable and human world. It was finite in extent. It was made to serve his needs. It was clearly and fully intelligible, being immediately present to the rational powers of his mind; it was composed fundamentally of, and was intelligible through, those qualities which were most vivid and intense in his own immediate experience—color, sound, beauty, joy, heat, cold, fragrance, and its plasticity to purpose and ideal. Now the world is an infinite and monotonous mathematical machine. Not only is his high place in a cosmic teleology lost, but all these things which were the very substance of the physical world to the scholastic—the things that made it alive and lovely and spiritual—are lumped together and crowded into the small fluctuating and temporary positions of exten-sion which we call human nervous and circulatory systems....It was simply an incalculable change in the viewpoint of the world held by intelligent opinion in Europe.[23]

What can we learn from the spirit of René Descartes? He was courageous. Not content to follow others like a lamb, he risked opening up new paths to knowledge. He ran deep, seeking the underlying metaphysical foundations for human knowing in science. He had a democratic faith in the rational powers of all men but insisted that, to reap its benefits, each of us must have a systematic method. He was audacious. Methodically doubting all in order to make a fresh start, his goal was to achieve rock bottom certainty for human knowing and thus make possible a valid science. But also he had some practical wisdom in warning us that, if we are to employ the method of systematic doubt, we should at the same time con-tinue to obey the laws and customs of our country and continue to practice our religion. Dedicated and disciplined, he remained focused throughout his life on his goal of seeking truth. He was extremely bright, but in the view of most modern thinkers, he claimed too many domains and too much certainty for innate ideas and human reason. However, in his systematic application of algebra to geometry, he made a decisive contribution to the rapid growth of mathematical physics. Both in his intuition of a universal mathematical science and his mechanical philosophy of nature, he was one of the giants on whose shoulders Newton stood. He was an outsider, never employed as part of the educational establishment, working quite alone and secluded most of his adult life in Holland, removed from his native France. This somewhat solitary nature may have contributed to his originality, but perhaps it also led to his frequent, stubborn resistance to critical feedback from his professional peers. Portraits of him as a young man seem to exude arrogance and aloofness. A portrait of him toward the end of his life depicts a more humane, rather tired veteran warrior, perhaps weary of wielding his sword of rationality in the pursuit of certainty. Like all of us, he had his limitations of character. Like few of us, he recognized his unique talents and concentrated them exceptionally well in his passion, perhaps even his obsession, for truth.

## PIERRE GASSENDI: MITIGATED SKEPTICISM AND THE SEPARATION OF THE NEW SCIENCE FROM METAPHYSICS

In answering the questions about what and how we humans can know, Pierre Gassendi (1592-1655) was a very different spirit than his contemporary, René Descartes. Whereas Descartes begins the epistemological quest in his mind as a pure rationalist, Gassendi is an empiricist, believing that all knowledge has its origins in sense experience, thus following the Scholastic motto that there is nothing in the mind that was not first in the senses. For Gassendi, no *a priori* innate ideas, no absolutely first principles or fundamental laws of physics are implanted at birth in the human mind by God. At birth, the mind is a blank tablet with nothing written on it. If we believe the axiom that the whole is greater than its parts, it is not because this idea is innate in our minds but rather because we have observed this phenomenon in nature. Similarly, if a person is born blind, that individual will never have an accurate idea of color. As their points of departure, Descartes is intuitive and then deductive, Gassendi is inductive and then generalizes from particulars.

While Descartes battled against skepticism and used it as a means to establish certainty, Gassendi embraced much of ancient Greek skepticism, accepting their argument that it is beyond human capacity to establish with absolute certainty any metaphysical foundation for knowledge of the natural world. For Gassendi, we can have knowledge of appearances but can never know the inner nature or real essence of things. We can know things as they appear to us, but not as they are in themselves. Certain knowledge beyond appearances is impossible; absolutely certain knowledge of nature is beyond our human powers. The best we can hope for is probable, provisional explanations, not demonstrative, certain knowledge. Though we do not need to indefinitely suspend judgment of all things, as with Pyrrho of Ellis, we do need to delay judgment until by induction we gather more sense data, and by experimental testing and critical reasoning we come to a clearer understanding about phenomena. Scientific knowledge is cumulative but not absolutely certain. Reason can give us knowledge beyond what the senses alone can provide. Gassendi gave the example of perspiration on human skin. Even though we cannot observe pores, we can infer their existence by the observable phenomenon of sweating. Yet such rational inferences are only provisional and must be later verified by more precise empirical observation and experimentation, which became possible during his lifetime with the invention of the microscope. However, he was acutely aware that we cannot arrive at absolutely certain and universal principles by induction from sense experience, because no matter how many identical observations are gathered, a negative instance may yet occur in the future. For example, even after observing one million swans to be white, we cannot know that the essence of swans includes the quality of white because sometime in the future we may discover a black swan. Also, he rejected Descartes' criterion of truth in clear and distinct ideas because there is no guarantee that what we clearly and distinctly perceive actually exists in external reality. Moreover, different persons can have subjectively certain, clear, and distinct but contradictory ideas about objective reality, and even the same person at a later time can change her mind as to what is clear and distinct.

Gassendi chose a middle path between the more radical of the Greek skeptics, who claimed that no valid human knowledge was possible, and the dogmatists, who believed that they had attained absolute, certain knowledge. For Gassendi, what is natural for the human species is empirical, experimental knowledge of phenomena. Knowledge of the inner essence of things and ultimate metaphysical truths of nature belong only to the mind of God. Though we humans cannot have absolute certainty about the valid foundations of knowledge, science does provide provisional and probable knowledge, which can be adequate knowledge to meet our practical human needs. This pragmatic knowledge, though not indubitable, is however a genuine epistemological achievement. It is all we can hope for in understanding nature. Because it is beyond human power to establish absolute criteria for certain knowledge, science is forced to go it alone without indubitable metaphysical foundations. Yet in its own restricted domain of working with appearances, science can provide systematic knowledge that is able to predict phenomena with various probabilities, provisionally adequate to guide our actions and promote human welfare. For Gassendi, Descartes was a dogmatist. For Descartes, Gassendi was too much of a skeptic. The two had an impatient and strong distaste for each other's views. Though Gassendi was known to be extremely tolerant and amiable, he considered Descartes a fanatic who made extravagant claims for *a priori* knowledge. Perhaps because of Descartes' apparent plagiarizing of some of Gassendi's ideas and the scathing criticism by Gassendi of

Descartes' work, they had some bad feelings toward each other. Gassendi dubbed him "the mind," and Descartes countered by calling Gassendi "the flesh," the latter of which is somewhat amusing because Gassendi was a vegetarian. The two represent the classic conflict between the rational, mathematical, deductive, and the empirical, experimental, inductive temperaments, reminiscent of the tension between Plato and Aristotle and certain modern theoretical and experimental physicists.

But who was Pierre Gassendi? Though during his lifetime and for some years following, he rivaled Descartes in fame, he has since been mostly forgotten in the English-speaking world except by a few specialists in the history of science and philosophy. Even among the French, he became overshadowed by Descartes, though in the twentieth century some outstanding French scholars followed by English-speaking researchers corrected this long neglect and reminded us of his importance. He was born at Champtercier, a village of Provence in southern France. His parents were peasants. A parish priest noticed his exceptional intelligence and guided him toward studies, with the result that at age twenty-one, he became a professor of rhetoric at Digne and by age twenty-five was given a chair of philosophy at Aïx and was also ordained a Catholic priest. During these early years in his career he totally rejected Scholasticism, was much influenced by ancient Greek skepticism, and began his lifelong practice of astronomical observations. Other interests included physics and humanistic studies of ancient philosophy and literature. He was a great admirer of Copernicus, Kepler, and Galileo and maintained active contacts with many leading scientists and intellectuals of his day. In 1645 he was appointed professor at the College Royal de France and was given the chair of mathematics, which actually was in astronomy. He is considered to be one of the founders of early modern science for his reviving the materialistic, atheistic atomic theory of Epicurus and baptizing it for Christian Europe by removing its most blatant antireligious elements and then using it as a hypothetical mechanical model for relating appearances and predicting observable phenomena.

Gassendi had two powerful currents running through him: a profound Christian spirituality rooted firmly in his Catholic faith and a great enthusiasm and commitment to the new emerging science. For him, there were two realms of truth, the natural and the supernatural, and he did not see any conflicts. In the natural order, we must limit ourselves to phenomena and endeavor to be as empirical as possible. Though he considered sense input and reason to be two necessary criteria for judging truth, when push came to shove he gave preference to the empirical over the rational. In the end, theory required empirical verification. In his empirical and pragmatic approach to knowledge and his intent to separate metaphysics from science, this seventeenth century devout priest, dedicated scientist, and professional philosopher sounds very modern.

## GALILEO GALILEI: PIONEER SCIENTIST IN OBSERVATIONAL ASTRONOMY AND MATHEMATICAL-EXPERIMENTAL PHYSICS

As a working scientist, one of the most influential founders of the scientific revolution was Galileo (1564-1642). Because science has absorbed so much of his methodology, his manner of doing science can today seem so familiar as to appear almost commonplace. Yet during his time the revolution that he pioneered in the scientific method, as applied to physics and observational astronomy, was new and controversial.

To more precisely discern the uniqueness of his radical innovations in the scientific method of his time let's begin with the indispensable function he assigned to the application of mathematical concepts for understanding nature. Rejecting the purely verbal descriptions of the qualitative aspects of nature that preoccupied medieval Aristotelianism, he pioneered the quantitative description and analysis of observed phenomena. As a beginning university student, he obeyed his father's wishes to pursue a practical career as a medical doctor, but he soon dropped out of medicine to follow his passion for applied mathematics. In studying Archimedes with a private tutor, he became fascinated with the way nature seems to follow mathematical, especially geometrical, laws. With a youthful enthusiasm that continued throughout his lifetime, he took great pride in seeing himself as continuing the mathematical physics of Archimedes. In contrast to most university mathematicians of his day, who rarely displayed any interest in the application of quantitative methods to terrestrial phenomena, and unlike the scholastic physicists, who, with the exception of the Jesuits, typically had little training or appreciation of mathematics and marginalized its application in physics, Galileo was convinced that without mathematics we would never understand nature as it really works. He thought that precise mathematical description, not wordy concepts, best revealed the laws that underlie and explain commonsense appearances. Philosophy, or natural philosophy as science was still called in his time, must understand that mathematics is the language of nature.

> Philosophy is written in this grand book, the universe, which stands continually open to our gaze. But the book cannot be understood unless one first learns to comprehend the language and read the letters in which it is composed. It is written in the language of mathematics, and its characters are triangles, circles, and other geometric figures without which it is humanly impossible to understand a single word of it; without these, one wanders about in a dark labyrinth.[24]

The mathematics of Galileo is applied, not pure, mathematics—the measurement and description of empirical phenomena. It is not the mathematics of the Pythagoreans, where number is an ultimate ontological reality. It is not Platonic, with form as the essence of reality and the material world as only a shadowy, imperfect imitation. It is not the sometimes mystical mathematics of Kepler. Rather, Galileo is more the hard-headed scientific realist as Aristotle was the descriptive biologist. For Galileo, a harmony existed between the world of sense experience and the mathematical forms of knowledge, a harmony that can be discovered by combining the two in a dynamic two-way interaction of empirical experimentation and mathematical analysis. Mathematics became a vehicle for scientific exploration and explanation. Mathematical demonstrations, especially for Galileo geometrical demonstration, replaced the syllogistic verbal demonstrations of the Scholastic scientists. Science was becoming quantified and henceforth advances in empirical science would be dependent on further progress in the discipline of mathematics, as for example in the development of analytical geometry.

Galileo was a brilliant experimenter who developed new experimental apparatus and procedures. His work and that of other contemporaries in the new sciences came to be sometimes called "experimental philosophy." In his new science of motion (for example, falling and projected bodies) he ingeniously forged a dynamic two-way relationship between theory and experiment, deduction and induction. Sometimes he would develop hypotheses out of his mathematical imagination and then test out their validity with empirical experiments. At other times he would perform experiments that would generate new hypotheses and which could be formulated in mathematical language. He used experiments to not only confirm theories but also to discover new laws of nature.

Another parting from the past was the high value Galileo placed on technical skills and technology to advance scientific knowledge, in contrast to the classical Greeks' typical aristocratic disdain for getting their hands dirty and the Scholastics' disinclination to leave the tranquility of their libraries for the noise and toil of the shop. It is no accident that Galileo, in the first two paragraphs of his *Two New Sciences*, set the opening dialog in the world-famous Arsenal of Venice. In this book, his most important publication and the first great work of modern physics, he begins by expressing his high esteem for the workmen and their technical hands-on knowledge, emphasizing how valuable their knowledge can be to physics, especially mechanics. Indeed, he explains, sometimes when the physicist is totally baffled and in despair of ever understanding how certain things can happen, a skilled tradesman has the answer and can

explain it with the finest reasoning, while also commenting that this
knowledge is commonly known as part of his practical daily work.
Galileo himself took a Dutch invention that was little more than a
toy and transformed it into a telescope, which as a scientific instrument revolutionized astronomy and cosmology. Also he had the
technical sense and excellent manual skills to design and build it
himself. By trial and error, he rapidly worked out certain principles
of magnification. Because the type of lens he needed could not be
purchased anywhere from artisans, he taught himself how to grind
and polish lenses to his own specifications, a painstaking job only
possible with deft hands. He also applied his technical talents to further develop several other scientific instruments, including the
microscope. In the tradition of Archimedes, he was mechanically
minded and technically gifted. Galileo was a trailblazer in understanding that the advance of physical science depended not only on
the progress of mathematics but also on the development of the
technology and techniques of scientific instruments.

Galileo was an observational, not a theoretical astronomer in the
grand manner of Kepler. He was not a systematic metaphysician like
Descartes, seeking new epistemological foundations for science. He
was not a speculative system builder. But this does not mean that he
was only technically minded or thought exclusively like a practical
engineer. Though he never wrote a formal treatise in the traditional
philosophical style on epistemology or metaphysics, we know that
he was much concerned with these two realms as they were directly involved with his revolutionary new science. He was a working
scientist and most often we learn of his philosophy of science as a
side commentary in polemical works defending himself against his
professional opponents or promoting himself and his work to the
educated public.

He gave much thought to the range and limitations of his new
mathematical-experimental way of knowing. As with some of his
contemporaries developing the new science, he did not seek to
know the intrinsic essence or final purposes of natural phenomena.
In his new science of motion, he sought to uncover natural laws

describing the interaction of observable events, not their ultimate purpose. For many scholastics, this was a controversial, even revolting approach because, for Aristotle, to explain an event was to explain its four causes, especially the formal and final causes. Typically, for the Scholastics, the goals of Galileo's physics seemed superficial, his results trivial. For Galileo, he knew the goals of his new scientific method were modest. Rather than seeking general, overarching ultimate principles of nature, he restrained his epistemological ambitions.

> Galileo selected certain well-defined and very restricted areas of inquiry within which mathematical analysis could clearly advance physics. Though now characteristic of science, his procedure of adhering to limited objectives and dealing with specific problems having precise solutions had little appeal to men schooled in abstract principles of great generality....If Galileo ever believed that all phenomena of nature could be explained, or even fully analyzed, he failed to say so; rather, he publicly expressed doubt that any phenomenon in nature, even the very least that existed, could ever be completely understood by any theorist.[25]

In his new physics, his range of inquiry was restricted to what natural properties could be counted, what could be described in mathematical terms. For Galileo, this did not mean that physical reality was limited to the quantified, but only that his way of knowing was limited to the quantifiable. Modest as were the goals of his method, he believed that the practical benefits of his new science would powerfully speak for themselves. Even in his own limited investigations, Galileo was usually reluctant to make generalizations, which is much in the spirit of modern science. Though aware of the broader implications of his new method, he was not at heart a metaphysician. He was not against philosophy, but he opposed the Scholastic habit of beginning with purposes and then deducing what must necessarily occur in nature, thus restricting in advance what may be actually happening. For Galileo, this was contrary to the empirical spirit of Aristotle who, at least in principle, gathered all possible data before theorizing about purposes. Galileo was convinced that Aristotle not only based his science on the most widely accepted empirical facts of his time, but also thought that if Aristotle had available the later observations of Galileo's telescope and his mathematical-experimental physics of motion, then Aristotle would have changed his cosmology and physics. For Galileo, the new science should be free from any submission to Scholastic philosophy so that it could investigate all the possibilities of events, properties, and laws that occur in nature.

Not only did Galileo want to liberate his new science from Scholastic natural philosophy, he also wanted to free it from any inappropriate control by religion. A sincere Catholic, he believed, like many of his religious and scientific contemporaries, in a dual theory of truth—the supernatural and the natural. Each had its own proper domain and thus one could not contradict the other. Supernatural truths were matters of faith beyond human power to know, with sources in divine revelation as contained in holy scripture and the sacred traditions of the Church. Natural truths were within our ability to know, with sources directly in nature and human reason. Science should not attempt to do religion, and religion should not attempt to do science. Galileo reiterated the famous saying of Cardinal Baronius, "The intention of the Holy Ghost is to teach us not how the heavens go, but how to go to heaven."

But Galileo did eventually run afoul of the official church. On the morning of June 22, 1633, the seventy year-old Galileo was brought before the Inquisition in Rome, required to kneel while his sentence of indefinite imprisonment was read to him and ordered to renounce his Copernican views. Continuing to kneel, the aging Galileo recanted in words including the following:

> I have been judged vehemently suspected of heresy, that
> is, of having held and believed that the sun is the center
> of the universe and immovable and that the earth is not
> the center of the same nor immovable.

*continues*

*continued*

> Nevertheless, wishing to remove from the minds of your
> Eminences and all faithful Christians this vehement sus-
> picion reasonably conceived against me, I abjure with a
> sincere heart and unfeigned faith, I curse and detest the
> aforesaid errors and heresies....And I swear that for the
> future I will neither say nor assert in speaking or writing
> such things as may bring upon me similar suspicion....[26]

Today, most church people acknowledge that the Inquisition's secret trial and condemnation of Galileo was a monumental blunder. But Galileo also contributed to precipitating this historical event. While he made modest claims about his new physics, nobody could claim that Galileo was modest in his personality! His feisty spirit was prone to polemics which over the years created many enemies. It may have been certain offended Scholastic philosophers who provided the principal push for the Inquisition's condemnation of Galileo's Copernicanism. At that time there was no irrefutable proof for a sun-centered universe, though for the new scientists there was a convincing preponderance of evidence. Nevertheless, for many years before the Inquisition's condemnation, Galileo had pursued a promotional campaign, sometimes in a quite devious manner to avoid church censors, to convert the world, including the church, to Copernicanism. His courageous enthusiasm for his Copernican beliefs, however, lacked a sociological sensitivity to the survival needs of the establishment science as well as a psychological sensitivity to the frightening impact of Copernicanism on the psyches of many Christians.

Galileo loved his new science, and he loved his old religion. He was a sincere believer in both. Yet it was clear that, if read literally, the sacred scriptures in various verses state that the sun revolves around a stationary Earth. In 1615 Galileo wrote a famous letter to Christina, Grand Duchess of Tuscany, who was disturbed by the contradictions between certain statements in the Bible and Copernicanism. In effect, Galileo's letter was a systematic presentation of the principles to be applied in the interpretation of biblical passages that seem to be in conflict with the discoveries of natural science, particularly Copernicanism. First, he affirms that "the holy Bible can never speak untruth whenever its true meaning is understood."[27] As part of its divine inspiration by the Holy Spirit, the sacred scribes accommodated their statements to the "capacities of the common people, who are rude and unlearned." This doctrine, says Galileo, is widely accepted by theologians. For example, Galileo continues, even though theologians and the educated know that it is contrary to the divine essence, the Bible describes God having "feet, hands, and eyes, as well as corporeal and human affections, such as anger, repentance, hatred, and sometimes even the forgetting of things past and ignorance of things to come." Also, "when speaking but casually of the earth, of water, of the sun, or of any other created things," the scriptures "condescend to popular capacity" for the purpose of "avoiding confusion in the minds of the common people which would render them contumacious toward the higher mysteries." Galileo then propounds the view that the Bible has no intention of teaching physical science, but rather its goal is to teach salvation. Both the Bible and nature come from God. Regarding "discussions of physical problems we ought to begin not from the authority of scriptural passages, but from sense-experiences and necessary demonstrations." In strictly natural matters, our human powers have primacy over scripture, which in turn must be interpreted so as to agree with scientific findings. "Nor is God any less excellently revealed in Nature's actions than in the sacred statements of the Bible." Furthermore, writes Galileo, without diminishing in any way the spiritual authority of the Bible, certainties arrived at in physics can help us better understand and express the meanings contained within sacred scriptures. The Holy Spirit in the Bible did not intend to enlighten us as to whether the sun goes around the Earth or the Earth goes around the sun. The Bible is not a science textbook.

Most scientists have not forgotten the condemnation of Galileo by the Inquisition. He has become in the minds of many a martyr for science. It has taken a long time for the official church to forgive

Galileo, though his "indefinite imprisonment" quickly became a rather benign house arrest. In 1820 the Church decided that Galileo's pro-Copernican work, *Dialogue Concerning the Two Chief World Systems*, was to be removed from the next edition of the *Index*. In 1992 Pope John Paul II stated, "Galileo formulated important epistemological norms indispensable in reconciling the Holy Scripture and science."[28] Back in Galileo's country, his trial and condemnation replaced freedom of inquiry with fear. Though several noteworthy Italian mathematicians and scientists would immediately follow him, the spirit of the new sciences moved north of the Alps into France, where the powers of the Inquisition were less consistent, and into Protestant Holland and England, beyond the reach of the Inquisition.

## FRANCIS BACON: PROPHET AND PROPAGANDIST OF A NEW VISION OF EXPERIMENTAL SCIENCE

If we were meeting with Sir Frances Bacon (1561-1626) in his elegant office as Lord Chancellor of England, and asked him his views about the purpose of scientific knowledge and the best ways to understand the natural world, his face might have turned crimson with rage. Explaining his strong emotional reaction, he might have begun by recalling that he entered Cambridge University at age thirteen, a young age even in those times for a precocious student, and began his studies in the Scholastic Aristotelianism so dominant in the universities. At age fifteen, disgusted with the Scholastic curriculum, he left Cambridge, never to graduate. He eventually qualified to practice law and served in Parliament for some thirty-six years. Living a full-time active life in politics beginning in the realm of Elizabeth I, he eventually obtained the high position of Lord Chancellor to James I. But all during his busy career, this practical man vividly remembered the two painful years at Cambridge where, in his opinion, he was subjected to wordy and worthless Scholastic disputations, that forever went around in contentious circles and contributed nothing to the advancement of learning or practical util-ity. At age fifteen, his intellectual repugnance toward Scholasticism and his moral outrage at its uselessness for relieving suffering and improving the human condition climaxed in the teenager's emotion-ally charged decision to use his future public power and private writ-ings to promote the intellectual and institutional reforms necessary to increase knowledge and contribute to human welfare.

Revolting against Aristotle's aristocratic notion that the most per-fect type of knowledge is contemplative enjoyment of the highest truths, an enjoyment possible only to a leisurely élite, Bacon passion-ately argued that the highest virtue was not intellectual gratification but rather the moral purpose of improving the human condition. Though he was only a conventional rather than a fervent Christian, Bacon insisted that the ultimate purpose of knowing is charity.

> I would address one general admonition to all—that
> they consider what are the true ends of knowledge, and
> that they seek it not either for pleasure of the mind, or
> for contention, or for superiority to others, or for profit,
> or fame, or power, or any of these inferior things, but for
> the benefit and use of life, and that they perfect and gov-
> ern it in charity. For it was from lust of power that the
> angels fell, from lust of knowledge that man fell; but of
> charity there can be no excess, neither did angel or man
> ever come in danger by it.[29]

Bacon proposed not only a new purpose but also a new method for obtaining knowledge. Rather than the barren, verbal disputations of the Scholastics, he argued for an empirical, experimental science. Rather than sterile, speculative, syllogistic deductions, which could not result in any new discoveries, he forcefully promoted an inductive logic, which would draw out from nature its full richness. Not ancient texts but nature itself is our best teacher, he claimed. Get out of the libraries and into the laboratories! Don't multiply words, multiply experiments!

It may seem such obvious ho-hum to hear Bacon promoting science as experimental, because most people today equate science with the experimental method. But keep in mind that during his time his proposal was revolutionary. His emphasis on the experimental violated the mental habits of centuries and met with hostile opposition from the educational establishment. For Bacon, careful observation was fundamental, but it was not enough. Raw input from the senses can mislead us, as when a lake appears on a distant desert flat when in reality it is only a mirage. Whenever possible, sense observations must be guided and corrected by the process of skillful and artificially designed experiments to accurately answer the questions we put to nature and unveil her hidden truths. He believed that he had developed an inductive logic beyond that of Aristotle. Bacon's inductive reasoning from particulars began with collecting as many observations as possible and then went further, to include also actively seeking out negative instances. Bacon stressed the crucial importance of seeking out negative instances in order to unmask generalizations that we might otherwise consider true. Only by many observations and varied experiments can the scientist cautiously and gradually ascend to generalizations and laws. Bacon thought that the Aristotelians precipitously jumped to constructing axioms based on scanty empirical evidence.

Bacon's inductive method is today often criticized as being almost a mechanical routine going from particulars to generalizations, neglecting the fundamental role of forming hypotheses to focus the search for facts and to decide which experiments need to be conducted. Generating productive hypotheses is a creative not a mechanical process which includes the person of the scientist and such processes as intuition, imagination, educated guesses, alert serendipity, and sometimes weird hunches. Also, from Bacon's own time into the present, he was criticized for not grasping the powerful role of mathematics in science, though in scattered passages he explicitly attributed an important if secondary role for mathematics in physics and certain other disciplines. By temperament he was empirical, not mathematical. However, he was innovative in calling for the application of experimental methods, not only in the physical and life sciences but also in psychology and the social sciences. His hope was that by extending the range of his experimental science, humans could transcend their subjective weaknesses and attain a greater objectivity. He was also acutely aware that the experimental method was a demanding discipline which needed to be learned. In the words of Loren Eiseley, a modern anthropologist and interpreter of science,

> Science exists only within a tradition of constant experimental investigation of the natural world. It demands that every hypothesis we formulate be subject to proof, whether in nature or in the laboratory, before we can accept its validity. Men, even scientists, find this type of thinking extremely difficult to sustain. In this sense science is not natural to man at all. It has to be learned, consciously practiced, stripped out of the sea of emotions, prejudices, and wishes in which our daily lives are steeped. No man can long endure such rarified heights without descending to common earth. Even the professional scientist frequently confines such activity to a specific discipline, and outside of it indulges his illogical prejudices.[30]

Bacon was not only a philosopher of science, he was also a prophet with a visionary ideal of what science could achieve and how it could help mankind. He was a man on a mission, inspiring succeeding generations with his revolutionary perspectives and program for the new science. First, he promoted a radical change in time perspective. Under various influences, including the Renaissance humanists, most of Bacon's intellectual contemporaries looked backward, yearning for the past glory of classical Greece and Rome as the golden age of human knowledge and wisdom. They considered the best era of secular human history to be in antiquity, an age that could not be equaled and certainly could not be surpassed in the present or future. Since those ancient times, they saw humanity as in decay. For some, like John Donne (1573-1631), the metaphysical poet and clergyman, all of nature was in its old age. Down through time, the human mind has been weakening in its powers, which explained the superiority of the ancient intellects. Renaissance scholars, feeling intellectually inferior to the ancients and almost worshipping antiquity, sought out Greek and Roman texts to recover the golden nuggets of the past superior minds.

Bacon had plenty of respect for the classical past, but he wanted to build on only the best of those times in laying new foundations for knowledge and advancing learning beyond a nostalgic looking backward. For him, the discovery of the New World by Columbus was a powerful symbol of a new era for humankind to be opened up by the new experimental science and practical inventions. He was opposed to the ancient belief in a cyclical notion of time, in which the eternal recurrence of events did not allow any possibility of progress in human history. Bacon, raised with a Judeo-Christian linear notion of time, was a futurist with a secular faith in progress toward man's ultimate fulfillment—a belief transformed from the religious faith of Moses, who pointed his people toward the promised land, and Jesus, who instilled in his followers the hope of a future messianic kingdom. Rather than despairing over our decaying human powers, the prophet Bacon electrified many with his proclamation of the dawn of a new era through experimental science and technology, governed by brotherly love for the welfare of all humankind.

Not only did Bacon draw from his ancient Judeo-Christian origins his belief in progress, but also he extracted from it his philosophy of human dominion over nature. Going back to Genesis, humans are described as made in the image of God, superior to all other creatures and with power over all of nature and every other creature. Nature was made for us. Then with the Fall, humans lost both their innocence and their dominion over nature. For Bacon, both could be recovered to some extent in this world, the first by faith and religion and the second by science and technology. Also from biblical sources, he believed that it is both an act of worship and a religious duty to study nature, because it is God's creation. In scripture, the two basic commandments are to worship God and to love one's neighbor. To love our neighbor means to actively do the person good. Science is not only the worship of God but also the love of one's neighbor, because it can practically help meet human needs and relieve suffering. Furthermore, Bacon emphasized that science, like religion, must be judged by its works. It is the religious duty of science not only to study God's creation but also to help God's human creatures. Science needs power to help people, and because knowledge is power, science must apply his experimental science to regain the dominion over nature that God had originally intended for humans before the Fall. With the mastery gained over nature through scientific knowledge, humans can transform the quality of life on earth and add to God's glory. Thus, Bacon gave science a new mission and an exalted meaning. He had no patience with those clergy who claimed that the study of nature was below humanity's spiritual calling.

In his vision of a science of practical benefits, Bacon was not, however, a pragmatic philistine who limited himself only to solving immediate, short-term problems. He was an advocate of both pure and applied research, believing that each could have practical value. As a Renaissance man with goals of universal knowledge and a wide spectrum of accomplishments, he promoted the idea of a broad liberal education, including philosophy and literature, as essential for evaluating alternative ends to scientific means. He had no objection to metaphysics and religion but believed that they and science could each best advance by restricting themselves to their own domains and methods. Final and formal causes best belonged to religion and metaphysics. The new experimental science, in restricting itself to efficient and material causes, could best provide new discoveries and power to humankind in this world. For Bacon, we need to know how nature works so that we can make nature work for us. Yet he believed we must approach nature with humility and the innocence of a child, as in his saying, "We cannot command nature except by obeying her."

Another revolutionary perspective introduced by Bacon, and today we take for granted is that because the complexity of nature is so great, it cannot be mastered by a handful of isolated individuals working independently. To be effective, science requires a collective, cooperative effort in a vast, organized enterprise. Bacon was also a pioneer in promoting the concept that the cooperative inquiry of many researchers could be more efficient through a division of labor of a variety of specialists, including even generalist theoreticians. In strong opposition to the private, secret work of the alchemists, occultists, and magicians of his era, he insisted that science be public. Research projects, procedures, and findings should be publicly presented and publicly criticized. Thus, his new experimental science not only had a social purpose to serve the public good, but the method itself had a social nature. Another astute, original observation of Bacon was that the science of his time was homeless. He was intent on finding an institutional home for science. This statesman–strategist for the new science used all his political influence and propaganda skills to convince the king that for the welfare of his subjects, the state should found and fund colleges, university departments, and institutes for research and teaching, where an organized community of scientists could be formed and sustained over time. During his lifetime, he was totally unsuccessful in realizing this goal, but his ideas took fire in succeeding generations. His inspiration led to the foundation of the first national scientific societies, including the Royal Society for the Promotion of Natural Knowledge (London, 1662) and the Académie Royal de Sciences (Paris, 1666). Many of Bacon's publications were an attempt to propagate his new, comprehensive vision and program for experimental science, not only among influential government officials but also with the general public. He was perhaps the first deliberate publicist for modern science.

As a person, it would be difficult to mistake Sir Francis Bacon for that other Francis from the little Italian town of Assisi. Sir Francis, the Baron of Verulam, Viscount St. Albans, not only had a passion for knowledge but also for power and possessions. He was notorious for his extravagant spending and enormous debts. Bacon had a reputation for not feeling any remorse for some of his most unprincipled behavior. At age sixty, at the very height of his career, he was accused of taking bribes from litigants in cases heard before him as Lord Chancellor. While not denying that he had accepted gifts, he insisted that they did not influence his decisions and also claimed that his actions were only part of a customary moral laxity among public officials. He was found guilty, fined, jailed, and banished from public life by his peers in the House of Lords. His fall into disgrace was only slightly softened by the king, who after only a few days canceled the fine and terminated his imprisonment. During the remainder of his life until his death five years later, he devoted much of his time to developing his ideas and publishing books promoting his ideal of experimental science.

Different as they were, Sir Francis and Saint Francis shared, each in his own way, a Christian aspiration for brotherly love. Though in his personal life Sir Francis was generally not very lovable or loving, the profound moral insight he so deeply experienced as a fifteen-year-old adolescent continued as a passion throughout his entire adult life. Part of his moral zeal to put science in the service of human welfare may have been influenced by his distinguished father, who promoted educational reform in the kingdom, and his devout Puritan mother. Though himself not of noble character, Bacon inspired others after him to pursue his vision toward a promised land made possible through a vast, organized, experimental science.

# ISAAC NEWTON: EXTRAORDINARY GENIUS WHOSE GRAND SYNTHESIS CLIMAXED THE SCIENTIFIC REVOLUTION

Fatherless and frail, the infant Isaac was born in a Lincolnshire farmhouse early Christmas morning, 1642—the same year that Galileo died. His father, a small but prosperous landowner who worked his farm and herds and who, like all his relatives, was completely illiterate, died only six months after his marriage and three months before the birth of his only child, Isaac. Dangerously premature, the little baby was given only a slim chance of survival. He was so tiny, it was said that he could have fit into a quart mug. He survived the physical ordeal of premature birth, only to experience three years later, the traumatic severing of the emotional bonds with his mother, when she married a sixty-three-year-old wealthy clergyman, moved to live with her new husband in a neighboring village, and left the child Isaac to be raised by his maternal grandparents. His stepfather never treated him as a son, never took him into his own home. Already without a father, the small child Isaac was now without a mother. Though evidence regarding the quality of his early relationships is sparse, it appears that, after his mother's remarriage, he never again developed an emotional closeness with her. There is no evidence of any warm bonding with his grandparents, and indications are that he felt bitter resentment toward his stepfather. A lonely and loveless little boy, he endured the painful experience of parental abandonment. His emotionally crippling upbringing helps us understand and to feel compassion for the adult Newton, so alone, secretive, fearful of criticism, and at times so cruel, hostile, and even paranoid. With a few tenuous exceptions, he was incapable of close friendships, of accepting an intimate community of love. So often alienated from his peers, he found a comfortable home in his mind, salvation in solitude. We can only be grateful to Newton for all he achieved in spite of his emotionally deprived life. And we can thank him for braving that lonely childhood, from which he grew up feeling content to live in almost total isolation, resulting in an almost superhuman capacity for long uninterrupted periods, even years, of intense scientific work—the harvest of which our entire species is a beneficiary.

When Isaac was eleven years old, his mother returned home, after eight years of absence. Widowed for the second time, she brought with her three young children, and a substantial inheritance from their deceased father. Though we have no documentation describing the quality of the relationship between mother and son during their reunion period, she must have been preoccupied with her youngest, an infant less than a year old, as well as with the next youngest, barely two. In any case, family life with his mother, half-brother, and two half-sisters was quite brief. In a little less than two years, when Isaac was only twelve, he was sent away to Free Grammar School in Grantham, seven miles from home. He lodged with Mr. Clark, a local apothecary, and his three stepchildren, two boys and a girl. Perhaps partly because he grew up in considerable isolation with his aging grandparents, Isaac did not get along well with the boys, foreshadowing his not infrequent conflicts with his peers throughout his adult life. Rather than playing games with the other boys, he displayed considerable manual skills and an intense interest in building mechanical models. When he was seventeen, his mother decided that he had enough education, withdrew him from school, and brought him home. This practical mother had a plan for her eldest son. Isaac could learn to take over the management of the farm. His enforced apprenticeship turned out to be a total disaster. He showed absolutely no interest in or aptitude for herding sheep and shoveling manure. His resentful behavior thoroughly alienated his family and the servants. Newton's schoolmaster, Mr. Henry Stokes, protested again, as previously, that it was a tragic waste of Isaac's academic abilities and utterly futile to try to make a farmer out of him. Sensing that Isaac's mother was rather tight-fisted with money, Stokes offered to waive the academic fees if Isaac returned to school and even proposed that he could board in his own home. Joining in on the assault against the mother's agrarian plans for Isaac was her clergyman brother, who was determined that his nephew resume his studies with Mr. Stokes, in preparation for entrance to his alma mater, Trinity College of Cambridge University. With all the difficulties caused by Isaac at home, his mother finally relented. Isaac returned to Grantham, lodging with Mr. Stokes, to prepare for the university. No one then spoke of Isaac in terms of being a genius. Rather, he was viewed as an excellent student who would be wasting his talents managing a farm estate. Since then, historians have diligently searched through his paternal and maternal ancestry looking for any individuals of genius or of clearly special achievement. They have found none. What we do know is that Cambridge, partly because of its lax academic discipline at that time, allowed Newton the freedom to find his own genius.

Early in June, 1661, eighteen-year-old Isaac Newton entered Trinity College at Cambridge. What they offered him was the standard Scholastic Aristotelianism ruling the curriculum of European universities. In this official course of studies Newton in no way distinguished himself. But then, beginning about halfway through his undergraduate years and continuing into 1666, a burst of extraordinary scientific and mathematical genius broke out in Newton, who at last found the freedom to discover and then pursue his own solitary, intensely driven, and brilliant way of seeking truth. None of this unprecedented creativity occurred within the official university curriculum. Rather, Newton and a handful of other especially inquisitive undergraduates, through their own private reading, had gotten a sniff of the maverick revolution in science that had been brewing since the sixteenth century. No other student was as stirred up as Newton. With a voracious appetite to learn and a perfectionistic temperament, he set out on a solitary, self-directed reading program to master the new science. He devoured the works of Descartes and as much as he could obtain of Kepler, Gassendi, Bacon, Galileo, Boyle, and Hooke, among others. With the same fierce single-mindedness, he taught himself the most advanced mathematics of his times.

The years 1664 to 1666 have been described as the *Anni Mirabiles*, the marvelous years. They extended from the time of Newton's undergraduate private reading program in the physical sciences and mathematics to the year following his bachelor of arts at age twenty-two in 1665. Among the marvels, was that the self-taught Newton, barely out of his teens, progressed from successfully assimilating the most sophisticated mathematics of his day to becoming an independent investigator contributing original innovations in mathematics, including the calculus, discovered prior to and independently of Leibniz. Newton's genius in pure mathematics, displayed in his famous Tract of October, 1666, helped make him the premier mathematician in all Europe. In only three youthful years, Newton laid the foundations for his epoch-making work in pure and applied mathematics, optics, mechanics, and celestial dynamics.

In 1667 at age twenty-four, Newton was elected a fellow of Trinity. Two years later, at the age of twenty-six, he became Lucasian Professor of Mathematics. During these years he perfected his optical experiments analyzing the nature and composition of light and demonstrated that white light is a mixture of many colors, each having its own index of refraction. This research led to the foundations of the science of spectroscopy. Following from his experimentally demonstrated theory of colors, he theorized (erroneously) that the telescopes with lenses then in use could never be perfected, because every image formed would be surrounded by a halo of colors. He then invented and built with his own hands a new instrument—the reflecting telescope, which eliminated the color contamination. In 1671 the Royal Society heard about his invention and asked to examine it. As soon as it was given a try, they could quickly appreciate its radically improved qualities and how it transcended the limitations of the refracting telescopes then in use. It created a sensation, and Newton, in 1672 at age twenty-nine, was elected a fellow of the Royal Society.

Among Newton's spectacular achievements, his crowning glory and grand synthesis climaxing the scientific revolution was his 1687 masterpiece, *The Mathematical Principles of Natural Philosophy*, usually referred to as the *Principia*, from the first word of its title in the Latin original. It was a creative synthesis that both rejected as false certain works of past geniuses but also took their positive accomplishments to another level, transforming not only their results but also their methods of inquiry. In demonstrating a unified framework for the world, he incorporated the revolution in astronomy initiated by Copernicus as advanced in Kepler's three laws of planetary motion, Galileo's new science of terrestrial motion, Descartes' mechanistic physics, certain discoveries of the great Dutch physicist Christiaan Huygens, and the work of a host of other illustrious pioneers of the previous 150 years. The time was ripe for an extraordinary genius to bring together and synthesize the best of this brilliant period.

Newton was equal to the challenge. Keeping within the self-imposed constraints of the new science, his "system of the world" does not attempt to explain the essence of things or the ultimate nature or final purpose of the universe. Rather, he limits himself to a mathematical description of phenomena and when possible of efficient and material causes in terms of mathematical laws. Metaphysicians looking for ultimate purposes, intrinsic vital principles, or warm spiritual realities will be sadly disappointed and will probably find vapid his cold mechanical philosophy explaining natural phenomena in terms of matter and motion following mathematical laws.

The main task of the *Principia* was to develop the basic mathematical principles of certain motions in moving bodies and the various kinds of forces required in different conditions to produce these motions. The goal was to develop a single exact science of motion that is both thoroughly mechanical and rigorously mathematical and which applies universally on earth and in the heavens. To attain this mathematical precision, Newton employed the model of Euclid's *Elements*, thus beginning the *Principia* with twenty-eight pages of definitions, axioms, and corollaries. In these opening pages Newton states his "basic concepts of mechanics and subsuming under the most general principles virtually all that had been accomplished in that science before 1687. Here Newton for the first time gives dynamics a clear, coherent foundation such as neither Galileo nor Huygens had offered. He defines mass, momentum, inertia, force and centrifugal force."[31] Along with six corollaries, he presents his celebrated three laws of motion: the law of inertia, first stated by Galileo and fully articulated by Descartes; the law that acceleration is proportional to force; and the law of the equivalence of action and reaction. Then the most astonishing intuition of Newton and most unique solution was his discovery of the law of universal gravitation. Bodies are attracted to each other by a single universal force of mutual gravitation. Brilliant mathematician that he was, he expressed this fundamental law in precise mathematical terms which may be written as follows:

$$F = G \, \frac{mm^1}{D^2}$$

This law says that between any two bodies whatsoever,
of masses $m$ and $m^1$, wherever they may be in the universe, separated by a distance $D$, there is a force of attraction that is *mutual*, and each body attracts the other with
a force of identical magnitude, which is *directly proportional to the product of the two masses and inversely proportional
to the square of the distance between them.* G is a constant of
proportionality, and it has the same value in all circumstances—whether in the mutual attraction of a stone and
the earth, of the earth and the moon, of the sun and
Jupiter, of one star and another, or of two pebbles on a
beach. This constant G is called the *constant of universal
gravitation* and may be compared to other "universal"
constants—of which there are not very many in the
whole of science—such as $c$, the speed of light, which
figures so prominently in relativity, of $h$, Planck's constant, which is so basic in quantum theory.[32]

This one universal law of gravitation, the centerpiece of the *Principia*,
is the cosmic force that uniformly controls motions in the heavens
and on earth. It explains with extreme accuracy the motion of the
planets in orbit around the sun, what maintains satellites in their
orbits, and why comets return from far off space to our region of the
solar system at predictable intervals. This single law explains why
objects on earth don't fly off into space from our twirling planet,
why the counterintuitive discovery of Galileo is true (that bodies on
earth, whatever their weight, fall freely with exactly the same acceleration), and how the rise and fall of ocean tides are caused by the
gravitational pull of the sun and moon on the seas.

Other remarkable achievements appear in the *Principia*, but none
is so stunning as his concept of a rationally coherent, intelligible
world unified by a few mathematically precise laws of motion and

universal gravitation. His "system of the world" applied Descartes' philosophy of nature as mechanical and advanced his vision of a universal mathematical science. For Newton, as he was discovering the universal laws of nature, it was as if he were rethinking the thoughts of God while creating the cosmos. In the Ode by Edmund Halley at the beginning of the *Principia* he says of Newton, "Nearer the gods no mortal may approach." The awe of so many for Newton was expressed by Alexander Pope in his famous couplet:

> *Nature, and Nature's Laws lay hid in Night.*
> *God said,* Let Newton be! *and All was* Light.

Like most of the other pioneers of the revolutionary new science, Newton was consciously much concerned with developing more valid methods of inquiry. With a fertile combination of brilliant intelligence, powerful intuition, and expansive imagination, his extraordinary genius took the work of his predecessors to a higher level, creatively synthesizing pure and applied mathematics with empirical experimentation and observation as well as critical reasoning. For Alexandre Koyré, Newton in the process and product of his inquires fulfilled the promise of the scientific revolution and was both its heir and highest expression. Furthermore, according to I. Bernard Cohen, Newton developed in the *Principia* a significantly new mode of using mathematics in science, a uniquely Newtonian style that was revolutionary.[33] While not completely Newton's original creation, he transformed its beginnings from Greek antiquity and the radical developments of the seventeenth century into a powerful new method of using mathematics that eventually became influential in our modern way of doing the exact sciences.

Now, I would like to share with you a deep, dark secret about Newton the truth seeker, a fact entirely hidden from most of his contemporaries and only begun to be publicly known during the second half of the twentieth century. Newton was an alchemist! Yes, I said alchemist, not chemist. Though not alchemy in the popular

stereotype of converting base metals into gold, neither was he a
Lavoisier pioneering modern scientific chemistry. Alchemy was *not*
an occasional side interest of Newton. Rather, he dedicated years of
intense study to alchemical texts and labored at his furnace which he
built with his own hands, almost always in strict secrecy. In episodic,
intense periods of time over almost thirty years, he set aside his scientific work including the *Principia* to pursue what he believed was
the secret knowledge of nature revealed by God as preserved in esoteric alchemical texts and to be discovered in alchemical experiments. Evidence of his extensive alchemical work includes papers in
his own handwriting of well over a million words devoted to alchemy. Scholarship indicates that he was hoping to show that mechanical principles alone are inadequate to explain all phenomena, and he
was attracted to alchemy for its vitalistic philosophy of nature which
asserted the existence of nonmaterial agents in nature and the primacy of spirit over matter in the universe, correcting the chilling
Cartesian mechanistic philosophy of matter in motion. And while
we are sharing secrets, here is another one. Newton, zealously and
mostly in secret, devoted massive efforts to biblical and patristic studies, theology and prophecy. His private religious writings, most of
which were not available for examination until about the beginning
of the last quarter of the twentieth century, total some several million words, dwarfing the quantity of his scientific works. Newton,
deeply religious although denying the divinity of Christ, did not let
the new science interfere with his religious mode of seeking natural
and supernatural truth.

Along with other Christian scientists who accepted Descartes'
mechanical philosophy of nature, Newton feared that if the material world was seen as a complete, absolute, and independent reality in
itself, then the result would be atheism. To avoid this, he not only
assumed with Descartes that God was the Creator First Cause but
also adjusted his mechanical philosophy so that matter had a certain
passivity requiring the continuing presence of God everywhere in
the universe. Neither matter nor gravity were independent of God.
Their continuing existence and action depended on the continuous

action of the divine will. Furthermore, based on calculations, he believed that he had discovered certain irregularities in the universe which he concluded provided evidence that God's corrective intervention was necessary from time to time in order to re-establish its usual lawful regularity. Less pious deists, who believed that they clearly saw through Newton's theological motivations, declared that the all-intelligent and powerful God had from the beginning created a perfectly designed world machine. Thus, no ongoing providential interventions were necessary or even possible in the already perfect universe. Little by little, Newton's claimed irregularities in the universe were found to be false. Pierre Simon de Laplace (1749-1827), the brilliant French mathematician and astronomer, demonstrated the complete lawful stability of the solar system within Newtonian mechanics, thus removing the need for any divine intervention to correct any so-called "irregularities." When asked by Napoleon, his former student, why he had not mentioned God in his *Mécanique Céleste*, Laplace was reported to have replied, "I have no need of that hypothesis." In buying into Descartes' mechanistic world view, even with his own modifications which he hoped would require both a creator and preserving God, Newton seems rather philosophically naive. He underestimated the depths of the apparent, perhaps irreconcilable contradictions between a mechanical universe following immutable mathematical laws and a loving, personal God providentially intervening in nature and human affairs. For Richard S. Westfall, an eminent Newtonian scholar, "Newton did not find God in nature. Quite the contrary, he imposed God upon nature. That is, [his] arguments did not so much derive from a study of nature as descend from the long tradition of Christianity in western Europe....Newton's arguments reveal above all a determination to find God in nature. They were the deposit of centuries of Christianity in the West, an inherited piety, that part of Newton's religion not yet disturbed by the rise of modern science."[34]

Newton's religious goals for the *Principia* backfired. As the theological implications of his world machine were gradually made more explicit, his goal to support religion eventually worked toward sabotaging Christianity as a living faith in an ever-present God. For many, the more they understood Newton's "system of the world," the less they believed in the God of Christianity. Had he lived long enough, what profound tragedy would he have painfully experienced when Voltaire lionized him as one of the glorious founders of the Enlightenment, and certain *philosophes* blasphemed the very God whose living presence Newton so deeply cherished. Though he was an extraordinary scientific genius who powerfully influenced our modern scientific world view, he could not have predicted the unintended but momentous spiritual consequences of his work, which further severed the medieval spirit from its foundations in a God–infused universe.

> In contrast to the medieval Christian cosmos, which was not only created but continuously and directly governed by a personal and actively omnipotent God, the modern universe was an impersonal phenomenon, governed by regular natural laws, and understandable in exclusively physical and mathematical terms. God was now distantly removed from the physical universe, as creator and architect, and was now less a God of love, miracle, redemption, or historical intervention than a supreme intelligence and first cause, who established the material universe and its immutable laws and then withdrew from further direct activity. While the medieval cosmos was continuously contingent upon God, the modern cosmos stood more on its own, with its own greater ontological reality, and with a diminution of any divine reality either transcendent or immanent. Eventually that residual divine reality, unsupported by scientific investigation of the visible world, disappeared altogether.[35]

Also, a radical shift occurred in the locus of epistemological power. In the medieval culture, religion was the final arbiter of truth. As the revolution in science pushed on and finally with Newton burst into public awareness, the new scientific method increasingly became the dominant criterion of truth. Science as an institution rivaled and eventually overshadowed the intellectual influence of the church. For many, science became the authoritative definer of reality. Newton's work had a powerful impact on the educated élite and even to a certain extent on the masses. For example, Edmund Halley applied Newtonian methods to boldly predict that a certain comet (now called, Halley's Comet) would reappear in 1758. When in fact it returned precisely on schedule, an entire civilization was awestruck. The new mechanical-mathematical science could not only understand but amazingly could also predict cosmic phenomena! Newton became the symbol of the astounding power of the new science to understand the rational order of the world, both in the heavens and on the earth. His exact, mathematically precise science became the model for all the other sciences, even the social sciences. Thus, his work gave us the hope that we can progressively understand and predict natural events and rationally take control of our lives. His monumental achievements provided powerful ideological foundations for the Enlightenment's strident confidence in human reason.

Science empowered us and gave us a new faith in ourselves. But historically, for so many of us, it also weakened our faith in the divine. In the generations following Newton, many scientists were less often people of Christian faith and more often deists, agnostics, atheists, or indifferent to any cosmic truth claims of religion. Though the mission of science was not to discover God in the universe, neither did it find a personal God who replies to our prayers and rituals and who intervenes in human history to help his people. In the mechanical universe of the Newtonians, there didn't appear much, if anything, to respond to the transcendent longings of the human heart. And why does everything else in the cosmos seem so utterly devoid of such human qualities as consciousness, intentionality, and our heartfelt spiritual aspirations for truth, goodness, beauty, compassion, and caring? In the Newtonian world machine there seems to be a split, or more accurately an alienation, between objective scientific facts and subjective human values, between matter and spirit, the secular and the sacred, reason and faith. Our warm inner life seems so totally estranged from the cold outer world. As a species, are we not metaphysical misfits? Epistemologically, so many of us in the new science wanted to free ourselves from the superstitious and the supernatural. We wanted to do it alone. We did it alone. And now we are alone. Alone in our sterile, cold cosmos, we are autonomous humans. With all the enlightenment provided by our conscious, rational brilliance, have we not somehow horribly blinded ourselves? Is it not futile to look for any personal or species-wide salvation in a science-based world view? Are there no ontological but only psychological solutions to our human dilemma?

Since the time of Newton's death in 1727, plenty of us as individuals and communities retain a residue of the religious spirit of the Middle Ages, but as a civilization the Medieval Age of Faith is well behind us. Enter the Age of Science and the birth of the modern secular era.

# THINKING CRITICALLY ABOUT THE RANGE AND LIMITS OF EMPIRICISM

## JOHN LOCKE: RATIONAL ADVOCATE FOR EMPIRICISM

During the winter of 1670-1671, John Locke and a group of five or six friends met on a fairly regular basis to discuss the principles of morality and revealed religion. Early on, they discovered themselves enmeshed in all kinds of unanticipated intellectual perplexities that blocked the group from coming to any firm conclusions. Locke came up with the suggestion that they had taken a wrong approach. Rather, he thought, it was first necessary "to examine our own Abilities, and see, what Objects our Understandings were, or were not fitted to deal with. This I proposed to the Company, who all readily assented; and thereupon it was agreed, that this should be our first Enquiry."[36] Shortly afterwards, he wrote out and took to the next meeting "some hasty and undigested Thoughts, on a Subject I had never before considered." Even after the group terminated their meetings, John Locke (1632-1704) kept thinking about the same subject, and some twenty years later in 1689 at age fifty-seven, he published his influential *Essay Concerning Human Understanding*. The expressed purpose of this lengthy book was to "enquire into the Original, Certainty, and Extent of humane knowledge; together, with the Grounds and Degrees of Belief, Opinion, and Assent."

The almost twenty years of incubation writing the *Essay* were necessary not only because the epistemological project was more difficult than expected, but also because he was thinking through his political theory. The result was the publication, also in 1689, of his *Second Treatise of Government*. This epoch-making work helped inspire the American and French revolutions, laying their intellectual foundations for democratic government in opposition to the divine right of kings, by placing ultimate sovereign power with the people and expressing an overriding concern to defend the individual against the state. He presented a reasoned theory for the inalienable natural rights of individual life, liberty, and property, the right to rebel against oppressive political rule, freedom of the press, and religious tolerance.

As a young man, Locke received both his undergraduate and masters degrees from Oxford and then stayed on for several years teaching various subjects, including moral philosophy, logic, rhetoric, and Greek. Deciding against a university career, he trained in medicine but never received an M.D. degree, though he did maintain an occasional part-time practice as a physician. He became immersed in the revolutionary politics of England through his work in the service of Lord Ashley, later Earl of Shaftesbury. Locke was comfortable and competent both in the world of ideas and in practical affairs. Though not a working scientist, he was thoroughly committed to the new science and was familiar with empirical-experimental methods through his close friendship with Robert Boyle, the celebrated British chemist and physicist and a major figure in the scientific revolution. Locke was influenced by, among others, Galileo, Bacon, and Newton. In 1668 he was elected a fellow of the Royal Society. He became one of the most important thinkers of his time, with influential publications not only in epistemology and political theory but also in economics, ethics, education, and religion. Before he died on October 28, 1704, at age seventy-two, he wrote an epitaph for his tombstone, which translated from the Latin included this self-description: "A scholar by training, he devoted his studies wholly to the pursuit of truth."[37]

A champion of human reason, he was also a founder of British empiricism. But he was not a pure empiricist. Influenced by Gassendi, he held that knowledge requires both sense input and reason. Though it was the work of Descartes that first energized his interest in philosophy, he, like Gassendi, completely rejected Descartes' doctrine of innate ideas. At birth, he thought, the human mind is a "white Paper, void of all Characters, without any *Ideas*."[38] Infants come into the world without any inborn knowledge stamped on their minds, without any innate speculative or practical principles. Furthermore, running counter to what was commonly taken for granted by most of his contemporaries, Locke maintained that we are born without any innate idea of God or moral principles. Not only are we lacking these innate foundations of knowledge, he also warned us against passively accepting tradition and others' opinions. Locke wanted each of us to think and judge truth for ourselves.

But how do we find truth? From where do we obtain knowledge? Locke replied, "I answer, in one word, From *Experience:* In that, all our Knowledge is founded."[39] He went on to explain that human knowledge is derived from two types of experience: sensation and reflection. Sensation means knowledge obtained from the external world through input from the five senses and also the awareness of internal bodily states, as for example, hunger and thirst. For the mind to know anything about the external world beyond its own mental creations, it requires input from the senses. Thus, Locke established himself as an empiricist. Though knowledge begins with sensory impressions, it does not end there. Knowledge also requires the second type of experience: inner reflection. The mind digests and works over the sensory input through its inner mental operations, including abstracting, comparing, combining, dividing, and generalizing. For the modern mind, "inner reflection" as a type of experience does not sound anything like a raw-minded notion of the empirical, and in fact it was the rational element in Locke's empiricism. Though the mind does not have innate ideas, it does have innate powers.

Sensory input and inner reflection are the two foundations of knowledge from which our ideas spring. Thus we have ideas of sensation and ideas of reflection. To explain how knowledge can be built from these two foundations, Locke distinguished between simple and complex ideas. The first are atomistic impressions passively received by the mind as sensory input, which in turn are actively formed by the mind into simple ideas and then combined into complex ideas. Raw sense input by itself is not yet knowledge. Rather, knowledge is the product of reason working out various relationships between our ideas of sensation and reflection. For Locke, knowledge was nothing but the perception of the connection and agreement or disagreement of any of our ideas. When the connection between ideas is directly perceived, we have intuitive knowledge. When the connection between ideas is indirect, i.e., perceived only through the medium of other ideas and connections of ideas, we have demonstrative knowledge. Though our knowledge is real, it extends only to the boundaries of our ideas. We can have knowledge no further than we have ideas. Though Locke was empirical about the original source of ideas, his definition of knowledge as the agreement or disagreement of our ideas was rational. For Locke, without reason we may have belief, but not knowledge. "*Reason* must be our last Judge and Guide in every Thing."[40]

Locke did not question the existence of an external world or of material objects. He believed that we can have an accurate knowledge of the external world through our sense input of such primary qualities as shape, size, weight, quantity, and motion or rest. Though this knowledge corresponds to something objective in the world, we cannot know the essential nature of matter. Also, he believed in the existence of independent material substances and that we can have a valid knowledge of their appearances, though we can never know their ultimate substrata or real essence.

A devout Christian, Locke was convinced that though our human capacity for knowledge has permanent limits far short of the full richness of reality, God has given us sufficient capacities for knowledge to adequately meet our practical human needs. While we do not have an innate idea of God, his existence can be demonstrated by a form of the "cosmological argument." Yet God's infinite essence will forever be unknown to us. While we also have no inborn conception of right or wrong, Locke believed that moral principles could be demonstrated by our natural reason, unaided by supernatural revelation. However, despite the urgings of friends and critics, he never provided such a demonstration. He believed in the divine revelation of religious truths beyond human reason but insisted that truths clearly contrary to reason must be rejected as not originating from God. Human reason, not tradition or ecclesiastical authority, is the final judge of whether a certain religious teaching or biblical interpretation is or is not a revelation from God. Locke, a very reasonable Christian gentleman, loathed what in his time was called "religious enthusiasm" and today we would equate with extreme religious emotionalism or fanaticism. For Locke, this type of religiosity based truth on feelings, mistaking the depth of emotions for the degree of inspiration, often resulting in exhibitionistic claims of infallible truth, zealous bigotry, and religious intolerance. For Locke, God and Christianity were reasonable, and we are obligated to use our God-given rational powers to judge the authenticity of revelation. The quiet dictates of reason and not high-pitched, irresponsible emotionalism lead us to religious truth and guard us from absurd errors. God "commands what reason does."[41]

Locke's carefully reasoned confidence in the powers of empiricism and the human mind helped create the Enlightenment's faith in science and reason. But he was also much concerned with defining the limits of human knowing. He was convinced that when we speculate about metaphysical realities, our speculations are restricted to ideas we obtain from our human experience. David Hume, a more extreme empiricist and skeptically minded young Scotsman, will restrict even further Locke's boundaries for human knowledge.

## DAVID HUME: A RADICAL EMPIRICIST'S SKEPTICAL ASSAULT

At eleven years old, David Hume (1711-1776) entered Edinburgh University, which at that time was more like a classical high school than a modern college. He received a solid grounding in the classical authors, especially Cicero and the major Latin poets, studied Latin and Greek, and took courses that included at least some elementary exposure to logic, epistemology, metaphysics, natural religion, moral philosophy, mathematics, and the new natural philosophy, particularly the work of Robert Boyle. Though apparently an excellent student, progressing successfully through the curriculum, he decided at age fourteen to leave school before obtaining his degree to follow his "passion for Literature which has been the ruling Passion of my Life, and the great Source of my Enjoyments."[42]

Already as a teen he ambitiously committed himself to career goals that would advance his "love of literary fame." With youthful enthusiasm, he launched into an extensive, self-directed program of private study to prepare himself to be a thoroughly educated writer. At age fifteen, and after only one year of reading whatever he liked, his family was concerned that he should pursue a more practical career and chose the law for him, given his serious, studious, and industrious disposition. David gave a try at legal studies but soon abandoned them as totally repugnant to his nature. Furthermore, he commented, "I found an insurmountable aversion to everything but the pursuits of Philosophy and general Learning." He returned to his private reading with even more determination. His most deeply felt need was to have the uninterrupted leisure to read and reflect widely and deeply so that eventually he would have something important to write about in his literary career. In a letter written to a friend when he was sixteen, David expressed his personal conviction that philosophy is an essential part of literature. Increasingly, he directed more attention to epistemology and the means and criteria by which truth can be discovered and justified. Because so many of the books he wanted to read in philosophy and history were written in French, he learned the language. He steeped himself in French skepticism, including the widely influential Pierre Bayle. Though as a young boy he had a rather religious nature and was raised in a strict Calvinist family, his readings and reflections little by little led him to become an atheist while still in his teens. However, during his entire life he never characterized himself as an atheist, an extremely pejorative term in the eighteenth century.

Hume's family supported his self-directed inquiries financially and emotionally. His father died when David was only two years of age, leaving him a small but regular annual inheritance that with careful frugality could provide for his basic needs of food and shelter plus some extras such as books. His mother never remarried and was much devoted to raising her three children. At best as we can determine from the available historical documentation, she was loving and emotionally supportive of her son's unconventional life, and their family home was always open to him as a place in which he could pursue his private studies. John, his practical older brother, successfully managed the modest family estate. Both brothers shared deep bonds with their sister and beloved companion, Katherine. Even as an adult, when he was a self-supporting writer, Hume would return to his family for emotional nourishment and an inexpensive place to reside. Though he enjoyed the company of women and they seemed to enjoy his friendship, he never married but rather concentrated on his literary ambitions.

As Hume was turning eighteen in the spring of 1729 and after almost four years of intense intellectual work, he felt that he had made an important discovery about a new means by which truth could be established. This discovery not only put into perspective his previous reading and reflection, it also resulted in an emotional experience "which transported me beyond Measure, and made me, with an Ardor natural to a young man, throw up every other Pleasure or Business to apply to it."[43] What exactly was this new discovery? We don't really know for certain, as Hume never left us any clear indications. The most likely hypothesis that scholars have put together goes like this: Hume was very much influenced by the Scottish philosopher Francis Hutcheson and other "sentimentalists," who considered human feelings, not abstract reason, to be the real foundation for ethics and aesthetics. Hume's discovery was that he *extended* human sentiment beyond ethics and aesthetics to all human beliefs about matters of fact. That is, human feelings are more fundamental and powerful than rational thinking in determining what we believe is real or not real in the world. For Hume, this new insight had revolutionary, practical consequences for all human knowing, including the new science of Newton.

All fired up by his new epistemological insight, eighteen year old Hume threw himself even more single-mindedly into his studies. But after six months he experienced what today we would call "burnout." In more clinical terms, he suffered from a depression which would wax and wane until he was twenty-three—some four years. Also, he began to experience a variety of psychosomatic complaints. Overworked by his inquiries, his brain revolted against the overload. No longer could he push his mind to pursue studies that only six months before gave him so much pleasure. He was stuck in a distressful conflict. At the very point where he had finally made a breakthrough discovery, his mind stopped working. He accused himself of laziness and tried to push on, but his brain balked, and he could not sustain any abstract thinking. In desperation, he consulted a physician, who turned out to be a wise clinician with a sense of humor and who quickly made the diagnosis. As Hume recalled in later life, the physician gently laughed at him and "told me I was now a Brother, for that I had fairly got the Disease of the Learned."[44] The physician recommended long horseback rides for exercise and enjoyment, a pint of red wine daily, and prescribed a "Course of Bitters and anti-hysteric Pills." Over the next four years, as soon as his mind and spirits lightened up, his tendency was again to push his intellectual work to the point of fatigue. Little by little, he recognized the importance of a more moderate study regimen, enjoying everyday pleasures, a good diet, and "a constant Rule to ride twice or thrice a week and walk everyday." Early in 1734, after four years and not yet fully "out of the cloud" of depression as much as he had hoped, he decided to try an experiment by completely setting aside his studies for a time to pursue a "more active Scene of Life." He traveled to Bristol and took a clerical job with an importer of sugar from the West Indies. Naturally sociable, he found some friends and fun in this busy city. However, our aspiring young writer, who so valued literary elegance, got into trouble with the owner by criticizing his letters for their grammar and style. After only four months on the job, he was fired. The active life in the business world and perhaps also his sudden discharge climaxed in the permanent cure of his depression! Energized, he decided to take the money he had earned plus his annual patrimony and travel to France to write the book that he hoped would bring him fame. At age twenty-three, after some nine years of intense self-directed studies, he had something to say and was ready to write. Also, he was ready to study the art of living, for which he was sure the French were justifiably famous.

Equipped with letters of introduction, he arrived in Paris, midsummer of 1734. After several social visits, he settled for one year at Rheims in the province of Champagne. Though graciously received into the city's social life and with private libraries opened up to him, the cost of living in Rheims was beyond the slim means provided by his inheritance. Thus, he resettled for two years in the provincial town of La Flèche in Anjou, some 150 miles southwest of Paris. Here he could live more economically, work quietly, and have access to the splendid library of the Jesuit College of La Flèche, alma mater of its most famous graduate, René Descartes. By the summer of 1737 and after three years of concentrated writing, he had substantially completed his *Treatise of Human Nature* and returned to London to find a publisher. After more than a year of obstacles and painful self-editing of his final manuscript, the *Treatise* was published as Volumes I &

II in 1739 and Volume III in 1740. After so many years of intense toil, the twenty-eight-year-old freelance thinker and writer had high hopes that his book would be a great intellectual event and reward him with literary fame. But as we would say today, the book completely bombed. In later life Hume looked back and commented, "Never literary Attempt was more unfortunate....it fell *dead born from the Press.*"[45] The book went almost unnoticed. The few reviews it obtained were mostly negative, some even abusive. Almost no one understood the book.

Little by little, the work did obtain more attention. He reworked and rewrote it in a shortened and more popular style as *An Enquiry Concerning Human Understanding* (1748) and *An Enquiry Concerning the Principles of Morals* (1751). He also produced two important critiques of religion: *The Natural History of Religion* appeared in 1757 and his *Dialogues Concerning Natural Religion* was published posthumously in 1779. Though both his reputation and notoriety as a philosopher grew during his lifetime, he established the literary fame he sought rather as a celebrated essayist and historian. His essays were published mostly between 1741 and 1752, and his six-volume *History of England* (1754-62) was for some hundred years the standard work. Also, he obtained a certain reputation as an economist and greatly influenced his close friend Adam Smith. As a person, he was known not only as bright, witty, and sociable, but also as exceedingly kind, generous, and modest. For these endearing qualities and the gentleness and good humor of his nature, his French friends called him "le bon David." For this non-Christian and closet atheist, amidst all the "religious enthusiasm" of his native Scotland, it seems no less than a minor miracle that the street in Edinburgh on which he lived was named after him and continues to be called St. David's Street.

Despite his admiration for Newton and his appreciation of the new empirical science, Hume believed that human beings and their daily struggles were of a far greater order of importance than the physical sciences. Moral philosophy concerned with human lives and human affairs was his dominant passion. In his time moral philosophy covered a broad domain, including not only ethics but also theories about the mind, the emotions, political theory, history, and economics as well as literary criticism and aesthetics. During the Middle Ages, much of moral philosophy had its ultimate foundations in the supernatural beliefs of the Christian faith. The atheist Hume, along with other nonbelievers in the Christian religion, were seeking new foundations for human morality. In the spirit of the new empirical science, he also rejected any *a priori* rationalistic, metaphysical theories that base reality on so-called axiomatic self-evident propositions and claims to then logically deduce specific rules of human behavior. Rather, Hume laid the empirical foundations of moral science in human nature; thus his *Treatise of Human Nature*. Furthermore, he emphasized that all human knowledge, including science and mathematics, is dependent on the nature of our knowing powers and limitations. The science of humans is the basic science, the foundation upon which all other science rests, the true science of sciences. In contrast to Descartes who designated metaphysics as the ultimate root of physics and the other sciences, Hume viewed human nature as the foundation not only of the moral sciences but of all human knowledge. But how do we come to understand human nature? Hume responded, "As the science of man is the only solid foundation for the other sciences, so the only solid foundation we can give to this science itself must be laid on experience and observation."[46] For Hume, so much of moral philosophy was still only rhetoric and speculation, just as it had been with the so called "science" of Scholasticism before Bacon and Newton. Hume's goal was to extend the empirical method to moral philosophy, just as they had applied it to natural philosophy.

As an empiricist, Hume believed that there is only one source of knowledge—sensation, which includes the five external senses and the internal sensations, like hunger and thirst. He rejected the belief that there are two orders of knowledge: a superior kind derived from religious supernatural or metaphysical truths obtained by an *a priori* pure intellect or Platonic transcendental eternal essences mystically recollected *and* an inferior type of knowledge gained through input from the senses. He thought such claims to a higher order of knowing were only lofty pretensions and superstitious fictions. We humans can never have metaemperical knowledge, because we are limited by sense input in what we can know. For Hume, all the contents of our minds are derived from our sense perceptions, which he divided between impressions and ideas. Impressions are the immediate sensory contents of our consciousness, either coming from the outside, such as light, sound, cold, pressure, smells, and taste, or coming from the inside, such as feelings of pleasure or pain, desire or aversion, and love or hate. The difference between impressions and ideas is not of kind, but only of quality. Impressions are more forceful and lively when they appear in our consciousness, whereas ideas are only faint images or copies of these impressions as they appear in our thinking and reasoning.

Hume then divided both impressions and ideas into simple and complex. All knowledge derives ultimately from simple ideas, which in turn derive from the immediate data of experience in simple impressions. Complex ideas are built by combining simple ideas, but because of the mind's active powers of imagination, complex ideas can become firmly believed, when in fact they may be erroneous or even blatant fabrications, to the extent that they do not correspond to the original sensory perceptions. Hume then went on to make a major assumption in accepting the psychological atomism so popular in his time, and which was an extension of the atomistic theory of physical reality dominant in the natural sciences. He took it for granted that each and every simple impression and idea in our consciousness is an independent, separate, and isolated atomic unit without any logical connection between them. The main job of psychology was to discover the simple Newtonian-like laws by which the presumably independent atoms of experience become associated. Hume did not invent association psychology, but he did compare his version of it to Newton's theory of universal mutual attraction in gravitation. Psychological association is a kind of gentle force of attraction uniting our independent impressions and ideas into systematic mental structures which constitute what we experience and believe is reality. Our minds do not directly know reality but rather directly know only our impressions and ideas which follow the laws of psychological association, like the physical world follows the laws of universal gravitation.

Hume's strict empiricism combined with his theory of how the mind works resulted in an extreme skepticism about what the rational mind can know with certainty. For example, let's begin with his critique of causality. He observes that the relation of cause and effect is crucial to making logical inferences in our everyday lives as well as in science and the other disciplines which seek to establish truth. In agreement with the new science of his time, the only type of causality he accepted was efficient causality. Final, formal, and material causality of Scholastic Aristotelianism was rejected. For Hume, the rationalists had not been able to demonstrate with absolute certainty that the relation of cause and effect necessarily exists or that it is a self-evident intuition requiring no further proof, such as the mathematical proposition that $1+1=2$. But also for Hume, a consistent empiricism cannot prove with absolute certainty that causality exists, because we have no direct impression of the relation of cause and effect and thus no valid idea of causality. For an idea to be true in external reality, it must have originated from a sensory impression, but our minds never experience cause and effect as a sensation. The only input our senses receive is a chaotic storm of independent, separate, atomistic impulses without any logical connection between them. But then where do we get our idea of causality?

For Hume, the answer lay in how our minds work by the psychological laws of association of ideas. He required three types of relationships to establish the presence of cause and effect. First, the phenomenon must show a regular succession of constant conjunction in space and time, and second, the cause should precede the effect in time. While these two relationships were essential, far more important for Hume was the third relationship of *necessary connection*, i.e., the cause inevitably produces that effect and not some other. Though we have sensory impressions of the first two essential relationships, we can have none of necessary connection. Rather, our repeated experience of the regular succession of phenomena in constant conjunction forms by association in our minds the conditioned habits of expectation that the same will occur in the future. Then our imaginations create in us the felt impression of a necessary connection, which we project out on reality as an objective fact. Our idea of necessary connection essential for the cause-and-effect relationship derives from a process in us, not from the events and objects themselves. Scientific laws, which we previously assumed were based on objectively observed cause-and-effect relationships are rather based on subjective human psychology. Hume did not necessarily intend to deny that the cause-and-effect relationship actually exists in reality, but rather he wanted us to know that we have no empirical or rational certainty of this common conviction so traditionally assumed to be necessary for human knowledge.

Following the same line of argument, Hume continued his skeptical assault. Regarding material substances, all we have are sensory impressions of such qualities as shape, size, and color, but none of any independent, self-existent substance itself. Thus we have no empirically verified idea of an objective substance and no certainty of its actual existence in reality. Also, there is no empirical basis for our belief in a substantial self that persists through time and change. If we will attentively introspect, we will note that all we directly experience is a continuous flow of different sense perceptions, rapidly succeeding each other in constant movement. Our felt belief in a permanent self as an underlying entity maintaining our same personal identity over time is an illusion created by our stored memories and active imagination in the process of our association of ideas. Space and time, which we subjectively experience and which Newton assumed were independent realities, are not given to us as empirically verified ideas but rather are created by the associative operations of our mind processing the flow of our independent, atomized sensory impressions. Hume's general principle is that we can only directly experience particular sensory impressions. Any relationship between them that we experience as reality is woven by the mind, not given to us by reality itself.

Even though as a critically thinking philosopher Hume was convinced that there is no rational or empirical certainty for our beliefs, such as causality, material substances, or a permanent self, he did not deny that they may exist in reality. In fact, he told us that as an ordinary person living an everyday active life, he shared in common with other humans the deeply felt conviction that they are entirely real. Also, he observed in himself that he only momentarily experienced his philosophical skepticism during the actual time sitting in his study, while doing the critical, abstract analysis, in contrast to his stable and deeply felt belief in their actual existence throughout his everyday ordinary life. Why is this? Hume replied that nature considers these various beliefs, including causality, so important for our human lives that it implants in us powerful instincts so that we have no choice but to believe in their reality. Stated in more modern terms, in order for our species to survive, nature programmed us with the felt conviction that causality is real, even though our rational minds find no certainty about its actual existence. In this struggle between the rational mind and natural instinct, it's no contest! "Nature will always maintain her rights, and prevail in the end over any abstract reasoning whatsoever."[47] As if by an automatic reflex, our natural instincts overwhelm our voluntary reflections. We firmly believe in ourselves as permanent entities not because we choose to, but because we are forced to by instincts. But even though our nature overcomes our intellects, it neither rationally refutes our skepticism nor guarantees infallibility to our instinctive beliefs about reality. Just because we naturally believe something doesn't mean it must be true.

In his investigation of the limits of human knowing, Hume made a distinction that had devastating consequences for both the rational metaphysicians and the confident new empirical scientists of his time. He divided all human understanding into only two kinds, one based on the pure intellect and the other based on sense input, which he called relations of ideas and matters of fact. One compares ideas, the other compares sense perceptions. Relations of ideas are discovered either by intuition or by demonstration in pure mathematics and formal logic. For example, the mathematical proposition $1+1=2$ is intuitively a self-evident certain truth. However, Hume insisted, this is only a formal relationship between abstract concepts, and no matter how certain in the domain of ideas, it tells us nothing and proves nothing about the facts of actual existence. Mathematics and deductive logic live in their own abstract self-contained world of empty rational certainties independent of and without any necessary connection with the concrete factual world. Thus, he directly attacked such rationalist philosophers as Descartes, who claimed to be able to use the intellect alone to derive metaphysical and natural truths about reality from intuitive, *a priori*, self-evident, axiomatic truths and subsequent logical deductions of necessary laws of nature. For Hume, the vast metaphysical systems of the rationalist philosophers were only empty fictions, not confirmed by experience and telling us nothing about actual existence in the real world. In contrast to the relations of pure ideas is the world of factual matters, which can be discovered by empirical observation and inference. But such inference must be based on cause and effect, and Hume had already presented his arguments to show that we have no certainty that causality exists in reality but rather it is only an internally felt belief created in the mind and projected upon reality.

However, he did acknowledge that we do empirically observe various natural phenomena in regular succession and constant conjunction. But Hume pointed out that the occurrence of past phenomena is no guarantee of its continuing in the future. To believe that past phenomena will necessarily repeat in the future is to believe in the uniformity of nature, which is only another subjectively experienced belief for which we have no objective certainty as to its actual existence, either by reason or sense impressions. Empirical induction from particular instances to universal conclusions can never attain demonstrative certainty. No matter how often they were confirmed in the past, we can never be certain that scientific laws will continue to hold true in the future. While the relation of ideas provides rational certainty, it is devoid of facts about existence. Matters of fact can provide knowledge of reality but without certainty. Neither by *a priori* reason nor by sensory experience can science hope to provide absolute certainty, but rather it must limit itself to fallible empirical generalizations. If we have the felt belief that empirical science can provide objective certainty, it is only a subjective certainty based not on nature itself but rather on our human psychology.

Let us now turn briefly to Hume's moral philosophy, which was his dominant interest and for which his epistemological investigations were a preliminary. In seeking new foundations not only for ethics but also for the other moral disciplines, including the social sciences, Hume rejected as invalid supernatural truths from a deity, transcendent principles from rational metaphysics, and practical rules derived from logical reasoning and abstract principles. Rather, he laid the foundations in our empirical observations of human nature. Skeptic that he was regarding the supernatural and the rational claims of metaphysics and empirical science, he had no doubts about the existence of a universal human nature and our abilities to empirically derive moral principles from observations of ordinary people in their everyday actions and internal states. As a generality, we might call him a moral realist or a common-sense moralist.

Hume's unskeptical faith in human nature as our best moral guide was in contrast to the stern Calvinist doctrines of original sin and the total depravity of human nature in which he was raised but rejected as a teenager. Much influenced by the Scottish philosopher Francis Hutcheson (1694-1746), he emphasized the dominant role of our emotions in determining both our moral beliefs and motivating us toward action. Reason alone can never move us to moral action. Emotions are the preponderant force in our moral analysis, decision making, and behavior, though reason also has an essential but subordinate role. Thus he was in opposition to the traditional notion that moral perfection lies in the triumph of reason over feeling and that rationality is part of our higher God-like nature, while the emotions are only a residue of our lower animal nature. Also, he opposed all the rationalists, who disregarded emotions or treated them as irrational, and the Puritans of his time, who feared emotions as morally dangerous. For Hume, we can have empirical moral knowledge, because in all nations and all places humans are observed to share common sentiments about basic moral principles. This internal moral sense is universal in all human beings. Because of emotionally bonding social experiences such as the family, we develop universal dispositions of sympathy, fellow feeling, and benevolence toward other humans which is a gentle binding force akin to the mutual attraction of gravitation acting universally in the material cosmos. However, Hume was not a naïve instinctivist. Some humans are deficient or lacking in the common moral dispositions through faulty upbringing and other distorting experiences. Also, to avoid errors in our moral judgments, critical reasoning is necessary in an instrumental mode to correct and refine our moral dispositions and actions. Over a number of years, Hume developed a sophisticated moral philosophy including certain utilitarian principles, but his main thrust was to establish affective foundations empirically and exclusively in human nature as manifested in the facts of ordinary lives in everyday human situations.

David Hume's moral philosophy partially opened the door to the Romantic movement's faith in instinctive human feelings, as a reaction to the Enlightenment's exaltation of reason. Also, as his skeptical critique of the fundamental rational claims of empirical science became better understood, he opened up some minds. For example, Einstein acknowledged that "the critical reasoning required for the discovery of the special relativity theory rejecting the [Newtonian] absolute character of time was decisively furthered by the reading of David Hume's philosophical writings."[48]

## IMMANUEL KANT: COGNITION INCLUDES CONSTRUCTION

Professor of philosophy at the University of Königsberg, Immanuel Kant (1724-1804) was born, educated, and lived his entire life in this provincial university town of East Prussia. Son of a saddler, the fourth of eleven children, his family was poor. His hardworking parents were deeply religious and raised Immanuel and all their children according to the stern discipline of a Lutheran pietist sect that emphasized stark simplicity and strict morality. As an adult, Kant retained a sincere but unorthodox Christian faith and a rigorous code of conduct. At his hometown university, he was educated in the rationalism of Leibniz and Wolff but was also introduced to physics, mathematics, and astronomy. He quickly became a convinced believer in the new empirical sciences, especially as personified in the extraordinary achievements of Isaac Newton. Though not a working scientist, his first publications were predominantly in physics and astronomy, and he maintained a deep-rooted interest in science throughout his lifetime. Later in life, as an established professor, Hume's skepticism and Rousseau's romanticism had a revolutionary effect on his thinking.

At age fifty-seven Kant published his masterpiece and greatest achievement, the *Critique of Pure Reason* (1781). This complex and systematic treatment of epistemology and metaphysics is usually considered to be the most important philosophical work of modern times. Following this epoch-making book were a series of other extraordinarily influential publications, including *Prolegomena to Any Future Metaphysics* (1783), *Fundamental Principles of the Metaphysics of Morals* (1785), *Metaphysical Foundations of Natural Science* (1786), a second and substantially revised edition of the *Critique of Pure Reason* (1787), the *Critique of Practical Reason* (1788) concerning morality, the *Critique of Judgment* (1790) treating aesthetics and teleology, *Religion Within the Limits of Reason Alone* (1793), and the *Metaphysics of Morals* (1797). Also, he published important articles on a wide variety of subjects, including political and legal theory, the philosophy of history, and educational reform. Well into his seventies, his last productive years were devoted to revising his ideas on the metaphysical and epistemological foundations of science. Perhaps the most comprehensive and systematic thinker since Plato and Aristotle, Kant is one of the giants of philosophy.

Given the vast range of his inquiries and the weighty issues he tackled, it may seem remarkable that during his entire lifetime a thinker so daring as Kant never once traveled outside his native province of East Prussia and was only little over five feet tall and extremely thin. While notorious for his abstruse writing style, he was a popular and stimulating lecturer who knew how to spice abstract ideas with humor and charming stories. Though he never married and much of his daily routine was dedicated to his studies and writing, he was not a recluse. He enjoyed social interaction, dining, and conversation with his circle of friends. Outwardly, his life was uneventful and undramatic. In contrast to his regulated life of restrained enjoyments, his most exciting and meaningful pleasures were in the adventures of the mind. He said of himself, "I am myself by inclination a seeker after truth. I feel a consuming thirst for knowledge and a restless desire to advance in it, as well as a satisfaction in every step I take."[49]

Our focus is to present some of Kant's fundamental theories about how we humans know and what we can and cannot know. Kant's traditional epistemological views were radically challenged during his midforties when he first discovered Hume's skeptical works which, as he later reported, aroused him out of his "dogmatic slumber." First, he was impacted by Hume's arguments that a purely rational metaphysics cannot provide any valid knowledge of actual existence in the real world. Second, he was shocked by Hume's radical empiricism, which claimed that we have no empirical or rational proof that science can provide universal, necessary knowledge of the natural world. He was especially disturbed by Hume's position that we have no proof that causality actually exists in reality and is not merely based on the subjective operations of the mind, thus making metaphysics impossible and science devoid of objective foundations. Powerfully impressed by the logic of Hume's skepticism and yet firmly convinced of the genuine knowledge attained by Newtonian science, Kant found himself in a fundamental, profoundly experienced contradiction. He was willing to grant most of Hume's skepticism regarding the impossibility of purely rational metaphysical knowledge, but he was convinced that something must be wrong, either in Hume's arguments or in our understanding of the theoretical foundations of science. What was urgently needed,

Kant believed, was an entirely new critical analysis of the role of pure reason itself and its relationship to sensory input, thus establishing valid epistemological foundations not only for science but also for our everyday forms of human knowing. Kant's ambitious project consumed almost twelve years of arduous intellectual toil, resulting in his epochal *Critique of Pure Reason*, which is our principal source for understanding his theory of knowledge.

Kant's solution to the conflict was revolutionary. His reconciliation of Hume's skeptical undermining of the epistemological foundations of science with its actual empirical success is often considered a radically new shift in perspective comparable to the Copernican revolution. In short, Kant proposed that rather than accepting the traditional assumption that all knowledge in the mind must conform to external objects, we should instead try the hypothesis that all objects must conform to the structure of the mind. He then developed the theory that the mind itself, prior to and independent of any sense experience, has its own inherent categories of sensing and thinking that it actively imposes on raw sense input, resulting in universal and necessary knowledge of natural phenomena. The mind receives, selects, and then organizes the inflow of sensory impulses according to its own internal processing forms. The world of phenomena that we and science know is already organized according to the mind's innate structure. We do not know objective reality independent of the mind, but only as dependent on the mind's intrinsic organizing forms. The resulting knowledge is real, not a dream because it is grounded in empirical data and the necessary and universal categories of human cognition so majestically exemplified in the certitudes of Newtonian physics.

In coming to this perspective that the mind's internal categories actively construe reality from empirical content, Kant took clues from Leibniz, who emphasized the mind as active, not passive in the knowing process, and from Hume's psychological operations of the mind weaving our experience of reality. However, Kant rejected Hume's psychological association of ideas, conditioned expectations, and active imagination as an inadequate explanation of the mind's constructive role. He was convinced that the very possibility of human knowledge could be explained only on the supposition that the mind makes an essential contribution to our experience of the external world. He sought to discover exactly what must be presupposed of the mind itself for knowledge to be possible. His systematic and complex analysis proceeded from the specification of the universal and necessary conditions for human knowledge to a critical analysis of pure reason itself, i.e., *a priori* reason, independent of and prior to any input from the senses—a form of knowledge that the mind has because of its own intrinsic nature and structure.

For Kant, there is no doubt that all our knowledge begins with sensory experience. This is the empirical component of his theory of knowing. But, he added, though all our knowledge begins with sensory experience, it does not follow that all our knowledge arises out of experience. The mind itself, absolutely independent and prior to any impressions from the senses, also adds knowledge. This is the rational component of his epistemology. The mind provides the form of knowledge; the sensory impressions provide the matter. The mind is active; the senses are passive. The mind does not have innate ideas, but it does have innate forms of understanding through which raw sensory input is processed, ordered, and given an interpretation. This dynamic synthesis produces what we call human knowledge.

For example, our experience of space and time derives not from raw sense input but rather from *a priori* intuitive forms of sensibility, i.e., innate, inner categories of sensing. Through the imposing of these internal forms on sensory matter, we all necessarily and universally have the spontaneous sensory experience of space and time. As humans, we cannot not experience the phenomenal world of appearances except through the simultaneous experience of space and time. Through these internal forms, we structure the raw sensory input in the very process of receiving it. Thus we have the experience and the conviction that we live in a world of objective space and time, a space of three dimensions, where events happen successively in a single, one-way irreversible time order. Space and time are our inescapable subjective modes of human sensibility, but we can never know if they are objective realities, independent of our perception.

Important at this point is Kant's essential distinction between noumena and phenomena, i.e., the world-in-itself and the world of appearances. Human knowledge is limited to the only world we experience, the world of sensory appearances. Our forms of understanding apply only to the phenomenal, not to the noumenal world beyond. The noumena, the world as it is in itself, conforms to its own laws and is independent of and not subject to our human modes of perception and understanding. All we can know is our phenomenal world, the world of appearances, not the world as it is in itself. All our experiences of the world are spatio-temporal, because this is the way sensory appearances are given to us by our *a priori* intuitions of space and time. We can think about but we have no way of knowing if space and time as we experience them are or must be universal characteristics of the world as it is in itself. It is beyond our powers to know if the noumenal world is a space of multiple or infinite dimensions, atemporal or reversible in time.

Kant then moves on from the *a priori* forms of space and time in the order of sensibility through other elements of his epistemological theory to the *a priori* conceptual categories in the order of understanding. Below is a list of his *a priori* cognitive categories, which are necessarily and universally inherent in the human mind and provide the conceptual forms of our knowledge, while sensory input provides the empirical content.

| Quantity | Quality | Relation | Modality |
| --- | --- | --- | --- |
| Unity | Reality | Substance & Accidents | Possibility— Impossibility |
| Plurality | Negation | Cause & Effect | Existence— Nonexistence |
| Totality | Limitation | Community— Reciprocity | Necessity— Contingency |

He always assumed that we know with certainty the truths of mathematics. For example, we know for sure that six and four add up to ten and that the angles of a triangle add up to 180°. Also, he assumed that Aristotle's forms of judgment in his syllogistic logic were valid. Moreover, he took for granted that we know for certain that the fundamental laws of physics are true; as for example, the conservation of matter and Newton's Three Laws of Motion. Yet Hume had demonstrated that no universal laws of nature can be established by induction from sensory experience, or if only logically certain, cannot be shown to be true in empirical reality. Kant's *a priori* perceptual forms of space and time and conceptual categories of understanding (for example, substance and causality) are not drawn from nature but rather are imposed on nature. Also, Kant tries to prove that any experience brought under the inner forms and categories must conform to the laws of arithmetic, geometry, and pure natural science. Kant doesn't question *whether* we can have genuine and certain knowledge of phenomena, but rather, in response to Hume's criticism, he develops his theory to show *how* we do have such knowledge.

We humans think categorically. Prior to the mind's conceptual categorization, the chaotic inflow of raw sensory intake was structured by the *a priori* intuitive forms of space and time. But this is not yet knowledge, because it has not yet been unified in a single consciousness. Neither is it empirical knowledge, because it has not yet acquired what Kant calls "relation to an object." Knowledge and objective experience arise only when the sensory representations are in turn mentally processed by the *a priori* conceptual categories. Human understanding is in the form of categorical ideas. A mind without conceptual categories would have no capacity to think. A mind without sensory input would have nothing to think about. Thought without empirical content is empty. The conceptual categories provide no knowledge of particular things but rather only provide the general forms of our knowledge. Categories are productive only when applied to empirical data. The mind actively imposes its categorical forms on empirical data to make it intelligible; the senses provide the content. Kant wants us to be very clear about the distinction between *a priori* categorical concepts, which are prior to and independent of any empirical content, and *a posteriori* concepts, which are discovered by empirical observation and experimentation. For example, the concept of substance is *a priori* and categorical, but our empirically discovered concept of a specific chemical substance is *a posteriori*. Human knowledge is based neither on pure intellect nor on pure sensation but rather on the spontaneous and simultaneous interaction of the two.

Kant felt an urgent need to defend the reality of causality against Hume's compelling arguments that we neither have empirical nor rational proof for the necessary connection that is essential for a cause-and-effect relationship. Causality is an indispensable condition to provide valid inferences for scientific explanation as well as to operate effectively in our everyday lives. For Kant, Hume, Aristotle, and a host of other philosophers, empirical induction alone can never provide necessary and universal knowledge. The future appearance of only one empirical exception invalidates the universality and certainty of the explanation. Rejecting the usual approaches to a solution, Kant argued that causality is found in the human mind as an *a priori* conceptual category not derived from but rather imposed on sense impressions. Causality is a pure form of thought inherent in our minds through which we conceptually interpret the world, but like the other categories may have no objective existence independent of our minds. Newtonian science discovered valid natural laws based not only on empirical experience but also on the application of the mind's pure conceptual category of cause and effect. Science can discover particular, empirically grounded laws in the phenomenal world, because our minds think in the formal category of cause and effect and their necessary connection, which it imposes on and by which it understands sensory input. Causality is a mental form through which we see reality. It is one of our categorical ways of understanding anything. If it were not for the formal category of causality inherent in the structure of our minds, we could never experience causality but at best only a constant conjunction of successive events.

Kant never claimed that causality or the other categories of understanding correspond to independent reality. The categories are the structures of our minds, but not necessarily the structure of reality. The categories are the forms of our consciousness through which we understand phenomena. All our knowledge is mind and sense dependent. We can know things only as relevant to ourselves, not as they are in themselves unmediated by our ways of knowing. We can never know what is "out there" as an objective reality undistorted by our sensory apparatus and forms of knowing. At least in part, "reality" is of our own making, of our own construction. Our human way of knowing has no completely independent, totally objective reference point in the phenomenal world and also has no access to any absolute foundations in the noumenal world.

As much as Kant was dedicated to establishing valid epistemological foundations for science, he was equally concerned with defining legitimate approaches to such metaphysical questions as the existence of God, human freedom, and immortality. In his analysis of the nature of human knowing, he assigned such questions to the realm of noumena, thus beyond the range of science and its phenomenal domain of sense appearances. For Kant, it is neither scientific nor unscientific to believe in God, human freedom, and the existence of an immortal self, because it is beyond the capacity of science to either prove or disprove such metaempirical realities. Also, he argued that it is beyond the power of traditional rationalistic metaphysics to prove their existence. For example, he demonstrated the invalidity of the three traditional proofs for the existence of God—the ontological and cosmological proofs and the argument from design. Rationalistic metaphysics claims to reach supersensible reality because it supposedly relies exclusively on pure reason entirely liberated from sense input. But for Kant, this is impossible because we humans are by nature creatures of sense experience and thus inescapably experience reality as spatio-temporal, whereas by definition God transcends space and time. Also, the divine transcends our human categories of understanding, such as substance and accident, cause and effect, possibility and impossibility. We humans cannot shake off our humanity by attempting to discard our intrinsic categories of understanding, and thus by unavoidably applying our human categories to God we pull the divine reality down to our sense level. To believe that we humans, even for a moment, can become creatures of pure reason and thus prove the existence or nature of God is a metaphysical illusion. Also, metaphysics can never be a science; it is a realm we can speculatively think about but can never know scientifically. Because of our limited knowing capacities, we can never have scientific knowledge of the ultimate reality of the universe, a complete and final explanation of the whole of reality, a world view in its own transcendent ontological categories. That is, we humans can never have a God's eye view of the noumenal reality. For Kant, any scientific or rational search for such transcendent knowledge was pretentious and futile and could only result in illusory myths.

Yet, as Kant also noted, even though the human search for transcendent knowledge is hopeless and doomed to failure, generation after generation of individuals continue the quest. And even after we understand that the pursuit is futile, some inner need often drives us on to persist. Why is this? Kant provided an answer. Our drive to seek metaphysical knowledge is a natural disposition originating from the purely rational component of our minds, which has an ineradicable impulse to discard the limitations of sense input in order to by itself seek a complete and rationally satisfying picture of the total world and our place and meaning in it. The synthesizing tendencies of our minds have a natural drive for systematic completeness, a total picture of the world that cannot be satisfied by specialized knowledge of particular realities. Pure reason has the impulse to function on its own, unrestrained by empirical verification. When our minds follow the tendency to pursue the impossible goal of functioning as pure intellect unconditioned by the senses, they no longer function as instruments of knowledge but rather instruments of illusion. Though Kant was convinced that metaphysics can never be a science, he believed that metaphysics as a natural disposition can be valuable. In the intellect's drive to obtain complete and systematic knowledge, it can be an inspiring ideal for scientists to strive for in their empirical investigations of the phenomenal world. Even though not epistemologically accessible to humans, the possibility of a metaphysical, noumenal world reminds us that science may not exhaust the possibilities of reality. Metaphysical speculation is not meaningless, not absurd only because it is metaphysical. Our judgment is that Kant would applaud those modern theoretical physicists who dream and work toward the ideal of a "theory of everything" unifying all physical laws into a single mathematical scheme, and who in the process might yield the creative potential of a synergy between metaphysical imagination and scientific investigation, providing that in the end they distinguish between speculative and scientific results.

Kant was as deeply concerned about human moral and religious life as the scientific quest for valid knowledge of the natural world. He was especially disturbed by the conflict between the dominant interpretation of the Newtonian world as a purposeless machine, deterministically following universal laws of mechanical necessity, and our subjective experience of human freedom and moral order as well as our religious faith in immortality and a purposeful, ultimately just universe governed by a personal and loving God. The science of his time revealed an ordered universe of matter in motion inexorably following laws of causation that excluded freedom while morality presumed freedom of choice. As a matter of fact, most humans subjectively experience not only moral freedom but also moral duty. Kant dedicated himself to reconciling the mechanistic world view of science with moral consciousness and religious faith. His strategy once again involved a revolutionary reversal. Previously, in order to establish new epistemological foundations for science, he rejected the traditional assumption that our minds must conform to objects and instead pursued the hypothesis that all objects, at least in part, must conform to our minds. Now, in order to establish new epistemological foundations for morality and religious faith, he rejected the traditional procedure of first demonstrating the existence and qualities of God, from which are deduced human freedom, the moral sense, and other metaphysical realities and instead began with human moral consciousness, from which he then used moral arguments for freedom of the will, the immortality of the soul, and the existence of God.

These metaphysical realities cannot be proven or disproven by science, because they are beyond its range of application, but arguments for their existence can be provided from the moral demands of practical reason. As Kant had previously sought the universal and necessary *a priori* elements in knowledge, he now sought the universal and necessary *a priori* elements in morality, because, for both knowledge and morality, the *a posteriori* inductive gathering of empirical input provides uncertain foundations. Kant noted that almost all humans have a consciousness of an innate moral law that makes practical demands on us. A universal moral law lives within us independent of our cultural conditioning and personal experience, independent of practical usefulness, pleasure or pain. An *a priori*, universal moral absolute exists within us, commanding us unconditionally and without exception, which Kant calls "the categorical imperative." Though he expressed the categorical imperative in different forms, it basically states that we should act only on that maxim which we can at the same time will that it should become a universal moral law. This absolute moral command derives from Kant's analysis of the *a priori* practical reason in its moral judgment, and it is imperative because its command is always valid and independent of any empirical circumstances. Kant then argued that the categorical imperative reveals a metaphysical realm of reason and freedom from which we derive our freedom to will rational moral actions beyond the determinism of natural laws. The human self has two different aspects: our phenomenal, spatiotemporal empirical self, part of the natural order like other natural objects, completely subject to and determined by the laws of nature, and knowable by natural science and our noumenal, metaphysical self, transcending space and time and other objects in nature, subject only to the moral law and beyond the range of natural laws and scientific ways of knowing. At our deepest level of moral and rational existence, we are free beings transcending the mechanical, deterministic laws of nature.

Kant built a metaphysics based on human moral consciousness. He was aware that his moral arguments for free will, the immortality of the soul, and the existence of God were not ironclad, objectively valid proofs. He did not claim to offer a scientific proof or an airtight demonstrative argument of the kind rationalistic metaphysics sought to provide. He argued that the innate moral law within, which gives us the consciously experienced obligation to obey the categorical imperative in our everyday practical lives, demands that we postulate free will, personal immortality, and the existence of God. The existence of these noumenal realities is a moral demand of our consciousness of being moral creatures, i.e., of our consciously experiencing the duty to act morally. It is a moral demand, not a scientific or rational proof. Essentially, it is a free act of practical faith, not compelled but supported by moral considerations and consistent with humans as moral creatures. This moral faith is not irrational in any logical way and not impossible in any scientific way because science cannot claim that its range of knowing is identical with the limits of reality. Kant sought to save science from skepticism and save faith from science. More specifically, his goal was to establish new epistemological foundations for science to overcome the radical skepticism of Hume and to define the limits of science in order to leave room for faith in a metaphysical realm beyond the Newtonian material cosmos following universal laws of mechanical causality. The astonishing fact of our human moral sense, a universal subjective consciousness of right and wrong, of moral demands beyond brute material existence, opens us up to the possibility of another and fuller dimension of reality—the noumenal realm beyond phenomenal spatiotemporal appearances.

◆ ◆ ◆ ◆ ◆

Professor Immanuel Kant had a revolutionary and enduring impact on epistemology. However, there have been several later developments impinging on some of his basic perspectives. He assumed that all geometry was Euclidean and all physical science was Newtonian, that both were final truths. Space was Euclidean and all science strictly deterministic. The subsequent developments of non-Euclidean geometry, relativity theory, and quantum mechanics undid

these absolute certainties. Also since Kant, the revolutionary perspective of evolution has permeated our thinking. Today, evolutionary epistemology denies the necessary, *a priori* origins of Kant's categories of perception and thought and explains their existence as a
product of an *a posteriori* evolutionary process over a vast duration of
time. The human categories exist not because of any universal *a priori* necessity but rather evolved because they increased the probability of the human species' survival. Similarly, if humans and other animals have two eyes rather than one, it is because two are necessary for
depth perception, thus increasing the chances of survival by avoiding
falling objects, escaping predators, and hunting down prey. To increase
our probability of survival, we humans as a species have evolved our
own epistemological niche, which in Kantian terms includes our five
senses, two intuitive forms of space and time, and the conceptual categories of understanding. Other terrestrial forms of life have evolved
their own epistemological niches. Living species of other galaxies will
have evolved their own forms of knowing, perhaps from one to hundreds of sensory forms and categories of understanding, but all sufficiently corresponding to reality to increase their probability of survival in their own specific environment.

Also since the work of Kant, there has been an explosive development in the neurosciences, which with rapid advances in technology are unveiling the structure and functions of the brain. Professor
Kant sat alone in his study thinking critically about the necessary and
universal *a priori* contributions of the mind for our actual experience
of the external world. He would have enthusiastically welcomed the
research of the modern neurosciences, and in turn we would whole-
heartedly welcome the application of his open spirit and comprehensive mind to help develop a systematic theory synthesizing our
empirical findings. But whatever advances in modern times and
despite whatever flaws in his theory, enduring is his central intuition
that the mind is not passive but rather actively imposes its own intrinsic forms and categories of understanding on the phenomenal world,
synthesizing the empirical and rational components of human knowing. Kant was a turning point in epistemology, especially

pre-Humean epistemology, in his revolutionary perspective that the object is to a certain extent the creation of the subject. The mind acts upon and is not merely acted upon. In contrast to the traditional view, the mind is not a mirrorlike reflection of external reality but rather imposes its own structure on the phenomenal world. The mind does not take photos mindlessly imitating objective reality, but rather it actively forms, at least in part, its own subjective interpretation of reality. Not only artists but also scientists, each in their own way and in their own domain, are creative interpreters of reality. The active, synthesizing powers of the human mind in a sense create another nature out of the material that actual nature gives us. Cognition includes construction. Human knowledge is humanized knowledge. And finally, Kant warns us that despite our natural impulses to seek metaphysical knowledge, the categories of the human mind are not the ontological categories of the universe as it is in itself.

# SOME OTHER WAYS OF KNOWING

Here is a brief description of some ways of knowing previously mentioned but not emphasized or entirely omitted.

*Authority* as a way of knowing is a practical necessity for most of us, because we don't have the time, talent, or resources to verify for our individual selves all that is necessary to know for our personal, work, and community lives. Necessity requires that we have a certain trust or provisional faith that certain persons or institutions, until proven otherwise, have a special competence or are in a position to know. We might judge a source to be authoritative based on its credentials, reputation, integrity, experience, power, the antiquity of a revered tradition, respect due to elders, the testimony of witnesses, or the validity of a process, as with the scientific method. In some religions, knowledge is obtained by direct transmission of an ancient tradition through a living master. For some of us, authority is based on the prestige or number of people who maintain a certain belief, group consensus, a charismatic leader, or reports in the mass media.

Another way some of us seek to know reality is by *revelation from a supernatural source*, which is variously described as inspiration, illumination, enlightenment, grace, mystical experience, religious conversion, ecstasy or divine intoxication. Sources of supernatural knowledge include dreams, visions, sacred scriptures, oral traditions, dogmas, priests, prophets, oracles, saints, gurus, and religious officials of the past and present. Individuals and groups can be chosen by God or the gods as the chosen elect to receive special revelations. Faith and obedience may be considered necessary conditions and paths to understanding, prayers for knowledge can be answered, and miracles can be proof for the validity of religious truth claims. A strictly observant and pious life, and devout participation in all the rites and rituals can be rewarded with sacred wisdom and supernatural knowledge of ultimate realities. Divination may be practiced to learn the will of the gods and to foretell the future.

Though the distinction between the *objective, detached* and *personal, involved* ways of knowing can easily be exaggerated in an abstract description, the basic contrast is between an observer as distant, cold, intellecting about and a participant as intimate, warm, feeling with. One way construes personal passion as contaminating truth finding, seeks to extricate the subject from the object, and emphasizes hard facts, and observable, measurable data from the outside; the other way requires personal passion for truth finding, seeks a oneness of the knower and the to-be-known, and values soft facts, and raw data from the inside. One path may live more in the head along the logical-illogical continuum, disentangling who we are from what we seek to know; the other path may live more in the heart along the relevant-irrelevant spectrum, recognizing the vital dependency of our knowing on our personal being.

*Introspection* is a looking within and observing our inner selves by attending to what we experience in our bodies as well as our mind's content and processes. It is an inner empiricism by which we learn from the wisdom of the body, discover emotional truth, and become aware of our mental phenomena, thus becoming more able to liberate ourselves from past conditioning. Psychodynamic psychotherapy and Buddhist insight meditation are examples of introspective disciplines. In some religious traditions introspection reveals not only personal but also ultimate realities.

The *contemplative way of knowing* is a quiet, gentle, and appreciative beholding of external and internal phenomena and also for some of us is a communion with spiritual and transcendent realities. The mood is receptive and profoundly respectful of what we are observing and experiencing. The mode is listening to and trusting in the realities we experience and our ability to receive them in the depths of our stillness. The approach is noninterfering, noninvasive and nonviolent. Never forcing, the goal is knowledge through union with the observed and experienced, not manipulating variables, not trying to twist answers out of reality. With effortless effort, we find almost without even looking. By letting the realities be, and letting them go, our hope is that they will flow within us and we will obtain objectivity by assimilation with the object.

While people disagree about its precise definition and domain, *intuition* is most generally viewed as a direct, instantaneous grasp of reality, not mediated by conscious reasoning. It is variously described as a gut-level feeling, a hunch, a total response, or a sudden, direct insight into truth. Operating below the level of conscious awareness, intuition is a dynamic gestalt of previous experiences and unconscious inductive and deductive reasoning. Thus we are only aware of the results of intuition, not the process. For example, a seasoned mathematician can spontaneously experience sudden insights into immediate solutions of extremely complex problems, and various scientists, most notably some eminent theoretical physicists, consider intuition the most important source for their Nobel-Prize-winning discoveries. For those of us who believe that the world we experience through our senses is only illusory, intuitive insight, not empirical observation or logical reasoning, may be the way to apprehend the ultimate reality. For some, moral intuition is the only valid foundation for our sense of right and wrong, good and evil. Religious mystics often describe their transcendental experiences as intuitive, direct apprehensions of God.

Throughout most of human history, many cultures have highly valued attaining *altered states of consciousness* as a way of knowing, entering into planes of existence beyond everyday baseline consciousness. The methods include such practices as fasting, self-flagellation, twirling, rapid breathing, isolation, sensory and sleep deprivation, along with an array of psychoactive substances that today include caffeine, nicotine, alcohol, marijuana, peyote (synthesized as mescaline), Mexican mushrooms (synthesized as psilocybin), LSD, cocaine, and heroin. In various indigenous cultures, psychoactive substances are sacraments and an integral part of their religion and rituals. In 1957 Humphry Osmond coined the term "psychedelic," which derives from the Greek, meaning "mind-manifesting" or "soul-revealing." By the use of this new word, he hoped to point out the positive, consciousness-expanding potential of certain drugs rather than viewing them as only pathologically hallucinogenic or psychosis-mimicking. William James (1842-1910), philosopher and a father of American psychology, personally experimented with inhaling nitrous oxide and was left with the conviction that

> ...our normal waking consciousness, rational consciousness as we call it, is but one special type of consciousness, whilst all about it, parted from it by the filmiest of screens, there lie potential forms of consciousness entirely different. We may go through life without suspecting their existence; but apply the requisite stimulus, and at a touch they are there in all their completeness, definite types of mentality which probably somewhere have their field of application and adaptation. No account of the universe in its totality can be final which leaves these other forms of consciousness quite disregarded. How to regard them is the question, for they are so

*continues*

*continued*

> discontinuous with ordinary consciousness. Yet they may
> determine attitudes though they cannot furnish formu-
> las, and open a region though they fail to give a map. At
> any rate, they forbid a premature closing of our accounts
> with reality.[50]

The *creative arts* can not only express but also discover realities. Sometimes the artist begins a project because of the personal way a basic question is experienced, and the creative process is a way of discovering the answer. The struggle is to come out of personal darkness and perhaps pain to a universal reality. The arts can cast a different light on reality because, in addition to using sensory input, abstract reason, imagination, introspection, intuition, and so on, they may also use images, metaphor, physical movement, aesthetic relationships, dramatic tensions, and harmonies and thus tap deep emotions and novel combinations of brain processes. For both the artist and the recipient, the creative process can transfer us from ordinary baseline reality to an expanded consciousness of present and possible realms of reality. In the artful aspects of science, beauty is viewed by some as a creative guide to discovering new realities, and various advances in theoretical physics have been made by seeking mathematical elegance and using aesthetic criteria especially when experimental tests are not yet feasible. For Paul Dirac, the Nobel laureate physicist, the aesthetics of a theory was crucial, and this approach led him to construct a mathematically more elegant equation for the electron which then led to the successful prediction of the existence of antimatter. In a famous quote he stated, "It is more important to have beauty in one's equations than to have them fit experiments....it seems that if one is working from the point of view of getting beauty in one's equations, and if one has a really sound insight, one is on a sure line of progress."[51]

*Personal experience* as a way of knowing derives a sense of reality from the totality of our lived lives. It is a synthesis of the truth and wisdom we have learned across our life stages, the physical changes in our bodies, our dreams and disappointments, joys and suffering, routines and crisis, our work, love, play, moral experience, and what we have come to believe is of indispensable value. It is what our human nature has assimilated through our own ways of knowing and where our complete person is the primary instrument of learning. What we learn from our total personal experience are lived truths, perhaps more implicit than explicit, tacit rather than precisely articulated. It is a personally biased summing up, skewed by the logic of our individual lives but perhaps at times deep and broad enough to touch the objective and universal.

Let us close by noting two pairs of possibly complementary or conflicting ways of knowing. Are there some typically different *female and male* ways of knowing? Not only culturally but also genetically, do men and women tend to ask different types of basic questions about life, prefer different ways of seeking answers, and have different criteria for meaningfulness and truth? Researchers are beginning to detect some gender differences in the brain and variations in cognitive abilities.

The neurosciences are increasingly providing empirical information on the various ways we humans know. For example, the pioneering researcher Roger Sperry shared the 1981 Nobel Prize in medicine and physiology for his famous split-brain studies. As a result of his work and that of other researchers, it is now more empirically established that *the right and left hemispheres of our brains* tend to have their own specialized functions, sometimes complementary with the other hemisphere but in other functions entirely independent. The left hemisphere is primarily verbal (speech, language), abstract, rational (logic, mathematics), and analytical, processing information sequentially in a linear mode. The right specializes more in nonverbal, sensual, perceptual (visual, spatial, and musical relationships), and synthesis, processing information simultaneously in a holistic mode. Though detailed research mitigates or disconfirms some of these neat dichotomies in actual individuals, the basic idea is that we have a dual brain with more or less two separate, simultaneous modes of consciousness with different cognitive information processing styles.

# HOW RATIONAL ARE WE?

Even from our casual observations of everyday human life, it doesn't take long to notice that we are not a species of pure rationality. Stephen Stich notes that a growing number of experimental psychologists who are empirically investigating human reasoning have discovered that "Human subjects, it would appear, regularly and systematically invoke inferential and judgment strategies ranging from the merely invalid to the genuinely bizarre." The empirical evidence supports the conclusion that "people are systematically irrational."[52] Among other investigations, he briefly describes the work of Ross, Lepper, and their colleagues which explores the irrational elements of belief perseverance. In these experiments, the subjects were given various evidence on which they were asked to form and record their beliefs. After this was completed, the subjects were given a thorough debriefing in which they were told that they had been intentionally duped by being provided with evidence that in reality was false. Yet even after being told that the evidence on which they had based their belief was totally contrived and erroneous, the subjects tended to retain by a substantial degree the beliefs they had formed on the foundations of the later totally discredited evidence. For Stich, this is only one among dozens of other empirical investigations that appear to demonstrate that human reasoning often deviates substantially from the standard provided by normative canons of inference.

A classic empirical study of belief perseverance in a modern group that prophesied the imminent destruction of the world was directed by Festinger, Riecken, and Schacter. Using the participant-observer method, they carefully followed the social and psychological developments of a small American group that believed that some of its members were receiving messages from the supernatural as well as from extraterrestrial creatures. The prediction was made that on December 21 of that year the world would be destroyed by a cataclysmic flood, but that they and certain other chosen few would be saved by superior beings from outer space who would arrive in flying saucers and transport them to other planets or to certain terrestrial safe places. The prophesied apocalyptic events never occurred. Objectively, their beliefs were totally disconfirmed. Psychologically, their reactions went beyond simply belief perseverance to, for the first time, actively proselytizing their unrealized beliefs. Here is the researchers' succinct description of the situation and the irrational consequences of individuals in this particular group, which elsewhere they note is also common to such apocalyptic groups down through history.

> Suppose an individual believes something with his
> whole heart; suppose further that he has a commitment
> to this belief, that he has taken irrevocable actions
> because of it; finally, suppose that he is presented with
> evidence, unequivocal and undeniable evidence, that his
> belief is wrong: what will happen? The individual will
> frequently emerge, not only unshaken, but even more
> convinced of the truth of his beliefs than ever before.
> Indeed, he may even show a new fervor about convinc-
> ing and converting other people to his view.[53]

A systematic way we deny and distort reality as well as deceive ourselves is through the various *ego-defense mechanisms*. Operating automatically and autonomously below the level of our conscious awareness, their goal is not detached, rational understanding of objective reality but rather our physical, psychic, and emotional survival. These mechanisms protect us from threats against our sense of self, as for example, our sense of being a good, honest, intelligent, rational, and competent person. They protect us from emotional pain by blocking from our conscious awareness such feelings as fear, anxiety, guilt, shame, and despair as well as socially unacceptable impulses such as incest, murder, and suicide. The ego-defense mechanisms are a sort of psychic reflex that pushes out of our conscious awareness threats from internal thoughts and feelings and perceived and believed external realities. Because they operate in the unconscious realm, we are unaware that, for the sake of survival, we are blocking out actual realities and thus being dishonest by telling lies to ourselves. In an evolutionary sense, the ego-defense mechanisms can have adaptive value by increasing our probability of survival, and thus are quite normal and even desirable. However, if our defenses excessively deny or distort actual internal or external realities, they can be maladaptive and thus decrease our probability of physical, psychological, and emotional survival. All of us use unconscious ego-defense mechanisms to various degrees. They can soften our subjective experience of the harsh realities of existence, protect us from the pain of failure and disappointments, alleviate our anxieties, maintain feelings of self-worth, and give us a sense of significance and a motivating hopefulness. Because the defense mechanisms operate basically on the unconscious level, we are not consciously aware of their actual functioning in us, but sometimes they can be woefully transparent to outside observers. When others bring to our attention the possible presence of certain ego-defenses in us, we often react with such feelings as anger, resentment, hurt, or disbelief, because not only may our integrity be brought into question, but also once the mechanisms become conscious their defensive powers evaporate.

Let us now briefly describe some specific ego-defense mechanisms and how they might be operating in us as truth seekers. Probably the most primitive and also a component in a number of the other defenses is the *denial of reality*. Here our minds push out of our consciousness external and internal realities that are experienced as too threatening to our psychic and physical survival. To relieve our anxiety, fear, and hurt, the autonomous and automatic powers of our mind bury the disturbing realities where we can no longer consciously experience them. For example, our minds may deny or diminish the painful inevitabilities of aging and death from our everyday consciousness. Yet when our minds bury such threatening realties, they bury them alive. Below the level of our conscious awareness, they can still impact our subjective experience of life and for plenty of us can be the most powerful, though unconscious, motivating force for our seeking some kind of hopeful remedy in religion, philosophy, or science. Entirely beyond or only with a vague awareness, our minds can reflexively deny disconfirming evidence or avoid cogent criticism of our assumptions, beliefs, and convictions, because it could damage or destroy our professional status, economic security, or family relationships. Also, the unconscious nature of the denial mechanism frees us from consciously and deliberately ignoring conflicting evidence and criticism, thus preserving our self-concept as honest and open-minded inquirers. Another way we unconsciously deny reality is to escape into a perpetual busyness with daily life with all sorts of ever so "necessary" major and minor projects, thus assuring us that we have absolutely no time left over to reflect, read, and experimentally inquire about life itself.

*Repression* as an ego-defense mechanism is a derivative of denial and is part of the dynamics of most, if not all, the other defenses. Repression of dangerous, painful, and forbidden thoughts, feelings, memories, and perceptions into the unconscious is usually beyond our conscious control and is distinguished from suppression, where we can consciously dismiss from our minds unacceptable external and internal input. *Fantasy* incorporates the denial of reality as we actually experience it to be and then goes beyond to construct a reality as we would like it to be. By involuntary mental processes beneath our conscious awareness, we deceive ourselves by screening out disappointing and threatening actual realities and instead imagine wish-fulfilling realities which we then experience as actual realities. At their best, the fantasy elements in our world views can add meaning, purpose, optimism, and excitement to our lives and motivate us to great acts of courage, sacrifice, and achievement. Among the worst consequences, we can waste our lives duped by our own or the fantasy dreams of others which we have assimilated.

In order to appear rational to ourselves and others, our minds without our conscious awareness operate a process of *rationalization*, which contrives "logical explanations" to justify the threatening contradictions among our beliefs and between our beliefs and actual reality as well as the incongruities between our declared beliefs and our actual behavior and between our claimed and real motivations. The attempt is to justify our beliefs as truly rational and our

motivations as genuinely righteous. Rationalizations are often difficult to uncover, because they usually have elements of truth and also
an internal logical consistency. Confronted with disappointment and
tragedy, we "explain" that everything always happens for the best.
Unable to provide rational reasons for the gap between our optimistic convictions and the cruelties of life, we "explain" that they are
mysteries beyond human understanding. Certain world views represented as authentic philosophy, theology, and science can be seen as
little more than sophisticated rationalizations.

Finally, the ego-defense mechanism of *intellectualization* occurs
when we attempt to deal with unacceptable emotions in an intellectual way. Automatically and without our conscious awareness, the
mind represses painful raw feelings or the threatening emotional
component of ideas and retains in our consciousness only rational
abstractions divested of their affective charge. Insulated from the
painful feelings at the conscious level, we are deceived into believing
that the relevant realities can be objectively comprehended as purely impersonal ideas with supposedly detached explanations. Split off
from the world of dangerous emotional realities, we believe we are
safe in our isolated world of words and concepts. But a difficulty
with the defense of intellectualization is that our quest for truth is in
fact personal and involved, and when we are unaware of our unconscious emotional agenda, we are completely unaware how powerfully it biases our investigations. With intellectualization, we can construe all kinds of consciously intended "objective" ideas, when in fact
they are radically driven and distorted by our unconscious motivations and emotional conflicts.

A number of disciplines exist to help guard us, at least to a certain extent, from some of our irrationalities and to train our minds
and emotions toward more honest and competent inquiry.
Philosophy can provide a practical apprenticeship in the skills of logical and critical thinking while unearthing our overlooked but most
fundamental assumptions, identifying unsupported assertions, and
exposing rational inconsistencies and contradictions. We can learn to
better detect our hasty generalizations, and avoid confusing cause and

effect, probability and causality. Thus, we can not only build valid rational arguments for ourselves and avoid passing on our logical fallacies to others, but also we can more competently assess the rational truth claims of others. Science trains us in its demand for rigorous standards of procedure to help reduce unintended irrational and emotional bias through its observational and experimental methods, hypothesis testing, critical rational analysis, quantification, peer review, and experimental replication by external investigators. When possible, controlled, double-blind experiments are further safeguards against hidden personal contamination. The public nature of scientific dialogue in readily available publications and other media rather than secret, esoteric knowledge open only to the chosen few tends to expose charlatans and methodological incompetence. At least as an ideal, the spirit of scientific inquiry is open and honest, accompanied by a robust skepticism rather than obstinate dogmatism. The psychologist George Kelly has remarked that the nice thing about the use of hypotheses in science is that we don't have to believe in them. "This is a key to the genius of the scientific method. It permits you to be inconsistent with what you know long enough to see what will happen."[54] According to Kelly, the creation and testing of hypotheses in science allows us some of the playfulness of a child, thus avoiding a grim, overinvolved determination to obtain experimental results which only confirm our adult, professional consistencies. The method of depth psychotherapy is training in the inner discipline of self-knowledge and emotional honesty which can help reduce the powerful influence of hidden ideational and emotional programming that otherwise can distort or destroy the rational objectivity of our inquiries. In many Eastern traditions, we seek answers to the basic questions of life more in our way of life and our experiments in living rather than in the abstract, rational analysis emphasized in the West and inherited from the ancient Greeks. Various ancient Eastern traditions require that personal truth seeking begin first with cleansing our minds from selfish desires, disturbing emotions, and immoral acts in order to develop self-discipline and self-control. Only after moral, emotional, physical, and intellectual training can we hope to have the mental clarity for valid insights into reality. Religious traditions, both West and East, emphasize spiritual practices as an integral part of seeking truth, including prayer, meditation, contemplation, sacred rituals, fasting, and retreats. All in common and each in its own way, the disciplines of critical and logical reasoning, scientific methods, depth psychotherapy, and Eastern and Western methods of purification and spiritual development aim to train us in more honest and competent inquiry and as much as possible protect us from our own personal distortions of reality.

♦ ♦ ♦ ♦ ♦

The aim of this chapter has been for you to become more informed about the different ways of knowing and more competent in judging which answers to your basic questions about life are possible, probable, true, or not true. I presented many of the classical ways of knowing from philosophy, science, and religion. The next chapter is more personal, emphasizing self-knowledge. The purpose of my describing twelve contrasting pairs of truth seekers is so you can better assess your own psychological reality and how this influences your truth seeking.

# 4

## *Some Types of Seekers: Know Thyself*

The primary instrument for our inquiries is ourselves. Who we are powerfully impacts the kinds of questions we ask, the way we go about our quest, and the kinds of answers we find true and meaningful. We bring to the search for truth no less than but no more than five senses, a three-pound brain filtering objective realities, feelings that have evolved to promote our individual survival and yet seek warm emotional bonding, plus social influences defining the true, good, and beautiful. As individuals and societies we not only passively assimilate objective realities, but we also actively construe what reality is or should be. No matter how objectively these realities may be experienced, they are, at least partly, the product of our output, not of pure input. However closely we approximate objective reality, our knowledge remains human knowledge. We are that species which lives not by reality alone but also by our conceptions of reality. Our observations are partly our constructions. To think otherwise would be to believe in what Nietzsche calls "the dogma of the immaculate perception." William James argues that our individual temperament strongly influences our philosophical convictions.

> The history of philosophy is to a great extent that of a certain clash of human temperaments....Of whatever temperament a professional philosopher is, he tries when philosophizing to sink the fact of his temperament. Temperament is no conventionally recognized reason, so he urges impersonal reasons only for his conclusions. Yet his temperament really gives him a stronger bias than any of his more strictly objective premises. It loads the evidence for him one way or the other, making for a more sentimental or a more hard-hearted view of the universe, just as this fact or that principle would. He *trusts* his temperament. Wanting a universe that suits it, he believes in any representation of the universe that does suit it. He feels men of opposite temper to be out of key with the world's character, and in his heart considers them incompetent and "not in it," in the philosophic business, even though they may far excel him in dialectical ability.
>
> Yet in the forum he can make no claim, on the bare ground of his temperament, to superior discernment or authority. There arises thus a certain insincerity in our philosophic discussions: the potentest of all our premises is never mentioned.[1]

James distinguishes two principle types of intellectual temperaments: the tender-minded and the tough-minded. The first he associates with the rationalist, the "devotee to abstract and eternal principles," and the second with the empiricist who is the "lover of facts in all their crude variety". He tabulates the traits of the two temperaments.

| *The Tender-Minded* | *The Tough-Minded* |
| --- | --- |
| Rationalistic (going by principles) | Empiricist (going by facts) |
| Intellectualistic | Sensationalistic |
| Idealistic | Materialistic |
| Optimistic | Pessimistic |
| Religious | Irreligious |
| Free-willist | Fatalistic |
| Monistic | Pluralistic |
| Dogmatical | Skeptical |

Furthermore, the psychologist and philosopher James notes,

> They have a low opinion of each other. Their antago-
> nism, whenever as individuals their temperaments have
> been intense, has formed in all ages a part of the philo-
> sophic atmosphere of the time. It forms a part of the
> philosophic atmosphere today. The tough think of the
> tender as sentimentalists and soft-heads. The tender feel
> the tough to be unrefined, callous, or brutal. Their
> mutual reaction is very much like that that takes place
> when Bostonian tourists mingle with a population like
> that of Cripple Creek. Each type believes the other to
> be inferior to itself; but disdain in the one case is min-
> gled with amusement, in the other it has a dash of fear.

Many are the psychological traits by which we color and even construct reality. I present below a preliminary sketch of twelve pairs of
truth seekers with some of their psychological characteristics. Some
of the types are characterological and endure through time and different circumstances; others are more contextual and vary with our
life situation. Almost none of us is a pure type; most of us are a mixture of these and other possible types. I dichotomize them into contrasting pairs for clarity, though the actual psychological realities are

far more complex and subtle. My goal is to begin to understand what you and I are about and how this influences what we think and feel the world is all about.

Much of this self-discovery is an inner quest. Often, however, the last thing we discover is ourselves. Plenty of us who are truth seekers are generally cognizant that the truth within people shapes their views of the external world, but in our own individual person and particular circumstances we often don't see the connection. Just as the eye cannot see itself, we are blind to ourselves. Also, for some of us, seeking the truth of the world out there can be a powerful but unconscious way of avoiding the truth of ourselves. Self-truth can be very threatening. Self-delusions, no matter how sincere, can be a painful discovery. Both the West and East have long traditions exhorting self-understanding. Inscribed over the entrance to the shrine of the god Apollo at Delphi is the age-old Greek precept "Man, know thyself." The Lao Tzu of ancient Chinese Taoism says, "To understand others is to be wise, but to understand one's self is to be illumined."[2] Montaigne puts it this way: "What can anyone understand who cannot understand himself?"[3]

# TRANSCENDERS AND INTRINSICS

Most truth seekers who ask some of the basic questions of life can be considered either transcenders or intrinsics. The transcenders can be subdivided into supernatural or natural transcenders; the intrinsics are nontranscenders either by innate disposition or by deliberate choice. Those of us who are supernatural transcenders believe in or consider that we have experienced an ultimate realm of Being that is entirely beyond, superior to, and different from the natural order. This transcendent reality is usually conceived as either impersonal or personal, indifferent to human life or in loving communion with humankind, even responding to prayer by interventions in human history and individual lives. Those of us who are natural transcenders are like the supernatural transcenders with a sixth sense, in that we also believe in or consider that we have experienced a reality beyond our five-sense consciousness of reality, but for us this greater reality is still within the natural order. Both types of transcenders might have the same experience of a reality apparently beyond ordinary sense experience, but each construes a different explanation. For example, the supernatural transcender might attribute the experience to a transcendent divine energy or a transcendent personal God intervening in nature, while the natural transcender might conceive of "God" as nature, perhaps in a very expanded understanding of nature but still within the natural order. For the natural transcender, the transcendent might be a universal life force, a cosmic intelligence, an absolute creative power manifesting itself as a progressive evolutionary unfolding—yet it is part of or the very essence of nature.

For those of us who have had the personal experience of transcendence, whether of a supernatural or natural interpretation, and even if only for minutes, the experience can be so utterly unexpected, overwhelming, subtle, or beautiful that our lives are never again the same. The experience can be a radical turning point in our lives. Our future commitments, what we consider sacred or special, essential or decorative, and the very meaning and mission of our lives can be explained only in terms of those minutes or hours of that transcendental experience. Within those fleeting instants, we typically believe that we experience the most real and illuminating moments of our entire lives. Most of us rarely talk to others about the experience, not only because it is so unusual and difficult to explain, but also because it is so very private and special. We know that we will never forget the experience, and the world will never seem the same. We don't feel the same, and for many of us, we will never again go back to our former way of life.

Though they construct different explanations, the occasions evoking transcendental experiences can be identical for both the supernatural and natural transcenders. Some typical occasions reported to us include military combat; nonviolent peace demonstrations in confrontation with brutal police power; exquisite natural beauty such as a sunrise, sunset, or walk through a silent woods at dawn; the delivery of a baby; sexual orgasm; moments of uniquely open and intimate sharing with a lover, spouse, child, or colleague; listening to music; sitting quietly in a temple, church, or car wash; physical trauma; near-death experiences; a moral crisis; revolutionary struggles; political, racial, or sexual oppression and abuse; imprisonment; torture; and chemically induced altered states of consciousness.

For those of us who are intrinsics by innate disposition, we wonder why all the fuss about what transcenders believe or claim to have experienced. We don't experience any sixth sense, and even though we might intellectually grant the possibility, our natural bent is to disbelieve transcendent claims. Though we might be accused of being Philistines or metaphysical hillbillies, we tend to view transcendental urges as a congenital excess of the brain or endocrine system, a possibly admirable but surely misguided idealism, a gratuitous and sentimental interpretation of reality, or for some desperately needy folks, metaphysical greed. For us, the "mystery" is how people can believe such nonsense! Life is to be lived as it appears. This is it! What you see is what you get. The ordinary, everyday reality is the real substance of life. Any claimed beyond is just fluff. If in any sense we are mystics, it is because we find the extraordinary in the ordinary; the daily life of our five senses is in itself a miracle. We accept reality as it appears. We are content with, concerned for, and celebrate the finite. It more than fills our cup. We have no great felt need for something beyond. We can feel deeply about the cosmos without sentimentalizing it, we can be romantic without romanticizing the world, and we can fight for ideals without demanding they be transcendent realities.

Also, we intrinsics have plenty of opportunities for altruistic heroism, because we don't believe in personal immortality or a just reckoning in an afterlife. Virtue is its own reward. We observe that neither supernatural nor natural transcenders are necessarily more moral in their actions. They can excuse themselves from the most basic of human decencies in the name of their ultimate ideals, and they may tend to sacrifice people and basic human needs and rights on the altars of their transcendent realities. Though as intrinsics our lives may require great courage, we can be hopeful for ourselves and our species without believing in God, gods, or a transcendent evolutionary *élan vital*.

We nontranscenders can be fully spiritual, but our spirituality is intrinsic in the real world itself and is not dependent on something exterior and superior. There is no split between this world and an imagined world beyond. We are not only in the world, but of the world. We can dedicate our lives to sharing the real possibilities and joys of this world. For some of us, "God" is people helping people, and our focus is on goodliness, not godliness. Our human lives and this planet are special and sacred because they are finite. As far as our innate instincts instruct us and the available evidence demonstrates, we are the sole custodians of the planet Earth, and it is for us to honor it, as we must honor ourselves.

Many of us who are intrinsics by deliberate choice have been emotionally or intellectually attracted to a transcendent world view, but we have rejected that position. For example, we might find a certain religion or philosophy emotionally appealing because it satisfies our transcendent yearnings, but after careful and critical examination we reject it as false. Yet we may still feel drawn to the transcendentalism of that view and perhaps also to the emotional bonding with a religious, spiritual, or philosophical community. To break these emotional ties, we deliberately choose by an act of will to reject that view and its community, and thus we are able to get on in other ways with our lives. This can be an heroic and painful decision involving disappointment and disillusionment, and thus much healing and psychological wisdom may be necessary. We need discipline and character to resist this "transcendental temptation."[4]

The meaning of life for transcenders and intrinsics comes from a different source. For transcenders, it is only by appeal to some transcendent ultimate that our lives have meaning. Without this transcendent frame of reference, a transcender can experience a profound emptiness, incompleteness, and radical loss of significance, dignity, and direction. We who are transcenders yearn to be part of a larger world and to have a greater identity. We believe in or have experienced more, expect or hope for more than our everyday, ordinary human reality. Without appeal to and a relationship with some positive determining ultimate, life has no worthwhile meaning. Without ultimate meaning, human life has little or no truly significant meaning. For us, "this world" attains significant value only to the extent that it participates in a reality that transcends itself. For intrinsics, daily life itself is full of meaning, and there is no need for any appeal to a transcendent ultimate.[5] The meaning of life is intrinsic within life itself and is to be found and created within the very structure and function of our lived lives. Though we who are intrinsics may be especially aware of the tragedies and limitations of human existence, we can also have a tremendous sense of fulfillment, significance, and worth, while fully involved in our human and planetary endeavors without reference to some Greater Beyond or Greater Within. This phenomenal world and our human lives are sacred within themselves and have so much intrinsic beauty, goodness, and challenge that we don't feel the need or willfully reject claims of any transcendent source of value. Transcenders require ultimate meaning, nontranscenders are satisfied with intrinsic meanings, and thus each will ask different kinds of questions about life and will be attracted to different types of answers.

# SEEKERS OUT OF DEFICIENCY AND SEEKERS OUT OF FULLNESS

Just as the pain of physical illness can impose upon us a somber view of the world, so can psychological depression paralyze us with the experience that not only we but all human existence is hopeless. If we feel lost and lonely, the world may seem a lost and lonely place.

We tend to paint our picture of the world with the colors of our physical and psychological health or deficiencies. Severe deprivation of basic needs can produce both emotional desperation and cognitive distortion. If we do not experience everyday meaning in our lives through meeting our basic human needs, we can be too hungry for "higher" meanings to fill our emotional emptiness and thus be vulnerable to many a clever charlatan, self-deluded group, and heartwarming, soul-satisfying, ego-inflating but fantasy world view. Most of us have certain unmet needs. This doesn't necessarily mean that we must postpone our quest, but it does mean that we should be acutely aware that major deficiencies in our psychological functioning can contaminate our objectivity by laying desperate demands on reality rather than letting reality speak for itself. Instead of being an accurate reporter of the facts, we may consciously or unconsciously be tempted to falsify the truth by rewriting the story to meet our urgent unmet needs. If we are too needy, we can be too greedy for almost any psychologically satisfying "truths" and be too anxious to find almost any quick and facile answers to the basic questions of life. Without a certain detachment, we diminish our psychological freedom and impair our reality judgment.

Maslow's psychological theory that we can be motivated out of deficiency or out of abundance can be applied to truth seekers. Most of the time we are deficiency motivated, i.e., we experience some dissatisfaction and tension until our unmet needs are met. With abundance motivation, we are not driven to find answers to the basic questions for our physical and psychological survival but rather are attracted to truth by love. Our goal is not to cope with life but to grow by exploring the universe. The spirit is that of delight, not desperation. The feelings are zestful, not fearful; our behavior is mostly spontaneous, not rigidly predictable. Our cup is running over; we seek truth not only for our personal pleasure but also to share with others. Awe and wonder ignite our inquiring spirits. Seeking out of our abundance, we don't have to be so needy, so tense, so grasping; we can be more playful, flowing, and not take ourselves so seriously. Truth is more a beauty to behold than a need to fulfill, having more to do with curiosity and celebration of reality and less to do with the survival and security of our personal selves.

# Optimists and Pessimists

Some of us seem to be almost unflappable optimists, others incorrigible pessimists. Whether by biological endowment, parenting, or childhood experiences, some of us early on develop a temperament that naturally inclines us to be cheerful, full of positive expectations, and seeing the bright side of life, while others of us are gloomy, expect the worst, and notice only the downside. Because of our positive or negative expectations, we tend to put an up or down spin on our interpretations of phenomena. As a self-fulfilling prophecy, we may actually create the events we so optimistically or pessimistically anticipated. We optimists have a certain faith that events will turn out well, and this can energize us to great accomplishments, while we pessimists may avoid new commitments to avoid repeating past disappointments. Both optimists and pessimists tend to ignore or resist evidence challenging their temperamental expectations.

I differentiate between reflective and sentimental optimists. The former have observed and experienced some years of adult life and with some critical skills and objectivity have reflected on the human condition. Their optimism is based not only on a positive temperament but on at least a beginning understanding of phenomena and some winnowed wisdom. Sentimental optimists may walk around with a glorious glow, but it is based not on observation and critical reflection of the actual world but rather is driven by internal upbeat feelings. They whistle in the dark, regardless of the actual realities. Their motto is always the same: "Everything always turns out for the best." Also I distinguish between authentic optimists, whose positive expectations and demeanor are not mere masks for their thorough but unconscious pessimism, and pseudo-optimists whose cheery, often unctuous declarations are a massive defense mechanism, of which they are unaware. Their optimism hides a profound sense of hopelessness, fear of the unknown, and the pain of past disappointments. Below conscious awareness is a deeply hidden, thoroughly convinced pessimist. However, at occasional unguarded moments, sometimes only in the presence of a skilled psychotherapist, the darkness will come to light. If we sometimes happen to rub pseudo-optimists the wrong way, a shocking burst of hostility can suddenly break out in the open, revealing their unconscious but bitter resentment of deeply experiencing the world as a doomed abode.

A distinction can also be made between the anguished and the accepting pessimist. The former looks at the wretched world with a heavy heart. We see all the misery around us and feel agony, because a part of us still yearns for a better world. We are drawn to hope, but our fundamental conviction and deepest feeling is despair that events can substantially improve. With a pervasive angst, we are still putting idealistic demands on reality, still seeking salvation. The accepting pessimist is not tormented by life's limitations. If we see the world as through dark glasses, it is because the world is in fact a dark place. Though we could conjure up all kinds of ideals of how the world should be, we accept the world that we experience as adequate enough to live a tolerable, perhaps even a quite enjoyable and meaningful life. Emotionally and intellectually we accept what life has to offer and do what is realistically possible to ameliorate our personal situation and humankind's welfare.

# INQUISITIVE AND INVESTIGATIVE

Most of our ancestors heard only one story about what life is all about. It probably was a religious story. So embedded in their psyche and daily routine, it never occurred to most of them to challenge that story. Besides, it may have been forbidden to question and even a sin to doubt. Few were literate, or had the leisure, resources, and support community to nurture honest and competent inquiry. In modern society, with worldwide travel and global communication networks, we are confronted with competing religions, diverse cultures, conflicting values, and assorted mega-stories. Some of us feel a need for consistency of beliefs in our daily lives, and so we quite quickly sort out the stories that have caught our attention and then with little inquiry choose one to guide us. But the more inquiring among us want to take a deeper look, and so we ask, "Is this really a true story?" and perhaps even further, "What is the ultimate story?" This more inquiring spirit can be expressed in the inquisitive or investigative modes.

Investigatives are much like the inquisitives but we take inquiry to another level. We ask many of the same questions but are more seriously committed to getting at the bottom of things. With an even greater passion for truth, investigatives can better tolerate the long, disciplined process required to advance knowledge of the very foundations of the realities under study. Inquisitives devote genuine but limited efforts and are less inclined to tough out the frustrations of extended, systematic inquiry and are more keen on quicker, bottom-line answers. Investigatives are more invested and willing to sacrifice time, comfort, and pleasure to obtain the necessary education and training to become more competent truth seekers. While inquisitives are authentic truth seekers asking and seeking answers to basic questions of reality and not mere dabblers, the personal sacrifices and disciplined inquiry usually required to research fundamental answers is beyond our depth of commitment.

# DESTINY SEEKERS
# AND DESTINY MAKERS

Destiny seekers believe that the universe and human nature has a pre-determined master plan and purpose dictated by God or inherent in nature itself. Our human calling is to conform ourselves to this fixed destiny. Destiny makers, taking clues from the interplay of chance and necessity in quantum mechanics, molecular genetics, and evolutionary biology, believe that the destiny of human nature and other life forms is partly open, not the predictable result of a Newtonian lockstep determinism. Not only necessity but also randomness rules nature and, whether by purely natural processes or divine intention, humans as a species and as individuals can to a certain extent create their own destiny. For destiny seekers, the book is already written; we only live out the pages. For destiny makers, we have an active, even if only a partial, possibility of writing our own life script. With genetic engineering and other biological interventions, we have the unprecedented power to modify human nature along with other life forms, thus opening up our destinies to new possibilities. Our future is not fixed but fluid. For destiny seekers, the claimed creative powers of the destiny makers are pretentious. More realistically, they say, the purpose and significance of our lives is to harmonize ourselves to God's awesome power or nature's pervasive lawfulness. For destiny makers, our calling is to respond to the grace of God or nature, which has bestowed us with intelligence and a moral sense, and to actively mold human nature and other biological species to even greater potential. We live not in a completely predefined but a rather open field. Our destiny, whether a golden or dark age, will be partly the result of chance and necessity, partly our own making.

# THINKERS AND FEELERS

All of us in most situations combine thinking and feeling in judging what is true, but like right- or left-handedness, it's natural for one of the functions to be dominant. The mode of thinking we are referring to here is rational analysis that seeks logical consistency based on objective criteria, while feeling evaluates reality on what we subjectively experience as true or false based on the logic of our emotions. We who are feelers trust more and follow our hearts, seeking out what has emotional significance. We who are thinkers trust more our heads and follow our conceptual understanding, seeking out objective knowledge. When we are in our thinking function, we may tend to prefer general principles rather than what has primarily individual impact and what may be universally true rather than only personally meaningful. Usually, feelers are more interested in warm personal relationships than cold conceptual connections. Religious seekers as thinkers value rational proofs for the existence of God, while feelers find God in their hearts. Thinkers may seek to understand the nature of the universe, while feelers may seek emotional bonding and belonging to the universe. The criteria for truth with thinkers is logical or illogical and objective cause and effect, while for feelers the criteria is like or dislike and what is personally experienced as real or unreal, good or bad. The route to truth for thinkers is their heads, for feelers their hearts. For head seekers, what can anyone know who cannot think? For heart seekers, what can anyone understand who cannot feel?[6]

Thinkers and feelers need each other, to caution each other about their possible excesses. In seeking answers to basic questions of existence, cerebrals can so preoccupy themselves with abstract concepts that their sterile search becomes irrelevant to human needs, while feelers may be so intent on emotionally appealing beliefs and attractive teachers that their rational, critical powers lie dormant before even the most glaring factual and cognitive contradictions. An extreme among feelers is a sentimentality which ascribes qualities to phenomena far beyond the objective facts. For example, we may remain loyal to no longer valid intellectual, cultural, ethnic, and religious beliefs because they provide warm community bonding, comfort, and security. Thus we can become pietists, sentimentally devoted to uncritically perpetuating traditions rather than seeking truth. Head seekers in the extreme can be insensitive, even oblivious, to the cruel consequences of their ideas on the feelings of others, while heart seekers, abhorring negative feelings and interpersonal conflicts, can strive for harmony with and among others at the price of logical consistency and factual data. While feelers, with their sometimes exquisite human sensitivities, tend to be peacemakers, thinkers, with their critical spirits, can be troublemakers. Within ourselves, the less dominant function can not only correct but also complement the more dominant, resulting in a more complete person who asks and seeks answers to basic questions of human existence. Competent thinking can provide more objectivity and perhaps more daring, while personal feelings can assure more meaningful truth seeking and perhaps more compassion. Painful and confusing conflicts can emerge between our thinking and feeling functions in judging reality, but this powerful psychic dynamic can also propel us to even more productive inquiries.

# VISIONARIES AND REALISTS

Plenty of us feel a need for a larger view of the world and ourselves than the mundane demands of our everyday lives. Whether experienced as vague unfulfillment from the unconscious or articulated anguish, we seek a more comprehensive vision to lift us up toward higher ideals and more meaningful lives. Some people call us dreamers, but in our vision quest we see far greater possibilities than conventional expectations. For those of us who are realists, we prefer empirical actualities rather than idealistic possibilities, specific attainable goals rather than imaginary hope. Great and glorious visions may make us feel special and lift us up above the ordinary, but down-to-earth practicality and perspiration benefit humanity more than pie-in-the-sky inspiration. We realists don't like to be fooled, don't want to waste time, and thus demand concrete proof. But we visionaries respond that just because something hasn't yet been proven doesn't mean it isn't real. Realists can be so trapped in their narrow world of precise facts and operational definitions that they are rendered incapable of envisioning any other than the dominant paradigm. Idealists can be so beguiled by their fantastic interpretations that they are totally resistant to examining disconfirming data. But visionaries can be dreamers who are thoroughly grounded in meeting their basic human needs while perceptively envisioning new horizons for humanity and the world, rather than the dreamy who are ungrounded, indulging in desperate magical thinking, and realists can be imaginative and innovative, but their point of departure is the established and empirical, not the visionary and idealist. Some scientists, artists, entrepreneurs, politicians, and religious leaders, among others, can combine the realistic and visionary, resulting in a creative blend of what is and what might be. In his famous speech "I Have a Dream," Martin Luther King was a visionary on several levels. His master vision was the Fatherhood of God and the brotherhood of man, his daily vision was racial equality and economic fairness, and his spiritual vision included nonviolence eclipsing our violent instincts. But he was not only a dreamer, he was also a doer. Street-smart, no-nonsense realism was at the heart of his tactics for change. Like perhaps many a visionary, he never entered the Kingdom, but he showed us the way.

# OPEN-MINDED
# AND CLOSED-MINDED

Here is a partial description of some contrasts between open and closed minds, which in actual humans range along a continuum of complex and interrelated characteristics.

| *An Open Mind* | *A Closed Mind* |
| --- | --- |
| Fluid, flowing, provisionally receptive to the reality in question. Flexible. | Fearful, fixed, attacking or avoiding the reality in question. Rigid. |
| Allowing, accommodating, accepting. | Controlling, constricting, rejecting. |
| Democratic, seeks dialogue, invitational. | Dictatorial, dogmatic, punishing. |
| Self-confident, welcoming, evidence-oriented. | Ego-defensive, threatened, self-centered. |
| Subtle, comfortable with ambiguity. Entertains alternate sources, methods and explanations. | Simplistic, tolerates only black and white categories. Limits inquiry to only one source, method, and explanation. |

As infants, all of us were open minded—and empty-headed. All prepped by nature to be programmed, our parents, family, tribe and cultural representatives dedicated themselves to filling up our heads. Our usually well-meaning and loving parents nurtured us with good food and safe shelter along with what we assumed was good truth and secure expectations. Totally dependent and trusting, we assimilated their subjective view of the world as the one and only objective world view. We didn't know any better. What is real and unreal, good and bad, what we should do and not do, feel and not feel—all this was absorbed into our impressionable little psyches. Many of these early imprints, intimately associated with our parents' love and warmth, became so instinctive that we can't imagine shaking them off, even if we want to. By early adulthood, most of us have been indoctrinated with an assortment of sense and nonsense. Childlike innocence carried into adulthood is perilous when we need to critically examine our early beliefs in light of adult realities, when we are confronted with new and conflicting beliefs, and when we are exposed to appealing but deluded or sociopathic "truth" purveyors. Adults with childlike trust and innocence can be easily duped—cult bait and ready prey for predators so cunning in exploiting our vulnerabilities. Open mindedness is not an unqualified virtue but rather requires emotional maturity, healthy skepticism, critical skills, and the ability to learn from experience.

A closed mind is not always a vice; it's a necessity. In turbulent times we don't necessarily need any more disturbing truths. Rather, our most urgent need may be raw physical and psychological survival. To avoid being overwhelmed, we may need to close down the onrush of incoming stimuli to maintain control of our lives. Also, the honest asking of basic questions is sometimes best postponed, because the consequences for our personal, family, and career lives are potentially too destructive. Because of the complexities of human life and our unique ability to lie to ourselves, no simple formula exists indicating when we should be more open- or closed-minded. Sometimes, it's a question of readiness. At a certain stage in our growing up, we may have sufficiently developed intellectually and emotionally to honestly and competently ask and seek answers to some of the basic questions. Also, the time may be ripe when at last we have the resources and a nurturing climate of inquiry to devote ourselves more fully to truth seeking. Being creatures of habit, sometimes only a crisis will open us up. In any case, let's remember that each of us was once an innocent little child, powerfully scripted by our own particular parents and cultures. As adults, let's be open to and tolerant of each other's beliefs and compassionate with each other as believers.

# SELF-RELIANT
# AND OVER-DEPENDENT

Self-reliant means we have a self to rely on. Regardless of whether the self is conceived of as an entity or process, it means we experience sufficient self-identity and self-confidence to question our own and other's reality stories as well as enough intellectual skill, emotional competence, and experience to at least provisionally trust our methods of inquiry. If we are especially ambitious truth seekers and are confronted by daunting challenges, we may also need exceptional courage and discipline. The bottom line for those of us who are self-reliant truth seekers is that, as far as our abilities can take us and our situation allows, we choose to think and feel for ourselves rather than letting others think and feel for us. Though we may seek truth for ourselves, we can't seek truth by ourselves. Complete independence from others is impossible. No matter how original we may be, all of us, at least to a certain extent, build on the work of others. However, some of us love and need to be alone most of the time; solitude is our most productive environment. Others of us are energized and do our most creative work in close collaboration with others, yet in the end we rely on our own judgment of reality. Self-reliance can welcome cooperation with others while avoiding clinging dependence; we can stand on our own feet while walking a path with others.

Overdependence can take many forms. For example, we can become truth junkies, addicted to questioning everything and obsessed with doubt and a drive for certainty—all in quest of an inordinate need for safety and security. God, philosophy, and science can all be abused in our desperate craving to escape the pain of our personal lives. Gurus, enlightened masters, and inspired teachers, laced with hidden agendas, can become our quick fix, as we abandon ourselves to their infallible guidance for our perhaps love-starved and aimless lives. Another way to become a clone is to be a groupie, giving over ourselves to the group, always hanging out with the group, because we haven't yet developed a life and mind of our own. In large organizations, group-think becomes the party line, perceived as the dependable way to meet our pressing needs for acceptance and belonging. Plenty of us have a longing to surrender ourselves to something greater, not only to our Creator in authentic religion, but also to powerful human authority. In the extreme, we experience a need for self-abasement, feeling more virtuous in submitting ourselves with blind obedience, covering our eyes, bowing our heads, kneeling before and kissing the ring of authority. If we are overdependent on the approval of others, it's safer being a follower than a leader, less risky paying homage to consensus authorities than holding out for a faith in ourselves. If we have a strong sense of self, we can be open to an honest study of the great traditions without losing ourselves. But for those of us who choose to be self-reliant truth seekers, we don't uncritically accept prepackaged answers to our individual questions. A Zen saying warns us, "Don't take other people's medicine." French novelist Marcel Proust says it this way.

> We do not receive wisdom, we must discover it for ourselves, after a journey through the wilderness, which no one else can make for us, which no one can spare us, for our wisdom is the point of view from which we come at last to regard the world.

# INTEGRATED AND ALIENATED

To be an integrated rather than an alienated person is to be fundamentally at peace rather than at war with ourselves and the world. However, alienation is not only an appropriate response to many adverse situations, it can also fuel our truth seeking inquiries. For example, if we are poor and oppressed by a power elite, not only might we become warriors for ourselves and our underclass, we might also become wise in not merely aiming to imitate the privileged but instead seek a deeper understanding of true human wealth and poverty—thus providing a beacon for both personal and social transformation.

One of the ways we become alienated from ourselves is when we have such massive defenses against feeling and are so unconnected with our inner life that we experience ourselves as hollow, strangers to our own souls. At this stunted stage of development, our personal inquiries may be quite mechanical, not yet in touch with our fluid depths, refined sensitivities, and the truths they can reveal to us. Another form of self-alienation is the internalized belief that unless we become a certain idealized, perfect person, we are a failure. We reject our actual selves because we have not yet achieved an imaginary ideal self. In our futile endeavor to become a perfect person, we may also attempt to seek perfect truth and wisdom not only beyond our personal abilities but beyond human capacities.

Some of us are *refugees*, fleeing from our origins which now seem so alien. We might feel that we were born to the wrong parents, raised in the wrong family, neighborhood, ethnic group, race, socio-economic class, nationality, or religion. Reacting, rebelling, we may with anger and shame reject even the most beautiful realities of our past and seek almost any truth that distances and disidentifies us from our origins. Some of us become lost souls. Some of us eventually realize that we need to lose ourselves in order to find ourselves, that we need to pass through the dark night of the soul, full of confusion and mistakes. Thus, we can begin a fresh assessment of who we are and what the world is all about. Some of us are *wounded spirits*: duped innocents, bruised idealists, and disillusioned intellectuals. As soon as we are able, we need to make peace with our past. We need to forgive the people and institutions that have wronged us, or they will continue to have power over us, and we need to forgive ourselves, or we will never be free of the pain. Liberated, we can then, much stronger and wiser, renew our inquiries.

Plenty of us are alienated from ourselves and the world by our narcissism. Spoiled by parents, grandparents, or significant others, we carry into adult life the feeling that we are so precious that the world revolves around us. We can only see things from our point of view. Truth is important only in reference to ourselves. We don't have to play by others' or reality's rules. Feeling so special, we may assume that we are entitled to know the answers to the big questions of life. Feeling so precious, we may resent that the world is imperfect and be stunned by the possibility of our own mortality. Thus, the driving but unconscious force behind our truth seeking may be our wish for immortality and eternal paradise. Typically, we are easily hurt, angry, or even enraged by criticism—more ego- than truth-centered. Some of us feel so remarkable that we want to be the genius or holy one above others, the enlightened master.

In a perfect world we would all be perfectly integrated persons. However, in the actual world, often it is only through the ordeal of resolving conflicts in our psyches and with our surroundings that we can develop the wisdom and knowledge to more compassionately and realistically embrace, not distance ourselves from, the world in its beauty and limitations.

# ROMANTIC AND CIRCUMSPECT

For romantics, truth seeking can be quite a ride! No ordinary bus seat for us. Instead, we hop on our Harleys and roar out, responding to the call of the open road—not only observing life but living it! Embracing all of human existence, especially the highs and the lows, is our reality school. Off to India seeking seers and saints, off to Paris plumbing the existential depths, crazed marathon months in the laboratory feverishly testing out our unconventional hypotheses, intimately exploring forbidden feelings and taboo relationships—we are risk takers, not overly concerned with possible downside consequences. Some people say we are thrill seekers and adrenaline junkies, and it is true that we like living on the edge, but only by taking ourselves to extremes can we discover the truth of who we really are, what we actually can be, and what life is all about. Our way of inquiry favors imagination and spontaneity over rational intellect and rigid structure. Truth seeking can be fun and exciting, and with sufficient discipline, we can brave the inevitable dangers and tough out the downtimes. Our tendencies, or perhaps our temptations, include the radical and revolutionary, the esoteric and exotic. Sometimes, like a butterfly, we are excited by and flutter about every new flower, and sometimes, in our dramatic gestures and colorful speech, we like to make an impression, often enchanting and entertaining.

As circumspect truth seekers, we are not instinctively attracted to dramatic extremes. We take risks, but usually only calculated risks, preferring to look before we leap. Life has no guarantees, but it seems only natural to estimate in advance the potential benefits and possible dangers of major truth seeking endeavors. Our watchwords are prudence, practicality and foresight. What romantics call spontaneity, we see more as impulsivity, sometimes even hysteria carried away by transient moods. Their heroic quests sometimes have a quixotic and self-conscious theatrical ring. But history gives ample examples of exceptional romantics who, by sheer audacity and sufficient unreasonableness, discovered what the more judicious said didn't exist or couldn't be found. Man does not live by prudence alone. At times we all need a healthy dose of romantic madness. Romantics can reveal to us the human spirit of adventure, inspire us to take some necessary risks, and give us permission to make some big mistakes. But we circumspect seekers need not be boring, even though by temperament and perhaps also by training we prefer methodical steps to mighty leaps and find no special virtue in the extreme swings between the heroic and tragic. Though in our truth seeking we might experience ecstasy, we do not consciously seek it. We are more long-distance runners than spectacular sprinters, and without feeling a need for flair and self-embellishment, our enthusiasm for discovery may be more firmly rooted and dependable than the romantics. Romanticism may be appropriate in various degrees to many stages of our lives, but it is often assumed that it belongs especially to our youth when we are still free of major responsibilities and have plenty of time to recover from our mistakes. However, romanticism may also be especially suitable toward the end of our lives when, having fulfilled most of our responsibilities, we can more fully take delight in our spirit of adventure and discovery.

# RELIGIOUS SEEKERS
# AND SPIRITUAL SEEKERS

Many of those we interviewed repeatedly stated, "I am spiritual, not religious." What's the difference? Most often we were told that religion means real estate, a rigid institution, oppressive authority, absolute dogmas, archaic moral demands, threats of hell and claims of being the exclusive ticket to paradise. With its prepackaged answers to the questions of life, it ignores our individual characteristics and real-life complexities, and thus no longer speaks to our spirits and is an obstacle to our spirituality. But neither theologians, nor our interviewees, nor almost anyone else shares a common, unambiguous definition of "spiritual," perhaps because it is fundamentally an experience, not a concept. However, many people seem to agree that the spiritual quest reflects a yearning for the "sacred," though this adds another term lacking a precise and universally accepted definition. For those of us who are spiritual seekers but not religious, spirituality is an innate, universal human phenomenon, not the exclusive possession of organized religion or traditionally religious persons.[7]

But for those of us who view ourselves as both religious and spiritual, we reply that our religious organizations are human, and thus, of course, imperfect and capable of making big mistakes. However, the very reason many of us have sought out and remain members of a formal religion is because its institutional structure, through the test of time, provides the most dependable means to the inner experience of the holy, as well as rites, rituals, and even real estate to express our sense of awe, wonder, mystery, and the sacredness and unity of all being. Our carefully sifted doctrines, formally trained and ordained clergy, and our moral demands are all intended to guide and develop our spiritual life. Some religions venerate and even canonize saints as models of exceptional spirituality for us to emulate. Religion is mankind's most reliable response to the longing expressed by St. Augustine: "God, Thou has made us for Thyself, and our hearts are restless until they rest in Thee."

However, for many of us who are spiritual seekers, religion is an unnecessary burden, with its heavy yoke of commandments, proscriptions, and regulations. Not only do we feel unsafe surrendering ourselves to fallible institutional authority, we don't believe that spiritual truth is limited to religion. We need the freedom to explore and test out for ourselves a variety of spiritual paths. The spiritual life justifies itself for those of us who live it; it doesn't need to be validated by outside authorities. We don't want to be made to feel guilty or be condemned because we choose to investigate spiritual alternatives. For those of us who are women, the needs of our soul can do without the male dominance so characteristic of traditional religions. However, individualistic spiritual seeking is not without its potential traps. Much as any religious truth seeker, we can succumb to self-righteousness, self-deception, and even spiritual snobbery. Also, we can become mere dabblers, superficially skimming the cream off a potpourri of traditions, resulting in a mishmash of self-serving spiritual goodies. We may avoid institutional religions because they often insist that authentic spirituality includes a major commitment, self-discipline, demanding practices, and some mighty inconvenient beliefs. All these religious demands, rules, regulations, rites, rituals, spiritual institutes, retreat centers, and even doctorates in spirituality, at least ideally, are not designed to suppress our spirits but to safeguard us from our narcissism and errors as well as nurture us toward a more soundly based spirituality. Whether religious seekers or spiritual seekers, our goal is to sanctify our individual, family, and community lives. Whatever name each of us assigns to the unseen but deeply experienced realm of the sacred, we all seek communion with that same source. We know that if we lose our inner spiritual core, we have lost the essence of ourselves.

◆ ◆ ◆ ◆ ◆

In contrast to this chapter, which looked inward to understand our personal psychology and how it impacts our truth seeking, the next chapter looks outward to alternative world views and the hope that each might provide us. First, I sketch the scientific world view, focusing on cosmology, physics, and biology. Then, I present a naturalistic and evolutionary philosophy and spirituality. Finally, I outline the world views of five living religions and the hope that each offers us.

# 5

## *World Views: What Can We Hope For?*

### THE SCIENTIFIC WORLD VIEW: INTRODUCTION TO THE STORY THUS FAR TOLD

We will present a brief nontechnical introduction to certain prominent scientific views of the world, limiting ourselves to perspectives from cosmology, physics, and biology. Each of these disciplines experienced its own golden age of discovery in the twentieth century, which in turn has revolutionized our concept of the physical universe and biological life. Also, let us not forget the revolutionizing impact of science-based technology. For example, which provides the more extraordinary view of the world: the Hubble space telescope or the

scanning electron microscope? For the very first time in the twentieth century, we humans and our machines ventured out beyond our
home planet into the immensity of the cosmos, and our brain
research with positron-emission tomography (PET) began peeking
into the mysteries of human consciousness.

# COSMOLOGY

## THE UNFOLDING UNIVERSE

It seems almost unbelievable that, as late as the beginning of the
twentieth century, astronomers had insufficient evidence to determine whether or not any galaxies existed beyond our Milky Way
galaxy. Back in the eighteenth century, astronomers observed faint,
fuzzy objects which, unlike comets, did not change in position or
appearance, but they were unable to provide an explanation for this
mysterious phenomenon. In 1755 Kant suggested that these "nebulae" might be island universes, i.e., independent systems of stars similar to but far beyond our own galaxy. Speculation continued into
the first two decades of the twentieth century. Even the sharper
images of the cloudy nebulae seen through improved observational
technology yielded not proof but only hotter debate as to their possible extragalactic location. Enter Edwin Hubble, Missouri-born
former Rhodes scholar freshly discharged from the Army in 1919
where he had been a major with the famed 86th Black Hawk division. With a prewar Ph.D. in astronomy from the University of
Chicago, he rushed from his military post to work at the Mt. Wilson
Observatory in Pasadena, California, with its new 100-inch reflecting telescope, at that time the largest in the world. By 1925 he provided the proof for the existence of other galaxies, and by the end
of the decade he also demonstrated that the universe is not static but
expanding, thus laying the cornerstone for the Big Bang theory. As
with Copernicus, the eventual implications of his discoveries revolutionized our world view.

Hubble was able to settle the debate over whether the nebulae were part of our Milky Way or self-contained galaxies beyond, because he was the first to provide measurable proof. Building on the work of predecessors, including the Cepheid variables research of the American astronomer Henrietta Leavitt, and aided by the unexcelled capabilities of the giant Mt. Wilson telescope and his own exceptional observing talents, Hubble obtained convincing measurements proving that the Andromeda Nebula (M31) was a self-contained galaxy located far beyond our own Milky Way. During the subsequent years of his galactic research, he further proved to astronomers and the public that our galaxy is not unique but rather is only one of millions of galaxies much like our own, each containing billions of stars—that we live in an unimaginably immense and awesome cosmos.

Within only five years of the shocking revelation that our galaxy is not the entire universe, Hubble delivered another jolt: the universe is expanding. Wait a minute! Surely, he knew that almost the entire scientific community, including Einstein, believed that the universe is static, neither expanding nor contracting. Following the tradition of Newton, the consensus belief was that the universe was unchanging in size and basic structure. Hubble's discovery was not without precedent. Back in 1914, Vesto M. Slipher of Harvard's Lowell Observatory in Arizona was surprised to discover that the spectral lines of most of the nebulae he observed showed significant redshifting to longer wavelengths, an indication that they are moving away from Earth at high velocities. Also, Hubble's discovery was not without a gifted collaborator—Milton Humason, who brought skills and a temperament that complemented the dynamic and increasingly celebrated Hubble. Working together using the Mt. Wilson telescope, they studied the redshift spectra of many galaxies and estimated their distances and speed moving away from us. The result was Hubble's Law, which states that the recession velocities of distant galaxies are directly proportional to their distances from our galaxy. Otherwise stated, galaxies recede from one another, and the most distant galaxies recede at the greatest rate. Consequently, the universe is expanding, not static, and thus open to the interpretation that at some time in the past it must have been compressed into an extremely small space.

Hubble's Law does not mean that we are at the center of an expanding universe. There is no center. The superclusters of galaxies do not expand into empty space. Rather, space itself expands. Space stretches out between the galactic clusters rather than the galactic clusters moving through space. In a sense, space is elastic. Observers in any supercluster would experience themselves at the center of the universe, as all the other superclusters would appear to be flying away from them. One of the popular images of the expanding universe is the rising of a loaf of raisin bread. Each raisin represents a galaxy supercluster, and the bread is space. As the bread dough rises through the action of the yeast and baking, it expands in all three directions, carrying the raisins to greater and greater distances from each other. The raisins (superclusters) do not move through the rising bread (space). Rather, the expanding bread carries along the raisins, stretching out the distances between them. Thus the superclusters aren't moving in relation to the universe but instead are being pulled away from each other in all directions by the swelling space.

A consequence of the finite speed of light is that when telescopes see out in space, they also look back in time. This is because it takes time for light to travel across the vast distances of the galaxies to reach us. The lighted image that the telescope receives is not of the object as it is now, but as it was when the light was emitted. Thus, the astronomer searching the heavens in the evening skies actually sees the cosmos as it was in the past, not as it is now. The most distant objects require the longest time for the light to reach us and thus take our observations the farthest back in time, to when the universe was much younger and smaller. Hubble was the first to estimate the expansion rate of the universe, which became known as the Hubble Constant. He not only described the expansion of the cosmos, but with Hubble's Law also devised a means to calculate its age —monumental discoveries.

## COSMIC ORIGINS AND EVOLUTION

The current scientific consensus is that some 12 to 15 billion years ago, originating from a single infinitesimal point (technically, an infinitely dense singularity), an enormous explosion of unimaginable violence created space-time, matter, and motion. At this primordial beginning of the universe, the first instant was essentially of infinite density, energy, and temperature. As best as can be extrapolated from theoretical and experimental physics, during the first infinitesimal fraction of a second after the big bang (before $10^{-43}$ seconds), all the physical forces (gravity, strong nuclear, weak nuclear, and electromagnetism) were unified in one force. This is considered to be the era of "quantum gravity," a theory for which has yet to be developed. The radius of the universe was incredibly tiny, less than $10^{-50}$ centimeter. At $10^{-43}$ seconds, the gravitational force separated from the other forces, and the universe expanded to $10^{-33}$ centimeter. Then, according to a widely accepted theory developed in the early 1980s, at between $10^{-35}$ and $10^{-33}$ seconds the universe underwent a sudden spasm of exponential inflation, rapidly ballooning out in all directions to billions of times its original tiny size, expanding to about the size of a beach ball. According to grand unified theories of elementary particles, the strong nuclear force separated from the weak nuclear and electromagnetic forces during the exponential inflationary event. The cosmos was now an intensely hot primeval soup of quarks, gluons, and leptons. At almost one microsecond ($10^{-6}$ seconds) after the big bang, the temperature of the universe dropped to a still extraordinarily hot $10^{13}$ K, and quarks and gluons could combine to make protons and neutrons. By the first three minutes as the universe was expanding, the plasma of particles and radiation cooled enough to allow the formation of simple atomic nuclei.

Three minutes after the big bang, the universe continued to expand and evolve at decreasing but still intensely hot temperatures. After 10,000 years, the mass density of the matter became bigger than the equivalent density of the radiation. At this time, the dark matter was able to start collapsing gravitationally into large-scale structures like galaxies and clusters of galaxies. Three hundred thousand years after the big bang, the electrons and atomic nuclei combined to make transparent hydrogen and helium gas. Behold, an epiphany: because hydrogen and helium gas are clear, the universe changed for the first time from opaque to transparent! The universe was yet only 1/1000 of its present size. A billion years after the big bang, the universe had expanded to one-fifth its present size, and almost all the existing matter consisted of the light elements hydrogen and helium. Giant clouds of hydrogen and helium primordial gas collapsed by gravitational force to form galaxies. Inside these galaxies, dense clouds coalesced into stars. Different types of stars formed with their own structures and characteristics. Today, astronomers can observe an array of stars in the process of birth, life, and death. Entire galaxies evolve, and interact with each other, sometimes colliding and even cannibalizing smaller galaxies.

Some 4.5 billion years past, our solar system evolved from a huge swirling cloud of interstellar gas and dust, which began to collapse in on itself under the force of its own gravity, eventually forming the Sun (a star of average size), Earth, eight other planets, the Moon, other satellites, and a debris of asteroids, meteorites, and comets. While some 99 percent of the mass of the entire universe consists of hydrogen and helium that emerged from the mega-heat of the big bang, the mass of our planet contains less than 0.15 percent of these two light elements, and 99 percent of all living bodies on Earth contain not only hydrogen but the heavier carbon, oxygen, nitrogen, calcium, iron, phosphorus, and sulfur. These heavier elements were forged by a natural alchemy of nuclear fusion in the furnace-hot core of stars. Massive stars end their lives by violent explosions called supernovae, which blow them apart and blast the newly synthesized heavy elements out into space to be incorporated into vast clouds of gas and dust, enriching the chemical composition of the cosmos. The spectacular deaths of these now-forgotten stars in supernova detonations scattered their rich elements throughout local star clouds, where new stars were being born, including our own star (the Sun) and its circling planets, on one of which—a small but extraordinary, wet, blue-green planet—organic chemistry and biological life became possible. We were once part of a star that gave its life in a supernova explosion. These stars were our parents. As scientific cosmologists often like to note, we are literally made of stardust. Perhaps even more amazing is that we are a piece of the universe that has become consciously aware not only of itself but also of its very cosmic origins and evolution.

## EVIDENCE FOR THE BIG BANG

Russian-born George Gamow was almost as well known for the playfulness of his personality as for the brilliance of his physics. He came to the United States in the 1930s with an already established reputation for his work explaining radioactive decay. Once here he focused on the astrophysics of nuclear reactions, especially the mechanism by which the first elements had been synthesized. As a result of research on the atomic bomb during World War II, physicists came to the realization that nuclear fusion provided an explanation for the origin of chemical elements. Gamow proposed the daring theory that the origins of both the heavy and light elements through nucleosynthesis required the extreme conditions of a stupendous explosion in the distant beginnings of an expanding universe. Plenty of physicists didn't take seriously the often joke-cracking Gamow. Fred Hoyle, the eminent English physicist and vigorous advocate for a steady-state universe, attempted to ridicule this rival hypothesis by dubbing it "the Big Bang theory," but the phrase was so catchy that Gamow adopted it, and it soon gained wide popularity. This new theory would eventually become a landmark in cosmology. But contrary to Gamow's original concept that all the elements were created in the big bang, we now know that, except for hydrogen and helium, most of the other elements were created much later inside stars.

By 1948 Gamow and his younger colleagues Ralph Alpher and Robert Herman predicted that the incredibly hot big bang must have produced a high-energy, short-wave radiation permeating the entire cosmos, an afterglow of which should continue to pervade the universe as low-temperature background radiation, detectable by low-power microwave emission. Robert H. Dicke, while working on the development of radar during World War II at the Massachusetts Institute of Technology, invented the microwave radiometer, which was capable of detecting low levels of radiation, though this fact was unknown to Gamow and most theorists. In the early 1960s Dicke, now at Princeton, and P. James E. Peebles began constructing an antenna to measure the residual cosmic background radiation predicted by their theories of the origin of the universe, theories that shared certain features with Gamow's big bang ideas.

Meanwhile, only some twenty-five-miles away in 1964 and 1965, radio astronomers Arno A. Penzias and Robert W. Wilson of Bell Laboratories were trying to figure out how to eliminate the omnipresent microwave background noise from their radio telescope, which was interfering with their research for improving satellite communications at microwave frequencies. They were puzzled to discover that, in every direction they pointed their antenna, they still picked up the same strange, faint background static. More than a little frustrated, they carefully cleaned the inside of the antenna to remove some pigeon droppings, which however only slightly diminished the stubborn signals. Then a colleague introduced them to the theoretical work of Peebles and Dicke at nearby Princeton, which proposed to explain the annoying signals. In a meeting with the Bell researchers, Peebles and Dicke soon realized that the radiation they were looking for had already been found, serendipitously, by Penzias and Wilson. Only after consulting with Peebles and Dicke did Penzias and Wilson realize the theoretical significance of what they had found, yet they deserve credit not only for their empirical discovery but also for their persistence in seeking out an explanation. For a number of crucial theoretical and empirical reasons, the discovery by Penzias and Wilson of the cosmic background radiation as the necessary afterglow from the big bang predicted by Peebles and Dicke and earlier by Gamow and his two colleagues eliminated the steady-state and other competing cosmological theories. Coupled with Hubble's discovery of the expanding universe, the findings provided decisive empirical evidence for the Big Bang theory. In 1978

Penzias and Wilson received the Nobel Prize in physics for their discovery.

Confirmation of the findings of Penzias and Wilson came from the more precise and extensive measurements made in 1990 by the NASA Cosmic Background Explorer Satellite (COBE, pronounced co-bee) in the work of John C. Mather of the Goddard Space Flight Center. In 1992 George F. Smoot and his colleagues at the University of California at Berkeley and the Lawrence Berkeley Laboratory, also using data from COBE, discovered small temperature fluctuations in different parts of the sky, which provided further crucial evidence for the big bang. A third foundation supporting the Big Bang theory comes from the application of particle physics to cosmology, beginning in the 1940s but especially since the early 1980s. The primordial explosion of the big bang resembled a cosmic experiment in high-energy physics and has proven to be the best theoretical model to explain the origins, observed abundances, and proportions of the basic elements in the universe.

## SOME MEGA-UNKNOWNS

The big bang is now the most widely accepted scientific model of the origin of the universe. Though it has answered some enormous questions, some mega-unknowns remain. What if anything existed before the big bang, or is there no "before"? What if anything created the universe in that primordial fireball? Any kind of conscious, intelligent force that pressed the big bang blast button? Did the cosmos originate itself out of a quantum space-time foam, randomly evolving its own physical laws as it unfolded? Or was there a Grand Designer? These mega-unknowns seem well beyond our present human capacities and scientific methods. They appear to be ultimate mysteries eternally beyond our grasp.

Another mega-unknown is whether we live in the sole existing universe or as one among a number of parallel universes? Are we only one among an abundance of sibling universes, cosmic brother and sister worlds beyond in the infinity of space-time? Speculations extrapolated out of inflationary theory allow for a multitude of other universes, but as yet we have no evidence for their actual existence. Also, it is presently unknown if we humans are alone in the cosmos or if advanced extraterrestrials with magnificent or terrifying civilizations exist within or beyond our galaxy. One popular story is that highly evolved aliens recently visited our planet. Searching exhaustively for intelligent life and finding none, they moved on to other galaxies. Would we likewise fail to recognize other forms of life and intelligence? At various sites, including Puerto Rico, California, and Australia, radio telescopes are being used to search for extraterrestrial intelligence (an endeavor also known by its acronym, SETI), but as yet they have apparently not obtained any positive findings. However, scientists are increasingly discovering throughout our galaxy the elements necessary to create life. Interstellar clouds contain the basic building blocks of life, including carbon atoms and other elements that, when combined, can produce an array of organic compounds. Organic substances have been found in meteorites fallen to earth. The search goes on!

What is the ultimate fate of the universe? Scientists don't yet know, but speculations built on incomplete knowledge have traditionally predicted two possible outcomes: the big crunch and the big chill. Presently, our universe continues to expand because of the powerful push given matter by the big bang and the subsequent inflationary surge. But in the big crunch scenario, if the average density of matter exceeds a certain critical value, gravity will eventually halt expansion, the universe will begin contracting, and it will ultimately vanish in a fiery apocalypse. In certain fundamental ways the big crunch plays out backward the evolution of the cosmos originating from the big bang. What before was a process of creation will reverse back, step by step, in a process of destruction. Biological life, planets, stars, galaxies, the heavy and light elements, each in their turn will be obliterated. The universe will continue its backward journey to the opaque, radiation-dominated plasma stage, to an unimaginably hot nuclear state, and then further back to the even more primordial quark, gluon, and lepton soup. The four forces will reunify into one force; matter and energy will be reunited. Finally, the violent, all-powerful implosion will crush all matter and space-time out of existence. Our universe will be no more.

However, if the average density of matter throughout space is below a certain critical value, gravity will be too weak to halt its expansion, and the universe will continue to expand indefinitely, traditionally believed to decelerate at a slower and slower rate. If the universe perpetually expands, it will thin out and, after billions of years, will cool down in a big chill. Most of what we know today as the universe, including ordinary matter, will decay and disappear. Energy will decline, and most physical processes will cease, resulting in a cold, dark, and dismal universe, virtually a vast void, featureless and failing—a great dying but never quite dead.

Cosmologists can't reliably predict the probability of a big crunch or a big chill, because they can't yet determine the density of matter in the universe. It may be embarrassing to admit, but astronomers know less than ten percent of what the universe is made up of—the objects that emit the kind of radiation we can visually observe, such as planets, stars, quasars, and galaxies. We have almost no knowledge of the nature and distribution of the dark matter that constitutes the other ninety to ninety-nine percent. The ultimate fate of the cosmos, whether it collapses or expands indefinitely, depends on the total amount of dark matter and its consequent gravitational effects. However, in 1997 a new ingredient was added to the speculative mix about the ultimate fate of the universe. Observations of the apparent brightness of distant exploding stars (supernovae) provided tentative evidence that the universe is permeated with some unseen matter or energy that produces a uniform antigravitational push, a cosmological constant, which would indicate that the universe will not only expand forever but also at an ever accelerating rate—the big chill.

## COSMIC CREATIVITY AND VIOLENCE

What could we possibly imagine to be more creative than creation itself? Think of it. A vast cosmos of billions of galaxies, each containing billions of stars, burst out from a single infinitesimal point in an incredibly distant past. Over billions of years, a dynamic, ever-changing world evolved out of what to our eyes would appear to be nothing. Everything that exists today was created out of that original instant and the resulting unfolding. It is an awesome, epic story told on an immense canvas—the ultimate work of art. Let us not forget that this same creative principle is also the original source of our own biological, intellectual, cultural, aesthetic, moral, and spiritual creativity. No wonder that some of us who are religious exclaim, "Lord, source of it all!"

But for the human sensibilities of perhaps most of us, the cosmic creativity is accompanied by a dominant, omnipresent megaviolence from the big bang blast, the stupendous collisions and even cannibalism of galaxies, the formation of heavy elements in the explosive supernova deaths, and the violent cataclysms that dominated the early formation of our solar system, reminders of which are the craters scarring the Moon's surface. Our planet has been the target of innumerable comet and asteroid impacts, one of which, some 65 million years past, destroyed the dominant dinosaurs and kick-started the expansion of mammals from which evolved the human species. Whether the ultimate fate of the universe will be a violent big crunch or a perpetual big chill, we need to be aware that today our home planet is vulnerable to crashing debris from outer space that could destroy not only human civilization as we know it but also all our sister and brother forms of life. We may never be able to wrap our three-pound brains around the massive mysteries of the universe, but if we wish to maintain our most truthful assessment of reality, it seems best that we not ignore, rationalize away, or sentimentalize the violence of the cosmos.

## A BRIEF TOUR OF THE UNIVERSE

As we are about to depart on our tour of the universe, let's reflect on our home planet. The circumference of Earth is 24,900 miles (40,100 kilometers). A commercial jet flying at a typical cruising speed of 600 mph at 35,000 feet (11,000 meters) altitude would take 41 hours to fly all the way around Earth. Looking out the window, we would see a deep blue sky. Most of the time we would be flying over water, because 70 percent of the Earth's surface is covered by water.

Our planet spins once on its axis every 24 hours, corresponding to a speed of 1,000 mph (1,600 kph) at the equator. This rotation of Earth determines the length of the day. The Earth takes one year to complete one orbit around the Sun, moving at a speed of 66,500 mph (107,000 kph). The orbit of Earth determines the length of our (solar) year, which is 365 days, 5 hours, 48 minutes, and 46 seconds. Leap years of 366 days every four years prevent the solar and calendar years from becoming out of step. The seasons of the year occur because the Earth's axis is tilted relative to the plane of its orbit around the Sun.

Now, fasten your seatbelt as our spacecraft takes us out into the vast dimensions of the universe. As we travel up through the 8 miles (13 km) of the troposphere (the lower atmosphere), the air pressure decreases, and the air becomes colder as we get farther from the warmth of the ground below. As the air gets thinner, the sky becomes a deeper shade of blue. In the higher levels of the atmosphere (the mesosphere, thermosphere, and ionosphere), the air actually gets warmer, due to direct heating by solar radiation, but the density of the air is so thin in these layers that an exposed person would quickly freeze. The color of the sky gradually changes to a deep purple, then to black, as we approach an altitude of 100 miles (160 km). This altitude is often thought of as the "boundary" of outer space.

The space shuttle commonly orbits Earth at an altitude of about 170 miles (270 km), traveling at a speed of 17,000 mph (27,000 kph), circling once every 90 minutes. From low Earth orbit, the atmosphere, visible near the edge of Earth, looks like a thin bluish shell of gases dotted with clouds. If we were crew members, we would witness a sunrise and a sunset every hour and a half in low Earth orbit. But there is no wind, no smell, no sound, because we are outside the thin blanket of air that envelopes Earth. In orbit, the side facing the Sun will burn, because we are above the ozone layer that protects the Earth from the Sun's sizzling ultraviolet rays. The side of us facing away from the Sun will freeze; without air to evenly distribute heat, anything not heated by direct or reflected sunlight will drop to a temperature just a few degrees above absolute zero (- 459.67° F, -273° C).

About 800 miles up (1,280 km), we encounter the first of two major rings of *ions*—charged particles trapped by Earth's magnetic field. These are the Van Allen belts. Looking toward the north or south poles, we may detect a soft red, blue, or green glow, as captured ions fall into the upper atmosphere, creating the auroras. About 100,000 miles up (160,000 km), traveling in the direction of the Sun, we encounter the *magnetopause*, a shock wave in space. It forms as the charged particles that make up the solar wind, traveling at 250 miles (400 km) per second, collide with Earth's magnetic field. The density of particles here is very low, about five per cubic centimeter.

Our spacecraft now heads toward the Moon. About 240,000 miles (384,000 km) from Earth, it is at a distance only ten times the circumference of our planet. A commercial jet, if it could fly through the vacuum of space, would take seventeen days to get there. The Moon orbits Earth and is our only natural satellite. Whenever we look at the Moon from Earth, we always see the same side, because the Moon turns on its axis in exactly the same time (29.5 days) that it takes to orbit Earth. The Moon is 1/4 the diameter of the Earth, only 2 percent of our planet's volume, and 1/80 of the mass of Earth. Fifty Moons would fit inside the Earth. Because it is far smaller and lighter than the Earth, the Moon has less gravitational force. As a result, on the Moon we would weigh only 1/6 of our body weight on Earth.

The Earth's Moon is an airless, dead world. Its surface is heavily cratered due to asteroid bombardment in the early history of the solar system. Without an atmosphere or volcanic activity, weathering and other forms of erosion have not worn away these ancient lunar craters. The "soil" is a layer of shattered rock fragments ground to powder size by the endless impacts of meteorites and micro-meteorites. Because there is no atmosphere to scatter sunlight, the Moon's sky is black. In direct sunlight, the lunar surface is very hot during the day (230° F, or 110° C) and very cold (-280° F, or -173° C) at night. Water ice has been detected in the permanently shadowed craters at the Moon's poles, probably deposited there by comets that have crashed into the lunar surface over the eons.

Let's continue our tour toward the Sun, which is a star—a huge, roiling furnace of hot gases 880,000 miles (1,400,000 km) in diameter. It is the largest and most massive physical structure in the solar system, containing 99 percent of the mass of the solar system. Over a million Earths would fit inside the Sun. It lies 93 million miles (150 million km) from Earth. A commercial jet would need 17.7 years to fly to the Sun.

The temperature at the surface of the Sun is 10,000° F (5,500° C), but the temperature is over 18 million° F (10 million° C) at the core. The Sun's life-giving heat is produced in its core, where atoms of hydrogen fuse to produce atoms of helium. This process, called nuclear fusion, creates a stupendous amount of energy, and it is the principal source of energy in all stars. It is the same process that produces the explosive energy of the hydrogen bomb. Energy generated in the core of the Sun takes a million years to get to the surface, due to the innumerable atomic collisions and ricochets a packet of energy must endure before it reaches the surface. The sun is extraordinarily bright. Its luminosity is equal to 4 trillion trillion (4,000,000,000,000,000,000,000,000) 100-watt light bulbs. Nuclear reactions in the heart of the Sun convert 5 million tons of matter into energy each second, but the Sun has another 5 billion years to live. Lucky for us, as life on Earth depends on the constant heat and light from the Sun.

Traveling away from the Sun, we can view all nine known planets of the solar system. Planets, unlike stars, do not generate nuclear fusion. Planetary materials exist in four basic forms: rock, ice, liquid, and gas. All the planets have distinct "personalities" reflecting their differences in size, chemical composition, rotation rate, atmosphere, and surface features. Four planets are larger than Earth and four are smaller, so our home is the median planet in size. However, it is the largest rocky planet and the only one with an atmosphere and surface temperatures that permit the existence of life as we know it. Earth, Mercury, Venus, and Mars are small and are called the "inner planets," because they orbit closest to the Sun, and are described as terrestrial, because they include an earthlike, rocky composition. The giant "outer planets" (Jupiter, Saturn, Uranus, and Neptune) are low-density balls of gas, though they may contain small rocky cores. The outermost but tiny planet Pluto is composed of equal amounts of ice and rock. All the planets travel in roughly the same plane and in the same direction around the Sun. The farther a planet is from the Sun, the colder its surface.

Let's take a closer look at the planets. Mercury is the innermost planet in the solar system, 4/10 of Earth's distance from the Sun. It is a little larger than the Moon, also heavily cratered, and has no appreciable atmosphere. Surface temperatures during the day average 800° F (430° C) and during the night −280° F (-170° C). Mercury has an iron core and a magnetic field like Earth. As on our Moon, ice has been detected in the permanently shadowed craters at Mercury's poles. Venus is 7/10 of Earth's distance from the Sun and has almost the same size, mass, and density as our planet, yet it is utterly inhospitable to life as we know it. Whereas our planet has temperatures and other conditions conducive to life, Venus is a dry, searing, high-pressure furnace, whose magnetic field is not strong enough to prevent the solar wind from stripping away the upper atmosphere. Beneath permanent clouds of sulfuric acid and a thick carbon dioxide atmosphere, surface temperatures can rise to 860° F (460° C). Mars is 1.5 times Earth's distance from the Sun. At the rust-colored surface, the thin atmosphere is about 1 percent of the density of

Earth's atmosphere and, much like Venus, is mostly (95 percent) carbon dioxide. The remaining 5 percent consists of 3 percent nitrogen, 1.6 percent argon and some traces of oxygen. There is evidence that Mars had a much denser atmosphere in the past and that water once flowed freely on its surface. Mars has two tiny potato-shaped moons, Phobos and Deimos, which probably are captured asteroids.

Continuing on our tour traveling away from the Sun, we come across the first of the outer planets, Jupiter, five times Earth's distance from the Sun. It is one of the four giant gas planets that dwarf Earth and have no solid surfaces. As the largest planet in the solar system, 88,846 miles (142,984 km) in diameter, it contains more than twice as much mass as all the other planets combined. Some 1,300 Earths could fit into it. Though predominantly hydrogen and helium, Jupiter apparently formed around a rocky protoplanet that has a mass ten times the mass of Earth but accounts for only 4 percent of Jupiter's mass. A hurricane-like storm in the Jovian atmosphere called the Great Red Spot, with wind speeds approaching 250 miles (400 km) an hour, spans a distance twice the diameter of Earth. Jupiter has seventeen known moons and also is attended by two major asteroid groups (called Trojan asteroids) that accompany the planet in orbit.

Saturn is 9.5 times Earth's distance from the Sun. Second in planetary size and mass only to Jupiter, it is best known for its magnificent system of rings. Although it has 95 times the mass of Earth, the overall density of Saturn is so low that it would float in water. Its surface and interior composition are similar to Jupiter. Saturn has eighteen known moons. Only seven are spherical, the others are oblong, suggesting that they are captured asteroids. Uranus is 19 times Earth's distance from the Sun. At 32,000 miles (51,100 km) in diameter, about 63 Earths would fit within it. The outer layers of Uranus are composed mainly of gaseous hydrogen and helium. Twenty-one known moons and a system of rings revolve around this rather placid and almost featureless planet. Neptune is 30 times Earth's distance from the Sun. It is about the same size and physically very similar to Uranus, but with eight moons. The atmosphere of

Neptune is swept by winds moving up to 2,300 feet (700 meters) per second, the fastest discovered on any planet. Pluto is almost 40 times Earth's distance from the Sun. A jet plane would need over 633 years to get there! At 1/3 the size of the Earth's Moon, this diminutive ball of rock and ice is the smallest planet in our solar system. The average surface temperature is a cold -370° F (-225° C). Its one known moon, Charon, is half the diameter of Pluto itself.

Having completed our tour of the nine planets, lets cautiously voyage out among the *vagabonds* of the solar system: the myriad asteroids, meteoroids, and comets that orbit the Sun and are debris left over from the birth of the solar system. Asteroids and meteoroids are pieces of interplanetary rock and metal, while comets contain large amounts of frozen ice. The space debris that falls through Earth's atmosphere as meteors lands on our planet as meteorites.

Most asteroids are concentrated between the orbits of Mars and Jupiter in what is called the *asteroid belt*. The millions of these "belt asteroids" range in size from four millimeters to about 1/4 the diameter of the Moon. The largest asteroid is Ceres, 590 miles (945 km) across. It is essentially a huge rock in space with no atmosphere. Even though they are numerous, the total mass of all the asteroids is only 1/10 the mass of the Moon, and the possibility of our encountering one as we fly through the asteroid belt is virtually zero—space is big! Asteroids also orbit outside the asteroid belt, some entering into the inner regions of the solar system, some crossing Earth's orbit. On March 23, 1989, an asteroid called 1989FC passed within 500,000 miles (800,000 km) of Earth, and on December 9, 1994, asteroid 1994XM1 (about the size of a large truck) passed within 65,000 miles (105,000 km)—a close encounter.

As presently determined, there are two reservoirs of comets. The *Kuiper belt* is made up of comets that lie between 30 and 1,000 times the distance from Earth to the Sun. These bodies of rock and ice are typically only a few miles in diameter, and are too far from the Sun to form the fuzzy coma and tail we normally associate with comets. There may be as many as a billion of these objects in our solar system. Another region of comets is the *Oort cloud*, 30,000 to 100,000 times the Earth-to-Sun distance—almost halfway to the nearest star. These sometime visitors from the far reaches of the solar system consist of a solid nucleus of dust and ice, so they are dubbed "dirty snowballs." They develop tails only when they enter the inner solar system.

The last type of vagabonds are meteoroids, which are rocky debris smaller than asteroids, scattered about the solar system. As some are pulled by gravity into Earth's atmosphere, air friction generates so much heat that their outer layer begins to vaporize. As the meteoroid approaches closer to Earth, leaving behind a fiery trail of dusty gas, it becomes a meteor—what we commonly call a shooting star. Though most meteors completely vaporize in the atmosphere, some hit Earth before totally disintegrating. Debris left on the ground is called a meteorite; it looks like a rock and may contain iron, nickel, and iridium.

Let's now turn our attention to the stars and our Milky Way galaxy. Our solar system has only one star—the Sun. But our galaxy contains at least 500 billion stars, ranging in size from *white dwarfs*, about the size of Earth to *red giants*, several hundred million miles in diameter. Seen from a truly dark location, the sky seems crowded with stars, but the space between them is vast. Travel to even the nearest stars is far beyond the reach of present technology. To express the almost unimaginable astronomical distances, it is convenient to think of such distances in terms of the time it takes light to travel. A beam of light (which travels at the speed of light: 186,300 miles per second; or 300,000 km/sec) could travel seven times around Earth's equator in one second, to the Moon and back in three seconds (a trip that took a week for the astronauts), from Earth to the Sun in eight minutes, and about a day to reach the outer planets of our solar system. A light-year is the distance a beam of light travels in a year, about 6 trillion miles—6,000,000,000,000 miles. Departing from Earth, it would take a beam of light 4.2 light years to reach the nearest star, Proxima Centauri. Otherwise stated, the star nearest our solar system is some 25 trillion miles (40 million km) away. The average distance between stars in our galactic neighborhood is about 6 light-years.

Our Sun and all the stars we see in the sky at night are members of our Milky Way galaxy. We see it as a band of light that crosses the sky on a dark night, but we and the Sun are inside, so our view is from the inside of the galaxy. If we could see our galaxy from afar, it would look like a slowly rotating flat pinwheel with a central hub. The Milky Way galaxy is about 100,000 light-years in diameter and about 2,000 light-years thick. Our solar system lies in a spiral arm about a third of the way from the center to the edge. A jet would take about 100 billion years to travel from one edge to the other, about seven times the age of the universe. For another way to appreciate the immensity of our galaxy, reflect on this: The Sun is orbiting around the center of the galaxy at speeds of 140 miles per second (230 km per second), taking 250 million years for each complete orbit.

Within the galaxy, stars are continually forming and dying. Huge, bloated red giant stars dominate space near the center of the galaxy. They furiously shed hot gases into space; the stars here are almost indistinguishable from the sea of hot plasma that surrounds them. At the center of the galaxy is an enormous *black hole*—a mass of matter so densely compacted that not even light can escape its clenching surface gravity. The galactic black hole contains 2 to 3 million times as much mass as the Sun. It is encircled by an *accretion disk* of swirling hot gas and dust, about the size of our solar system, drawn from nearby stars. Before matter from the accretion disk is pulled into the black hole, it kicks up fountains of radiation that shoot into space and stream away from the poles of the black hole, spraying out like a fire hose thousands of light-years away from the center of the galaxy. A black hole is formed when a very large star dies and collapses under its own weight. It shrinks down into an infinitely dense point called a *singularity*, around which space curves back on itself, and time stands still. Present scientific opinion favors the view that not only our galaxy but almost all large galaxies have huge black holes at their centers.

Until recently, we knew of the nine planets in our solar system but could only speculate as to whether other stars had similar planets. Beginning in 1995, astronomers have been discovering planets orbiting other stars. Some may be terrestrial planets like Earth; those discovered thus far are Jupiter-size or larger, because big planets are easier to detect. There are probably billions of planets in our galaxy. A new era in human exploration may be emerging when we will discover other planets like ours in their own solar systems. Is our planet a common or unique type of planet?

Once or twice in a century, a star in our galaxy explodes as a supernova. The core of a supernova collapses to form a neutron star—a rapidly spinning ball of neutrons about 10 miles (16km) in diameter—or, if the core is massive enough, a black hole. Thousands of neutron stars and black holes are scattered throughout our galaxy.

The space between the stars is not empty. Gas (mostly hydrogen) and dust particles float throughout space, forming the interstellar medium (ISM). For the most part, this gas and dust is spread very thin, just a few particles per cubic meter. But in some places the ISM aggregates into immense clouds called nebulae. Often spanning several light years, stars and planets are born in nebulae. The gases in a nebula often fluoresce in delicate shades of red, blue, and green, due to ultraviolet light from nearby stars.

About two hundred compact families of stars known as globular clusters orbit the Milky Way. Each cluster is spherical in shape and contains several hundred thousand to several million stars. Two small, irregularly shaped companion galaxies, the Magellanic Clouds, orbit the Milky Way, about 180,000 light-years away. The Small Magellanic Cloud contains a few hundred million stars; the Large Magellanic Cloud a few billion. They are to the Milky Way what moons are to planets.

Now, let's travel even farther out into space and visit our inter-galactic neighborhood. Tens of thousands of light-years from our galaxy we find rarefied hydrogen and helium clouds, but intergalac-tic space is mostly a very cold and empty space. Our galaxy is one of several dozen that make up the *Local Group*. Each of these galaxies contains tens of millions to hundreds of billions of stars and proba-bly billions to hundreds of billions of planets, as well as nebulae and other interstellar denizens of our own galaxy.

The nearest big galaxy is the Andromeda galaxy, a spiral over 2 million light-years away. It is the most distant object we can see with the naked eye from Earth. Gravity is pulling Andromeda and the Milky Way toward one another at a speed of 600,000 mph (1 million kph). If we were positioned directly between our galaxy and the Andromeda galaxy, each would look like a faintly luminous, swirl-shaped patch of light, like a snippet of the Milky Way as seen from a dark mountaintop here on Earth. Each would appear to span a patch of sky several times the diameter of the full Moon as seen from Earth. Other, fainter galaxies would appear here and there throughout space, some elliptical in shape, others with irregular shapes. The farthest galaxies we could see with our naked eye would look like faint, fuzzy stars.

Astronomers have learned that most of the matter that makes up our universe is invisible to telescopes. The presence of this so-called *dark matter* can be inferred by the gravitational influence it exerts on stars and galaxies. The dark matter may consist of rogue planets, burned-out stars, isolated black holes, subatomic particles we haven't yet discovered, some exotic form of matter fundamentally different from anything we know of today, or some combination of all these things. We don't yet know what dark matter is, but we do know that it accounts for 90 percent to 99 percent of the mass of the universe.

All of the galaxies in the local group are being pulled in the direction of a huge, invisible mass of matter known as *the Great Attractor*. This could be a huge cluster of galaxies, obscured from our view by intervening dust in the Milky Way, or it could be dark matter.

Astronomers estimate that there are some 50 to 100 billion galaxies in the universe, each containing billions of stars. Traveling out hundreds of millions of light-years, we would realize that galaxies are not uniformly distributed throughout space but form clusters and clusters of clusters ("superclusters"). Astronomers have discovered great voids between "sheets" of galaxy clusters, suggesting that the structure of the universe, on a scale of a billion or so light-years, resembles a block of Swiss cheese! Galaxies in a cluster can collide and combine. Astronomers use the term *galactic cannibalism* when a large galaxy captures and "devours" a smaller one.

The farther we look out into the universe, the farther back we see in time. Thirteen billion light-years out, near the edge of the visible universe, we see the universe as it was 13 billion years ago, when the universe was very young. At these distances, we find perhaps the most distant, most luminous objects in the universe—*quasars*. Even though smaller than our solar system, they generate more energy and are far more luminous than an entire galaxy. Astronomers believe quasars are in fact massive black holes located at the centers of ancient galaxies. Like the black hole at the center of the Milky Way, black holes with billions of times the mass of the Sun devour surrounding stars and pour tremendous amounts of energy into space in the process. It appears that such massive black holes were commonly found in the centers of galaxies when the universe was young.

The universe is expanding. Space is stretching, increasing the distances between galaxy clusters over time. This expansion is the continuation of the "big bang" that created the universe some 12 to 15 billion years ago, but there appears to be an extra repulsive force helping push the expansion along. The nature of this force is unknown. The universe may expand forever, or it may slow down, stop, and contract, eventually collapsing to form a black hole that contains all the matter in the galaxies. Which it will be—continual expansion or a "big crunch"—depends on how much total matter there is in the universe and the strength of the repulsive force that's accelerating the expansion rate. Some cosmologists are now proposing the idea that our universe may be just one infinitesimal part of a "multiverse" in which branching bubbles of space-time contain different physical realities.

Astronomy and astrophysics have discovered such extremes in the cosmos that they are truly beyond the powers of our three-pound brains to imagine. We can pile metaphor on metaphor, analogy on analogy, and we will never be able to experience the immensity of space. But, here are some comparisons to help us imagine the vast distances of space. If the Sun's diameter were one inch, it would be nine feet from Earth. The solar system (out to Pluto's orbit) would be 700 feet across, the nearest star would be 450 miles away, and our galaxy would be 10 million miles across. The Andromeda galaxy (part of our Local Group) would be 300 million miles distant, and the radius of the observable universe would be a trillion miles.

With the billions of galaxies and billions and billions of stars, one might think that the universe is crowded. Not so! Because the distances between these objects are enormous compared to their size, most of the cosmos is empty space. If we found ourselves in some typical locale of the universe, we would be millions of light-years from the nearest source of light. We would be deeply enveloped in an inky blackness, pierced only here and there by the tiniest pinpoints of light, which would be images not of stars but of galaxies that are so far away as to be all but invisible. Our typical cosmic locale would be extraordinarily cold. The average background temperature in outer space is three kelvins, i.e., three Celsius degrees above absolute zero (about-454° F)—the rock bottom temperature for matter. Not only would we find ourselves in darkness as black as black can be and in frigid coldness but also in a bone-dry vacuum. As far as what we might sense, space is basically 99 percent nothing. The density of interstellar gases is so low that it is virtually empty—better than the best vacuum we can create in a lab on Earth. In the typical cosmic locale we would hear nothing, only experience a deafening silence because there is virtually no matter to produce sound waves. We would smell nothing because the concentration of molecules would be too sparse to trigger our olfactory receptors. There would be nothing to touch, nothing to taste.

Is there life out there? Although no life has been discovered beyond Earth, the chemical building blocks of life exist throughout our Milky Way galaxy. Organic molecules have been discovered in interstellar clouds and in some meteorites. Though we may eventually discover little or no life on the other planets of our solar system, there are hundreds of billions of other stars in our galaxy. If only a fraction of those stars have suitable planets, and only a fraction of those planets contain life, then our galaxy could have thousands of life-bearing planets.

Is anybody out there? A small cadre of scientists with limited resources are looking for intelligent life beyond our planet. As of yet they have no positive findings, but absence of evidence is not evidence of absence. If intelligent societies do exist elsewhere, they could be unimaginably more advanced than we are. Here's why: Our Earth is 4.5 billion years old, and that's how long it took us to develop our civilization. It is unlikely that we would encounter a civilization at *exactly* our level of development. If they advanced at the same rate but their planet is 1 percent older than ours or if their life progressed at a 1 percent faster rate, they are 45,000,000 years ahead of us! Just imagine the potential achievements of such a civilization. Their technology would be magic to us. They might appear to us as almost divine beings.

# PHYSICS

## EINSTEIN'S SPECIAL AND
## GENERAL THEORIES OF RELATIVITY

Typically, science plods along with an army of well-trained, hard-working, and bright, even exceptionally bright, workers. Then out of the blue comes an extraordinary genius like Albert Einstein—no ordinary mortal. The first half of the twentieth century brought a revolution in physics through a handful of epoch-making talents like Einstein, plus a roomful of other physicists, who in more ordinary times would have been regarded as geniuses. In 1905 the twenty-six-year-old Einstein published five remarkable papers, three of which were turning points in physics. One of these papers described the quantum nature of light, for which he received the Nobel Prize, and two others laid out his special theory of relativity, which is our concern here.

Prior to the special theory of relativity, Newton's classical concept and our commonsense notion that space and time were independent and unrelated was unquestioned. In fact, even today this idea remains valid in our everyday experience of walking, driving an automobile, and even launching spacecraft to the moon, because Einstein's theory applies only to situations where matter moves at tremendous velocities approaching the speed of light; i.e., nearly 300,000 kilometers (186,000 miles) per second. In these conditions, space and time are not viewed as independent variables existing in isolation from each other but rather as inseparably connected in a relationship of union. Space and time are not independent but are united in a space-time continuum. Thus, since Einstein, physicists no longer speak of time plus three-dimensional space, but instead of four-dimensional space-time. Among the amazing consequences of his theory is that time past and future does not pass uniformly and universally for all observers but varies, depending on their physical frame of reference. An event that is past for one observer can still be in the future for another, depending on the relative speed between each of the observers and the measured event. Time is relative, not absolute, and it depends on the motion of the observer. However, for any two events that are causally connected (for example, if a light signal passes between them), the order of before and after is the same for all possible observers. An effect cannot precede its cause. There is no way to influence the past or to change history. Time dilation becomes apparent at exceedingly high speeds not only in the cosmos at large but also for subatomic particles moving near the speed of light as, for example, in an accelerator. Motion in space affects motion in time. However strange its consequences may appear to us, it is important to keep in mind that a central tenet of the special theory was that the laws of physics are the same in all physical frames of reference in uniform motion.

In his special theory of relativity, Einstein not only shows the intimate relationship between space and time but also between matter and energy. His famous equation, $E=mc^2$, states the equivalence of mass and energy. In contrast to Newton's immutability of mass,

Einstein showed that mass can be transformed into energy, as well as the reverse. Mass and energy are different forms of the same thing. His equation states that for each unit of matter there is a quantity of energy, i.e., the amount arrived at by multiplying the corresponding mass (m) by the square of the speed of light ($c^2$). However, he did not initially believe it would be technically possible for humans to actually convert significant quantities of matter directly into energy. Ruefully, for this dedicated pacifist, it was achieved in the atomic bomb, when a little less than one gram of matter was transformed into enough energy to kill hundreds of thousands of people. Other principles in the special theory of relativity include the experimentally verified notion that the speed of light in a vacuum is an absolute quantity: The speed of light never changes, no matter how it's measured or who is measuring it, no matter what the motion of the observer. Also, the speed of light is the speed limit of the universe: nothing can move faster than light, regardless of how much force is applied. The special theory of relativity has been confirmed by an array of empirical tests. Today Einstein's equations have applications in various technologies, including medical instruments, electronic products, and nuclear reactors producing electricity. They also provide theoretical foundations for nuclear, particle, and astrophysics and for the origin and evolution of the universe, including the creation of matter and antimatter.

In 1916, after ten years of exhausting labor, Einstein presented his general theory of relativity. It was an extension of his special theory and a radically new theory of gravity. Newton had adopted Galileo's principle of inertia, as later refined by Descartes, which stated that an isolated body, free from external forces or friction, moves uniformly in a straight line at a constant speed. Newton's theory of mechanics explained that departures from this uniform motion were caused by the force of gravity, which acts at a distance as a mutual attraction between separate material bodies. In other words, distant bodies are pulled toward each other across empty space. His mathematical theory brilliantly quantified celestial motion resulting from this gravitational force, but in response to those who accused him of introducing an occult force into science, he stated that he made no claims about the actual nature of this invisible, mysterious gravitational force.

While Newton assumed gravitation is a cause, Einstein presented the revolutionary idea that rather it is an effect of the curvature of space-time, which in turn is a result of the concentration and distribution of mass and energy. For Einstein, there was no Newtonian gravitational force, no mutual attraction acting at a distance between bodies. Matter bends space-time, and then it moves along the shortest path in this bent space-time. Moving bodies follow the contours of space-time, following the curved paths of a non-Euclidean geometry. Such geometries were developed in the nineteenth century and were not available to Newton, who was thus limited to describing only Euclidean flat space. Rather than depicting gravitational forces pulling bodies toward each other, Einstein spoke of the curvature of space in a certain vicinity, which results in gravitational effects. For example, the closer it is to the Sun, the more sharply curved is space, and thus the planets closest to the Sun revolve in more tightly curved orbits than more distant planets. Furthermore, massive material bodies not only curve nearby space but also the flow of time in its vicinity—time passes more slowly in regions of strong gravity.

Newton's gravitational theory is sufficiently precise for our planet, because we are in a weak gravitational field, and thus it is adequate for the types of calculations we make in our earthly lives, including propelling objects, building bridges, and flying airplanes. Einstein's theory is essential for understanding bodies of extremely large mass and high density that curve space and produce intense gravitational fields. Einstein's theory can predict the behavior of objects moving at speeds near the speed of light, and it also describes the motion of matter near black holes as massive stars collapse under their own unimaginably powerful gravitational influences. Einstein's theory has been empirically tested by different methods which have confirmed a variety of seemingly bizarre predictions, including the bending of light rays by gravity. It has successfully explained the deviations from Newtonian predictions of the orbital motion of the planet Mercury around the Sun, the delay of radio signals from space missions, and a host of other phenomena. The accuracy of the global positioning system depends on corrections from general relativity. As of yet, no astronomical observations or experimental tests have disconfirmed Einstein's predictions. Both the special and general theories of relativity represent a radical departure from Newton's "system of the world" and have been critical to the development of scientific cosmology during the twentieth and our present century.

## QUANTUM MECHANICS AND INDETERMINACY

The year was 1900. Max Planck, a conservative German professor doing conventional research, announced a new theory that came to be known as quantum mechanics and that gave birth to a revolution in science. Years later, Werner Heisenberg described the situation:

> When Planck tackled the subject he had no desire to change classical physics in any serious way. He simply wanted to solve a particular problem, namely, the distribution of energy in the spectrum of a black body. He tried to do so in conformity with all the established physical laws, and it took him many years to realize that this was impossible. Only at that stage did he put forward a hypothesis that did not fit into the framework of classical physics, and even then he tried to fill the breach he had made in the old physics with additional assumptions. That proved impossible, and the consequences of Planck's hypothesis finally led to a radical reconstruction of all physics.[1]

In his study of black body radiation, Planck was focusing on one of the outstanding problems of physics of his day. It was known as the "ultraviolet catastrophe." Classical theory predicted a frequency spectrum that yields an infinite result for the amount of black body radiation emanating from a hot cavity. However, experimental results indicated that the radiation is quite finite. Its spectrum is measurable. Planck resolved the problem by a mathematical artifice, constructing an equation to fit the experimental results. But he didn't stop there. After some years of frustrating work, he came to the realization that his artificial mathematical description suggested an actual physical phenomenon! Contrary to the accepted theory of his time, that the wave modes in such radiation may have any energy, Planck proposed that in fact a radiation mode may not have any energy at all but rather only discrete allowed energies, which are multiples of a certain quantity—a quantum—of energy. The energy quantum of a light wave is given by the wave's frequency multiplied by a universal constant, h=6.63 x 10$^{-34}$ joule-seconds, now called Planck's constant. He invented the term "quanta" for these packets of energy, and he spoke of the radiating atom as being "quantized," because it could only contain discrete quanta of energy. Thus originated the revolutionary idea of "quantum," that energy can be emitted or absorbed only in discrete energy quanta. This new view of a fundamental process of nature resulted in his receiving the Nobel Prize. Yet the deeply radical character of his quantum theory was only fully understood during the following several decades.

Inspired by Planck's discovery, Einstein in 1905 presented his Nobel Prize-winning theory of the photoelectric effect. He proposed that light travels in discrete packets of energy called photons, which act like particles rather than waves. He enlarged Planck's theory by showing that the idea of quantized electromagnetic waves—photons—could explain not only black body radiation but also the photoelectric effect. In contrast to most physicists in 1900, who viewed Planck's quantum theory as merely an artificial mathematical manipulation rather than a physical reality, and the resistance of many in 1905 to his own quantum theory of light, Einstein welcomed quantum theory as a profound scientific truth that could be applied to all areas of physics. As his career developed, Einstein made other fundamental contributions to quantum physics. Over three decades, but especially in the 1920s, quantum mechanics deepened in theory, multiplied in confirmations, and widened in applications, through the pioneering work of physicists like Niels Bohr, Werner Heisenberg, Max Born, Erwin Schrödinger, Wolfgang Pauli, Louis de Broglie, and Paul Dirac.

In both classical and quantum physics, mechanics is the study of matter, motion, energy, and forces. Quantum mechanics is a fundamental physical theory which treats waves and particles as two aspects of the same underlying reality. All matter and energy in the quantum realm is dualistic, combining the complementary properties of particles and waves. Quantum mechanics is potentially applicable to all scales of reality, from the smallest to the largest, though it originated with the study of the microscopic constituents of atoms, subatomic particles, and molecules. Classical physics is clearly not accurate in the realm of the very small. Newtonian mechanics was developed to deal with objects available to the naked eye or with limited magnification. Nonordinary conditions, such as extremes of high velocity and temperature, tiny atomic and subatomic size, were not available for study by the classical physicists. Newtonian physics had entirely adequate precision with bits of dust, objects falling from trees, and speeding automobiles; objects of ordinary size, speed, and temperature have negligible quantum effects. However, as Niels Bohr explained, it is hopeless to try to understand the atom with classical physics. There was no possibility of developing twentieth-century cosmology with Newtonian principles. A host of amazing phenomena would remain a mystery today except for quantum theory. Physicists have not discarded classical physics; rather they now understand its limitations. Quantum mechanics does not displace classical physics but includes it as a limiting case in a far more comprehensive theory. Physicists seek to discover fundamental laws of physical reality. Because the basic Newtonian laws have been established in their own restricted domain, most physicists no longer do theoretical or experimental work in classical physics, but instead this is now more in the realm of engineering.

The scientific and technological applications of quantum mechanics have been astonishingly successful and provide powerful confirmations of the theory's validity. Without quantum mechanics, we would not have the enormous wealth of knowledge found in atomic, nuclear, high-energy, and condensed-matter (solid state) physics. Quantum mechanics undergirds all of chemistry, explaining the periodic table, the properties of the chemical elements, and molecular bonds. Quantum mechanics has had a monumental impact on our personal lives through electronics in the form of transistors, integrated circuits, and the associated technology of computers and telecommunications. Lasers are quantum mechanical devices. Radioactive dating depends upon quantum findings, and in medicine we have the benefits of magnetic resonance imaging (MRI) and radioactive tracers.

According to quantum theory, wave-particle duality is found throughout atomic physics. Werner Heisenberg was a twenty-five-year-old postdoctoral assistant to Niels Bohr in 1927 when, reflecting on the wave-particle duality of an electron, he realized that despite the classical expectation that we ought to be able to measure simultaneously and precisely the position and momentum of a particle, in fact we cannot do so. He recognized the existence of incompatible measurements for pairs of quantum phenomena. Measuring at the same time the position (a particle property) and momentum (a wave property) of a moving particle inevitably involves a limitation in precision—the more precise the measurement of position, the less precise the measurement of the momentum, and vice versa. In the subatomic domain of quantum mechanics, we cannot know at the same time both the position and the momentum of a particle with absolute precision. We can know both approximately, but the more we know about the one, the less we know about the other. In the most extreme situation, absolutely perfect precision for one would result in complete ignorance for the other. This is Heinsenberg's Uncertainty Principle, which has been verified by numerous experiments, though it appears paradoxical if we continue to think in terms of our everyday experience, as in classical physics. Heinsenberg codified his findings in an equation involving Planck's constant. Eventually he applied the uncertainty relation to other pairs of conjugate variables, such as energy and time. No matter how perfect our experimental apparatus, Heinsenberg showed that an uncertainty will always exist in measuring these pairs of incompatible variables. The name *uncertainty* principle is somewhat misleading. The uncertainty does not refer to our subjective uncertainty due to our human limitations in knowing, but rather means that the uncertainty is an objective property of nature.

Niels Bohr is often quoted as saying that anyone who is not shocked by quantum theory has not understood it. One of those jolts is indeterminacy. On the scale of the microcosmos, individual events can occur by chance. For example, in the subatomic world of individual electrons, events are random; they may or may not happen. Yet the cosmos is not chaotic. There is an order in the universe, but it certainly wasn't the order physicists were expecting. Though random events occur at the microscopic level, a statistical pattern will emerge which on repeated trials will accurately and consistently describe and predict the behavior of the ensemble. Quantum mechanics describes the behavior of particles and atoms in terms of probability distributions within which their individual behaviors will occur at random. While individual behaviors appear to be indeterministic and can only be known with probability, the pattern is determined and can be known with certainty. Nature is not irrational; it follows an overall mathematical order, more specifically a statistical lawfulness. Nature is intrinsically statistical. At its most fundamental level, the universe may be indeterministic. In classical physics nature at every level is strictly deterministic, following a rigid chain of cause and effect. Classically, if we know each and every initial position and momentum, we can with absolute certainty predict the future in every detail. One of the favorite metaphors of classical physics was that the world is a machine. Einstein during his entire lifetime remained a staunch determinist. He believed that quantum mechanics could only be an incomplete description of physical reality and that eventually a more comprehensive theory would explain away its apparent randomness and statistical character. He explained that God does not play dice with the universe, to which Niels Bohr responded that it is not for us to tell God how to run his universe.

The indeterminacy of quantum mechanics has different inter-pretations. Today, only a small minority of physicists maintain Einstein's position that the randomness of quantum phenomena is only apparent, not real. The so-called indeterminacy is only the result of our present human ignorance. Eventually we will discover the more fundamental physical laws demonstrating that subatomic mechanisms are rigidly causal and deterministic, and thus their exact prediction will be possible. Most physicists are pragmatic instrumen-talists as they go about their daily work, using the apparent random-ness of individual quantum events and the statistical lawfulness of the aggregate to observe, predict, and achieve productive results leaving aside metaphysical speculations as to whether the indeterminacy is an aspect of nature or only a useful human construct. For a group of more philosophically reflective physicists, such as Heisenberg in his later writings, indeterminacy is an objective feature of nature and not the result of our present ignorance or a permanent limitation of human knowledge. That is, indeterminacy is ontological, not merely epistemological. Nature has tendencies that include a potential range of possibilities. Future events are not all decided. More than one alternative is possible, and there is some opportunity for unpre-dictable novelty. Thus, for some physicists, if we roll back the film of the universe to its beginning and then start it up again, the same exact movie would not necessarily repeat itself. A different world would unfold, reflecting quantum indeterminacy and its tendency to be open to unpredictable creativity.

To fully experience the power of quantum theory, we need to do its mathematics. To limit ourselves to a verbal-conceptual approach results in a much reduced understanding. Quantum mechanics is a formal mathematical theory that describes and predicts physical phe-nomena to incredible levels of accuracy. It is based on observation and measurements that seek pragmatic results, not philosophical insights into the ultimate essence of nature. With Newtonian physics, we can personally experience the mathematical laws of gravity when we fall and visualize planets orbiting in space as a result of gravitational forces. Quantum mechanics seems mysterious, because it transcends our human categories of immediate sensory experience. We can't picture its mathematical abstractions; we can't feel its realities. The more we attempt to understand the realities behind the mathematics, the more it seems to elude our conceptual powers. But quantum theory is not the first time we have been shocked by physics. Before Newton, people assumed that objects could influence each other only if they were physically touching. Newton came along and said this isn't necessarily so. Both heavenly bodies and earthly objects can affect each other without physical contact, even from afar, through a mysterious action-at-a-distance force called gravity. So people adjusted their common sense until gravity seemed natural, just as physicists in the twentieth century adjusted their common sense until the quantitative description of quantum physics seemed natural. At least for now, quantum physics has no rivals. It is an established theory. For university students using his textbook in quantum mechanics, physicist Marvin Chester provides this guiding perspective.

> Our entire understanding of nature's way is founded on the subject called *quantum mechanics*. No fact of nature has ever been discovered that contradicts quantum mechanics. In its existence of over 60 years, quantum theory has experienced only success in describing the physical world. It has survived a stunning multitude of tests on its validity. We must accept it as the soul of nature. Quantum mechanics is nature's way.[2]

During the first half of the twentieth century, the two grand theories of relativity and quantum mechanics created modern physics and transformed our view of the world. If they have taught us anything, surely it is that physical reality is far deeper, richer, vastly more complex and mysterious than classical physics understood or even dreamed.

# BIOLOGY

## EVOLUTION BY CHANCE AND NECESSITY

Before the impact of Darwin, the dominant belief was that the marvelous structures, ingenious adaptations, and resplendent diversity of all life forms could only be explained as the result of divine design. As revealed in Genesis, the all-good, powerful, and intelligent God from the very beginning separately created each and every now-existing species. Each species was created independently from the other species, and its nature was immutably fixed for all time. The life forms we now observe are exactly as they were at the instant of their creation. From the very beginning, God had given gills to fish to breathe in water, wings for birds to fly, and legs for animals to walk. The widely influential English theologian William Paley argued convincingly in his *Natural Theology* (1802) that if we happened to find a watch on the ground and noted all its ingeniously coordinated parts, it is only logical to conclude the necessity of a watchmaker. Even more marvelous is the design of the human eye, with its diverse parts perfectly functioning together for the purpose of sight. Surely, he argued, all the complex designs found in nature could not be attributed to blind chance but rather required an intelligent Designer. Where there is a design, there must be a designer. Paley, along with eminent scientists and philosophers of his time, laid out a mass of empirical evidence for the existence of a grand organized design and also detailed rational proof for the necessity of an omniscient and benevolent Grand Designer. Earlier thinkers, including the theologian St. Thomas Aquinas in the thirteenth century, had used much the same argument from design to demonstrate the existence of God.

Among the revolutionary consequences of Darwin's theory, the most disturbing to many religious thinkers was his idea that all the wonderful structures, adaptations, and diversity of biological organisms do not need to be explained as the direct intervention of a Divine Designer. Rather they are more accurately explained as the result of a strictly natural, autonomous, and impersonal process—evolution by means of natural selection. He proposed an alternative interpretation of nature as not static and fixed for all time, but dynamic and unfolding. For religious believers, God could be viewed as the original source of creation, but ongoing creation is accomplished through the independent and entirely natural mechanism of natural selection, elaborated gradually across a vast canvas of time. In the final sentence of *On the Origin of Species*, Darwin concluded,

> There is grandeur in this view of life, with its several
> powers, having been originally breathed into a few
> forms or into one; and that, whilst this planet has gone
> cycling on according to the fixed law of gravity, from so
> simple a beginning endless forms most beautiful and
> most wonderful have been, and are being, evolved.[3]

Ernst Mayr, one of the deans of modern evolutionary biology, noted that from the ancient Greeks down to the nineteenth century, a great controversy persisted as to whether changes in the world are due to chance or necessity. "It was Darwin who found a brilliant solution to this old conundrum: they are due to both. In the production of variation, chance dominates, while selection itself operates largely by necessity."[4] In other words, nature dances an evolutionary two-step: chance and necessity. Darwin had observed small, spontaneous variations among individual members of species that were inherited by subsequent generations. Modern molecular genetics shows us empirically that mutations arise spontaneously by chance, and these random changes accumulate in the gene pool of a population. The random gene mutations are blind in the sense that they are entirely unrelated to the adaptive needs of the organism to survive in its own particular environment. Randomly produced genetic variation is the raw material of evolutionary change, the engine and original source of biological novelty, diversity, and creativity. But evolution by natural selection does not work by chance alone. The second step is nonrandom. By necessity, those individuals of a species will be eliminated or remain alive (and perhaps reproduce) depending on how well their genetic makeup happens to facilitate survival in their local environment. Darwin's use of the terms "natural selection" and "selection" is somewhat confusing. Evolution by natural selection is a two-step process: random variations and nonrandom selection. The second step of "selection" in everyday language can imply some active agent in nature that intentionally selects for survival or extinction, whereas Darwin intended it to be mechanical, not deliberate, passive, not active.

It seems almost shocking that a mechanism so simple in concept as evolution by natural selection can be so powerful in creating the luxuriant panorama of biological phenomena. Awesome is the accumulative power of the interplay between chance mutations and the necessity of nonrandom selection over millions of years to bring about evolutionary change. Across eons of time, minute variations build to such momentous consequences.

Rapid advances in molecular genetics during the second half of the twentieth century revealed that variations within species are much more abundant than Darwin had estimated, and thus the influence of chance in the evolutionary process is far more extensive than he had supposed. For example, we now know that in sexual species, contrary to Darwin's assumption, most of the genomic variation in populations arises not from new mutations at each generation, but rather through the reshuffling of existing mutations and recombination via sexual reproduction. The result is an often massive supply of genetic variation. Sexually reproducing organisms, which represent the vast majority of known species, by producing much greater genetic variation increase the possibility of a faster rate of evolutionary change than asexual organisms. Both for random mutations and the recombination of genes in sexual reproduction, chance dominates. Also, what Darwin could not have even guessed in his time, we now have detailed knowledge of external triggers of mutations, including radiation from the Sun's ultraviolet light, X rays, gamma rays, and chemicals known as mutagens.

## EXTINCTIONS: THE GREAT DYING

The extinction of entire species is one of the most pervasive phenomena in evolution. Darwin was acutely aware that through the process of natural selection species appear and disappear over time. New species arise by splitting off from an already existing species, which in turn may become extinct. Though Darwin identified extinction as one of the ways of nature, he lacked our present knowledge of the five major and various lesser mass extinctions that pivotally impacted evolutionary events and trends. The well known "Big Five" of mass extinctions, according to their geologic time and estimated percentage of species killed, are the end of the Ordovician, 440 million years past, 85 percent killed; the end of the Devonian, 367 million years past, 82 percent killed; the end of the Permian, 245 million years past, 96 percent killed; the end of the Triassic 210 million years past, 76 percent killed; and the end of the Cretaceous, 65 million years past, 76 percent killed. The end-Permian is called the "mother of mass extinctions," because it approached the total destruction of all species and caused such fundamental changes in the evolution of life. With the exception of the end-Cretaceous, the other four mass extinctions are attributed to various combinations of natural catastrophes, including climatic instability, drops or rises in sea levels resulting in loss of habitat and flooding, changes in ocean chemistry, diminished oxygen levels, volcanic eruptions that spewed dust and gas into the atmosphere causing global climate changes, continental drift, and increased glaciation. Time durations of the extinctions vary. For the end-Permian, estimates range between 1 and 10 million years. Whatever the killing time, the species totally disappeared forever.

Interest in mass extinctions was enlivened in 1980 when Nobel Laureate physicist Luis Alvarez and his colleagues published their startling theory that it was a large extraterrestrial object, perhaps an asteroid at least six miles in diameter, that crashed into Earth and caused the last of the big five mass extinctions 65 million years past.[5] Their "far out" theory was greeted with abundant professional skepticism but subsequently, as evidence accumulated, including the identification of the undersea crash site off the Yucatan Peninsula on the south side of the Gulf of Mexico, it has become an accepted theory among most scientists. Almost 125 miles in diameter, it is the largest impact crater known on earth. Philip Dauber and Richard Muller, physicists and former students of Luis Alvarez, describe the unimaginable violence resulting from the extraterrestrial's impact.

Within a few seconds of the impact, energy equivalent to millions of thermonuclear bombs was released, much of it as heat. Temperatures within a few hundred meters of the impact soared to over 1 million degrees Celsius. Mud, water, and even some rock vaporized; more rock melted. A huge fireball exploded out of the sea in ghostly slow motion, because of its enormous size. In truth it carried destruction with it at faster than the speed of sound.

Expanding through the Earth at more than 4 kilometers per second, the shock wave dug out a monstrous crater nearly 200 kilometers wide. Earthquake tremors roared outward from the epicenter. Even those dinosaurs and other animals that took it as a warning could do little to protect themselves

Rebounding chunks of asteroid and debris hurtled upward and outward. The mass of dust alone totaled 100 trillion tons—the equivalent of a billion large ships. Countless pieces shot far out into space as glowing meteors. These missiles cooled temporarily, then flared up again as they rained back down to Earth.

Forests and jungles within a thousand miles or more burst into flame. If any burning trees were left standing, a blast wave of pressurized air knocked them down. As secondary fragments bombarded the Earth, distant forests and grasslands also burned. Intense heat from the reentering meteors baked many animals alive.[6]

Dauber and Muller continue their description, including mile-high tsunami waves spreading across the oceans at hundreds of kilometers per hour, storms approaching supersonic speeds, severe acid rain, dust and debris blocking the sun and causing a widespread "nuclear winter," like a shroud of darkness over the entire Earth.

Among the 76 percent of species annihilated was the entire array of active and alert dinosaurs who had reigned as the dominant species on Earth for more than 150 million years. For some 100 million of these years, mammals had coexisted with them, but they were unable to evolve beyond rat size, due to competition with the dominant dinosaurs for ecological niche space. The impact of the extraterrestrial rock, 6 miles in diameter, crossing Earth's path at 50,000 mph, destroyed the dinosaurs but allowed the mammals, whose tiny size was better adapted to survive the catastrophe, to rapidly evolve into diverse terrestrial, aerial, and aquatic species, including our ancestors.

Ordinary everyday extinction by natural selection can be seen as an indication of the success of evolution. Poorly adapted species do not survive, while their better adapted transformations thrive. Paleontologist David Raup, a pioneer in the resurgent interest in extinction, proposes that without extinction biodiversity would at first increase exponentially but rather soon the evolutionary system would saturate, leaving no room left over for new species. Without extinction, many innovations, such as new body plans, behaviors, survival strategies, and novel kinds of organisms, would not have the opportunity to appear. The result would be that evolutionary diversification would slow down to some type of steady-state.[7] For Raup, the same principle applies to the big five mass extinctions, after which bursts of speciation occurred. But a dramatic difference exists between the two types of extinction. Ordinary extinction by natural selection results from a combination of chance and necessity, but mass extinctions are mostly the result of pure chance, almost entirely unrelated to the species' past successful adaptations necessary for everyday survival. Most species were doing quite well until they were annihilated by the unprecedented events of overwhelming environmental magnitude. These mass killings were not caused by bad genes but rather by bad luck. Mass extinctions add an even greater element of chance to the drama of life.

For those of us living on the planet today, what are the chances that we too will be annihilated by a crashing asteroid or comet falling from the sky? Scientists disagree on the probabilities, but most would concur that it is only a matter of time until something devastating will happen, whether it's the destruction of a city or the end of civilization and a return to the Stone Age. How much time do we have? Some estimate hundreds of thousands of years, and thus we shouldn't worry. Others calculate that the probability of a catastrophic impact might be greater than the risk for an individual dying in an airplane crash. Tom Gehrels, principal investigator of the Spacewatch Program of the University of Arizona at Kitt Peak, is one of a small group of specialists attempting to assess our vulnerability. He concludes, "After years of studying the problem, I have become convinced that the danger is real. Although a major impact is unlikely, the energies released could be so horrendous that our fragile society would be obliterated."[8] He believes that most of the danger to Earth comes from asteroids. He estimates that there are 100,000 near-Earth asteroids 100 meters and larger in diameter within the solar system, deeper than the orbit of Mars. For Gehrels, these are a threat. One of these, only 60 meters wide, exploded in 1908 four miles above the Tunguska Valley in Siberia, with a force around 2,000 times that of an atomic bomb. It flattened thousands of square miles of forest. More dangerous are the 1,000 to 2,000 near-Earth asteroids, approximately one kilometer (0.6 miles) and larger in diameter, crossing Earth's orbit, one of which is estimated to crash into Earth about every 300,000 years. This is only a statistical average. An actual collision with our planet could happen at any time, today or not in a million years, but probably once in 300,000 years. Even more perilous are the largest near-Earth asteroids, some 10 kilometers in diameter, but luckily for us, only ten of these probably exist and asteroids of this size are estimated to collide with Earth only once in every 100 million years.

As director of the Spacewatch Program, Gehrels and his staff search for and track threatening asteroids and comets. His colleague, Jones Scotti, discovered an asteroid in 1994 that passed within 65,000 miles of Earth. Presently, efforts are intensifying to identify potential doomsday and less apocalyptic objects heading our way from space. For example, since 1998 a then little known but radically advanced military telescope in New Mexico run by scientists from the Massachusetts Institute of Technology's Lincoln Laboratory has exponentially increased our ability to detect previously unknown near-Earth asteroids and comets. The number of observations has been stunning in both quantity and quality. Interestingly enough, the LINEAR observatory (short for Lincoln Near-Earth Asteroid Research) is located on the White Sands Missile Range, about a mile from Trinity Site where the first atomic bomb was detonated on July 16, 1945. Also, a few researchers are investigating possible means of destroying or deflecting Earth-targeted asteroids and comets using rockets and nuclear devices. For the first time in evolutionary history, the human species, as representative of all life forms, might be able to detect and destroy the extraterrestrial source of our potential mass extinction.

Though our extinction may be coming in from space, our salvation may come by going out into space. We have only incomplete knowledge of potentially Earth-crossing asteroids and comets, and we may not even have the time and technology to block known threats. We may not have a fighting chance. The long-term survival of our species may depend on some of us departing Spaceship Earth and colonizing the cosmos in space stations, bringing along with us natural and genetically engineered biological species—a modern Noah's Ark. And while asking how safe our planet is for us, we might also ask how safe it is from us. Our reckless excesses in population growth and arrogant consumption of Earth's resources might shatter all hopes of order and fairness in our economic, political, and other life-sustaining social systems. Are we not becoming an out-of-control biomass of locusts devastating the planet?

## OPPORTUNISTIC TINKERING
## FOR LOCAL ADAPTATIONS

Is evolution going anywhere? Is it progressive and moving toward perfection? Is evolution following any advance plan and overall goal? Mighty big questions. The ultimate answers are beyond the power and aims of science and more properly belong in the realm of religion and metaphysics. However, most scientists today generally agree on the answers to these questions as pertaining to natural phenomena. For example, regarding the question of progress, the eminent paleontologist and evolutionary theorist George Gaylord Simpson expresses the general consensus in this statement.

> Evolution is not invariably accompanied by progress, nor does it really seem to be characterized by progress as an essential feature. Progress has occurred within it but is not of its essence. Aside from the broad tendency for the expansion of life, which is also inconstant, there is no sense in which it can be said that evolution *is* progress.[9]

No systematic and universal progress appears to occur in evolutionary history. Empirical investigations are unable to demonstrate that the totality of advances exceeds the number of regressions. Furthermore, no pervasive perfection principle appears to be operating on or within the evolutionary process. Natural selection produces sufficiently successful adaptations for the survival of certain species in particular environments but does not create perfect species. Natural selection promotes survival and reproduction, not perfection. Mayr describes nine constraints on natural selection that prevent optimal responses.[10] Chance, i.e., bad luck, can impede progressive trends across many levels, from adverse mutations to unlucky encounters with unexpected diseases and predators as well as mass extinctions. With 99.9 percent of all species now extinct, the evolutionary process seems dreadfully inefficient in yielding its exquisite instances of progress and beauty.

Simpson views opportunism as an outstanding characteristic of the evolutionary process. Nature follows available opportunities rather than a fixed plan. French biologist and Nobel Laureate François Jacob used the metaphor of "tinkering" to further elucidate the opportunistic workings of evolution. He notes that the process of natural selection is often considered to be like the work of an engineer. However, he maintains that this is not appropriate for several reasons. In contrast to what happens in evolution, the engineer follows a preconceived plan in doing his work. Also, an engineer who constructs a new structure is not required to build it from an older one. For example, the electric light does not derive from the candle or the jet engine from the internal combustion engine. To construct something new, the engineer begins with original blueprints for that particular project and uses specialized materials and machines for its completion. Finally, the engineer aims for the highest level of perfection in his new product by using the most recent technology and materials. In contrast, as Darwin emphasized, evolution does not produce perfection, but rather often results in all kinds of structural and functional imperfections, oddities, and strange solutions. Jacob explains why.

> In contrast to the engineer, evolution does not produce
> innovations from scratch. It works on what already
> exists, either transforming a system to give it a new
> function or combining several systems to produce a
> more complex one. Natural selection has no analogy
> with any aspect of human behavior. If one wanted to use
> a comparison, however, one would have to say that this
> process resembles not engineering but tinkering, *bricolage*
> we say in French.
>
> While the engineer's work relies on his having the raw
> materials and the tools that exactly fit his project, the
> tinkerer manages with odds and ends. Often without

*continues*

*continued*

even knowing what he is going to produce, he uses whatever he finds around him, old cardboards, pieces of string, fragments of wood or metal, to make some kind of workable object.

In some respects, the evolutionary derivation of living organisms resembles this mode of operation. In many instances, and without any well-defined long-term project, the tinkerer picks up an object which happens to be in his stock and gives it an unexpected function. Out of an old car wheel, he will make a fan; from a broken table, a parasol. This process is not very different from what evolution performs when it turns a leg into a wing, or a part of a jaw into a piece of ear.[11]

Jacob lists the evolution of the mammalian brain as one of his examples of how evolution will add new structures to old ones rather than replace them. Citing the work of neuroscientist Paul MacLean, he notes how the neocortex thinking brain was added to the paleo-mammalian feeling brain, which in turn had been built over the reptilian brain. The result, especially in the human brain, is a lack of systematic coordination. For Jacob, this is typical of how evolutionary tinkering works, but with the human brain, "It is something like adding a jet engine to an old horse cart."

Life scientists today totally shun vitalist and finalist explanations of biological phenomena. The assumption is that the mechanisms of physics and chemistry are or will be entirely adequate to explain all biological processes, and their laws apply without any fundamental distinction to both living and nonliving natural events. Vitalism takes the opposing view that there is an ultimate difference between the organic and inorganic, and that an invisible nonphysical force operates only in biological life, which radically distinguishes it from the other physical forces in the universe. Vitalism has a long tradition, going back to ancient authorities including Aristotle. Thus, vitalists were shocked when in 1828 the chemist Friedrick Wöhler first made urea, a simple organic substance, from inorganic chemicals. Subsequent discoveries have shown that chemicals are interchangeable between the inorganic and organic, thus unifying the living and nonliving worlds at the atomic and molecular levels. Nevertheless, the vitalist tradition continues to have its proponents.

The French philosopher Henri Bergson (1859-1941) became widely influential with literary and general audiences for his vitalist interpretation of evolution. In his immensely popular 1907 book *L'Évolution creatrice*, he argued for a cosmic-wide creative evolutionary process to replace scientific materialism and mechanism. He postulated an immanent, nonphysical vital impetus (*élan vital*) as the driving force directing biological evolution toward more complex and higher levels of structure and organization. In later writings he explicated his view that God is love and that the divine purpose in the evolutionary process includes creating creators so that He can have, besides Himself, creatures worthy of his love.

French Jesuit and paleontologist Pierre Teilhard de Chardin developed a unique theology of cosmic and biological evolution, partly influenced by Bergson and purportedly based on scientific findings and Christian tradition. Though he quietly formulated his ideas for some thirty years beginning in the 1920s, his cosmic vision did not become publicly known until shortly after his death, when in 1955 his *Le Phénomène Humain* was published in France and in 1959 the English translation appeared as *The Phenomenon of Man*. This endeavor to integrate evolutionary phenomena and Christian spirituality had a powerful appeal to a vast audience. His optimistic message was thoroughly teleological: A divine creativity immanent in the entire cosmos directs a progressive evolution toward its final goal of bringing together all of nature into a redemptive union with a personal God.

Science aims to explain nature functionally through efficient causes, not by an ultimate purpose through final causes. At the level of natural phenomena, science finds no empirical traces of a pre-planned teleological goal. Evolution seems more like the work of a master tinkerer who gets rather inconsistent results. Sometimes the result is increased complexity, at other times static simplicity, sometimes an explosion of species diversity, at other times mass extinction. Even the evolution of consciousness in animal and human life was not preplanned and is not a dominant and inevitable trend but rather the unique result of a rare series of chance events. Natural selection cannot know the future, does not plan future goals, but rather only passively reinforces positively or negatively past variations in present circumstances. Natural selection gives the illusion of a planned goal but in reality lacks any foresight into future needs. In its most stark portrayal, natural selection is mindless and mechanistic. From its most restricted biological perspective, the purpose of life is survival for reproduction. From the viewpoint of the gene, the purpose of life is to replicate.[12] As best as most life scientists can discover, evolution has no grand, preplanned end state and no guarantee of overall improvement. In the words of evolutionary scientist R. C. Lewontin, "Evolutionary theory in general no longer incorporates notions of progress or of unidirectional change. Evolution, at least in the modern view, is going nowhere in particular."[13]

## DIRECTED EVOLUTION: THE NEW GENESIS

The last half of the twentieth century experienced epoch-making discoveries in molecular biology and explosive developments in the potent new technology of genetic engineering. Not only do we know that we and all other organisms evolved from a common ancestor, but we can trace the outlines of that unfolding at the molecular level. And now we have an increasing power to design, at least to a limited degree, the evolutionary future of many life forms, including ourselves. Human-made evolution is not only a turning point in the history of life, but also a revolution of the human relationship to nature. But altering nature is not something entirely new for our species. Some twelve to fifteen thousand years ago, during the transition from hunting-gathering to settled agriculture, ancient farmers noted the taste and appearance of wild grains, fruits, and vegetables and then selected seeds from only the best for later planting, thus developing better varieties. In the same slow and unpredictable manner, wild animals were selectively bred and domesticated. In their own elementary way, our agrarian ancestors were engineering genetic changes to improve nature.

Today, we have a wealth of knowledge about how organisms inherit and pass on the detailed instructions for their particular nature and operations. These inherited instructions are encoded in an actual chemical substance—most often deoxyribonucleic acid (DNA). Genes are the units of the inherited instructions and are made up of DNA. With very rare exceptions, stashed inside each somatic cell of an organism is a DNA molecule. Any one somatic cell contains complete DNA instructions to, at least theoretically, create an exact copy of the entire organism. Thus, a single cell of an animal contains all the genetic information for growing a new, perfectly duplicated animal. Early in the 1970s it was discovered how certain molecules in the cell can cut a DNA chain. These chemicals, called restriction enzymes, cut through the double DNA strand at a precise point in the sequence. Another enzyme reattaches DNA fragments. With the discovery of how these enzymes could "cut and paste" fragments of DNA, recombinant DNA technology was born. Novel DNA sequences could now be created in the laboratory by artificially joining pieces of DNA from different sources. "Genetic engineering" refers to the variety of techniques by which recombinant DNA can be produced to change the makeup of cells or individual organisms by deliberately inserting, removing, or altering individual genes, typically moving genes from one organism or species to another.

The era of genetic engineering is well underway. Applications are multiplying in plant and animal agriculture, medicine, pharmaceuticals, and a variety of other areas, including waste treatment, environmental protection, and the preservation of endangered species. Millions of acres of U.S. farmland are being sown with the seeds of genetically modified corn, soybeans, potatoes, tomatoes, and cotton. Bananas, cloned to perfection, are shipped throughout the world from Central America. Fruits, vegetables, and grains are engineered to be tastier, more consistent in size and appearance, higher in protein, more resistant to pests and disease, and thus less dependent on toxic pesticides and herbicides. Plants are being developed that better retard frost damage and that can be irrigated with seawater. With fish, chickens, cows, and sheep, our new technology of life is beginning to insert genes so that these organisms will grow bigger, faster, and produce leaner meat. Transgenic animals can be created by transferring desirable genes from one species to another, including from nonfarm animals to farm animals. Cows, sheep, rabbits, and rhesus monkeys have been cloned from embryonic cells. In 1997 researchers in Scotland cloned an adult sheep to create a lamb (Dolly) with no father. This virgin birth was produced from a single cell of an adult ewe which was genetically programmed to make a whole new body. If successful on a mass scale, cloning will eliminate the need for conventional breeding while producing entire herds of precise copies in a single generation.

Over four thousand genetic disorders have been recognized in humans. Every year we hear of breakthrough discoveries identifying yet another defective gene causing a specific disease or abnormality. Hopefully the new specialization of genetic medicine will eventually cure numerous inherited diseases by replacing the patient's defective genes. It is theoretically possible that many hereditary diseases can be permanently eradicated in humans and animals by making genetic changes in embryos, thus eliminating the possibility that they will be passed on to succeeding generations. Meanwhile, millions of people are benefiting from genetically engineered medicine to control diabetes and heart disease, treat cancer, and diminish the effects of stroke. Many thousands use genetic screening to assess susceptibility to chronic diseases and evaluate the health of unborn children. Behavioral genetics seeks to discover specific genes or combinations of genes that contribute to alcoholism, drug addiction, and other behavioral disorders. Genetic vaccines crafted from genetic material may one day prevent AIDS, malaria, and even help treat cancer. Eventually, people may not die for lack of spare parts. The new technology of tissue engineering has taken the first steps toward growing new organs, sometimes using only one of our own cells as the raw material to replace worn-out or damaged organs. In 1998 the first engineered living-tissue skin product became commercially available, mercifully helping patients with severe burns. Astonishing progress is being made in our understanding of how and why we get older; perhaps in the not too distant future we will be able to halt and even reverse the aging process. Though generally rejected as morally unacceptable, the cloning of humans is theoretically possible and technologically perhaps almost feasible now.

Nature makes mistakes. As part of nature, the chances are that we humans will make mistakes in our efforts to correct and improve nature. Genetic engineering puts an unprecedented power in our hands to direct biological evolution. In fifty, two hundred, or five hundred years, where will all this new technology take us? Will it be like a genie that we eagerly release out of the bottle to magically grant our every wish, who becomes our cruel master that we are unable to squeeze back into the bottle? Genetic engineering may have risks and perhaps unanticipated dangers to the health of all life on the planet, including biological warfare. What aspirations and values, what spiritual and moral principles, can guide us? Will we have the disciplined wisdom to follow our principles?

Nature invents. Space-time evolved successively into chemical, biological, conscious, and cultural realities. Chance mutations and sexual recombination create novelty, including the human species, who in turn can now deliberately and nonrandomly create original variations that previously did not exist. In this second genesis we become not only cocreators but also cotrustees of the evolutionary process. Despite the dark history of eugenics,[14] and by an inevitability perhaps beyond our powers to constrain, we may use the new genetic knowledge and technology to change our own nature. Perhaps already our nature is to transcend our nature, combining high risk with great opportunity in another dramatic chapter of the evolutionary epic.

## The Diversity and Unity of Life

A very different world might have happened. Had only a few critical variations occurred in the physical and chemical dynamics, Earth today could have a flat and featureless terrain of mostly mud, interrupted only by splotches of gray-green slime consisting of a single species of a primitive, eternally unchanging bacterium—the first, final, and only form of life on our planet. Instead, Earth gave birth to a dazzling multitude of ingeniously variegated species, that surprisingly survived and even thrived in specialized niches, from tropical forests to Antarctic ice and from sandy deserts to deep-sea vents—so many species that, after 250 years of systematic research, we still don't know how many inhabit our planet. Estimates of the number of species vary from 3 million to more than 30 million. Perhaps the best estimate is 10 million. In any case, taxonomists have only identified 1.8 million species.[15] Edward O. Wilson lists among the known species 248,400 higher plants, 751,000 insects, 18,800 fishes and lower chordates, 4,200 amphibians, 6,300 reptiles, 9,000 birds, and 4,000 mammals.[16]

Yet undergirding this widespread diversity is a profound unity. A mighty kinship unites all life forms, because we all have common cosmic origins and have shared the same extraordinary unfolding of the universe. Some 12 to 15 billion years past, we were all primordially there in that incredible instant creating space-time, matter and motion, and we expanded along with the universe in the formation of galaxies and stars. The heavy elements necessary for our lives were forged in the hot cores of giant stars and then seeded out into the cosmos by mega-violent supernova explosions. Parented by these mighty stars, we are literally made of stardust. All life forms including ourselves follow the same laws of the universe and live by the same physical and chemical rules. We are all built up from subatomic particles, atoms, molecules, cells, and tissues. Nature provides us with the same ninety-two naturally occurring chemical elements, but as living organisms we are all mostly composed of oxygen, carbon, hydrogen, and nitrogen. All living bodies are astonishingly similar in chemical composition, not only containing atoms of the same elements, but also in similar proportions. All life on Earth shares a powerful bond by being totally dependent on water. Between 70 and 90 percent of all living tissue is water, and the chemical reactions in life processes all occur in a water-containing medium.

All living organisms, from bacteria to humans, use the same raw materials and have the same basic way of doing things. For example, every living being is either a cell or is made up of cells. Cells of all living species are pretty much alike in the way they are built and the way they work. Structurally, all living beings, without exception, are made up of proteins, nucleic acids, and lipids. Invariably and universally, the proteins are made up from one set of the same twenty amino acids. DNA is composed of four nucleotides: tyrosine, cytosine, guanine, and adenosine. All cells use ATP (adenosine triphosphate) as the molecule that energizes their life systems. All cellular organisms use DNA to store and transmit information, building from the same nucleotides which in turn are translated into proteins using the same twenty amino acids.

What can explain the universality underlying such immense diversity? Why are the same biochemical raw materials and mechanisms found throughout life? The answer goes back to Darwin's daring hypothesis that all organic beings that have ever lived on Earth descended from perhaps only one primordial form. Today, all of biochemistry and molecular biology confirms that the underlying oneness of all life forms is because we all originated from one common ancestor, probably a single-celled creature of many millions years past. We all have the fundamental oneness, because we all come from the same one. Also, it is essential to remember that evolution proceeds by the modification of existing characteristics, thus contributing to the basic continuities among species, past and present. Nature creates not by starting up new species from scratch but rather by retaining the same foundations, while tinkering about with new forms. For example, when our human species and the chimpanzees branched off from each other some 5 million years past, we each evolved some novel variations, but we retain much of the same body plan, and about ninety-nine percent of our genes are identical.

Hemoglobin A is identical in the human and chimpanzee species. Thus, while distinct in certain characteristics, we remain blood brothers or at least close cousins. The underlying unity of life is a scientific fact, not biological romanticism. Cosmologically and biologically, we share the same origins and evolutionary process. Humankind, like all other species, is not homeless. Our home is in nature, and we are kin to all that lives.

## Evolution of Evil and Good

Ideas of evil and good cannot be defined in biological terms, because they imply value judgments, which are beyond the goals and powers of the scientific method. More appropriately, the criteria for these values are provided by religion and such human endeavors as philosophy, the arts, and personal ethics. For example, science can empirically identify the biochemical mechanisms by which cigarettes cause lung cancer as well as the smoking pleasure centers in the brain, but it cannot prove if a longer, healthier life is superior or inferior to a shorter but more pleasurable life. Science may be able to empirically demonstrate that the mass extinction of the dinosaurs allowed the eventual evolution of the human species, but it cannot provide any objective criteria proving that this phenomena was evil or good, progress or regression. For several thousand years religious thinkers and philosophers have devoted enormous efforts to explaining the ultimate origins of cosmological and terrestrial good and evil. While science may be able to explain the immediate, natural mechanisms of what other disciplines evaluate as good or evil, it is beyond the range of science to identify their ultimate religious or metaphysical origins. Presently, as in the past, different definitions of evil and good abound. Some associate evil with such natural disasters as floods, drought, and earthquakes; others emphasize more human relationships, sometimes limiting the domain of evil to malicious intent. Our purpose here is to present a few perspectives from evolutionary biology that might shed some light on the natural origins of what we humans in our ordinary, everyday lives often judge to be evil and good. Among all sentient beings, it appears that the human species has evolved a pre-eminent capacity for consciously experiencing physical pain, mental and emotional suffering, and intense happiness. Though I do not wish to equate evil with suffering and good with happiness, it seems that in our practical, personal, and social lives, suffering and happiness are often an essential component or consequence of what we judge to be evil and good.

"Mother Nature" is a common metaphor expressing the wide-spread belief that nature and its evolutionary unfolding is wise, nurturing, and has a kind concern for our human welfare. Often the assumption is that whatever is natural is good, and nature can do no wrong. For many evolutionary biologists, natural selection occurs primarily at the level of the individual; however, this does not necessarily result in a benefit for the individual. Natural selection favors survival for reproductive success, not a perfect or even the best available solution to an adaptive demand. Adaptations can occur that are eventually useless or harmful to individual organisms. Established adaptations are not necessarily optimized, maladaptations can arise that are not always and invariably eliminated, and residual adaptations without present functions may not disappear. Random mutations are classified as deleterious, neutral, nearly neutral, or beneficial. The proportions in which these mutations fall into these classifications is under dispute. However, in humans alone, over four thousand genetic disorders have been recognized, including various forms of mental retardation such as Down and Williams Syndrome, dwarfism, deafness, Alzheimer's, Huntington's, Parkinson's, Wilson's and Tay-Sachs disease, cystic fibrosis, sickle-cell anemia, and hemophilia. The initial random mutations causing these and the thousands of other genetic abnormalities were the first step of evolutionary change which, however, were not eliminated in its second step. As Theodosius Dobzhansky, the great geneticist and one of the founders of modern evolutionary biology, explains, "Natural selection is the guiding agent of evolution, but it is not an all-seeing and all-wise pilot. It adapts, as best as it can, a living species to the environments prevailing in a given place at a given time, but it cannot know the future. Hence biological species frequently combine excellence in some of its parts with astonishing imperfections in others. The human species has both."[17] With the massive pain and suffering inflicted on all sentient beings as a result of the limitations of natural selection, might we not ask if Mother Nature could have evolved a wiser and kinder agent than natural selection?[18]

Thomas Huxley in 1892 delivered his famous Oxford guest lecture in which he provided his moral evaluation of nature.[19] The bottom line is that nature and its evolutionary processes are morally indifferent. For both the animal and human world, neither the pleasures nor the pains of life are distributed according to anything they might deserve. Nature is entirely indifferent to the fact that the wicked flourish and constantly escape the punishment they deserve, while the innocent, who are without evil intent, are universally punished for their ignorance. Amoral nature and human ethics are entirely distinct, in conflict, and alienated from each other. Evolution, which he also calls the cosmic process, lacks any special sensitivity to human needs and ethical concerns. Our moral duty is to revolt against the very process that gave us birth. "Let us understand, once and for all, that the ethical progress of society depends, not on imitating the cosmic process, still less in running away from it, but in combating it."[20] Huxley acknowledges that it may seem "an audacious proposal thus to pit the microcosm against the macrocosm and to set man to subdue nature to his higher ends," but for modern humans with their intelligence, energy, and developing natural and social sciences, there is "the hope that such an enterprise may meet with a certain measure of success." In view of past cultural advances, he believes that "much may be done to change the nature of man himself," but he warns us that progress is not inevitable, and to accomplish all this would require a great common effort over a long period of time. For Huxley, evolution may teach us how human tendencies for good and evil originated, but it is incompetent to provide valid ethical norms for human behavior. "Social progress means a checking of the cosmic process at every step and the substitution for it of another, which may be called the ethical process; the end of which is not the survival of those who may happen to be the fittest…but of those who are ethically the best."[21]

In a sociobiological expansion of Huxley's lecture, the biologist George C. Williams faults him for not sufficiently distinguishing the ethical effects of physical versus biological evolution.[22] While physical evolution can be described as morally indifferent, biological evolution by natural selection instills such cruel competitive instincts that it must be characterized as gross immorality. Most often, natural selection maximizes selfishness. The survival of any one organism is possible only at great cost to others. He cites Annie Dillard, who deplores the wretched predator-prey system that gives us a "world in which half the creatures are running from—or limping from—the other half." Books describing parasite life cycles are "hellish hagiography…the devil's summa theologica."[23] Williams notes that several scientists see a parallel between the adverse consequences of natural selection and the doctrine of original sin as an explanation for human immoral conduct, and another scientist proposes that the goal of morality should be the ultimate negation of the commandment of natural selection. For Richard Dawkins, genes are selfish because all they care about is their own survival. DNA is not capable of independent existence but rather is locked up in living creatures. The only value of their living hosts is that they are survival machines engineered by natural selection to live long enough to reproduce and thus propagate DNA, which in turn are in competition with other genes for survival. As long as DNA is passed on, it doesn't know or care who or what gets hurt in the process. But we humans have the power to defy the selfish genes of our birth and, if necessary, our cultural indoctrination to hopefully create a "pure disinterested altruism—something that has no place in nature, something that has never existed before in the whole history of the world.…we alone on Earth, can rebel against the tyranny of the selfish replicators."[24]

In our everyday lives most of us have ample opportunity to observe in ourselves and others a deeply rooted instinct for selfishness, an innate drive compelling us to seek above all our own survival. In the struggle for existence, this selfishness has had an adaptive value for the individual in the competition with others for limited resources. But we also observe widespread cooperation among individuals. This social cooperation may have evolved, at least partly, out of the predator-prey system—not especially noble origins. To be more efficient in hunting down prey as well as more successful in defending against predators, our ancestors increased their chances of survival and reproduction by collective rather than individual efforts. Cooperation evolved because it was in our biological interest to cooperate. As a successful adaptation, social cooperation may have evolved into a human instinct along with individual selfishness. Though cooperation may be part of our nature, it is not unique in nature. Genes, molecules, cells, organs, physiological systems, and various other species cooperate. Common in complex organisms is a division of labor necessitating cooperation and where the fate of the individual components is inextricably tied to the fate of the collectivity. Though each creature acts in its own interest, the living world also works through cooperation. Not only humans but also most other life forms require a degree of enlightened selfishness to survive and thrive.

However, cooperation does not guarantee that we humans do the morally good. After all, couples, families, groups, gangs, tribes, corporations, and governments can and do oppress and victimize in their efforts to survive and flourish. Cooperation alone does not seem to be the evolutionary source of our moral sense. At least partially, our norms for good and evil seem to derive from the advanced capacity of humans to feel empathy for other humans. Empathy is one of the defining traits for being human. Most psychologists agree that empathy consists of both an affective aspect, feeling what another is feeling, and a cognitive aspect, understanding what another person is feeling and why. We take in and experience as our own the other person's suffering and joy, motivating us to treat others as we wish to be treated, thus explaining, at least in part, the biological origins of a universal human norm for moral good, traditionally expressed as the Golden Rule. Human empathy can move us beyond our own individual and group survival to help others in their own, perhaps even competing groups, and thus represents a novel, emergent evolutionary phenomenon. Psychological research demonstrates that our human capacity for empathy varies among individuals, may be greater in girls than in boys, can be increased or decreased by different parenting styles and environments, and also seems to be influenced by biological dispositions. Sociopaths are the human exceptions, because they lack the capacity for empathy and thus in doing their crimes lack any feelings of remorse or regret.

Though empathy may provide us with moral intentions and a fundamental moral norm, it does not necessarily discern for us the particular good and evil in our complex personal and social lives. We also need to apply another defining human trait—conscious intelligence. At least to a certain extent and in certain circumstances, we have the capacity to rationally assess the moral situation, to gather practical moral wisdom from the experience of others through personal consultation and reading, and to sort out the objective relevance of our empathetic and other feelings. Unlike natural selection, we have the ability of conscious foresight in imagining possible alternative actions and consequences, which we then can morally evaluate by rational analysis. Some of us have an evolved social consciousness transcending individual, family, and tribal boundaries that may move us to create and sustain economic and political systems to manage the conflicts between individual and institutional survival instincts, competition and cooperation, as well as design conditions in which it is easier to do the good and avoid the bad. With a versatile and reflective consciousness as well as a more open, less genetically programmed behavioral repertoire, some of us, at least some of the time, have the hope of transcending an all-encompassing biological and cultural determinism.

Down through recorded history we are reminded of man's inhumanity to man. Furthermore, some of us today have a more acute awareness of human cruelty to nonhuman sentient beings as well as our destruction of the environment. Now, as in the past, the question constantly reappears: Are humans fundamentally depraved?

Judging from empirical studies limited to natural phenomena, it seems that any indictment of human nature is eventually an indictment of nature itself and its evolutionary process by natural selection. Human moral consciousness apparently evolved as an emergent property but was not an antecedent characteristic of nature itself. In so many ways, physical and biological nature are glorious, but from a human perspective they seem morally deficient. Evolution cannot take the place of Providence. Our best assessment of man's alleged moral depravity is that most of us do not intentionally and directly choose evil, but rather in following our instinct to survive, meet our needs, and satisfy our wants in competition with others for limited resources, conflicts inevitably occur. Some of us win. Some of us lose. Except with malicious sociopaths, evil is usually a byproduct. Nature has given us this morally imperfect setup. Humanity has neither fallen from a perfect state nor adequately risen to overcome its amoral natural origins. As Katharine Hepburn tartly replied to Humphrey Bogart in The African Queen, "Nature, Mr. Alnutt, is what we were put in this world to rise above."

# A NATURALISTIC AND EVOLUTIONARY PHILOSOPHY AND SPIRITUALITY

## A REALITY-BASED VISION TO INSPIRE AND GIVE DIRECTION TO OUR LIVES

The tradition of naturalistic philosophies in the West goes back to the ancient Greeks, including but not limited to Thales, Democritus, Epicurus, and Aristotle. Now, as then, we find differences among these philosophies but also certain common threads. Ontologically, naturalistic philosophies are monistic, not dualistic. In the entire universe there is only one fundamental reality, and that is nature. It is self-existent and self-contained and is not derived from or dependent on any supernatural or transcendent powers. No supernatural world exists. Thus, no split or alienation occurs between this world and an ultimate realm of Being entirely different and superior. Our lives in this world are not merely means to an ideal domain beckoning from beyond. Good and evil, the spiritual and the natural, and the mind and the body are not separate realms of being but are different dimensions of one integral nature. From our particular perspective, naturalism does not necessarily equate with materialism or physicalism, and the present methods of science do not necessarily exhaust all possible descriptions of reality. One thousand, or five thousand years in the future, our understanding of the basics of nature may be revolutionized and the methods of science radically evolved. Epistemologically, the only way to know reality is by natural means. For us, however, human knowing does not necessarily equate with the scientific method. Scientific instruments usually find only what they are designed to find. Other natural ways of knowing exist, applicable to specific domains and with greater or lesser validity. In truth seeking and fulfilling practical needs, naturalists do not seek power, privilege, knowledge, wisdom, love, compassion, or any other kind of help from a supernatural being. No supernatural power interferes with natural phenomena or intervenes in our personal lives. No nonnatural causes exist. Human ideals, values, and spiritual aspirations emerge solely from nature without any supernatural guarantees, rewards, or punishments.

For those of us who are naturalists, our view of human life offers realistic hopes, not fantasy expectations. Many religious supernaturalists seem childish in their magical solutions to the human condition. For example, they may believe that beyond all the pain and suffering of this world dwells an all-powerful and loving Cosmic Parent who, if we are good, rewards us with everlasting life in a heavenly paradise. What human, including most any naturalist, would not yearn for such an enchanting dream of eternal bliss? Naturalist philosopher Paul Kurtz claims that the fact of our inevitable death makes many people feel that life is meaningless, and thus they seek—futilely—religion's promise of immortality.

> This quandary and the despair that such reflections can generate is no doubt the deepest source of the religious impulse, the transcendental yearning for something more. Can one extend his present life-world and those of his loved ones and community indefinitely in some form throughout eternity? People ask in torment and dread, "Why is there not something more to my existence?"....At some point there is the recognition of one's finitude, as one gradually realizes that he or she is growing old and is not eternal. The lines on one's face and the sagging body point to the fact that one's powers are not eternal. Prayers to an absent deity will not solve the problem or save one's soul from extinction. They will not obviate the inevitable termination of one's life-world. They merely express one's longings. They are private or communal soliloquies. There is no one hearing our prayers who can help us. Expressions of religious piety thus are catharses of the soul, confessing one's fears and symbolizing one's hopes. They are one-sided transactions. There is no one on the other side to hear our pleas and supplications.[25]

From a naturalistic perspective, death is an integral part of the gift of life. It is a natural event. Death is a homecoming, returning to our original source. We do not die alone; we are part of a universal process of birth, growing, and dying. Even stars and galaxies do it! In dying we can experience a solidarity with all of nature, a shared experience with all of life, including our parents, grandparents, great-grandparents, and all who came before. Our dying is going with the flow of life, a natural not an alien experience. We can make peace with death by living full and beautiful lives and then graciously passing on our spirits and accomplishments to others who can thus take their turn at a more evolved level.

Mortality is our great teacher, confronting us with fundamental questions: Why am I living? What can I best do with this great gift of life? What is really most important to me? Am I throwing away my peace and happiness by being caught up in nonessential things? The tragedy of life is not so much in the fact of death as what dies inside us while still living. Am I realizing and enjoying what is most beautiful inside me? Am I giving my special gift to the world? When did I stop singing? Shall we dance!

Along with all the potential joys of living a fully human life, not one of us escapes pain and suffering. Nature makes no exceptions. Who among us would not wish for eternal life in another and perfect world? But no matter how much a naturalist might compassionately understand the human yearning for eternal salvation, it still remains for us only a wish, not a reality. Ideal as it might be, we find no convincing evidence for immortality from a loving transcendent power. Today, the life sciences are beginning to understand the genetic and biochemical causes of aging as well as how we can grow new organs to replace worn-out organs. Thus some of us living today or our children may become the first of the immortals. Such a scientific breakthrough will present humanity with unprecedented potential and problems, but even at its best it will never match the supernaturalist's idealized fantasies of eternal bliss. Nature is not perfect.

Our home is here on earth, not in heaven. It is only natural to be drawn to the supernatural promises of eternal happiness, a loving God and Cosmic Companion who we can talk to in prayer, who will help us in our daily lives, and who also provides a transcendent guarantee that the world is fundamentally all right and that ultimately everything makes sense. But in the version of naturalism we present here, our belief is that in the long run we humans will be happier and live more meaningful and productive lives if we base them on actual realities rather than understandable but wish-fulfilling fantasies. Also, we can live lives of greater spiritual integrity. By the grace of nature we have evolved out of this world. Science has not diminished but rather has increased our appreciation of the wonders of humankind, the marvels of nature, and the ultimate miracle of existence itself. The cosmos unfolds in us and we evolve the cosmos in us. Whether truth, goodness, and beauty are transcendent entities somehow informing nature, we do not know. But it does seem that sparks of truth, goodness, and beauty sometimes emerge from within our nature, crying out to be realized. We don't need an external commandment to follow our love of truth in science and the humanities. We don't need a supernatural revelation to see and want to relieve the massive pain and suffering that confronts us everywhere in the world. We don't need external threats to follow our urge to create beauty. Born in the womb of the earth, we are children of nature, mighty companions to all that lives, and now more than ever cotrustees with nature of our home planet. As we continue to unveil the secrets of life, we can only deepen our reverence for all life and intensify our awe that ultimately we live in a mystery of mysteries. The beautiful part is that each of us in our daily lives can participate in this mystery, and hopefully more of us can live lives inspired by love and compassion and guided by knowledge and wisdom. Recent discoveries in cosmology, physics, and biology reveal to us that our blue-green planet with its sometimes puffy white clouds is a sensational and perhaps even a singular experiment in cosmic evolution. In the twentieth century for the first time in the history of humanity, a few humans dubbed astronauts and cosmonauts were privileged to experience a radically new view of our planet. For astronaut Russell Schweickart, it was also a new personal relationship.

> For me, having spent ten days in weightlessness, orbiting our beautiful home planet, fascinated by the 17,000 miles of spectacle passing below each hour, the overwhelming experience was that of a new relationship. The experience was not intellectual. The knowledge I had when I returned to Earth's surface was virtually the same knowledge I had taken with me when I went into space. Yes, I conducted scientific experiments that added new knowledge to our understanding of the Earth and the near-space in which it spins. But those scientific extensions of technical details I did not come to know about until the

data I helped to collect was analyzed and reported. What
took no analysis, however, no microscopic examination,
no laborious processing, was the overwhelming beauty...the stark contrast between bright and beautiful
home and stark black infinity...the unavoidable and
awesome personal relationship, suddenly realized, with all
life on this amazing planet...Earth, our home.[26]

But if we reflect on the astronomical vastness of the universe with its
billions of immense galaxies and stars, doesn't our planet with its
human life add up to virtually nothing? The answer depends on how
we view our identity. If we see ourselves as entirely separate, self-contained entities excluding all connectedness with the universe, then it
seems that we are truly such trivial creatures. But if we can let our
egos relax and experience ourselves as part of the ongoing cosmic
flow, we expand as the universe expands. Mystics down through the
ages have described their experience of the oneness of all being.
Modern science in its discoveries of the fundamental unity of all
physical reality shows us how right they were. Our ultimate belonging is with all nature, as we are all connected by the same evolutionary unfolding and the same physical laws and components. If we
withdraw from the totality of nature, we withdraw from our total
selves. We transcend our narrow ego boundaries to the extent that we
become active partners with nature, bonding with all life. As active
participants, we are part of and in communion with the whole.

The cosmic significance of humanity and our planet is qualitative,
not quantitative. Floating in the cold, dark immensity of space, Earth
is a multifaceted jewel, and at our best we humans are an abode of
warmth and a spark of light. Our planet has been blessed. Sustained by
energy from the sun, graced with essential chemical elements, water,
and nurturing atmospheric conditions, it was able to evolve an astonishing diversity of life forms. The human species has been blessed. We
are that part of nature that has become conscious of itself, the vast cosmos, and its stupendous evolutionary story. Humankind has been
bestowed with unique capacities to be cultivated and celebrated,

including intelligence, imagination, memory, passion, creativity, courage, determination, humor, aesthetic awareness, and, perhaps most essential in the long run—spiritual aspirations, compassion and a moral sense. If, as it appears, biological evolution has no predetermined end state, then our duty and destiny are not all spelled out. At least to a certain extent, we have an open destiny. If no divine Providence exists to help us and there are no evil powers to hinder us, it's up to us to work out our own destiny. With the accelerating advances in the life sciences and biotechnology, we are already beginning to transform biological nature and even our own human nature according to what we judge to be more evolved values. Nature has given us much, and it appears that we have much to give back. The human species is unfinished, not yet complete, still evolving. Our full story has not yet been told. As we become cocreators of future biological evolution, we are not only beginning to author our own story but also the future story of life.

Now, more than ever, many of us in certain parts of the world have opportunities for a greater variety and degree of human fulfillment, including meaningful work, enduring pleasures, and loving relationships. The hope is that science, including the biological and social sciences as well as medicine and psychology, can improve the quality of our lives, and the arts can continue to enlighten and enchant us. Though future progress is a hope, not an inevitability, we can see that in recent centuries humankind has in certain parts of the planet expanded education, diminished ignorance and superstition, extended basic freedoms to think, speak, and organize, and empowered oppressed women, classes, and races. Hopefully, worldwide communication and travel will help dissolve totalitarian regimes and also promote economic and social fairness. A variety of disciplines and practices is now available to develop our inner lives. Opportunities abound for us to dedicate ourselves to important and meaningful ideals, lifting ourselves and others above brute existence. Where there is despair, we can bring hope, where sadness, joy, and where hatred, love. Naturalist philosopher Corliss Lamont frames his hopes for humanity in terms of humanism.

Humanism is an *affirmative* philosophy. It is essentially
yea-saying. It says: Yes, this mighty and abundant Nature
is our home; in it we ever live and move and have our
being. This Nature produced the marvel of life and the
race of man. It sustains us with its varied goods and stirs
us with its wonderful beauty. Yes, this is a good earth and
upon it we can create a worthwhile and happy existence
for all humanity. Yes, we humans possess the glory of
mind and the power of freedom; we know the grace of
body and the splendor of love. We are grateful for the
many simple pleasures that are ours, for the manifold
enjoyments which art and culture and science bring. We
mortals delight in the sweetness of living rather than
lamenting over its brevity. And we rejoice in being able
to hand on the torch of life to future generations. Yes,
this life is enough; this earth is enough; this great and
eternal Nature is enough.[27]

# THE SPECIALNESS
# OF THE HUMAN SPECIES

Why us? Of the estimated 10 million surviving species existing
today, how is it that only we have evolved a type of consciousness
that can wonder about our origins, purpose, and destiny? How is it
that we who are offspring of evolution are so remarkably unlocking
the secrets of our own cosmological and biological story? John
Barrow asks, "What is man that he is mindful of the universe?" He
notes how strange it is that our minds, which are a product of the
laws of nature, can yet reflect upon them.[28] Is it not astonishing that
our three-pound brains are beginning to uncover the apparent hidden order of the universe? The conceptual and mathematical categories of our minds can discover to a wondrous depth the underlying laws of a bewildering flux of phenomena. Isn't it almost miraculous that nature is so profoundly intelligible to our species? The

stunning discoveries of science seem so improbable for only a primate. George Gaylord Simpson views humans as a unique species.

> Man is the result of a purposeless and natural process that did not have him in mind. He was not planned. He is a state of matter, a form of life, a sort of animal, and a species of the Order Primates, akin nearly or remotely to all of life and indeed to all that is material. It is, however, a gross misrepresentation to say that he is *just* an accident or *nothing but* an animal. Among all the myriad forms of matter and of life on the earth, or as far as we know in the universe, man is unique. He happens to represent the highest form of organization of matter and energy that has ever appeared. Recognition of this kinship with the rest of the universe is necessary for understanding him, but his essential nature is defined by qualities found nowhere else, not by those he has in common with apes, fishes, trees, fire, or anything other than himself.[29]

Humankind is a unique flowering of nature on the planet. Our special significance is defined not by our animality but by our humanity. Because of our unparalleled capacities, it has been in humans that a new kind of evolution began—cultural evolution, with its own set of rules and expressing an astounding range and richness of human pursuits. While the sources of variability in biological evolution are mutations and genetic recombination, the sources of change in cultural evolution are individual and social creativity. As best as science can presently determine, biological evolution is an unconscious process without a predetermined plan and purpose other than survival for reproduction. By contrast, cultural evolution is more a conscious process with deliberate human purposes and plans toward intended goals. At least before the arrival of genetic engineering, biological evolution was something that happened to humans, whereas in cultural evolution we have the potential for making things happen. While in biological evolution change tends to occur over eons of time, cultural change in today's world can be explosively rapid and achieved in less than one generation. Information is transmitted not physically through genes but symbolically through ideas and forms abstracted from things and communicated linguistically in speaking and writing as well as in the language of mathematics and artistic images. The speed of cultural change is accelerated today through international travel, print media, television, movies, and computer networks.

The best available evidence indicates that the human brain capacity and body form have not changed in the last 170,000 years. However, some fifteen thousand years past, modern cultural evolution began with the revolutionary innovation of agriculture, which transcended the hunter-gatherer way of life and eventually resulted in crop and livestock surpluses, systematic trade, the division of labor, complex social organization, permanent cities, and the leisure necessary for the birth of civilization, the arts, and sciences. Culture is not something we add on to our lives by occasionally visiting a museum or going to the theater but rather is an integral part of our daily lives in which we enjoy in ourselves and others our diverse expressions of truth, goodness, and beauty. This culture can be manifested in myriad ways, including the mode in which we walk, talk, and listen; the manner in which we care for our mates and family, our colleagues and customers, as well as other sentient beings and the planet itself. The justly celebrated great works of the arts and sciences remind us, as most of us need to be reminded above the din of our everyday lives, of the privileged endowments of the human spirit.

## A NATURALISTIC SPIRITUALITY

Among many of those we interviewed, the spiritual refers to a quality or dimension behind or beyond our ordinary everyday lives, something sensed but not seen, deeply experienced but impossible to precisely define, yet often described as having to do with the sacred. In the experience of the spiritual and sacred some of us feel opened up to a larger world, more deeply connected to the totality of reality, and more in harmony with the ultimate source of it all. Some of us primarily experience an energizing solidarity with all humanity and all of life. In bonding with these realities experienced as transcending our individual selves, we may feel larger, more at peace, more pure, profound, or powerful. For the supernaturalist, the something beyond is the divine, a reality entirely different and superior to natural reality. For the naturalist, the spiritual is also a sacred reality, perhaps not only transcending everyday human experience but also representing higher realms of being, yet all within the domain of nature. For the naturalist, there is something naturally spiritual in most humans, but even in our spiritual qualities and dimensions we are part of nature.

Natural spiritual values can include a profound sense of the miracle of existence, awe of the vast universe revealed by modern scientific cosmology, an appreciation of the unity and sacredness of all life and celebration of its diversity. In gratitude for the special gifts of our human species, our most appropriate spiritual attitude might be that of personal responsibility to nurture our own individual lives and all life forms on the planet. We can consecrate our lives to the values of truth, goodness, and beauty. Where there is pain and suffering, we can work to bring joy and happiness. If we yearn for peace, we can dedicate our lives to economic and social justice. We can base our personal lives on only what we truly need rather than on all the things we can want, thus not confusing our standard of living for the quality of our lives. In our human relationships, we can honor the fact that all of us have a common evolutionary story, not tied to any one race, religion, or nation. We can devote our lives to create and preserve freedom of inquiry and expression, freedom of religion and nonreligion, as well as promote equality of opportunity for all. For these and other possible naturalistic spiritual values, we cannot claim that they have absolute foundations or are found universally in the cosmos, but we can claim that in our domain they are genuine values worth living, fighting, and sometimes dying for.

Natural rites of passage can celebrate the sacredness and seasons of our lives, including pregnancy, the birth of a child, the first day at

school, adolescent coming of age, graduation, marriage, our first
house, the beginning of a new career, successes, birthdays, retirement,
and finally passing on our stories, wisdom, knowledge, and acquired
goods to our family, friends, colleagues, and the community. Where
possible, a nurturing rite of passage for divorcing could be healing
and hopeful for the couple and their children. Spiritual practices can
train and reinforce us to live our spiritual values. Meditation can
quiet our minds and open our hearts. Retreats can be sanctuaries for
our spirits, allowing the muddy waters of our daily lives to settle and
thus gaining a clearer perspective on where we have been, where we
are now, and where we need to go in relation to our talents and calling in life. Music and the other arts can transport us to domains of
greater beauty and help transform our everyday lives. Walks in nature
and wilderness experiences can bring us back to the basics of life and
ourselves. For some of us, naturalistic prayer is possible in which we
acknowledge our creaturely limitations and open ourselves to the
possibility, even the reverent hope, that transcendent and benevolent
powers can bless us while we rely solely on natural means to manage our daily lives. Never before in history have so many natural
spiritual practices been available to transform our inner lives, including many types of meditation and contemplation, but also yoga, t'ai
chi, the martial arts, vision quests, massage, chanting, sweat lodges,
guided imagery, sensory awareness, and personal journal writing.

We humans have twenty-first-century science and technology
and yet some Stone Age emotions. A variety of modern psychother-
apies help evolve our inner natures by liberating us from unrealistic
fears, anxieties, anger, hostility, guilt, and depression as well as speeding our recovery from traumas and tragedies and developing the self-
knowledge, confidence, and skills to better realize our personal and
spiritual potential. Both professional and self-led support groups can
be powerful and beautiful means to free ourselves from addictions,
heal emotional wounds, learn to love ourselves and others, acquire
the power to deal with sickness, and discover graceful and meaningful ways of passing on our spirits in the process of dying. All this
inner work helps us be more at home with ourselves and at home

with nature. For Erich Fromm, our human fulfillment and even our very sanity depends on being able to unite with the world in a relationship of love.

> There is only one passion which satisfies man's need to unite himself with the world, and to acquire at the same time a sense of integrity and individuality, and this is *love. Love is union* with somebody, or something, outside oneself, *under the condition of retaining the separateness and integrity of one's own self.* It is an experience of sharing, of communion, which permits the full unfolding of one's own inner activity. The experience of love does away with the necessity of illusions....In the experience of love lies the only answer to being human, lies sanity.[30]

This naturalistic and evolutionary philosophy has a rather plucky and passionate spirituality. If science is correct that we are partly or almost entirely the result of chance, then let's take our chance! Rather than waste our lives, let's take a chance on life! In one way or another, each of us has the opportunity to use the powers nature has given us to participate with our heads and our hearts in the vast wonder and mystery of the universe. We can both discover in and create from nature and the human situation the purpose and meaning of our lives. The challenge is to rise to our highest potential, to express our creativity, not our destructiveness. In our striving and sacrificing for our highest ideals we achieve our greatest worth and dignity. For those of us who are especially privileged with such gifts as exceptional intelligence, wisdom, emotional maturity, good health, attractive physical appearance, financial means, social skills, and leadership abilities, it is our moral responsibility to share our blessings by helping others rather than merely feathering our own nests. Much have we all received from nature and perhaps much have we to give back. Where nature is cruel we can give compassion; where mindlessness, mindfulness, and where purposeless, purpose. In our own domain and with all our limitations, our human calling may be to evolve our own nature and bring certain spiritual dimensions to the world. This is an adult spirituality; the responsibility is ours. Sustained by nature, we are the stewards of our own spirits.

# RELIGIOUS WORLD VIEWS

In a beginning way, we will sketch the basic world views and hopes of five living religions. Because each has ancient origins that over time developed a rich panorama of diverse and sometimes conflicting beliefs, it is impossible to generalize in this brief introduction without omitting certain important qualifications that could only be included in a more detailed presentation. Nevertheless, you can obtain an over-all sense of each religion's vision and how in the past and present it can transform individual lives and impact human history.

## TWO MULTIFACETED RELIGIONS FROM THE EAST

### HINDUISM

No one knows exactly when or where in the ancient past the idea began, but a master key to understanding the diverse religious traditions that form modern Hinduism is the belief that we live in a cyclical world—both at the cosmic and human level. In Sanskrit they call it *samsara* which literally means "wandering." For Hindus, the universe is of infinite time and infinite space. Ultimate existence has no beginning and no end. Within this universe, our world and an infinite number of other worlds pass through endless cycles of coming in and going out of existence, following a regular rhythmic pattern, like breathing in and breathing out. Each cycle consists of four great ages called *yugas* which in successive order decline in time and virtue, and last 1,728,000, 1,296,000, 864,000, and 432,000 years, for a total cycle of 4,320,000 years, called a *mahayuga*. A *kalpa* consists of 1,000 of the mahayuga cycles for a total of 1,555,200,000,000 years. But this immense cycle is part of an even greater eternally recurring cycle of 155,520,000,000,000 years. We humans are now living in the *Kali yuga*, the last and most degenerate of the four yugas, and which eventually will be destroyed by fire and floods. After a period of dissolution, our world will again begin a new mahayuga and continue in endless cycles.

That human existence is a series of endless, recurring cycles became widely accepted as a fact by about the eighth century B.C. Our individual souls have existed from beginningless time, wandering from one life form to another in eternal cycles of life, death, and rebirth. Furthermore, our physical and social situation in each lifetime is determined by the *karmic* moral law of cause and effect. Depending on our ethical or unethical actions in past lives, we can be reborn in vegetable, animal, or human forms. If we have earned sufficient karmic merit, we could be reborn as a handsome, wise, and wealthy prince blessed with good health and a long life or, with accumulated karmic demerit, we could be reborn as a pig or worm. According to some traditions, if we have acquired extraordinary merit or demerit, we can be reborn and exist temporarily as heavenly beings and minor gods or suffer painfully in hell before again dying and being reborn. As we sow, so shall we reap. Each of us has free will and is personally and totally responsible for our present life situation. We alone determine our future situation in successive reincarnations. Each of us gets exactly what we deserve. The law of karma is objective and impersonal, part of the structure of the universe—a judgment without a judge. As conceived by the eighth century B.C., there is no escaping the ceaseless rounds of birth, death, and rebirth, no getting off the eternal wheel of karma.

Many modern scholars postulate that by the end of the eighth century B.C. a cloud of despair had settled over many religious spirits because they could never hope to be free from the relentless laws of karma and samsara. How oppressive a feeling to realize that our every act mercilessly determines our future happiness or agony. As we do not live perfect lives, we can expect lifetime after lifetime of suffering. Grueling is the prospect that our souls will never stop wandering. No final security, no end to all this. Heavy are our spirits, crushed by the ever-turning wheel of karma, ever on guard that we do not create more bad karma in our grinding round of endless lives—a sort of eternal purgatory.

How different had been the adventuresome and life-loving spirit of the conquering Aryans as they stormed into northwest India on their thundering chariots earlier in the second millennium B.C., many centuries before the appearance of such ideas as an unending chain of reincarnations and the law of karma. They brought with them their own friendly and benevolent nature gods who were evoked to bring and celebrate the good things of life, including robust health, wealth, power, and a long life. Along with their goals of success and happiness in this world, they had expectations of immortality in heaven. The Vedas, those most ancient sacred scriptures of Hinduism, originated with the Aryans and express their life-affirming beliefs and practices. Their sacrificial rituals, believed to be absolutely necessary to control nature and maintain the order of the universe and society, contributed to Aryan society's optimism and sense of power.

But many generations later, in the eighth century B.C., religious spirits could not recapture the zest for life of their Aryan predecessors, because they had lost faith in the efficacy of the sacrificial rituals and felt trapped in unending reincarnations and the system of moral merits and demerits. The solution to their world-weary despair needed to be discovered within the context of their new but unquestioned assumption of samsara and karma. Enter the Upanishads. Though scholars are unable to date their origins more precisely than by a century or two, a good generalization is that the classical Upanishads considered to be part of the Vedas appeared as early as the eighth century B.C. and continued to be composed until the fourth century B.C.. Other texts called Upanishads were written up to sixteenth century A.D. The classical Upanishads are the last of the four great parts that constitute the Vedas, though in popular terminology the term "Veda" is usually confined to the first part, the Vedic hymns. For many modern Hindus, the essence of their beliefs is found in the Upanishads, which traditionally are called Vedanta, which in Sanskrit literally means "end of the Veda" but is more loosely interpreted as the end or goal of knowledge.

The solution in the Upanishads was both ontological and epistemological. Its inspired contributors sought to discover the ultimate reality behind all appearances and also beyond the gods and ritual sacrifices of the Aryans. Their adventure was not by thundering out with sound and fury to conquer distant lands but rather to gently embark on an inward journey to the inmost silence of their souls, thus unveiling the very foundations of reality. Their quest resulted in revolutionary conclusions: an eternal, unchanging ultimate reality exists which though supporting and pervading the changing phenomenal world yet transcends it; and furthermore, our most fundamental inner self is of the same essence as this cosmic Ultimate. The essence of our personal self, called Atman, is identical with the essence of the cosmic Ultimate, called Brahman. Called God in certain other religions, Brahman should not be sought out as something distant and separate from us but rather as dwelling within our inmost being, our most profound and true Self. The Real as the foundation of the universe is reflected in the infinite depths of our souls. The eminent twentieth-century Indian scholar and statesman Sarvepalli Radhakrishnan beautifully expresses this Ultimate kinship.

The word used in the Upanisads to indicate the supreme reality is *brahman*. It is derived from the root *brh*, "to grow, to burst forth." The derivation suggests gushing forth, bubbling over, ceaseless growth, *brhattvam*.

The word suggests a fundamental kinship between the aspiring spirit of man and the spirit of the universe which it seeks to attain. The wish to know the Real implies that we know it to some extent. If we do not

know anything about it, we cannot even say that it is
and that we wish to know it. If we know the Real, it is
because the Real knows itself in us. The desire for God,
the feeling that we are in a state of exile, implies the
reality of God in us. All spiritual progress is the growth
of half-knowledge into clear illumination. Religious
experience is the evidence for the Divine. In our
inspired moments we have the feeling that there is a
greater reality within us, though we cannot tell what it
is. From the movements that stir in us and the utterances
that issue from us, we perceive the power, not ourselves,
that moves us. Religious experience is by no means subjective. God cannot be known or experienced except
through his own act. If we have a knowledge of
*Brahman*, it is due to the working of *Brahman* in us.
Prayer is the witness to the spirit of the transcendent
divine immanent in the spirit of man. The thinkers of
the Upanisads based the reality of *Brahman* on the fact of
spiritual experience, ranging from simple prayer to illu-
minated experience. The distinctions which they make
in the nature of the Supreme Reality are not merely
logical. They are facts of spiritual experience.[31]

The Upanishads not only revealed that we can come to know the
identity of Ultimate Reality (Brahman) and our Ultimate Self
(Atman), but also that this knowledge frees us once and for all from
the endless reincarnations of samsara and the unrelenting consequences of karma. This salvation is called *moksha*, which literally
means "release" or "liberation." Our ultimate spiritual goal is moksha, which we achieve by our deeply experienced understanding of
the Atman-Brahman identity. By this saving knowledge we transcend this world of appearances and free ourselves from the bondage
of our egocentric worldly desires which have fueled our karmic
wheel and consequent reincarnations. Our ultimate salvation is
beyond time in union with the Timeless. What survives is not our
apparent self with all its ignorance and desires but our true Self, the

divine in us. Our divine Self continues to exist blissfully forever, absorbed eternally in the Divine itself, somewhat like a raindrop sinking into a silent sea.

A tradition of Hindu philosophies called Vedanta developed from the Upanishads; the most influential among intellectuals has been Advaita Vedanta (the ontological absence of dualities), whose most brilliant and systematic thinker was Shankara (A.D. 788-820). In his philosophy the fundamental idea is that Brahman is the one and only ultimate, independently existing reality, and what we experience in our ordinary empirical lives is *maya*, an illusion like a nighttime dream in which we experience events as real, but that in fact have no independent, objective existence. Only when we achieve that higher consciousness in which Brahman is mystically experienced do we correctly understand that the phenomenal world of ordinary consciousness, while practically real in our everyday lives, is only deceptively real and ultimately illusory. For Shankara, the empirical world does exist, but it is only derivatively, not fully real. It is unreal when compared to the one, eternal, ultimate reality that is Brahman. Our true, essential self (Atman) is one with the Ultimate Reality (Brahman) and independent of our physical body and its mental, emotional states. As individuals, we are not ultimately real; ultimately we are really Brahman. As long as we continue in our attachments to the world of maya, we cannot attain the higher understanding that we are ontologically identical with the Absolute and that, ultimately, reality is one, indivisible, and without any dualities.

By Western standards, Advaita Vedanta is more than a philosophical system; it is also a theology and practical guide to spiritual experience and higher states of consciousness. Its path to moksha is by both spiritual and intellectual discipline and includes the intensive practice of meditation as well as renunciation of sensual pleasures that disturb our mental tranquility and self control and diminish our yearning for the wisdom to discern the ultimately real from the apparently real, the eternal from the temporal. Shankara urged celibacy and founded monasteries so that seekers could single-heartedly pursue liberation unfettered by conflicting loyalties and worldly attachments. This sort of discipline is not for the many. As Eliot Deutsch notes, "It requires a radical change in the natural direction of consciousness that leads one to a passionate involvement with the things of the world. Advaita Vedanta is explicitly aristocratic in its contention that, practically speaking, truth or genuine knowledge is available only to the few who, by natural temperament and disposition, are willing and able to undertake all the arduous demands that its quest entails."[32]

The Upanishads contain some of the earliest texts in Hinduism exhorting meditation, ascetic practices, and withdrawal from the world as necessary for the religious quest. During the same period when the Upanishads were being written, the practice of yoga was emerging. The word *yoga*, meaning "yoke" or "discipline," first appeared in the Upanishads. Though a variety of yoga schools and practices developed, its classical expression was the systematization by Patanjali (c. third century A.D.), based upon earlier yoga traditions, and called Raja Yoga. Patanjali incorporated from the Shankara philosophical school the sharp dualistic distinction between matter (*prakrti*) and spirit (*purusha*). Through intensive training in an array of physical and mental techniques, the practitioner aims to control the body and quiet the mind by halting its constant inner chatter and turning it away from alluring external stimuli. Thus free from distractions, one can serenely enter into the inner realm of eternal pure spirit. The persistent and well-trained practitioner can progress by specified stages, eventually developing the capacity to advance from ordinary consciousness, which always has an awareness of something, to pure consciousness, which is devoid of any object of awareness. In this state of pure consciousness, the yogi can finally achieve *samadhi*, the absolute independence of his spirit (purusha) from matter (prakrti), thus attaining moksha's final release from samsara and karma as well as the realization of eternal bliss.

Yoga and Advaita Vedanta continue to be vital traditions, but overwhelmingly today and during the last thousand years the dominant religious path of Hinduism is Bhakti—the loving devotion to a personal god or goddess. Unlike the austere discipline of yoga, this is a way that comes naturally to most humans. In contrast to the intellectualism of Advaita Vedanta, this is the way of the heart. In Bhakti our goal is not a vague identity with a remote, anonymous Ultimate, but rather a warm, personal relationship in which we transcend our selfish egos by unceasing devotion and service to our personal god, both in this world and the next for all eternity. Unlike the self-help rigors of Advaita Vedanta and yoga, we can pray to our chosen savior divinity for assistance, as for example in this invocation to the goddess Durga.

> O Goddess who removes the suffering of your suppli-
> cants, have mercy!
> O mother of the whole world, be gracious!
> O mistress of the universe, protect the world!
>      Have mercy!
> You are the mistress of all that moves and moves not!
>
> You alone are the foundation of the world,
>      residing in the form of earth.
> O you whose prowess is unsurpassed,
>      you nourish the world in the form of the waters.[33]

Among the multitude and luxuriant variety of personal deities, the Hindu typically feels especially attracted to one or only a few. However, the three great divinities today are Shiva or one of his family; Vishnu or one of his *avatars* (incarnations), of which the most popular are Krishna and Rama; and Devi, the goddess in a variety of names and forms. Beyond the self-effort disciplines of Advaita Vedanta and yoga and their promise of a vague oneness with a remote essence of Being, faithful Bhakti devotees can expect the assistance of divine grace by which they are not only released from the bonds of samsara and karma but also granted an eternal afterlife of devoted, blissful union with their beloved god or goddess. Ideally, the focus of Bhakti love is not what we might gain in this or the next world but rather our selfless devotion and service to the deity.

Otherwise stated, our ultimate attachment is to our god, not to our-selves. This altruistic love is graciously expressed by the Bengali saint and mystic Chaitanya (1485-1536) in his devotion to his god, Lord Krishna.

> I pray not for wealth, I pray not for honours. I pray not
> for pleasures, or even the joys of poetry. I only pray that
> during all my life I may have love: that I may have pure
> love to love Thee.[34]

The greatest theologian of Bhakti was Ramanuja (c. A.D. 1017-1137). As with Shankara, he was thoroughly rooted in the Vedanta tradition, but unlike him was also a fervent champion and practitioner of devo-tionalism, in particular, to Vishnu. Based upon a systematic study of sacred scriptures, he concluded that Shankara's strict nondualism (Advaita Vedanta) was incorrect and furthermore reduced to virtual nonreality Bhakti's religious practices and hopes for a truly personal salvation. Ramanuja, who described his theology as a qualified nond-ualism (Vishishta Advaita), shared Shankara's view of the ultimate dependence of all phenomena on Brahman, but in disagreement with him argued that the physical world and the individual self, though ultimately indivisible from Supreme Being, are also distinct and have their own genuine reality and are not a mere illusory reflection of human ignorance. Furthermore, the ultimate reality is not impersonal and without attributes, as Shankara claimed, but rather is personal, with such attributes as omniscience and omnipotence, all loving and all merciful. Moksha is obtained not only by knowledge gained by meditation and the study of scriptures but also by God's act of divine grace, which destroys our karma and samsara in response to our lov-ing dedication and devotional practices such as home and temple wor-ship, religious festivals, visiting shrines and temples, pilgrimages to sacred places, and religious songs and dances. According to Ramanuja, Bhakti is a valid path to salvation. The Ultimate Self rewards our lov-ing devotion and grants our genuinely real selves eternal bliss with our god or goddess in a heavenly paradise.

Another path to moksha's release is the way of selfless action (Karma Marga) according to our *dharma*; i.e., the duties of our place in society and stage in life. In the powerful and beautiful religious classic the Bhagavad Gita, the god Krishna explains to the warrior prince Arjuna that he (and by implication all of us who are necessarily involved in the world) has obligations to do certain deeds in order to sustain the social order and thus should not renounce the world by withdrawing from it. But, warns Lord Krishna, in order that his actions avoid accumulating negative karma, it is absolutely necessary that he renounce any egotistical desires that may have first motivated him to take the actions as well as any desires for resulting benefits. As with Arjuna, we must detach our eternal self (Atman) from our necessary social role and then perform this role without any regard for personal consequences. By offering our actions and entire lives as a loving sacrifice to God, we are able to discipline ourselves in selfless work and consequently avoid accruing negative karmic consequences.

Selfless work according to our place in society means doing the set of duties proper to our social rank. The ancient Aryan invaders from the north originated the four major ranks (which Indians refer to as *varna*, or "color") in their subjugation of the darker-skinned indigenous peoples. The four major varnas, ranked in a descending hierarchy, are the Brahmins (priests who perform ritual sacrifices and are responsible for religious knowledge and learning), the Ksatriyas (warriors and rulers responsible for political order), the Vaisyas (business and trades people) and the Sudras (who serve the higher three varnas as serfs, servants, menial craftsmen, and laborers). Eventually, over two thousand castes (*jati*, or "birth groups") developed within the varna framework and quite often represent specialized occupations. The untouchables, which comprise about a fifth of India's population, are the lowest group of castes and represent an underprivileged class who do such "impure" work as garbage collection, sewage disposal, animal slaughter, and scavenging; they are physically avoided by other castes to prevent pollution. The basic Hindu belief is that each individual is born with a certain temperament, intellectual and spiritual capacities that result from his or her accumulated karma from previous lives, and thus one reincarnates into a specific caste with its own fixed social role and responsibilities. The caste system is sacred and part of the cosmic order. Everything in the universe has its proper place, and the entire universe works best when everything and everybody plays its assigned role. The Bhagavad Gita teaches that it is better to do badly the duties of one's own caste than perform well the duties of another's caste.

Ideally, upper-class males progress through four life stages, each of which defines a specific set of duties and responsibilities. Beginning between the ages of eight and twelve, and then lasting for some twelve years, the first stage is that of the celibate student, whose responsibility is to study, especially the Vedic scriptures. This stage is open to the three highest classes (varnas), but is forbidden to the lowest, the Sudras. After completing this stage, the student returns home to begin the second stage of his life as householder with the demands of marriage, raising children, career, and civic involvement. The duties of a householder not only assure the continuation of society but are often seen as essential lessons for personal spiritual development. With the arrival of the first male grandchild, retirement from many social commitments becomes possible, and the individual is beckoned by the opportunity for the more intense spiritual life of the forest dweller. In this third life stage, the person withdraws from society and retires to the forest to live a hermit life to concentrate on spiritual development, including such means as meditation, study, pilgrimages and seeking out holy people for guidance. Wives may join their husbands if they wish, but they must maintain celibacy. Otherwise, husbands go alone, though perhaps still maintaining some loose family ties. Even more severe and directly focused on achieving moksha in this lifetime is the final stage of world renouncers called Sanyasin. Ceasing all family contacts and giving away all possessions, this liberation-seeker performs his own funeral ceremony symbolizing his death to the world and the end of his phenomenal self. As a solitary wandering beggar, nude or almost nude, free of all attachments and desires, he seeks that state of higher consciousness that can achieve his final release from samsara and karma and the realization of the identity of his eternal self with Ultimate Reality.

Hinduism prescribes four legitimate goals for human life. The first is sensual pleasure, especially sexual pleasure, which is to be fully enjoyed when within the moral and social guidelines of dharma. We should not feel guilty or ashamed and thus suppress our erotic desires but rather cultivate sensual delights. During our entire lifetime or through many cycles of lives, sensual pleasure may be fully satisfying, but Hinduism assumes that eventually we will feel a certain emptiness and a desire to expand our enjoyment to include success in the world in the forms of wealth, power, possessions, and reputation. In this second legitimate group of life ambitions, we expand ourselves and our range of desires from private to social satisfactions involving many other persons. Once again it is assumed that during this present or some future lifetime we will experience a certain malaise and need to move beyond to something more. The third aim of life, which is more properly religious and begins to involve self-renunciation, is our duty to serve and maintain the dharmic moral and social order by right conduct appropriate to our station and stage of life. To conform our personal and community lives to the dharma is to follow the natural order of the universe. The desires for pleasure and success, though they must be within the rules of dharma, are primarily self-serving. In this third goal of following the dharma, we further enlarge ourselves by including our duty to serve the community. This is a more mature stage of spiritual development, where our impulse is more to give than to get, more to serve than to be served. The first three goals of human life are supportive of the householder way of life and the dharmic order at the individual, family, social, and cosmic levels—life-affirming values typical in the early Vedic scriptures rather than the later, more ascetic and mystical emphasis of the Upanishads. After accomplishing the first three life goals, it is expected that again we will feel something lacking, and during our present or some future lifetime will be drawn to directly seek moksha, the final and supreme goal of human existence. Different in kind

than the three previous steps, the achievement of moksha is not by
affirming but by renouncing this world. Salvation is found not by
looking for fulfillment within time but beyond time. Finally, we are
free to be our true Self—Atman is Brahman.

What is the purpose of this world? According to Huston Smith,
Hindus both welcome and prepare to say farewell to the world. They
see us living in a "middle world."

> This is so, not only in the sense that it hangs midway
> between heavens above and hells below. It is also middle
> in the sense of being middling, a world in which good
> and evil, pleasure and pain, knowledge and ignorance,
> interweave in about equal proportions. And this is the
> way things will remain. All talk of social progress, of
> cleaning up the world, of creating the kingdom of heav-
> en on earth—in short, all dreams of utopia—are not just
> doomed to disappointment; they misjudge the world's
> purpose, which is not to rival paradise but to provide a
> training ground for the human spirit. The world is the
> soul's gymnasium, its school and training field. What we
> do is important; but ultimately, it is important for the
> discipline it offers our individual character. We delude
> ourselves if we expect it to change the world fundamen-
> tally....The world can develop character and prepare
> people to look beyond it—for these it is admirably suit-
> ed. But it cannot be perfected.[35]

Hinduism is an accumulation of diverse religious traditions, which
to the Western mind may seem much like an unwieldy collage of not
fully and logically integrated parts. To risk any generalizations about
Hinduism is to invite an avalanche of criticism from specialist scholars and devout practitioners who emphasize this or that tradition,
this or that practice. Nevertheless, we would like to share several
general impressions. In the Hindu world view, our ultimate goal is
not to transform the world but to transcend it. But for most house-

holders, who in fact constitute the vast majority of Hindus, this does not mean that the world is unimportant. The joys of sensuality, success, and service are real, even though not ultimate values. Furthermore, as a manifestation of the playful creativity of God (*lila*), it is part of our nature to rejoice in the wondrous expressions of our bodies, minds, and spirits. In the Advaita Vedanta tradition, it could be said that we don't need to change the world; we only need to change our perception of it—meaning that the world is already perfect, and to discover this we only need to penetrate behind its appearances. Hinduism's resounding message is that we live in an ultimately sacred and benign reality which transcends our ordinary human consciousness, and that we all have an ultimate calling to this transcendent dimension. Each of us in our own due time can hope to obtain moksha. No one, not a single one of us, need fear eternal damnation. Eventually, all of us will be saved, because something of the divine dwells within every living being. For most of us who are religious, how beautiful is the gentle greeting and parting (*namaskar*) between Hindus, who bring the palms of their hands together as in prayer and bow slightly and reverently to each other, thereby acknowledging the divinity in each other. This simple, elegant gesture symbolizes a world view which is ultimately divine, ultimately hopeful.

## BUDDHISM

Siddhartha Gautama was a truth seeker. By modern historical standards, little is known about him with any certainty, but ancient tradition testifies that he was born around 560 B.C. in modern Nepal close to the border of northeast India. Though wondrous legends later developed that he was born miraculously as the princely son of a powerful ruler in a sumptuous kingdom, the truth seems that he was indeed born into the aristocratic warrior-ruler Ksatriya caste and that his father was a local chieftain of the Sakya clan. The young Siddhartha was apparently raised in a certain amount of luxury and perhaps grew up in a pampered lifestyle, spared of most of life's hardships. But judging from his later teachings, he was both a thinking person with a keen, analytic mind and a sensitive spirit who felt extraordinary compassion for human suffering. According to the famous legend of the Four Passing Sights, the young and sheltered Siddhartha was emotionally traumatized the first time he became aware of sickness through an encounter with a person in painful agony from a repulsive disease (perhaps leprosy), learned of aging by meeting a decrepit old man, and discovered death in coming across a human corpse lying alongside the roadway waiting to be cremated. He felt profound sorrow that the human condition involves such pain. Also deeply distressing was his maturing awareness of humankind's unending misery in samsara's eternal cycles of life, death, and rebirth. Realizing that not even palace walls can prevent humanity's dreadful destiny of sickness, aging, death, and rebirth, torment overwhelmed his previous tranquility. But then he came upon the fourth sight—a wandering religious ascetic, homeless and begging for food, yet with an extraordinary serenity. Inspired by the inner calm of the homeless mendicant, Siddhartha reasoned that if he followed the ascetic's path, he too could regain his peace of soul and somehow free himself from the sorrows of life. That very night, twenty-nine-year-old Siddhartha beheld for the last time his sleeping wife and infant son, and left his family and former way of life to become a wandering renunciate, thus freeing him to single-mindedly pursue answers to the questions about human suffering that had come to dominate his life.

For six years Siddhartha pursued his great quest for truth and salvation. In addition to practicing the usual spiritual disciplines of his day, including meditation and self-mortification, he followed the established but nonconformist tradition of the wandering, mendicant philosopher and spiritual seeker. He visited various teachers and ascetics, and though presumably he was influenced by their views, he never became a permanent disciple of any of them. In his part of India it was a time of religious and spiritual unrest intensified by the emergence of conflicting philosophies and theologies, including the Ajivakas, who though believing in the transmigration of souls through millions of lifetimes denied the notion of karma and taught

that we are purely creatures of fate. The Jains practiced vegetarian-
ism, opposed the taking of life in any form (*ahimsa*), and taught that
by choosing morally good actions it was possible to wear out bad
karma and eventually be released into the highest heaven, a pure,
eternal, nonmaterial state of being. Both the Ajivakas and Jains practiced severe ascetic austerities. The materialists, known as Lokayatas,
taught that consciousness was the product of chemical interactions,
and totally rejected karmic moral causation and any form of immortality. However, they did believe in complete freedom of the will, that
humans are entirely free to act as they choose. The only proper criterion for our actions is whether it increases pleasure, including both
pleasures of the senses and human relationships. The philosophy was
optimistic in the sense that it viewed human existence as potentially
more full of pleasure than pain but warned that it is necessary to
develop practical wisdom in order to discern ways to maximize
pleasure and avoid pain. Also, it seems very likely that Siddhartha was
well acquainted with atheistic views, both from his home region's
pre-Vedic traditions and atheistic Sankhya doctrine which had a
major similarity with the atheism of early Buddhism. Another major
school of thought was generally known as the agnostics, or skeptics.

> These appear to have been men who rejected the tradi-
> tional way of life, the Vedic doctrines, and the priestly
> system on the grounds that the speculative doctrines of
> priests and teachers were contradictory of one another,
> and that no final position of "truth" could ever be
> reached. They avoided all argumentativeness, which, they
> said, was productive only of ill-temper. Their positive
> emphasis was on the cultivation of friendship and of
> peace of mind.[36]

Perhaps discouraged by the dissension among the competing schools
of thought, none of which provided a satisfying answer to his questions about the cause and cure of suffering, Siddhartha decided to
pursue truth by even more severe ascetic practices. Fasting to the

point of starvation, his body emaciated and turning black, ignoring heat and cold, he followed a rigorous regimen of yogic exercises and meditation. Impressed by his heroic determination and extreme austerities, he attracted a community of five fellow ascetics. But for Siddhartha, his methods were not working. They gave him neither inner peace nor spiritual enlightenment. Rather than elevating his awareness to higher realms of truth and wisdom, his consciousness was trapped in a tortured body racked by physical pain and debilitating headaches. Then, he suddenly remembered. Once when he was a healthy, carefree child sitting under a shady tree, he spontaneously slipped into a serenely pleasant and energizing trance free of desires, which now as an adult he recognized as the classical first step of *dhyana* (meditation). With this insight, he immediately rose up and took solid food, rice and yogurt, to nurture his enfeebled body. He had discovered the Middle Way for truth seekers, avoiding the extreme self-indulgence of his aristocratic origins but also the extreme self-deprivation of the renunciant life. His companions were scandalized, assuming that by relinquishing the most harsh of his austerities he had abandoned the spiritual quest. They left.

Alone, Siddhartha decided to go it on his own. Sensing that the opportune time had arrived, he seated himself at the foot of a large fig tree to meditate, vowing not to rise until he had found the answers to the cause and cessation of human suffering. Far into the night, he entered into deeper and deeper levels of trance, obtaining clearer and clearer insights into the nature of reality. In the depths of his being he found the answers to his questions. It was such a profound experience that Siddhartha was never the same. Ancient legends tell us that when he arose from meditation and walked about, his appearance was transformed. People would ask him if he was a god, an angel, or a saint, to which he simply answered, "No." "Then what are you?" they asked. The Buddha replied, "I am awake." His answer became his title. The Sanskrit verbal root *budh* means "to awake," thus his titles, the awakened or enlightened one. From a heartfelt compassion, the Buddha wanted to share the truths and consciousness that he had so deeply experienced, but he wondered if it would be at all possible to teach others what he had discovered. One legend tells us that Brahma, the highest god in the popular religion of his time, appeared to the Buddha and convinced him that at least some would understand. Encouraged, he decided to search for his five former companions and found them at Deer Park, near the holy city of Benares. At first they were hesitant, but sensing his serenity and radiance they opened up to him and his message. The Buddha explained to them the wisdom of the Middle Way and what he had learned in his enlightenment experience. They became his first disciples and the core of what came to be the community (*sangha*) of celibate monks, who along with the Buddha followed a way of life that was homeless, mendicant, meditative, and gently missionary.

What truths did the Buddha discover? Like a physician, he carefully observed the patient and then specified a diagnosis, cause, cure, and treatment program for humanity's ills, which are summarized in the Four Noble Truths. First, life is permeated by suffering or dissatisfaction (*dukkha*). Second, the causes of dukkha are the Three Unwholesome Roots (or "three poisons") which are (1) craving, clinging, and grasping, (2) anger, envy, and hatred, (3) ignorance and confusion. Third, the cure to eliminate the suffering or dissatisfaction is the cessation of the craving, clinging, grasping, anger, envy, hatred, ignorance, and confusion. Fourth, the treatment program is the Noble Eightfold Path, which aims toward the eradication of the unwholesome roots and can be divided into three categories: moral conduct (right speech, right action, right livelihood), mental discipline (right effort, right mindfulness, right concentration), and wisdom (right views, right intentions). The prognosis is good if we follow the eight-point regimen. There is hope for humanity.

The Buddha was a practical seeker looking for useful ways to relieve suffering in our present life and the endless cycle of future lifetimes. In his part of India, philosophers and religious thinkers were hotly debating such questions as whether the world is infinite or finite, timeless or temporal, and if the soul is identical or separate from the body. He had no interest in such cosmological and metaphysical speculations, because he considered them unanswerable and unprofitable for liberation from suffering. However, he clearly accepted the Hindu beliefs in samsara's ceaseless reincarnations, the karmic moral law of cause and effect, as well as the pressing need for liberation from their relentless realities, though he gave all three a different interpretation. Incorporated from Hinduism into early Buddhism are the six realms of rebirth (the wheel of life), which, beginning with the lowest, are the hells, the place of the hungry ghosts, the animal world, the level of the violent, warlike Titans, the human world, and the heavens of the gods. These are all possible but temporary rebirth destinations where our bad karma is worked off or good karma is rewarded. None provides final liberation from the wheel of karma. Eventually, Buddhism developed a complex cosmology of three spheres of existence: the sphere of sense desires (where passion rules), the sphere of subtle form (where the mental predominates but with a subtle physical component) and a sphere of formlessness (purely mental without any physicality). Ultimate liberation (nirvana) is beyond all three spheres of existence.

Though the Buddha shunned the rampant philosophical and theological speculating of his times, he did teach a group of metaphysical doctrines that critically define the possibility and nature of our liberation. For him, all phenomenal existence was impermanent (*anicca*). Some three hundred years later, the Sri Lankan version of Sthaviravada-Theravada modified the doctrine to mean that everything is always changing, in flux at every moment. There are no enduring entities, no underlying physical or spiritual substances. In spite of our experience of permanent, fixed things, all is an ongoing, ever-changing series of transitory states. Consequently, there is no permanent entity or thing that we erroneously experience as our "self" or "soul" (*anatta*). As with the rest of the universe, our essential nature is change, impermanence, and insubstantiality. What we really are is a dynamic process of impermanent, temporarily connected, loose bundle of five types of events (*skandhas*): bodily events that give us physical form, sensations (feelings), perceptions (mental images inferred from sense input), dispositions (inherent impulses derived from our karmic inheritance of past lives), and states of consciousness. The repetition of momentary but similar physical forms, sensations, perceptions, impulses, and thoughts interact in a way that makes us experience ourselves as separate, individual entities that we call the "self." But as a matter of fact, there is thinking but no thinker, feeling but no feeler, acting but no actor. Our "self" is a case of mistaken identity analogous to the pre-Copernican deeply experienced but ignorant illusion that the Sun revolves around Earth. Furthermore, there is no salvation in our realization of an identity of the essence of a personal self and a cosmic self (the Upanishads "Atman is Brahman") because no such entities exist. For the Buddha, the common belief in the self as a permanent entity is a pernicious delusion, because it creates an addictive attachment to our experienced self and an egotistic craving for sensual pleasure, power, reputation, and wealth. Clinging to our continuing existence results in actions that generate bad karma, unending rebirths, and consequent suffering. When we die, there is no "self" that is reborn. Rather, at death the five aggregates disintegrate, but the accumulated karma continues to exist with all of its consequences in a newborn living being, which thus is not identical with the previous living being but not entirely different because of the inherited karma of many previous lives. To illustrate this, the Buddha pointed out that when a flame (the accumulated karma) is transferred from one candle to another, the continuous light is one and the same, but the two candles (different combinations of aggregates) are not the same. Our ultimate salvation (*nirvana*) is to be liberated from the profound unsatisfactoriness of this world and the wheel of karma by totally extinguishing our delusion of the self as an entity and its consequent cravings. Thus the Buddhist saying, "No self, no problem."

The Buddha also taught that even in this world we can begin to psychologically experience within "ourselves" the peace and insight of nirvanic consciousness through meditation, possibly even advancing to the craving-free enlightened state of the monk saint (*arhant*), but we can only ontologically abide in nirvana itself after death when we are free of the possibility of rebirth. For the Buddha, the final nirvana after death completely transcends the human capacity to conceptualize or express in words. At best, its description can only be approached in terms of what it is not. It is not a place or a thing, there are no delusions of a self and thus no self-centered attachments and desires with their consequent suffering. When his followers pushed him for a positive description, the Buddha steadfastly kept a "noble silence." From earliest times, however, Buddhist thinkers have argued for and against a fuller picture of nirvana. Some have claimed that in the nirvanic state only personality and struggle disappear. For others, nirvana is extinction but not total annihilation. Some claim that it is a permanent state of transcendent bliss and insight, totally free of misery bringing delusions, desires, hatred, and fear. In the last analysis, the nature of final nirvana, remains a mystery until we actually experience it. The Buddha discouraged our trying to describe the indescribable nature of nirvana but rather stressed our need to strive for its realization.

Hope for attaining nirvana is provided by the Buddha's doctrine of the causal interdependence of all things, technically called "dependent origination." This universal causation extends not only to the physical world but also to the mental, moral, and spiritual domains. It is an objective reality, whether or not we are subjectively aware of its presence. Events occur not just by chance or the arbitrary will of a supernatural power. Basically, "dependent origination" means that every event is the result of numerous causes and conditions, and nothing is independent. There is a network of causes and conditions for each event. As one application of this general principle in our human lives, the Buddha demonstrated a twelve-linked chain of causation which begins with our ignorance (of the Four Noble Truths, impermanence of the world, and nonexistence of the self) and then in turn continues with the consequent causalities of the *skandhas* (also called Five Groups of Grasping) and certain other causal links, resulting in the painful cycles of birth, death, and rebirth. Once we gain knowledge of this causality sequence and because of our freedom to choose, we have the power to determine our destiny by reversing the chain of causation and thus liberate ourselves from the suffering in this and future lives, eventually attaining nirvana.

The Buddha was an atheist or at least an agnostic. He did not believe in a personal or creator God. As to the gods who exist in one of the six realms of rebirth, he spoke of them as inferior, because they can only attain nirvana by first being reborn as humans. Never claiming to be God, a manifestation of God, a savior, a privileged recipient of a transcendent revelation, a miracle worker, or a mystic, he told us that he was simply a human. The starting point for his inquiries was not asking the soaring metaphysical questions of ultimate existence but observing for himself the down-to-earth human situation. Limiting himself to creating as few metaphysical principles as possible, he had great confidence in his human reason and preeminent trust in the powers of introspection. With an independent and skeptical spirit, he found inadequate all appeals to authority or tradition. In the process of his truth seeking, he rejected the supernatural inspiration of the Vedic sacred scriptures, the inherited privileges and caste system of the Brahmin priesthood along with the power of their sacrificial rituals, the requirements of religious purity, and the Upanishad's doctrine of the existence and identity of Brahman and Atman. For the Buddha, each person is his or her own master; there is no transcendent power to help or judge us. We are responsible for ourselves.

Though the Buddha discovered and showed us the path to freedom, each of us must tread the path ourselves. Even though we may have the vital support of a Buddhist community, no one can walk the path for us, no divine grace will save us. In the last analysis, our own personal experience, not the experience of others, is the final test of truth. The Buddha tells us in the Kalama Sutta not to believe in traditions simply because they have been handed down for many generations or believed by many, to reject truth claims based on specious reasoning or simply because they were written by ancient authorities or revered teachers, and to discard old "truths" that we have retained only because we're attached to them by habit.[37] Included in the Buddha's farewell address when he was eighty years old and dying is this instruction: "Be ye lamps unto yourselves.... Those who, either now or after I am dead, shall be a lamp unto themselves, relying upon themselves only and not relying upon any external

help, but holding fast to the truth as their lamp, and seeking their salvation in the truth alone, shall not look for assistance to any one
besides themselves, it is they...who shall reach the very topmost
height."[38]

The Buddha refused to appoint a supreme leader or create a central authority to continue his work after his death, apparently having
faith in the power of his teaching (Dharma), the richness of his psychological and spiritual training, as well as the intelligence, discipline,
and self-reliance of his community. Eventually monks organized and
laity supported a vast network of monasteries, which became spiritual, educational, and cultural centers radiating an influence out into
the surrounding population.

Buddhism frees us both from life and for life. That is, it wakes us
up from our cultural trance of what we hypnotically believe is the
good life and shows us another, more real way of life. Our root problem is not that the world is evil or that we are sinners alienated from
God, but rather that we have a fundamental misunderstanding of
what we are and the human condition. Buddhism has inspired
countless persons and diverse cultures with its high ideals of truth,
wisdom, generosity, peace, nonviolence, and regard for all life forms.
Its four cardinal virtues are compassion, equanimity, loving friendship (also called loving kindness), and joy. For Buddhists, the result of
living their values is happiness. The Venerable Dr. Walpola Sri
Rahula, Buddhist monk and scholar from Sri Lanka (Ceylon), puts
it this way.

A true Buddhist is the happiest of beings. He has no
fears or anxieties. He is always calm and serene, and cannot be upset or dismayed by changes or calamities,
because he sees things as they are. The Buddha was never
melancholy or gloomy. He was described by his contemporaries as "ever-smiling" (mihita- pubbamgama). In
Buddhist painting and sculpture the Buddha is always
represented with a countenance happy, serene, contented

*continues*

*continued*

and compassionate. Never a trace of suffering or agony or
pain is to be seen. Buddhist art and architecture, Buddhist
temples never give the impression of gloom or sorrow,
but produce an atmosphere of calm and serene joy....

Buddhism is quite opposed to the melancholic, sorrow-
ful, penitent and gloomy attitude of mind which is considered a hindrance to the realization of Truth. On the
other hand, it is interesting to remember here that joy
(*piti*) is one of the seven *Bojjhamgas* or "Factors of
Enlightenment", the essential qualities to be cultivated
for the realization of Nirvana.[39]

Thus far we have been describing early Buddhism as understood by
and surviving as the Theravada tradition (Way of the Elders). It is
found today in Sri Lanka (Ceylon), Myanmar (Burma), Thailand
(Siam), Cambodia and Laos. From about the beginning of the first
century B.C. and into the second century A.D., a major division
occurred in Buddhism with the rise of the Mahayana tradition (The
Great Vehicle), which eventually spread from India to China, Korea,
Japan, Tibet, Mongolia, and Vietnam. Among its criticisms of the
older orthodoxy, it claimed that the spiritual goal of the Theravada
*arhants* (saints) was essentially selfish, seeking nirvana only for themselves, contrary to the Buddha's compassionate effort to bring salvation to all suffering humanity. Also it rejected the Theravada doctrine
that only monks could be liberated, while lay persons can only attain
nirvana by first becoming monks and following their austere monastic discipline, withdrawn from the world and exclusively focused on
salvation. Rejecting the monk arhant model as the supposedly highest perfection, the Mahayanists introduced a new, altruistic spiritual
ideal in their doctrine of savior *bodhisattvas* who compassionately
dedicate themselves to helping all creatures attain nirvana.

   The literal translation of the word *bodhisattva* is "a being for
enlightenment," i.e., a Buddha in the making, a Buddha to be. While
in both the Theravada and Mahayana traditions any human who

sincerely seeks enlightenment, even if only in a beginning way, is a
bodhisattva, the Mahayanists exponentially elevated the most spiritual, advanced bodhisattvas to the position of divine saviors for all
mankind. Rather than (in their view) the self-centered, emotionally
detached monk arhants, the supremely enlightened bodhisattvas, fully
eligible for and on the brink of attaining nirvana, instead look back
to suffering humanity and heroically vow to delay their entry until
winning nirvana for all mankind. For the Mahayanists, the supposedly enlightened arhant in seeking nirvana only for and by himself had
not yet completely freed himself from attachment to an individualistic "I" and "mine." By contrast, the ultimate bodhisattvas in their
extraordinary compassion for all beings have transcended any distinction between their and our salvation, thus manifesting their complete
enlightenment as to the radically nondualistic, no-self (anatta). These
ultimate bodhisattvas live in celestial realms. Because of their spiritual achievements over millions of rebirths, the bodhisattvas have
amassed inexhaustible stores of karmic merit which they happily
transfer to suffering beings for their relief, enjoyment, and progress
toward enlightenment. Partly influenced by the emerging Hindu
Bhakti movement, widespread devotional cults developed to lovingly worship their favorite bodhisattva, be granted karmic merit for
more fortunate rebirths, and pray for everyday help and favors.
Beyond merely transferring his karmic merit and helping from afar
or only an example of one who has conquered the causes of suffering, the loving bodhisattva joins humanity by sharing and taking on
the burden of their suffering. From the pages of the Mahayana holy
scriptures, the self-sacrificing, suffering savior declares:

> All creatures are in pain…all suffer from bad and hinder-
> ing karma….all that mass of pain and evil karma I take
> in my own body….I take upon myself the burden of
> sorrow; I resolve to do so; I endure it all. I do not turn
> back or run away, I do not tremble…I am not
> afraid…nor do I despair. Assuredly, I must bear the

*continues*

*continued*

> burdens of all beings…for I have resolved to save them
> all. I must set them all free.…I resolve to dwell in each
> state of misfortune through countless ages…for the salva-
> tion of all beings.…for it is better that I alone suffer than
> that all beings sink to the worlds of misfortune.[40]

While the bodhisattvas were elevated to deities, Siddhartha Gautama
was divinized. Even during his lifetime, disciples began to make him
an object of devotion, but the Buddha warned them to focus on his
teaching, not his person. Soon after his death, legends flourished
exalting his supermundane nature. For example, it was claimed that
he was miraculously conceived when his mother dreamed that a
white elephant entered her body. At the time of his birth, the newborn immediately stood up, walked seven steps, and declared that he
would be an enlightened Buddha. An aged sage, noting the marks on
the infant, prophesied that indeed he would become a Buddha.
However, according to the most strict of the earliest traditions, the
enlightened Siddhartha never claimed to be more than a human like
any other human, and also as the Buddha in nirvana, he is neither
aware of nor able to help beings still trapped in the samsaric scene of
endless sorrow and rebirths. Yet for many believers, it was inconceiv-
able that a being so compassionate as the Buddha would abandon
suffering humanity. He must be existing somewhere, both concerned
and working for our welfare. Little by little, devotional cults appeared
where religious spirits could lovingly honor and seek help from a
supernatural Buddha existing in a transcendent realm.

Momentum for the divinization of the enlightened Siddhartha
culminated in the Mahayana doctrine of the three bodies of the
Buddha (Trikaya), each of which is a distinct mode of existence. At
one level the Buddha appears in his "transformational body"
(Nirmanakaya) as a historical person in mortal physical form like any
other human. At the next level, the "heavenly body" (Sambhogakaya),
Buddha takes on a celestial form in a blissful mode of existence as the
heavenly gods and celestial bodhisattvas. Finally, and radically most

important, is the Dharmakaya (literally, "body of dharma or truth") where the Buddha existence is identified with the Absolute, Formless, Ineffable Reality underlying all phenomena. In the last analysis, Buddhahood is identical with ultimate truth and reality, the transcendent ontological and moral principle immanent and operating in the world. In the billions of other worlds like ours scattered across the infinite, eternal cosmos, innumerable Buddhas assume temporary, worldly forms to manifest the Ultimate Dharma to sentient beings. In our own world during each previous era, historical Buddhas have appeared revealing the Dharma. Also, the belief developed that the future Buddha was Maitreya, a glorious and benevolent bodhisattva now residing in the Tusita Heaven, only awaiting the appropriate time to enter the human domain. Messianic hopes resulted from the belief that the historical Buddha had prophesied that Maitreya would someday appear and purify the world with his teaching. Among the new perspectives flowing from the Mahayana Triple Body doctrine, the most consequential for our spiritual life is the realization that because of the omnipresence of the Dharmakaya, the ultimate Buddha nature is innate in all sentient beings. As each of us has a Buddha nature, all of us can become a Buddha, not only an elite few. To be our true self is to realize our Buddha nature. Furthermore, all sentient beings are one because all are manifestations of the same Dharmakaya.

In the first century A.D. religious philosophers began developing "wisdom teachings about ontology, or the nature of reality [which] constitute the inner core of Mahayana doctrine. These teachings are extremely subtle, abstruse and elusive and defy any attempt at summarizing them."[41] Two main philosophical schools emerged, the Madhyamika, founded by Nagarjuna in the second century A.D., and the Yogacara, established by the brothers Assanga and Vasubandhu in the fourth century A.D. Nagarjuna, one of the greatest minds in all of Indian history, elaborated and systematized the labyrinthine but fundamental doctrine of emptiness (sunyata), which basically means "empty of essence" or "empty of substance." No object anywhere has any inner essence or substance. Rather, every object is simply "dependently originated." Every object exists in causal dependence upon its various causes and conditions. Thus, the concept of emptiness signifies that all forms of existence are relative, not only impermanent but never existing as independent substantial realities. A radical ontological conclusion is that our phenomenal world of samsara with its rebirth, karma, and suffering, and the transcendent world of nirvana, where these three types of events cease, are both equally empty at their most fundamental reality. Thus, the phenomenal world of samsara and nirvana are not two opposed but one and the same reality.

This new ontology had revolutionary spiritual implications. It rendered false the Theravada claim that only by eliminating ignorance and bad karma do we attain nirvana. Rather, to be enlightened is to understand that already here and now we live in nirvana, and our task is to realize in ourselves and the entire phenomenal world our Buddha nature. Our spiritual path is not to retreat from the world, but instead, like the great bodhisattvas, to embrace the world with loving compassion. Truth is discovered through entering into the flux and flow of everyday living. The Mahayana way is not to first become enlightened and then help others, but rather in the very process of helping others to become enlightened, you manifest the radiance of your own Buddha nature. Mahayana is truly "the Great Vehicle" as it opens up salvation beyond the elite monks to all lay persons.

Extending and transforming Nagarjuna's perspective, the Yogacara school developed a religious philosophy of metaphysical idealism, describing ultimate reality as Mind. For one tradition of Yogacara, pure consciousness is the only reality; physical objects have no independent existence but rather are the mental creations of consciousness, while the second tradition holds that all we can ever know is our own ideas. By the practice of meditation and yoga, we can come to understand the unreality of the world and experience things as they truly are. The essential nature of reality is emptiness, as all the world is ideation only. The doctrines of emptiness, nirvana-samsara identity, the presence of the Buddha nature in all sentient beings, and the metaphysical idealism of mind only, spread to and powerfully influenced the Mahayana tradition that dominated the Buddhism of China, Korea, and Japan.

Two of the most important schools of Mahayana practice, both originating in India and further evolving in China, Korea, and Japan, are the Pure Land School, emphasizing devotional piety with salvation by faith and grace, and Ch'an (Zen in Japan), stressing meditation, intuitive insight, and self-effort. Most Pure Land sects focus their loving devotion on the cosmic Buddha Amitaba (Amida in Japan), who while yet a bodhisattva gained Buddhahood on the express condition that all humans with sincere faith who call upon his name will be reborn in his Pure Land, a marvelous heavenly paradise of peace and happiness and a more favorable place than earth to attain Nirvana. Thus the ideal of the historical Buddha's compassion is elevated to the gift of saving grace, generously bestowed to all those of faith by a virtual deity. In Japan the two greatest personalities in the Pure Land tradition are Honen (1133-1212), founder of the Jodo-shu (Pure Land sect), and Shinran (1173-1262), founder of the Jodo-shin-shu (True Pure Land sect). The school called Ch'an in Chinese (a transliteration of the Sanskrit *dhyana*, meaning focused concentration) fused elements of Indian meditation, Taoist nature mysticism, the religious philosophies of Madhyamika and Yogacara, plus the practical, antispeculative Chinese temperament. It emphasized that the essence of Buddhism is the inner experience of realizing the Buddha nature within. As with the Buddha himself, meditation is the method to obtain enlightenment. Scripture study, philosophical understanding, and even liturgical rituals may have a certain value, but they can also be an obstacle if mistakenly considered to be equivalent or a substitute for enlightenment, which is a radically direct, intuitive experience of our true nature as the ultimate Buddha nature. It utterly transcends the power of words, analytical reason, or sacred gestures. Our mind is Buddha mind, innately pure, clear, and radiant; enlightenment is our natural state of mind. Our task is to cleanse the mind from defilements that come in from the outside. By meditation we can look within ourselves with an immaculate Buddha mind and discover that our real nature is the

Buddha nature. Because enlightenment is inherent within all minds, all of us have the innate potential for enlightenment. In Zen, as in Ch'an, we don't need to seek an outside savior; we are our own savior. Also, because the Buddha nature is everywhere, we can experience the radiant and miraculous even in the everyday and ordinary. Samsara is nirvana.

Beginning in the seventh century, a type of Mahayana Buddhism heavily influenced by tantrism entered Tibet from India, known as Vajrayana (the Diamond or Thunderbolt Vehicle). It exists today in Tibet and among refugees in northern India, Mongolia, Nepal, and Bhutan. Though incorporating elements from Tibetan shamanism and the indigenous Bon religion, it might be best described as Buddhist tantrism. Among other and sometimes unique elements, it includes esoteric scriptures and such sacramental practices as the recitation of mantras with enormous powers for good or evil and ritual gestures of the body, hands, and fingers (*mudras*) by which devotees can contact deities. Sacred diagrams (*mandalas*) contain mystical meanings which can only be unveiled by the consecrated elite. Initiation ceremonies include baptism by water and receiving a secret name. Based on the Mahayana teaching that there is no difference between nirvana and samsara, all of human life including sexual passions and practices can be powerful means toward enlightenment.

Let's summarize some of the differences between the Theravada and Mahayana traditions, keeping in mind that both share common roots, including such fundamental beliefs that we live in an infinite universe without beginning or end, containing an infinite number of other worlds like ours, which pass through endless cycles of coming and going out of existence, and that we humans are born and die in endless cycles with karmic consequences until becoming enlightened and attaining nirvana. The Theravada never claimed that Siddhartha Gautama was anything more than a human, however much an enlightened saint and supreme teacher. In the Mahayana, his humanity and our self-efforts as the only hope to free ourselves are eclipsed by celestial bodhisattvas and cosmic Buddhas, who (except in Ch'an/Zen) in response to our faith and prayers, gracefully bestow upon us heavenly bliss and help toward final liberation. Instead of skeptically shunning philosophical speculations, elaborate meta-physics were constructed and savior deities discovered. While in the Theravada enlightenment traditionally requires the full-time com-mitment of monks and nuns withdrawn from the world, the Great Vehicle sees us as already possessing the Buddha nature, which can be manifested in the everyday life of the lay person. Instead of the spiritual ideal of the perfected arhant who after death disappears into nirvana, a new model of perfection appears in the bodhisattva, who after enduring millions of rebirths and finally standing before the open door to nirvana, delays his own entry until all suffering humanity can be saved by his loving service to the world. Though essential virtues in both traditions, Theravada is usually considered to emphasize more the wisdom that gives us profound insight into such truths as the impermanence of reality, the no-self, and the causes and cure for suffering, while Mahayana focuses more on compassion. Both paths, however, lead to the same goal of enlightenment and final nirvana for all sentient beings.

# THREE MAJOR RELIGIONS WITH FAMILY ORIGINS FROM ABRAHAM

## JUDAISM

Hope based on several evolving core beliefs has sustained the spirits of the Jewish faithful since the founding father Abraham and the ancient Hebrews some four thousand years past. Significantly, the national anthem of the modern state of Israel is entitled "Ha-Tikvah"—the hope. Especially between the revelations to Moses on Mount Sinai about 1250 B.C.E. (Before the Common Era) and not later than the sixth century B.C.E., the belief eventually crystallized that the God of the ancestors is the only true divinity, the one and only eternal Supreme Being, the creator and controller of the universe, the judge and ruler of history. God is all powerful and all knowing, all creation is completely subject to his will. Nature is orderly not because of any inherent law, but because the creator wills its regularities. Though ultimately transcendent, this God is not abstract and remote but rather a personal and good God intimately present and actively committed to the welfare of human beings. A moral God, He demands morality from us and rewards goodness and punishes evil.

The God of all creation is also the God of a unique bond with a particular people. Beginning with Abraham, God established a covenant with him and all his descendents which later culminated in further revelations to Moses at Sinai that gave the Jews a unique identity, destiny, and duties as the chosen people. In Exodus 19:5-6, God declared to Moses and the children of Israel, "Now then, if you will obey Me faithfully and keep My covenant, you shall be My treasured possession among all the peoples. Indeed, all the earth is Mine, but you shall be to Me a kingdom of priests and a holy nation."[42] In announcing that they will conquer and come to possess the Promised Land, the Book of Deuteronomy (7:6-8) continues to describe God saying through Moses, "For you are a people consecrated to the LORD your God; of all the peoples on earth the LORD your God chose you to be His treasured people. It is not because you are the most numerous of peoples that the LORD set His heart on you and chose you—indeed you are the smallest of peoples; but it was because the LORD favored you and kept the oath He made to your Fathers [Abraham and his descendents] that the LORD freed you with a mighty hand and rescued you from the house of bondage, from the power of Pharaoh, King of Egypt." The dominant Jewish tradition is that God chose the Jewish people not because of any merit they earned or because they are inherently superior to other people but instead for his own reasons and as a free act of grace. The Jews were not chosen for any special favors but rather for special responsibilities: through their unprecedented relationship with God to bear witness to his sovereignty, law, and love and thus be an instrument for the redemption of all mankind.

During the final centuries of the Biblical era, the idea of a coming Messiah emerged which during its subsequent development and
diverse interpretations has provided a crucial hope for traditional
Jews. Beginning with the Books of Isaiah and Daniel, the expectation grew that God would consecrate a descendent of King David
who would liberate Israel from foreign bondage, restore its past
glory, and inaugurate God's kingdom of peace and justice. The
expected messiah would be a national savior, sometimes seen as having extraordinary political abilities, wisdom, and righteousness; at
other times a gifted warrior who would conquer Israel's enemies and
build a powerful state. Whatever the remarkable characteristics of the
messiah, the constant Jewish tradition is that he will be a human
being, not divine. By the time of the Common Era, a split developed
in the messianic expectations. Some simply hoped to restore the
Kingdom of David in all its splendor, while others had eschatological yearnings for a utopian religious Kingdom of Heaven on earth,
in which the present sinful and imperfect world will come to an end
on a great and terrible Day of the Lord when all mankind will be
judged by God. In some versions, the end days will include the resurrection of the dead so that they also can be judged. With the world
thus purged, God will initiate a universal Messianic Age, "A New
Heaven and a New Earth" in which all creatures will be at peace
with God, each other, and nature as they were in the Garden of
Eden. For some two thousand years, the promise of a messiah and a
messianic age in one interpretation or another has been a literal
truth for every traditional Jew. The liturgy and daily prayer book
express the age-old expectation of the ultimate deliverance and vin-
dication of the Jewish people and the redemption of all mankind.
Today, it is primarily the strict traditionalists who continue to believe
in the sudden and miraculous coming of a personal Messiah, a
descendent of King David, who will be sent by God to reestablish
the Davidic Kingdom in the Holy Land and commence an entirely
new era in which human history will find its fulfillment on earth.
Jewish modernists tend to reject the notion of a personal messiah
and instead believe that all of humankind by working together using

its God-given natural powers can slowly bring about a messianic age of peace and justice.

Up until about the second century B.C.E., the Jews had a vague notion of life after death in which the individual's animating principle descends into Sheol, a Hades-like underworld where it lives a shadowy semiconscious existence. It was a place of no return where the mighty and the weak, the good and the bad descend into a dismal, ghostly existence, seeing no light, feeling no movement, and experiencing neither joy nor pain. It was a place of no hope where even the blessings of God could not reach. The good and the bad, side by side, shared the exact same existence. The idea of the resurrection of the body after death received its first clear biblical expression in the Book of Daniel, dated around 165 B.C.E. during the time of the Maccabees. From this time onward, the Pharisees, who will be the wellspring of the future Judaism after the destruction of the second temple in 70 C.E., elaborated the doctrines of the resurrection, eternal life, and also that in the world to come the righteous will receive their reward and the wicked their due punishment as required by God's justice. Under the influence of the Greeks, some Jews including the great Jewish philosopher Philo (c. 20 B.C.E.-50 C.E.), and possibly even Maimonides (1135-1204 C.E.) reinterpreted the resurrection in terms of an immortal soul surviving a temporal body. Though, for almost two thousand years, the resurrection and eternal life have been constant core beliefs of Judaism, neither has received an entirely systematic and dogmatic expression as to their precise relationship and temporal sequencing with the Last Judgment and the Messianic Kingdom. In daily practice, belief in the afterlife is so fundamental that the Amidah, one of two central prayers in most Jewish services, includes the verse, "Blessed art Thou O Lord, who calls the dead to life everlasting."

Unifying all religious Jews is the Torah and their aspiration to live the way of Torah. In its most restrictive sense, the Torah consists of the first five Books of the Bible, often called the Books of Moses or the Pentateuch. Later the Prophets and the Writings (including the Psalms, Proverbs, Job, Daniel, etc.) also became accepted as authentic

revelation from God. These three components, which comprise the
complete Hebrew Bible, are called the TANAKH. Around 200 C.E.,
Rabbi Judah, the Patriarch of the Land of Israel, promulgated the
Mishnah, which was a collection of laws and normative rules of
practice developed between about 200 B.C.E. and 200 C.E. by rabbinical teachers and scholars (i.e., Pharisees) and based upon what
they believed was an oral tradition going back to Moses at Sinai. The
Mishnah document was soon regarded as a sacred text and became
the foundational starting point for further commentary and development by successive generations of learned interpreters and sages at
the rabbinic academies of Palestine and Babylonia. Both centers
were in constant communication, as both were doing essentially the
same work. The result was two great compilations of teachings—the
Palestinian and Babylonian Talmuds, completed about 400 and 600
C.E. respectively, though the latter became the more comprehensive
and authoritative source for Jewish law and theology. Both Talmuds
contain two kinds of material: (1) Halakhah, translated as "law," laid
out the normative rules about what one must do and not do in every
situation of life and every moment of the day. In a spiritual sense it
means the way people live their daily routines to sanctify every detail
of their lives according to divine revelation and to ultimately attain
redemption: (2) Aggadah is all the nonlegal material including theology, biblical exegesis, ethics, history, medicine, folklore, and legends. After the destruction of the second temple, the whole Torah
(both the written and oral parts, i.e., the Bible plus the Talmud)
eventually replaced the temple, and Torah study replaced its sacrifices. For those of us who are religious Jews, the Torah is God's most
precious gift, because in it we come to know God and the laws of
life for this world. To know and love the Torah means that we can
better do God's will in this world. It is a divinely revealed way of
truth and salvation to make holy and meaningful our individual and
community lives. Torah is our hope, coming from God and leading
us back to God. When a Jewish boy first starts Torah studies, sometimes a drop of honey is placed on the page to indicate that his
sacred duty is also his wondrous joy.

What is the Jewish attitude about this world? Basically, Judaism is very much at home in the world. Its founders were not meditators, mystics, or wandering mendicants. When Abraham was wandering in the desert, it was not for his spiritual enlightenment but rather because he was a nomad. His hope and that of his descendants was to find a settled home in the Promised Land of milk and honey. Self-mortification and self-denial are not the higher paths to salvation. Traditional Jews take seriously the Book of Genesis when after the completion of creation, it is stated, "God saw all that He had made, and found it very good." (Gen 1:31). Not only good, but "very good." Celibacy is not part of Jewish spirituality. In the process of creating Eve, the Lord God said, "It is not good for man to be alone." (Gen 2:23) Marriage and the family are sacred; children are a blessing. Ideally, the home is the house of the Lord, and the family table is an altar where the weekly Sabbath meal and the annual Passover Seder are celebrated. As creatures of God, our bodies, not only our spirits, are good. Both are expressions of God's bounty; both are to be enjoyed. The body is not the prison of the soul. Mortification of the flesh and monasticism's withdrawal from the world are not ways to express the goodness of God's creation.

> Life is good and a gracious gift of God. Man should
> enjoy it in all ways which do not transgress the moral
> law and which do not impair his spiritual growth....One
> should not experience any sense of guilt in the legiti-
> mate enjoyments of life. They are of God. Man can wor-
> ship God with his total being—with body, mind and
> soul....Rab, who together with Samuel established the
> leading academies in Babylonia and made it a center of
> Rabbinic studies, is quoted as saying: "A man will some
> day have to give an account to God for all the good
> things which his eyes beheld and of which he refused to
> partake."[43]

The Hebrew Bible tells us that "God created man in His image, in the image of God He created him." (Gen 1:27) Though Adam and Eve sinned against God and suffered the consequences, there is no mention of any inherited guilt or corrupted nature automatically transmitted to all mankind from which we need to be redeemed by divine intervention in order to be saved. Judaism finds no Biblical justification for the idea that the human race is born in sin and only the grace of God can save us. Rather, born in the image of God, we all have free will and thus are personally responsible for our own moral behavior. Predestination is rejected. Though Judaism looks forward to an afterlife, its focus is not so much to prepare us for the next world as to guide us in this world. Its principal passion is not metaphysical speculation about ultimates but practical ethics—discovering and doing God's will in our everyday lives as revealed in the Torah. For Jews, a person's calling is not to reject or escape from the world, not to renounce or abandon the self, but rather to be an active partner with God, embracing all life and fully engaged in completing his creation—keeping covenant with God in history.

The Jewish belief in linear time and a future messianic age has decisively shaped the Western psyche in its expectation and passion for progress. In contrast to the Hindu and Buddhist concept that the world is without beginning or end and ceaselessly repeats itself in eternal cycles of coming in and going out of existence, the Jewish view is that the world was created by God at the beginning of time and is moving forward toward a final culmination at a definite end point in time. The world is not going around in endless circles, it is going toward a unique climax. Human life is not a continuous series of transmigrations of the soul from life form to life form, but a one-time event with eternal consequences. For both Hinduism and Buddhism, there is no hope for final salvation within time itself, but rather it is necessary to be released into a timeless existence. The God of Judaism is the ultimate reality and though radically transcendent is also the immanent Lord of history. This world is not a mere illusion but rather is so important that God at critical times intervenes in the world to guide the Jews and thus all humanity according to a divine plan, eventually achieving a messianic age in a very real world. This positive world view passed into Christianity and Islam and thus into Western civilization. All human history has a purpose, a meaningful direction and goal. Our individual lives have a sense of purpose, meaning, and significance to the extent that we actively participate in the progress toward the goal of history. The Lord of history is also the God of hope. If we faithfully follow God's commandments and respond to his love, as well as collectively use our God-given powers, we can hasten the arrival of the promised Messianic Age. God is not passive but active and creative in the world; thus we should not be passive but active and creative in the world. The Lord is not an abstract universal being remote from the world, but instead a personal God involved with the world. We are not a mere collection of energies, but real persons with intelligence and will engaged in the world—creatures made in the image of God who are "little less than divine" and "Master over Your handiwork." (Psalms 8:6&7) The goal is more to transform than transcend the world; the messiah will usher in the new era in this, not another, world. The Jews have a lively memory of God's past interventions, a love of their traditions, and a powerful orientation to better times in the future, thus bequeathing to the West, an acute historical consciousness. With the prophets as models, a passion for social justice developed in the West, resulting in political revolutions and the secular messianism of Marxism, which shaped Western history. In contrast, an ever-repeating cyclical world with no beginning or end offers no lasting hope for historical progress and thus no fundamental incentive to improve the world. In the Jewish world view, the messianic goal of history will not arrive solely by the gift of divine grace descending from above. Rather, we humans must energetically work for it in cooperation with God's commandments and interventions in history. Humans are not merely objects of history but also the subject of history. Humans are active coworkers with God in forging our future, thus fulfilling the divine will for us in history and the creative destiny of humanity. The ancient Greeks developed a variety of world views, including cyclical or linear concepts of time. When linear, everything proceeded in a horizontal line, but with no expectation of the world improving. For the Greeks, if there is a Golden Age, it was in the past, not the future. Generally, they had no notion of historical progress and thus little hope for the improvement of the human lot. The Greeks discovered the rational cosmos; the Jews gave us a vision of history.

Today, Judaism is expressed in four religious movements, which, ranging from the most strictly traditionalist to the most decidedly modernist, are the Orthodox, Conservative, Reform, and Reconstructionist. Though their beliefs stretch from fundamentalist to naturalistic, their emotional divisions are generally quite mild to nonexistent due much to Judaism's emphasis on being a practical religion focusing more on correct action than correct beliefs. The identity of being a Jew, the strong sense of community, and the thousands of years of shared traditions and tribulations are a powerful bond allowing for a variety of religious beliefs. In the twentieth century, two epochal events occurred in Jewish history—the unimaginably evil and systematic extermination of six million Jews by Hitler's Nazis, and in 1948 the establishment of the state of Israel. The Holocaust has raised questions, perhaps unanswerable, such as how could God let this happen. The homeland offers the possibility of a safe haven and the opportunity to be a light to all nations. Let us close this presentation of Judaism with a concluding prayer (Alenu) for worship services which summarizes some basic Jewish beliefs and hopes.

> Let us praise Him, Lord over all the world;
> Let us acclaim Him, Author of all creation.
> He made our lot unlike that of other peoples;
> He assigned to us a unique destiny.
> We bend the knee, worship, and acknowledge
> The King of kings, the Holy One, praised is He.
> He unrolled the heavens and established the earth;
> His throne of glory is in the heavens above;
> His majestic Presence is in the loftiest heights.

*continues*

*continued*

He and no other is God and faithful King,
Even as we are told in His Torah:
Remember now and always, that the Lord is God;
Remember, no other is Lord of heaven and earth.
We, therefore, hope in You, O Lord our God,
That we shall soon see the triumph of Your might,
That idolatry shall be removed from the earth,
And false gods shall be utterly destroyed.
Then will the world be a true kingdom of God,
When all mankind will invoke Your name,
And all the earth's wicked will return to You.
Then all the inhabitants of the world will surely know
That to You every knee must bend,
Every tongue must pledge loyalty.
Before You, O Lord, let them bow in worship,
Let them give honor to Your glory.
May they all accept the rule of Your kingdom.
May You reign over them soon through all time.
Sovereignty is Yours in glory, now and forever.
So it is written in Your Torah:
The Lord shall reign for ever and ever.[44]

## CHRISTIANITY

Jesus was a Jew. The Gospels give ample evidence that he was deeply
Jewish, firmly rooted in his Jewish heritage. Born around 4 B.C. in
Palestine, he was brought up in Nazareth, a small village in the hill
country of Galilee about a hundred miles north of Jerusalem.
Though little is known of his childhood and early adult years, scholars surmise that he attended synagogue school in Nazareth, with its
emphasis on reading and writing, employing the Torah as the primary text. It is generally assumed that his family was at least minimally devout, and thus Jesus learned the prayers, stories, and customs
of Jewish tradition and celebrated the Jewish holidays and some of

the pilgrimage festivals in Jerusalem. He probably became a wood-worker, in Greek a *tekton*. Marcus Borg notes that "In terms of social standing, a *tekton* was at the lower end of the peasant class, more mar-ginalized than a peasant who still owned a small piece of land. We should not think of a *tekton* as being a step up from a subsistence farmer; rather a *tekton* belonged to a family that had lost its land."[45]

Judea had been conquered in 63 B.C. by Pompey, and soon all of Palestine became part of the Roman Empire. Powerful Hellenizing influences flourished in certain neighboring cities, including Sepphoris less than four miles from Nazareth. However, no evidence exists that Jesus sought out knowledge of Roman law and literature or Greek science and philosophy. Gentile gods did not interest him. Rather, his world view was profoundly Jewish. Ultimate reality was the God of Abraham, Isaac and Jacob, Moses, the Torah, and the prophets. His loyalty was to the one, true God of his people—Israel. From the beginning of time to its eventual climatic end, all of histo-ry was seen as threaded with the will of an eternal, all-wise, good, and omnipotent personal being—the God of the Jews.

With the exception of a brief sojourn to neighboring Phoenicia, Jesus never traveled beyond the borders of his native Palestine. He began his healings and teaching in the synagogue on the Sabbath, and only after his reputation grew did he preach in open areas to accommodate the crowds. Jesus spoke as a Jew to his fellow Jews. His ministry and message was to the Jews. He made no effort to seek out and win Gentile converts. He did not intend to found a new reli-gion. His chosen disciples were Jews, twelve in number symbolizing the twelve tribes of Israel. His followers were considered a Jewish sect, the Nazarenes. According to the Gospel of Matthew (5:17), Jesus came not to abolish but to fulfill the Law and the prophets. He began his public ministry in his late twenties or early thirties, and it lasted perhaps as little as one year or at most only four years. He died somewhere around the age of 33. He was so young, with a life so short and a ministry so brief—how can one explain his powerful imprint on millions of lives over two thousand years? His death was brutal and humiliating. As best as can be deciphered from the New

Testament and scanty historical documents, the ruling Jewish authorities in Jerusalem arrested Jesus and judged him to be a leader of potential riots by his followers and thus a danger to the precarious peace with Roman power and one more threat to the survival of the Jewish people. The high priest and the chief priests recommended the death sentence when they handed him over to the local Roman administrator, who considered him a political troublemaker and ordered his execution by crucifixion, the most disgraceful type of death penalty according to Roman Law. The Gentile soldiers mocked him as they nailed to the cross: "This is Jesus, the King of the Jews." (Mt 27:37)[46] Born a Jew, Jesus died a Jew.

Most biblical scholars agree that the central message of Jesus was the coming kingdom of God. However, the same equally expert scholars sharply disagree about what Jesus believed to be the nature of the kingdom and its expected time of arrival. After carefully examining the scriptures, some conclude that Jesus expected the immediate, apocalyptic end of the world and the dramatic arrival of a radical new age when God's will would be done on earth, as it is in heaven. Certain other scholars, examining the same scriptures, conclude that the message of Jesus was primarily spiritual and that in his person and ministry the Kingdom of God was already and continues to be realized in the present. Some experts deduce that Jesus believed that he was the promised messiah, while others hold that Jesus thought of himself as only a prophet proclaiming the soon and sudden appearance of the messiah and his kingdom, which would finally vindicate God's justice and mercy for the faithful of Israel. Some biblical specialists are convinced that we can never resolve all these differences, because the New Testament is not an objective historical record but rather the devout testimony of the early Christians' faith in the risen and soon-to-return Lord.

One of the events in the Gospels that seems certain is that Jesus in his late twenties left Nazareth and became a follower of John the Baptist, an apocalyptic prophet who lived in the desert wilderness of Judea. This solitary ascetic, wearing clothing of camel's hair and surviving on locusts and wild honey for food, preached the urgent message, "Repent, for the kingdom of heaven has come near." (Mt 3:2). The end of the present age was at hand, the messiah was about to appear and judge the world in the day of wrath. "His winnowing fork is in his hand, and he will clear his threshing floor and gather his wheat into the granary; but the chaff he will burn with unquenchable fire." (Mt 3:12). Many, including Jesus, responded to John's powerful warning and followed him to the Jordan to be baptized in water, signifying their repentance and the washing away of their sins. Biblical scholars conjecture that Jesus' encounter with John was a profound religious experience and a turning point in his life, because shortly after John's arrest and imprisonment, Jesus began his own public ministry, proclaiming the imminent coming of the Kingdom of God.

Convinced that the end would soon arrive, Jesus returned to Galilee and launched his career as an itinerant preacher and healer, "proclaiming the good news of God, and saying, 'The time is fulfilled, and the Kingdom of God has come near, repent, and believe in the good news'." (Mk 1:14-15). "I must proclaim the good news of the kingdom of God…For I was sent for this purpose." (Lk 4:43). His tone was urgent, his person sincere, and his message compelling to many who had eschatological yearnings for better times. Especially the poor, the disenfranchised, and the rejected must have resonated with his electrifying message of hope beyond their difficult, even desperate times. At last, the long-awaited messiah was coming, and God's radical new order will be established. It will turn the world upside down. The last will be first and the first will be last. In the famous Beatitudes of the Sermon on the Mount, Jesus gave hope for a just new world, God's will to be done on earth as it is in heaven.

> Blessed are the poor in spirit, for theirs is the kingdom
> of heaven.
> Blessed are those who mourn, for they will be comforted.
> Blessed are the meek, for they will inherit the earth.

*continues*

*continued*

Blessed are those who hunger and thirst for righteousness, for they will be filled.
Blessed are the merciful, for they will receive mercy.
Blessed are the pure in heart, for they will see God.
Blessed are the peacemakers, for they will be called
children of God.
Blessed are those who are persecuted for righteousness'
sake, for theirs is the kingdom of heaven.
Blessed are you when people revile you and persecute
you and utter all kinds of evil against you falsely on my
account. Rejoice and be glad, for your reward is great in
heaven, for in the same way they persecuted the prophets
who were before you.

(Mt 5:3-12)

In Luke's Sermon on the Plain, there are four Beatitudes and four
"woes" which are followed by some of the spiritual qualities that
Jesus taught his disciples in preparation for the coming kingdom of
God. Unlike Matthew's "Blessed are the poor *in spirit*," Luke begins
with the more radical, "Blessed are you who *are poor*."

Blessed are you who are poor, for yours is the kingdom
of God.
Blessed are you who are hungry now, for you will be
filled.
Blessed are you who weep now, for you will laugh.
Blessed are you when people hate you, and when they
exclude you, revile you, and defame you on account of
the Son of Man. Rejoice in that day and leap for joy, for
surely your reward is great in heaven; for that is what
their ancestors did to the prophets.
But woe to you who are rich, for you have received your
consolation.
Woe to you who are full now, for you will be hungry.

Woe to you who are laughing now, for you will mourn
and weep.
Woe to you when all speak well of you, for that is what
their ancestors did to the false prophets.
But I say to you that listen, Love your enemies, do good
to those who hate you, bless those who curse you, pray
for those who abuse you.
If anyone strikes you on the cheek, offer the other also;
and from anyone who takes away your coat do not
withhold even your shirt. Give to everyone who begs
from you; and if anyone takes away your goods, do not
ask for them again.
Do to others as you would have them do to you.

(Lk 6:20-31)

Though scholars dispute whether Jesus understood himself to be the
messiah or was rather proclaiming the imminent arrival of the messiah, it is clear that he conveyed a sense of crisis—the end was near.
The sun will be darkened, the moon will stop giving its light, the
stars will fall from the sky and the powers in the heavens will be
shaken. People will see the Son of Man coming in the clouds with
great power and glory. Then he will send out the angels to gather his
elect from the ends of the earth to the ends of heaven. "Truly, I tell
you, this generation will not pass away until all these things have
taken place.... Beware, keep alert; for you do not know when the
time will come." (Mt 13:24-33). Jesus conveys a sense of urgency. A
man invited by Jesus to follow him says, "Lord, first let me go and
bury my father." But Jesus replies, "Let the dead bury their own
dead; but as for you, go and proclaim the kingdom of God." Another
says, "I will follow you, Lord; but let me first say farewell to those at
home." But Jesus says to him, "No one who puts a hand to the plow
and looks back is fit for the kingdom of God." (Lk 9:59-62). To his
disciples whom he has sent out to proclaim the good news of the
coming kingdom, he declares "If anyone will not welcome you or
listen to your words, shake off the dust from your feet as you leave

that house or town. Truly I tell you, it will be more tolerable for the land of Sodom and Gomorrah on the day of judgment than for that town." (Mt 10:14-15).

The sudden, unexpected, and humiliating death of Jesus left his followers in a state of shock and confusion, but later his resurrection and ascension into heaven vindicated their faith in him. Yet the expected apocalyptic end of the world had not occurred. The belief grew in the early Christian community that at any moment Christ himself would return in glory to judge the living and the dead, end the present world in a universal cataclysm, and establish the kingdom of God. The tense expectation of the imminent return of the Risen Christ dominated the spirituality of the early Christians. When will the Lord come? Paul writes to his converts, "For you yourselves know very well that the day of the Lord will come like a thief in the night." (I Thess 5:2). But they were worried. Some among them had already died. Would they be excluded from the kingdom of God because they had died before Christ's glorious return? In this first preserved Christian text (written 50-51 A.D.), Paul assures them that when Christ returns their deceased will be resurrected, and even before the living, they will be the very first to greet the Lord and thus be with him forever in his kingdom. (I Thess 4:13-18)

As time passed and the return of Christ was delayed, the teaching developed that the kingdom of God had already begun in the person of Christ, though final salvation would only be complete when he returns. In one of the latest books of the New Testament (written about 120-130 A.D.), it is noted that because Christ had not yet returned, some people scoff and say, "Where is the promise of his coming?" In response, the writer assures the Christian community, "But do not ignore this one fact, beloved, that with the Lord one day is like a thousand years and a thousand years are like one day. The Lord is not slow about his promise, as some think of slowness, but is patient with you, not wanting any to perish, but all to come to repentance. But the day of the Lord will come like a thief, and then the heavens will pass away with a loud noise, and the elements will be dissolved with fire, and the earth and everything that is done on it will be disclosed…. But, in accordance with his promise, we wait for new heavens and a new earth, where righteousness is at home." (II Peter 3:4, 8-10, 13) For many of us who are devout Christians, we have already experienced the saving grace of Christ and the beginnings of the kingdom of God in our personal lives, yet we also look forward to our Lord's return. In this world, Christ is a model for us in his particular love for and mystical identity with the poor, the sick, the suffering, the underclass, and the outcast. We will be judged, and our fate in the afterlife will depend on how well we live in the image of Christ.

When the Son of Man comes in his glory, and all the angels with him, then he will sit on the throne of his glory. All the nations will be gathered before him, and he will separate people one from another as a shepherd separates the sheep from the goats, and he will put the sheep at his right hand and the goats at the left. Then the king will say to those at his right hand, "Come, you that are blessed by my Father, inherit the kingdom prepared for you from the foundation of the world; for I was hungry and you gave me food, I was thirsty and you gave me something to drink, I was a stranger and you welcomed me, I was naked and you gave me clothing, I was sick and you took care of me, I was in prison and you visited me." Then the righteous will answer him, "Lord, when was it that we saw you hungry and gave you food, or thirsty and gave you something to drink? And when was it that we saw you a stranger and welcomed you, or naked and gave you clothing? And when was it that we saw you sick or in prison and visited you?" And the king will answer them, "Truly I tell you, just as you did it to one of the least of these who are members of my family, you did it to me." Then he will say to those at his left hand, "You that are accursed, depart from me into the eternal fire prepared for the

*continues*

*continued*

devil and his angels; for I was hungry and you gave me
no food, I was thirsty and you gave me nothing to drink,
I was a stranger and you did not welcome me, naked and
you did not give me clothing, sick and in prison and you
did not visit me." Then they also will answer, "Lord,
when was it that we saw you hungry or thirsty or a
stranger or naked or sick or in prison, and did not take
care of you?" Then he will answer them, "Truly I tell
you, just as you did not do it to one of the least of these,
you did not do it to me." And these will go away into
eternal punishment, but the righteous into eternal life.

(Mt 25:31-46)

Unique to Christianity is the doctrine of original sin. The concept
originates in the epistles of Paul, in which he states that because of
the original sin of disobedience by Adam, all of humanity has inherited his sin and so all of nature is fallen, i.e., estranged from God and
prone to evil. All people are sinners, not only by inheriting the state
of sin from Adam's fall, but also because as a consequence we cannot
keep ourselves from sinning in our personal lives. Furthermore, death
entered the world as a consequence of Adam's sin. We humans are
powerless to break out of our bondage to sin and death. Only the
special intervention of God can free us. In Paul's words, "Sin came
into the world through one man, and death came through sin...so
death spread to all because we all have sinned." (Rom 5:12). But God
sent one man, Christ his obedient son, to reconcile us with Him, free
us from sin, and restore our natural state of immortality. "Just as one
man's trespass led to condemnation for all, so one man's act of righteousness leads to justification and life for all. For just as by one man's
disobedience the many were made sinners, so by one man's obedience the many will be made righteous....so that, just as sin exercised
dominion in death, so grace might also exercise dominion through
justification leading to eternal life through Jesus Christ our Lord."
(Rom 5:18-19, 21). As both ritual and moral uncleanness were

purged by the shedding of animal blood in the temple sacrifices of
Jerusalem, so did Christ by the bloody sacrifice of his crucifixion and
death atone for the sin of Adam and all the resulting personal sins of
mankind, thus reconciling us with God and restoring us to eternal
life. Christ came as a "merciful and faithful high priest in the service
of God, to make a sacrifice of atonement for the sins of the people."
(Heb 2:17). He is "the Lamb of God who takes away the sins of the
world." (Jn 1:29). Christ "is truly the Savior of the world." (Jn 4:42).
In Hinduism it might be said that the basic problem is that we usually don't see beyond appearances. In Buddhism the basic problem is
suffering. In Christianity the basic problem is sin. Christianity is the
religion of salvation from sin. The fundamental miracle is the incar-
nation of God in Christ, his sacrificial death, and his victorious resurrection by which all humanity received the hope that they can be
free of Adam's sin and personal sin. Christians have taken the cross as
the sacred image of their faith, symbolizing the redemptive sacrifice
of Christ and the evidence of God's love for humanity—the
B.C./A.D. crossroads of salvation history.

Love is the primary Christian virtue. John's first epistle taught
the early church, "Beloved, let us love one another, because love is
from God; everybody who loves is born of God and knows God.
Whoever does not love does not know God, for God is love….those
who abide in love abide in God and God abides in them." (4:7-8,
16). John's gospel states further, "For God so loved the world that he
gave his only Son, so that everyone who believes in him may not
perish but have eternal life." (3:16). Jesus instructs his disciples, "This
is my commandment, that you love one another as I have loved you.
No one has greater love than this, to lay down one's life for one's
friends. You are my friends if you do what I command you." (Jn
15:12-14). God's love transcends race, nationality, gender, and socioe-
conomic status, and embraces even our enemies. God's love gives us
the hope that our prayers will be answered: "Ask, and it will be given
you; search, and you shall find; knock, and the door will be opened
for you. For everyone who asks receives, and everyone who search-
es finds, and for everyone who knocks, the door will be opened."

(Mt 7:7-8). According to the beliefs of certain Christian denominations, God's love is also bestowed through the sacraments and the intercession of the saints in heaven for the faithful on earth. The classic Christian statement on the primacy of love is by Paul.

> If I speak in the tongues of mortals and of angels, but do not have love, I am a noisy gong or a clanging cymbal. And if I have prophetic powers, and understand all mysteries and all knowledge, and if I have all faith, so as to remove mountains, but do not have love, I am nothing. If I give away all my possessions, and if I hand over my body so that I may boast, but do not have love, I gain nothing.
>
> Love is patient; love is kind; love is not envious or boastful or arrogant or rude. It does not insist on its own way; it is not irritable or resentful; it does not rejoice in wrongdoing, but rejoices in the truth. It bears all things, believes all things, hopes all things, endures all things.
>
> (I Cor 13:1-7)

Though salvation comes from the Jews, it culminates in Christ, who is not only a man but also God. In the later texts of the New Testament, its inspired writers began to formulate the superhuman nature of Jesus. For example, in the famous opening prologue of John's gospel, the Greek philosophical concept of the Logos (in English, "the Word") as the universal reason permeating and governing the world was applied to Jesus as the Eternal Cosmic and Divine Creative Word. Over the following 350 years, theologians struggled to define Christ's nature, resulting in the General Council of Nicaea's declaration in 325 that Christ is of one substance or essence with God the Father, and in 451 the Council of Chalcedon's affirmation that Christ is both True God and True Man, two natures conjoined in one Person. Also, the idea of the mystical presence of Jesus with his followers began in the New Testament with such verses as "Where two or three are gathered in my name, I am there among them," (Mt 18:20), and Paul's statement, "It is no longer I who live, but it is Christ who lives in me." (Gal 2:20). As best as we are able to observe among most devout Christians, more important than determining the precise facts about the historical Jesus or explicating an exact theological understanding of his divinity is their personal relationship with Jesus. For most of us who are fervent Christians, we have experienced the living power and presence of Christ, and this has sanctified and made meaningful our personal existence. In all the big and little events of our daily lives, Jesus is "the way, and the truth, and the life." (1 Jn 14:6). Here is a popular Christian hymn adapted from a poem by Saint Bernard of Clairvaux, a twelfth-century mystic and theologian.

### Jesus, the Very Thought of Thee

Jesus, the very thought of Thee, With sweetness fills my breast;
But sweeter far Thy face to see; And in Thy presence rest.

Nor voice can sing, nor heart can frame, Nor can the memory find
A sweeter sound than Thy blest name, O Savior of mankind!

O Hope of every contrite heart, O Joy of all the meek,
To those who fall, how kind Thou art!, How good to those who seek!

But what to those who find? Ah! this Nor tongue nor pen can show,
The love of Jesus, what it is None but His loved ones know.

## ISLAM

A few months before his birth, his father died. While only six, his
mother died. Orphaned, his grandfather raised him for a while until
his uncle, though with very limited means, warmly adopted him, but
soon put him to work as a shepherd tending his flock. As typical for
his time and place, he received no formal schooling and according to
Muslim tradition was illiterate. His father had been a trader, but his
uncle trained his teenage nephew to be a caravan manager, a highly
respected but dangerous profession. At twenty-five, his employer, who
was a wealthy widow of about forty, was so impressed by his moral
integrity and management skills that she proposed marriage. He
accepted. During their close and monogamous marriage until her
death twenty-five years later, they had two sons, who unfortunately
did not survive infancy, and four daughters. All this life history appears
to be inauspicious background for Muhammad becoming the
beloved, the last and greatest of the prophets, God's messenger of the
definitive and final revelation. When he died at age 62 in 632 A.D.,
the community he formed was already on its way to becoming a vast
religious and political state and was soon to expand into an empire.

Until age forty, Muhammad lived a private life, edifying but not
noticeably eventful. He rose from poverty to prosperity in a quiet but
conventional way, enjoying success in his career, marriage, and family, along with social status in the community. But by his late thirties,
a hidden life was ripening. Experiencing spiritual yearnings, he began
to periodically leave the commercial bustle of his native Mecca and
withdraw to mountain cave retreats to pray and meditate, far removed
from everyday responsibilities, the noise of busy merchants, and pilgrim crowds milling around innumerable polytheistic idol shrines. At
age forty, during one of his solitary month-long wilderness retreats in
a cave on Mt. Hira outside Mecca, he unexpectedly experienced a
frightening and life-transforming experience. The Archangel Gabriel
gave Muhammad orders to "recite," thus beginning a series of many
revelations from God that he continued to receive over a period of
twenty-two years and which were collected and written down in the

Quran, Islam's sacred scripture.

God revealed to Muhammad through the Archangel Gabriel that he was the last in a long line of prophets chosen by God to receive divine messages. The Quran names at least twenty-five prophets, including Abraham, Moses, Job, Jonah, and Jesus. Muslims, Christians, and Jews are all the Children of Abraham, because they all trace their origins back to him. But the Jews and Christians lost or altered part of their original revelations and consequently have distorted the divine Word and deviated from God's path. Like past prophets in the Hebrew and Christian traditions, Muhammad did not intend to nullify their scriptures or create a new religion but rather only aimed to restore their original purity. God in his mercy chose Muhammad to correct the corruptions in the Old and New Testaments, and furthermore, not only to continue but to complete the original divine revelations. Muhammad is the last or the "Seal" of the prophets, and the divine messages he received as recorded in the Quran are the pure, literal, and infallible word of God, his final revelation to the world, and source *par excellence* of all Islamic spirituality.

The Quran proclaims an uncompromising monotheism. There is no god but God.

He is God;
there is no god but He.
He is the knower of the Unseen and the Visible;
He is the All-merciful, the All-compassionate.

He is God;
there is no god but He.
He is the King, the All-holy, the All-peaceable,
the All-faithful, the All-preserver,
the All-mighty, the All-compeller,
the All-sublime.
Glory be to God, above that they associate!

*continues*

*continued*

He is God,
the Creator, the Maker, the Shaper.
To Him belong the Names Most Beautiful.
All that is in the heavens and the earth magnifies Him;
He is the All-mighty, the All-wise.
(Sura 59:22-24)[47]

God is absolutely one, in no way three. Though Jesus was a great prophet, in no way is he divine. Muslims have never believed and Muhammad never claimed that he was more than a human. God is transcendent yet immanent in creating and sustaining the world. The one God is a personal God, the Ultimate Reality, all powerful, all knowing, and all just. He is beyond human comprehension, yet he knows us intimately and intervenes in human history. Allah (literally "God" in Arabic) cares for us and has given us in the Quran the straight path to be fully human and enjoy the bounty of his creation in this world and the next. The world was made for the benefit of mankind but is under the absolute rule of God. As creatures, our relation to God is that of a servant or slave to a sovereign Lord. God is the provider; all that we have, our very existence comes from God. Recognizing our creatureliness, our radical dependence on God, the Prophet Muhammad called his religion *Islam* which in Arabic means "surrender." A Muslim is one who submits to the will of God. We who are Muslims are God's servants. Submitting to the majesty, the just and merciful rule of God is not humiliating but liberating. It frees us from slavery to the human idols of ego-driven selfishness, status seeking, and greedy consumerism. Surrendering to God's guidance in his commandments is not self-denying but self-fulfilling; it shows us the way to blossom both spiritually and materially in this world and attain paradise in the next. Fundamental to Islamic spirituality is *Shukr*, gratitude and thankfulness for the very gift of life and all the bounty and blessings the Creator has bestowed on us. We who are Muslims express this gratitude in worship and right conduct. To be ungrateful is to be an unbeliever. A fundamental virtue is *Dhikr*

*Allah* meaning "the remembrance of God" in his greatness and goodness, which is so beautifully expressed five times daily in the Salat prayers and also emphasized in Sufi mystical practices. Underlying sinful disobedience to God is not any inherited depravity from the original sin of Adam and Eve but rather forgetfulness of our divine origins, and thus we become distracted or indifferent to the reality of God and heedless of his guidance. Repentance is remembering the one, true God and the path He has revealed for us.

The Islamic worldview confirms the Judeo-Christian doctrine that one God created one universe out of nothing. While God as the Ultimate Reality is eternal and timeless, the created world had a definite beginning in time and moves not in endless cycles but rather toward a culminating climax. God is not vague and abstract but rather personal and real; humans are not a temporary collection of energies but personal entities consciously enduring for all eternity. God is not absent but rather actively sustains the world and intervenes in human history. The universe consists of three realms: heaven, earth, and hell. In addition to human inhabitants in the visible world, several kinds of spirits populate the invisible: angels, devils, and jinn. Most angels are good creatures doing important work as messengers and helpers of God. However, one of these, Iblis (the personal name for the devil, Satan) was cast out of heaven for refusing God's commandment to pay homage to Adam. Also, because he tempted Adam, he bears the guilt for Adam's sin. Satan has a host of other fallen angelic followers who tempt and try to mislead humans. Lower in nature than the angels are the *Jinn* (singular is *Jinni*, which became known in the West as genies), who like humans are intelligent with free will and can be good or bad. They live in a subtle immaterial world and take visible form from time to time. Some jinn are helpful to humans, others are harmful. At the Last Judgment at the end of the world, all deceased humans will be bodily resurrected from the dead, and then both the jinn and humans will be judged by God and assigned to either eternal paradise or eternal hell fire.

The Muslim faith has a positive and meaningful view of this world. By Allah's deliberate act, all of nature was created as real and important. Because its Creator is all good and perfect, so is the natural world. The study of nature has a sacramental quality and is helpful in our spiritual life, because it unveils the grandeur and goodness of God.

> Islamic spirituality is therefore based not only upon the reading of the written Quran…but also upon deciphering the text of the cosmic Quran…which is its complement. Nature in Islamic spirituality is, consequently, not the adversary but the friend of the traveler upon the spiritual path and an aid to the person of spiritual vision in his journey through her forms to the world of the Spirit, which is the origin of both man and the cosmos. The Quranic Revelation created not only a community of Muslims, but also an Islamic cosmic ambiance in which the signs of God (Ayat Allah) adorn at once the souls of men and women and the expanses of the skies and the seas, the birds and the fish, the stars and the creatures living in the bosom of the Earth.[48]

The doctrine of *Fitra* teaches that the primordial nature of humans is essentially good and in harmony with God and nature. Though we humans may forget, repress, or ignore this fact and thus can err and do great evil, our fundamentally good nature as creatures made in the image of God can never be entirely erased. For Muslims, all of nature including human nature can be celebrated, but, of course, only God is to be adored. According to the Quran, humans are the viceroys of God, entrusted as his representatives to protect and manage the earth, thus realizing God's will in history. God has made all of nature subservient to humans, and we will be judged on how well or badly we have carried out our stewardship. According to traditions handed down from the Prophet, we humans should use all our talents to profit from God's creation. God likes to see the traces of His bounty in his creatures. Islam teaches the goal of success both in this world and the next.

It is well known that the motto of Islam is summed up in the expression of the Quran (2:101), "Well-being in this world and well-being in the Hereafter." Islam will certainly not satisfy the extremists of either school, the ultra-spiritualists (who want to renounce all worldly things and mortify themselves as a duty) and the ultra-materialists (who do not believe in the rights of others), yet it can be practiced by an overwhelming majority of mankind, which follows an intermediate path, and seeks to develop simultaneously the body and the soul, creating a harmonious equilibrium in man as a whole. Islam has insisted on the importance of both these constituents of man, and on their inseparability, so that one should not be sacrificed for the benefit of the other. If Islam prescribes spiritual duties and practices, these contain also material advantages; similarly if it authorizes an act of temporal utility, it shows how this act can also be a source of spiritual satisfaction.[49]

Muhammad is the ideal model for Muslim life, "the living Quran." A universal human, he was not only deeply religious and a contemplative but also a man of action—a successful businessman, husband, father, spiritual guide, skillful negotiator, political organizer, founder of a state, chief judge, ruler, and brilliant military strategist. Following Muhammad's example, the Muslim ideal is to live both a full and integrated life, never compartmentalizing the material as independent of the spiritual or the secular as distant from the sacred. Islam is a total, all-embracing way of life. With God as sovereign Lord of all creation, Muslims have traditionally maintained the ideal that no separation should exist between the state and religion. All of life should be ruled by religious values as specified by the Quran, tradition, and Islamic Law.

The heart of Islam includes its mission to create a moral social order.

> There is no doubt that a central aim of the Qur'an is to establish a viable social order on Earth that will be just and ethically based....the Qur'an's goal of an ethical, equalitarian social order is announced with a severe denunciation of the economic disequilibrium and social inequalities prevalent in contemporary commercial Meccan society....The economic disparities were most persistently criticized, because they were the most difficult to remedy and were at the heart of social discord....The Qur'an is certainly not against earning wealth. On the contrary, it sets a high value on wealth, which it terms "the bounty of God"...it counts peace and prosperity among the highest blessings of God...But the abuse of wealth prevents man from pursuing higher values...the Meccans' single-minded pursuit of wealth is said to be "the height of their knowledge" (53:30), since they knew only the "exterior of life, being heedless of its higher ends" (30:7). In the absence of concern for the welfare of the poor, even prayers became hypocritical...This lack of consideration for the economically needy is the ultimate expression of pettiness and narrowness of mind—the basic weakness of man. The Meccans contended that they had earned their wealth, which they, therefore rightfully owned and which they could spend or dispose of as they wished. The Qur'an insisted, first, that not all wealth earned was rightfully the earner's; the needy had also a "right" in it. "In their wealth there is a definite right of the indigent and the deprived." (70:25; also 51:19). Secondly, the Qur'an told the Meccans that even the wealth they rightfully owned they could not spend just as they wished, for they could not become islands of plenty in a sea of poverty.[50]

One of the methods in the Quran to promote economic justice is the *Zakat*, an obligatory tax that Muslims pay at the end of the year according to their means that is used to help the needy. So central is this tax to religious practice that it is one of the five Pillars of Islam. In addition, voluntary charity is strongly encouraged and is highly meritorious. Beginning with the prophet himself, Islam teaches the brotherhood of all Muslims and the equality of the entire human race. Muhammad instituted many social reforms, some of which were radical for his time, including strengthening family life and expanding women's rights. As Allah is just, so all Muslims should strive to establish a just society.

Exquisitely symbolic of our relationship with the Creator and the bond of brotherhood uniting all Muslims is the Salat ritual prayer, required of the faithful, both male and female, five times daily. Performed at daybreak, noon, midafternoon, sunset, and evening, and in the same simple, formal way throughout the world, faithful Muslims pause from their busy daily lives to remember and express gratitude to their sovereign Lord. After preparing for prayer by doing a few brief ritual ablutions to clean their outer bodies and purify their inner souls, they face Mecca, the holy city and center of Islam, in exactly the same manner as the prophet Muhammad. In uniformly prescribed cycles of standing, bowing, kneeling, sitting, and prostrating with the forehead and palms of the hands touching the ground or carpet, accompanied by specified prayers performed in Arabic, Muslims reverently acknowledge their profound thankfulness for existence, their creatureliness and total submission to the will of their Creator. When Salat is performed with others, especially at the Friday noon Mosque congregational service, Muslims line up in rows shoulder to shoulder as equals before the same God and brothers in the same worldwide family of Islam. Repeated among the Salat prayers is the *Fatihah*, the opening *sura* of the Holy

Quran expressing the heart of the Muslim's devotion to the one true God.

> In the Name of God, the Merciful, the Compassionate
> Praise belongs to God, the Lord of all Being,
> the All-merciful, the All-compassionate,
>     the Master of the Day of Doom.
>
> Thee only we serve; to Thee alone we pray for succour.
>     Guide us in the straight path,
> the path of those whom Thou hast blessed,
> not of those against whom Thou art wrathful,
>     nor of those who are astray.

# 6

# *On Our Way*

The roads we have traveled in this book have been a considerable journey. In the Preface I stated that this work is intended for those who want to make up their own minds and hearts about some of the basic questions of life and who may wish to develop their own philosophy within or outside the major traditions of philosophy, science, and religion. My goal has also been to provide some practical psychological wisdom to better equip persons for the truth seeking paths they choose for themselves.

In the opening chapter I laid out many of the basic questions raised by individuals in my interviews as well as gathered down through time from philosophy, religion, and science. I recommended that you reflect on these questions as well as your own so that you can identify which of them are most important to you. The purpose of the remainder of the book is to assist you to become more informed and competent as you seek answers to your questions. In the second chapter I provided some of the historical reasons why people today are seeking fundamental answers about their existence and outlined the impact of religion's decline and the advance of science. Then I took up the question of whether truth should be of any great importance, alerted you to dangers of asking basic questions, and provided practical wisdom to better prepare you for your inquiries. I concluded by describing different points of departure for truth seekers and also provided a wide range of answers that people have discovered.

The focus of Chapter 3 was epistemology: the ways of knowing, and how we know when we know. I began with our evolutionary context of millions, even billions of years, provided some perspectives on the evolution of the human brain, and then traced the origins of Western science and philosophy from the ancient Greeks and the scientific revolution of the sixteenth and seventeenth centuries. Then I presented the critiques of empiricism by Locke, Hume, and Kant. Finally, I sketched out some important but less emphasized ways of knowing and raised the question: how rational are we? In Chapter 4, I emphasized that we as persons are the primary instruments of our inquiries because who we are powerfully impacts the kinds of questions we ask, our methods of inquiry, and the answers we find true and meaningful. I described some psychological characteristics of twelve contrasting pairs of truth seekers to help us better assess our own inner reality and how it can influence our truth seeking. Chapter 5 presents the world views and hope provided by science (cosmology, physics, and biology), a naturalistic and evolutionary philosophy, and five living religions.

We are tiny creatures living in a vast cosmos. With a reflective consciousness unparalleled among the other species on our planet, we ask foundational questions about our existence and the universe. Among our many limitations is that we are territorial creatures, so often defending ourselves and our beliefs and fighting off others and their views of life. When operating in its territorial mode, the ego can be a lonely place, a narrow, fearful world, often drawing too narrow a circle around reality or creating imaginary realities. To more objectively assess reality, we need to develop a certain detachment. But objectivity requires not only detachment but also respect. And at best, we not only respect each other's beliefs, but we also have compassion for each other as creatures so capable of error and self-delusion. We all live in the mystery called human existence; some of us also seek to live in communion with the mystery of mysteries — The Great Ultimate. To more accurately understand reality and create lives of greater truth, goodness, and beauty, we need all the help we can get. In this mighty undertaking, why don't we all pull together, not apart, help not harm each other? Rather than fighting over our beliefs, let's keep our minds open and public forums available to all for open dialogue, a joint venture in the spirit of collaboration, not competition. As truth seekers, each of us may follow our own individual way, yet we are all members of the same remarkable species—the same family that sometimes asks, "What's it all about?"

# *Notes*

## CHAPTER 1
### *Some Basic Questions*

1.  To encourage open and honest sharing, I usually interviewed people in the comfort and security of their own homes. Also, I signed an Interview Consent Agreement assuring them that I would not reveal their identity. Generally, I avoided persons with whom I had any personal relationship as well as celebrities, who understandably may need to maintain a certain public image. I never interviewed persons in the presence of their mates, though sometimes I would follow with a couples interview. To avoid being distracted by note taking, I used professional but quite unobtrusive recording equipment. I began the interview by briefly explaining its purpose. From then on, most of the interview was open-ended and nondirective. Thus, I could evoke the interviewee's thoughts and feelings expressed in their own way and at their own pace. Near the end of the interview, I usually did a deep relaxation procedure along with some sentence completions as a way of eliciting responses from the unconscious. Most interviews lasted about two hours. My task was not only to listen but to really hear, not to judge but to understand what this particular human being was so graciously sharing with me.

## CHAPTER 2
### *Why and Why Not Ask These Questions?*

1.  William Barrett, *Irrational Man, A Study in Existential Philosophy* (Garden City, New York: Doubleday Anchor Books, 1962; originally published 1958), pp. 24–25.

2.  Sigmund Freud, *The Future of an Illusion*, translated and edited by James Strachey (New York and London: W.W. Norton, 1961; originally published in 1927), pp. 30, 43, and 49.

3.  Wallace first developed his version of natural selection in 1858 and described it in a brief paper that he sent to Darwin, who recognized immediately that it was virtually the same theory which he had privately formulated twenty years earlier. By a gentlemen's agreement, the two men received equal credit for the new theory, though Darwin was the actual predecessor. I will focus on Darwin's work because subsequently their views developed along divergent paths, and Darwin and "Darwinism" became the more dominant influence.

4.  Cited in Henri F. Ellenberger, *The Discovery of the Unconscious: The History and Evolution of Dynamic Psychiatry* (New York: Basic Books, 1970), p. 207.

5.  This is Willis W. Harman's description of the views of David Lorimer's "Towards a New Science—A Critical Appraisal of Scientific Knowledge," 17th Annual Conference on the Unity of the Sciences, Los Angeles, November 24-27, 1968. Willis W. Harman, *A Re-examination of the Metaphysical Foundations of Human Science* (Sausalito: Institute of Noetic Sciences, 1991), pp. 85-86.

6.  Friedrich Nietzsche, "The Gay Science" in Walter Kaufman, editor and translator, *The Portable Nietzsche* (New York: Penguin Books, 1976; originally published 1954), p. 95.

7.  Thomas Berry, *The Dream of the Earth* (San Francisco: Sierra Club Books, 1990), pp. 123-124.

8.  T.Z. Lavine, *From Socrates to Sartre: The Philosophic Quest* (New York: Bantam Books, 1984), p. 5.

9.  Cited in, "Russell, Bertrand Arthur William" by Paul Edwards and William P. Alston in Paul Edwards, ed., *The Encyclopedia of Philosophy* (New York: Macmillan, 1967), vol. 7, p. 256.

10. The phrase, "the soul's high adventure" is by Bill Moyers in Joseph Campbell with Bill Moyers, *The Power of Myth* (New York: Doubleday, 1988), p. xviii. The other expressions are from Joseph Campbell, *The Hero with a Thousand Faces*, second Edition (Princeton: Princeton University Press, 1968).

11. From a letter to Marie Bonaparte, August 13, 1937, in *Letters of Sigmund Freud*, Ernst L. Freud, ed., Tania and James Stern, trans. (New York: Basic Books, 1960), p. 436.

## CHAPTER 3
### Ways of Knowing: How Do We Know When We Know?

1. Carl Sagan, *The Dragons of Eden: Speculations on the Evolution of Human Intelligence* (New York: Ballantine Books, 1977), pp. 13-17.

2. Paul D. MacLean, *The Triune Brain in Evolution: Role in Paleocerebral Functions* (New York: Plenum Press, 1990), p. 9.

3. MacLean, 1990, pp. 448 and 577.

4. MacLean, 1990, p. 578.

5. From an interview by the authors Judith Hooper and Dick Teresi, *The Three-Pound Universe* (Los Angeles: Tarcher, 1986), pp. 48-49.

6. David C. Lindberg, *The Beginnings of Western Science* (Chicago: University of Chicago Press, 1992), pp. 23-24.

7. Edith Hamilton, *The Greek Way* (New York: Time, Inc. Book Division of Time Magazine, 1963. Reprinted from 1942 revised edition published by W.W. Norton), p. 26.

8. W.K.C. Guthrie, *The Greek Philosophers: From Thales to Aristotle* (New York: Harper and Row, 1975. First published in 1950 by Methuen), p.23.

9. W.T. Jones, *The Classical Mind, vol. I: A History of Western Philosophy*, second edition (New York: Harcourt Brace Jovanovich, 1970), p.32.

10. R. Hackforth, "Great Thinkers, I. Socrates," *Philosophy, The Journal of the British Institute of Philosophy*, vol.VIII, no. 31, July 1933, pp. 259-272.

11. W.K.C. Guthrie, *Socrates* (Cambridge: Cambridge University Press, 1971. First published as part 2 of *A History of Greek Philosophy*, vol. III, Cambridge University Press, 1969), p. 156.

12. Hamilton, *The Greek Way*, p. 279.

13. The "Phaedo" of Plato in *The Last Days of Socrates*, translated by Hugh Tredennick (Harmondsworth: Penguin Books, reprinted with revisions, 1969), p. 183.

14. Aristotle's *Metaphysics*, 991$^a$23 (p. 1566). All references to the works of Aristotle are from *The Complete Works of Aristotle, The Revised Oxford Translation*, vols. I and II, edited by Jonathan Barnes. (Princeton: Princeton University Press, 1984). The first numbers cited are from Aristotle's text in the Berlin Academy Edition (1831-70). The second number, which is in parentheses, refers to the page numbers in the Revised Oxford Translation.

15. Aristotle's Nicomachean Ethics, as above. 1103 $^a$24-25 (p. 1743).

16. Aristotle's Nicomachean Ethics, 1106 $^b$36-38 (p.1748).

17. W.T. Jones, *The Classical Mind*, vol. *I, A History of Western Philosophy*, as above, p.310.

18. Stephen Gaukroger, *Descartes: An Intellectual Biography* (Oxford: Oxford University Press, 1995), pp. 110 and 111.

19. *Principles of Philosophy*, part one, as collected in *The Philosophical Writings of Descartes*, vol. I, translated by John Cottingham, Robert Stoothoff, and Dugald Murdoch (Cambridge: Cambridge University Press, 1985), p. 193.

20. *Discourse on the Method*, part four as above in Cottingham, Stoothoff, and Murdoch, vol. I, pp. 126-127.

21. *Principles of Philosophy*, Preface, in Cottingham, Stoothoff, and Murdoch, vol. I, p. 186.

22. *Discourse on the Method*, part five, in Cottingham, Stoothoff, and Murdoch, vol. I, p. 131.

23. E.A. Burtt, *The Metaphysical Foundations of Modern Science*, revised edition, (Atlantic Highlands: Humanities Press, 1980. Originally published in 1924, revised edition 1932.), pp. 123-124.

24. *The Assayer* in Stillman Drake (trans.), *Discoveries and Opinions of Galileo* (New York: Doubleday Anchor Books, 1957), pp. 237-238.

25. Stillman Drake (trans.) in his introduction, *Two New Sciences* (Madison: University of Wisconsin Press, 1974), p. xxi.

26. Cited in William R. Shea, "Galileo and the Church," David C. Lindberg and Ronald L. Numbers, eds. *God and Nature: Historical Essays in the Encounter Between Christianity and Science* (Berkeley and Los Angeles: University of California Press, 1986), p. 131.

27. Citations for Galileo's "Letter to the Grand Duchess Christina" are from *Discoveries and Opinions of Galileo*, pp. 181-183, referenced above.

28. Michael Sharratt, *Galileo: Decisive Innovator*, (Oxford: Blackwell, 1994), p. 131.

29. From Bacon's Preface to *The Great Instauration* in Fulton H. Anderson, (ed.), *The New Organon and Related Writings* (New York: Macmillan, 1960), pp. 15-16.

30. Loren Eiseley, *The Man Who Saw Through Time* (New York: Charles Scribner, 1972), p. 19.

31. A. Rupert Hall, *From Galileo to Newton* (New York: Dover, original 1963, republished with corrections in 1981), pp. 298-299.

32. I. Bernard Cohen, *The Birth of a New Physics*, revised and updated (New York: Norton, 1985), pp. 164-165.

33. I. Bernard Cohen, "Newton's Method and Newton's Style" in Frank Durham and Robert D. Purrington (eds.), *Some Truer Method: Reflections on the Heritage of Newton* (New York: Columbia University Press, 1990), pp. 15-57. A later adaptation of this article retaining the same title can be found in I. Bernard Cohen and Richard S. Westfall (eds.), *Newton: Texts, Backgrounds, Commentaries* (New York: W. W. Norton, 1995), pp. 126-143.

34. Richard S. Westfall, "Newton and Christianity" in I. Bernard Cohen and Richard S. Westfall (eds.), *Newton: Texts, Backgrounds, Commentaries* as above, p. 359.

35. Richard Tarnas, *The Passion of the Western Mind* (New York: Ballantine Books, 1991), p. 285. For an insightful summary of some of the religious and philosophical consequences of Newtonian cosmology, see pp. 270-271, 280-281, and 285-288.

36. John Locke, *An Essay Concerning Human Understanding*, Peter H. Nidditch (ed.), (Oxford: Oxford University Press, 1975. Reprinted with corrections as a paperback 1979). This and the following citation are from "The Epistle to the Reader," lines 23-27, p. 7. The third citation is from Book I, Chapter I, Section 2, Lines 13-16, p. 43.

37. Maurice Cranston, *John Locke: A Biography*, (Oxford: Oxford University Press, 1985. First published in 1957 by Longmans, Green and Company.), p. 482.

38. John Locke, *An Essay Concerning Human Understanding*, Book II, Chapter I, Section 2, Lines 15-16, p. 104.

39. Locke's *Essay*, Book II, Chapter I, Section 2, Lines 20-21, p. 104.

40. Locke's *Essay*, Book IV, Chapter XIX, Section 14, Lines 20-21, p. 704.

41. Locke cited in article, "Locke's Influence" by Hans Aarsleff in Vere Chappell (ed.), *The Cambridge Companion to Locke* (Cambridge: Cambridge University Press, 1994), p. 252.

42. From Hume's short autobiographical account, "My Own Life," in Ernest Campbell Mossner, *The Life of David Hume*, second edition (Oxford: Oxford University Press, 1980), p. 611. The following two citations are from pp. 615 and 611, respectively.

43. Mossner, 1980, p. 65, who cites as the original source vol. I, 13 of *The Letters of David Hume*, 2 vols., edited by J. Y. T. Greig, Oxford University Press, 1932.

44. This and the following quotations regarding Hume's health are from Chapter 6 of Mossner, 1980.

45. Hume's "My Own Life" in Mossner, p. 612.

46. David Hume, *A Treatise of Human Nature*, second edition, edited by P. H. Nidditch (Oxford: Oxford University Press, 1978), Introduction, p. XVI.

47. David Hume, *An Inquiry Concerning Human Understanding*, Section V, Part I, p.41 in P.H. Nidditch (ed.) *Enquiries Concerning Human Understanding* and *Concerning the Principles of Morals*, third edition (Oxford: Oxford University Press, 1975).

48. Mossner, 1980, p. 5. The citation is in the words of Mossner, not a direct quotation from Einstein. I have added in brackets the word "Newtonian."

49. Cited in article "Kant's Intellectual Development: 1746-1781" by Frederick C. Beiser in Paul Guyer, ed., *The Cambridge Companion to Kant* (Cambridge: Cambridge University Press, 1992), p. 43. This book contains articles covering the broad range of Kant's work as well as a selective bibliography.

50. William James, *The Varieties of Religious Experience* (New York: The New American Library, 1958) p. 298.

51. K.C. Cole, *First You Build a Cloud and Other Reflections on Physics as a Way of Life* (San Diego: Harcourt Brace & Company, 1999), p. 73. Cole does not provide the original reference.

52. Stephen P. Stich, "Could Man Be An Irrational Animal?," *Synthese, An International Journal for Epistemology, Methodology and Philosophy of Science*, vol. 64, no. 1, July, 1984, pp. 115-135. This article is also reprinted in Hilary Kornblith, ed., *Naturalizing Epistemology* (Cambridge: MIT Press, 1985), pp. 249-267.

53. Leon Festinger, Henry W. Riecken, and Stanley Schachter, *When Prophecy Fails* (New York: Harper and Row, 1964. Originally published in 1956 by the University of Minnesota Press), p. 3.

54. George Kelly, cited in D. Bannister, ed., *Perspectives in Personal Construct Theory* (London and New York: Academic Press, 1970), p. 258.

## CHAPTER 4
### *Some Types of Seekers: Know Thyself*

1. William James, *Pragmatism and the Meaning of Truth* (Cambridge: Harvard University Press, 1975; originally published in 1907 and 1909). This and the following quotations of James are from pp. 11-14.

2. Herrlee G. Creel, *Chinese Thought from Confucius to Mao Tse-Tung* (Chicago: University of Chicago Press, 1953) p. 105.

3. Michel de Montaigne, *An Apology for Raymond Sebond*, M.A. Screech, trans, (London: Penguin Books, 1987, Original written 1576) p. 136.

4. Paul Kurtz entitled his book, *The Transcendental Temptation* (Buffalo: Prometheus Books, 1986).

5. Highly recommended is the insightful article, "Living Without Appeal: An Affirmative Philosophy of Life" by E. D. Klemke in his book *The Meaning of Life* (New York and Oxford: Oxford University Press, 1981), pp. 162–174.

6. Some of the characteristics that I ascribe to thinkers and feelers are partly drawn from C.G. Jung, *Psychological Types*, Collected Works, volume 6 (Princeton: Princeton University Press, 1971. Originally published in 1921). I use the term "feeling" in a somewhat different sense than Jung.

7. David Elkins, humanistic psychologist and former Protestant minister, has devoted over twenty years of study and research to identifying and developing spiritualities not dependent on institutional religion. See his *Beyond Religion: A Personal Program for Building a Spiritual Life Outside the Walls of Religion* (Weaton, Illinois: Quest Books, 1998).

## CHAPTER 5
### *World Views: What Can We Hope For?*

1. Werner Heisenberg, *Physics and Beyond* (New York: Harper & Row, 1971), pp. 147–148.

2. Marvin Chester, *Primer of Quantum Physics* (New York: John Wiley, 1987), p. 1.

3. Charles Darwin, *On the Origin of Species*, A facsimile of the first edition (Cambridge: Harvard University Press, 1964, original published in 1859), p. 490.

4. Ernst Mayr, *This Is Biology: The Science of the Living World* (Cambridge: Harvard University Press, 1997), p. 189.

5. L.W.Alvarez,W.Alvarez, F.Asaro, and H.V. Michel,"Extraterrestrial Cause for the Cretaceous-Tertiary Extinction," Science 208 (1980): pp. 1095–1098. Walter Alvarez is a geologist and son of Luis. Frank Asaro and Helen Michel are nuclear chemists.

6. Phillip M. Dauber and Richard A. Muller, *The Three Big Bangs: Comet Crashes, Exploding Stars and the Creation of the Universe* (Reading, Mass.: Addison-Wesley, 1996), p. 14.

7. David M. Raup, *Extinction: Bad Genes or Bad Luck?* (New York: W.W. Norton, 1991) pp. 16–20 and 187–188.

8. Tom Gehrels, "Collisions with Comets and Asteroids," Scientific American, vol. 274, no. 3 (1996), p. 54.

9. George Gaylord Simpson, *The Meaning of Evolution: A Study of the History of Life and Its Significance for Man* (New Haven: Yale University Press, 1967 revised edition of 1949 original), p. 260.

10. Ernst Mayr, *Toward a New Philosophy of Biology* (Cambridge: Harvard University Press, 1988), pp. 106-110.

11. For this citation and his description of evolutionary tinkering, see François Jacob, *The Possible and the Actual* (New York: Pantheon Books, 1982), pp. 25-46.

12. See Richard Dawkins, *The Selfish Gene*, new edition (Oxford: Oxford University Press, 1989). The original edition was published in 1976.

13. R.C. Lewontin, "Organism and Environment" in H.C. Plotkin (ed.), *Learning, Development, and Culture: Essays in Evolutionary Epistemology* (New York: John Wiley, 1982), p. 165.

14. See Daniel J. Kevles *In the Name of Eugenics: Genetics and the Uses of Human Heredity* (Cambridge: Harvard University Press, 1985). The more recent 1995 edition has a new preface by the author.

15. These estimates are from Robert M. May, "*How Many Species Inhabit the Earth?*" Scientific American (vol. 267, number 4), October 1992, pp. 42-48.

16. Edward O. Wilson, *The Diversity of Life* (New York: W.W. Norton, 1992), p. 139.

17. Theodosius Dobzhansky, Francisco J. Ayala, et al., *Evolution* (San Francisco: W.H. Freeman, 1977), p. 43.

18. A detailed, documented, and at times passionate argument tracing the origins of human suffering to evolution by natural selection can be found in Timothy Anders, *The Evolution of Evil: An Inquiry into the Ultimate Origins of Human Suffering* (Chicago and La Salle: Open Court, 1994).

19. T. H. Huxley, *Evolution and Ethics* (Princeton: Princeton University Press, 1989). This is a reprint of his 1892 Romanes lecture at Oxford University published in 1893.

20. T. H. Huxley, 1893, p. 83. The following three quotations are from pages 83 and 84.

21. T. H. Huxley, 1893, p. 81.

22. George C. Williams, "A Sociobiological Expansion of Evolution and Ethics" in T. H. Huxley, *Evolution and Ethics* (Princeton: Princeton University Press, 1989), pp. 179-214.

23. Williams refers to the original source, Annie Dillard, *Pilgrim at Tinker Creek* (New York: Harper's Magazine Press, 1974), p. 229.

24.  Richard Dawkins, *The Selfish Gene*, 1989, p. 201. The preceding perspectives are from his article "God's Utility Function," Scientific American, vol. 273, no. 5 (1995) pp. 80-81.

25.  Paul Kurtz, *The Transcendental Temptation: A Critique of Religion and the Paranormal* (Buffalo: Prometheus Books, 1986), pp. 21-22.

26.  Russell L. ("Rusty") Schweickart, American astronaut, was on the Apollo 9 mission, March 1969. The quotation is from the Preface of *The Home Planet*, conceived and edited by Kevin W. Kelly for the Association of Space Explorers (Reading, Mass.: Addison-Wesley, 1988).

27.  Corliss Lamont, *The Philosophy of Humanism*, sixth edition (New York: Frederick Unger, 1982), p. 145.

28.  John D. Barrow, *Theories of Everything: The Quest For Ultimate Explanation* (Oxford: Oxford University Press, 1991), p. 172.

29.  George Gaylord Simpson, 1967, p. 345.

30.  Erich Fromm, *The Sane Society* (New York: Fawcett World Library, 1967; originally published 1955), pp. 36-38.

31.  Sarvepalli Radhakrishnan, *The Principal Upanisads* (Atlantic Highlands, N.J.: Humanities Press, 1992. First published in 1953 by George Allen and Unwin, London), pp. 52-53.

32.  Eliot Deutsch, *Advaita Vedanta: A Philosophical Reconstruction* (Honolulu: University of Hawaii Press, 1969), p. 106.

33.  From the Markandeya Purana, 88:2-5, Cornelia Dimmit and J.A.B. Van Buitenen (trans.), *Classical Hindu Mythology: A Reader in the Sanskrit Puranas* (Philadelphia: Temple University Press, 1978), p. 219.

34.  Juan Mascaro (trans.), *The Upanisads* (New York: Penguin Books, 1965), p. 33. Cited in the Introduction. No reference given for the original text.

35.  Huston Smith, *The World's Religions* (San Francisco: Harper, 1991), pp. 68-69.

36.  Trevor Ling, *The Buddha* (New York: Charles Scribner's Sons, 1973), p. 82. Our presentation of the conflicting philosophies and theologies is drawn primarily from this work, especially pp. 76-83 and 92-93.

37.  Soma Tera (trans.), *Kalama Sutta: The Buddha's Charter of Free Inquiry* (Kandy, Ceylon: Buddhist Publication Society, 1963), pp. 6-10.

38.  E.A.Burtt, *The Teachings of the Compassionate Buddha* (New York: Mentor Books, 1955), pp. 49-50.

39.  Walpola Rahula, *What the Buddha Taught*, revised and expanded edition (New York: Grove Press, 1974), pp. 27-28.

40.  William Theodore de Bary (ed.), *The Buddhist Tradition in India, China, and Japan* (New York: Vintage Press, 1972), pp. 84-85.

41.  Edward Conze, *A Short History of Buddhism* (London: Unwin Paperbacks, 1980), p. 50.

42.  All biblical quotations are from the new J.P.S. translation, *TANAKH, The Holy Scriptures* (Philadelphia: The Jewish Publication Society, 1985).

43.  Abba Hillel Silver, *Where Judaism Differed* (New York: MacMillan, 1956), pp. 256, 261.

44.  Rabbinical Assembly of America Prayerbook Committee (ed.), *Weekday Prayer Book* (New York: Rabbinical Assembly of America, 1962), pp. 97-98.

45.  Marcus J. Borg, *Meeting Jesus Again For the First Time* (San Francisco: Harper-SanFrancisco, 1994) p. 26. A well-known and highly respected Biblical scholar, Borg presents a noneschatological interpretation of Jesus as an enlightened master with an emphasis on his wisdom and spirituality. In our presentation, we follow more the distinguished scholar E.P. Sanders, who views Jesus as an eschatological prophet emerging out of his Jewish tradition. For example, see his *The Historical Figure of Jesus* (London: Penguin, 1993).

46.  All our biblical citations are from the most widely accepted interdenominational translation, *The Holy Bible, New Revised Standard Version* (New York: Oxford University Press, 1989).

47.  Muslim belief strongly asserts that the Quran was dictated verbatim by God in Arabic and consequently any attempted translation can never convey its exact meaning and poetic beauty. Granting these limitations, many of the Muslim and non-Muslim scholars with whom we are familiar prefer one of these two translations: For readability (and source for our citations), A.J. Arberry, *The Koran Interpreted* (New York: Simon and Schuster Touchtone, 1996. Original 1955); for accurate translation and original Arabic side by side plus a helpful commentary, Abdullah Yusuf Ali, *The Meaning of the Holy Qur'an*, new edition with revised translation and commentary (Beltsville, Maryland: Amana, 1989).

48.  Seyyed Hossein Nasr, "The Cosmos and the Natural Order" in the book edited by him, *Islamic Spirituality, Foundations* (New York: Crossroads, 1997), pp. 345-346.

49.  Muhammed Hamidullah, *Introduction to Islam* (Paris: Centre Culturel Islamique, 1969), p. 35.

50.  Fazlur Rahman, *Major Themes of the Qur'an*, second edition (Minneapolis: Bibliotheca Islamica, 1989), pp. 37-39.

# *Acknowledgements*

I deeply appreciate and would like to again thank the anonymous persons who, in formal or informal interviews, so generously shared with me their basic questions about life and why and how their questions and beliefs have changed. Also, I would like to gratefully acknowledge the intelligent and good-humored expertise of Sally Van Meter, academic services coordinator of the UCLA BookZone, and her former associate Jennifer Groener, who recommended and obtained key books across a range of disciplines. To achieve a book of this breadth, I had the indispensable guidance of specialist consultants—who sometimes vigorously disagreed among themselves. Finally, however, the contents of this book are my sole responsibility and are based on what seemed to me to be the actual facts, most accurate interpretations, and at a level of analysis, language, and tone appropriate for this introductory book.

Following the sequence of the book chapters, here are the specialists and their areas of consultation. Brain scientist Arnold B. Scheibel provided a final reading of the manuscript section describing Paul Macleans's theory of the triune brain and also confirmed its current validity and relevance. In several conversations, psychiatrist Eugene d'Aquili elucidated the most recent developments in his theory relating transcendental experiences and brain functions. Experimental psychologist and neuroscientist Eran Zaidel shared with me his knowledge of the latest research indicating possible gender differences in the right and left hemispheres of the human brain.

Adrian Johns and David C. Lindberg provided a final reading of both the Greek origins of Western science and the scientific revolution of the sixteenth and seventeenth centuries. For Aristotle, G.A. Spangler early on and at several later stages engaged me in constructive dialogue and recommended relevant books. Final readings were furnished by these philosophers: Richard McKirahan and William J. Prior (Socrates, Plato, and Aristotle), John Carriero (Descartes and Gassendi), Don Garrett (Locke and Hume), and Michael Friedman (Kant). For the types of seekers, I benefited from the discussions and insights of psychologists Greg Bogart, David Elkins, Tom Greening, Jeffrey Hutter, Christopher F. J. Ross, and Jonathon Young.

For Chapter 5 on world views, astronomer Edward L. Wright did a final reading of the section on scientific cosmology. For the brief tour of the universe, I incorporated the specialized knowledge of astronomer Samuel B. Larson, space consultant Andre Bormanis, and Griffith Observatory program director John E. Mosley. From the very beginning and at several stages along the way, including a final reading, physicist Marvin Chester has been a consultant on Einstein's relativity and quantum mechanics. Peter Kosso, a philosopher of physics, gave a challenging final reading. Early on, physicist Arthur H. Huffman described several classical experiments and some of the basics of quantum mechanics. Molecular biologist Richard E. Dickerson, in an afternoon meeting, discussed with me some of the philosophical implications of the most recent developments in biology and genetics. Francisco J. Ayala kindly referred me to biologist and evolutionary geneticist Victor R. Defilippis, who did the final review of the biology sections.

For the religious world views, I was fortunate to receive the counsel of specialized scholars. Glenn Yocum shared his expertise on Hinduism from the beginning through the final draft, and on two occasions Thomas J. Hopkins provided some critical insights. For Buddhism, meditation teachers and Buddhist thinkers Jack Kornfield and Shinzen Young described the questions asked and answers often sought by people inquiring into Buddhism; Robert Buswell gave scholarly input, and Robert Zeuschner furnished a final reading. I would like to thank Rabbi Yitzchok Adlerstein and philosopher and Rabbi Elliot N. Dorff, who met with me and gave initial direction and reading recommendations. Phil Goldin and I engaged in ongoing discussions, and he did the final reading on Judaism. For Christianity, Christine M. Thomas was with me at every major stage, including the final reading, and on two occasions Gregory J. Riley shared some of his research and insights on the early Church and its cultural context. I am grateful to Zayn Kassam, who started me out with lively discussions and reading suggestions for Islam and also furnished the final review, as well as Dr. Aslam Abdullah of the Islamic Center of Southern California, who met with me to clarify some of my understanding, and who at my request, demonstrated for me with my active participation the Salat prayers and prostrations.

Many thanks to editor Caroline Pincus, who gave me her impressions of the book manuscript, Doug Childers, who provided editorial suggestions and much good humor, and Holly Hammond, who applied her talents as line and copy editor. Jane Sutton demonstrated her exceptional skills and stamina in computer typing the book manuscript. I would like to acknowledge the careful reading of the entire book manuscript and valuable feedback from Kathleen Caldwell, Marvin Chester, and Robert Zeuschner. I was fortunate to receive counsel on the publishing process from Byron Belitsos, Brad Bunnin, Bob Erdmann, Tony Little, Dan Millman, Wes Nisker, Richard Tarnas, and Dick Teresi. Linda F. Radke, President of Five Star Publications, provided exceptional expertise as publishing consultant, and her personal commitment to the book often went far beyond what any author could expect. It was a pleasure working with Barbara Kordesh, who as book designer, provided both creativity and a collaborative spirit. Also, I would like to thank our neighbor Jethro Bodine for his spontaneous impressions of the book manuscript, which he stumbled across while joining our family for morning coffee at our kitchen table.

In a category all by herself is my wife and life mate, Esther. Her beautiful spirit and healing love have powerfully influenced my life, and I hope her qualities at times manifest themselves in this book. In her own flowing way she is also a philosophically reflective person. As the first reviewer for each section, her feedback helped keep me in focus and with the reader. In this work I have emphasized the importance of acquiring both knowledge and wisdom in our inquiries. Fortunate also is the truth seeker who has a partner like Esther on the path of life.

♦ ♦ ♦ ♦ ♦

Grateful acknowledgement is made to the following publishers and authors
for permission to reprint excerpts from their books:

*The Triune Brain in Evolution: Role in Paleocerebral Functions* by Paul D.
MacLean, 1990. Reprinted by permission of Kluwer Academic/Plenum
Publisher and the author.

Drake, Stillman. *Galileo Galilei, Two New Sciences.* Copyright © 1974. Reprinted by permission of The University of Wisconsin Press.

David Lindberg, Ronald Numbers. *God and Nature: Historical Essays in the
Encounter Between Christianity and Science.* Copyright © 1986 The Regents
of the University of California.

*The Home Planet* by Kevin W. Kelley. Copyright © 1988 by Kevin W. Kelley.
Reading, Mass.: Addison-Wesley.

*The Buddhist Tradition in India, China and Japan,* William Theodore de Bary,
ed., 1972. (Vintage Press).

*Weekday Prayer Book,* edited by Moses Hadas. Copyright © 1962 Rabbinical
Assembly of America. Reprinted by permission.

Scripture quotations are from the New Revised Standard Version of the
Bible, copyright © 1989 by the Division of Christian Education of the
National Council of the Churches of Christ in the USA. Used by permis-
sion. All rights reserved.

"The Cosmos and the Natural Order" from *Islamic Spirituality: Foundations.*
Copyright © 1997. Reprinted by permission of The Crossroad Publishing
Company.

# Index

# About the Author

Richard de la Chaumière Ph.D., is a licensed psychologist. In addition to his doctorate in psychology, his studies include philosophy, science, and religion. He and his wife, Esther, reside in California. Their children are young adults, each following a unique path in life. Dr. de la Chaumière can be contacted at wisdomhousepress@aol.com.